Darling, Yours Always

Darling, Yours Always

The World War II Letters of Peggy and George Steiner
Algeria, 1943–1944

Volume II

Compiled, edited, and annotated by
ART MENDOZA-BALLESTEROS

Copyright © 2022, Mind of Mandrake Publishing

All rights reserved. No part of this publication may be reproduced or transmitted in any form or by any means, electronic or mechanical, including photocopying, recording, scanning or otherwise, or through any information browsing, storage or retrieval system, without permission in writing from the publisher.

ISBN: 978-1-7355659-0-3

Letters and photographs from the collection of Georgia Steiner

Cover design by AMB

This book is dedicated to the brave and diligent men and women behind the front lines who were responsible for keeping the troops supplied.

— Georgia

Table of Contents

Abbreviation Guide ix
Steiner/Gillette Family Tree xii
Introduction. 1
Editor's Note 3
The Algeria Letters 7
Afterword. 383
Acknowledgments 384
Primary Sources 386
Secondary Sources 389
Index. 393

Abbreviation Guide

AAF:	Army Air Force
AC:	Air Corps
AFHQ:	Allied Force Headquarters
AMGOT:	Allied Military Government for Occupied Territories
ASC:	Air Service Command
ASTP:	Army Specialized Training Program
ATC:	Air Transport Command
AUS:	Army of the United States
CBS:	Columbia Broadcasting System
CGSC:	Command and General Staff College
CIA:	Central Intelligence Agency
CIO:	Congress of Industrial Organizations
ETO:	European Theater of Operations
FA:	Field Artillery
FBI:	Federal Bureau of Investigation
HBS:	Harvard Business School
LCT:	Landing Craft, Tank
LST:	Landing Ship, Tank
Mpls.:	Minneapolis
MSP:	Minneapolis-St. Paul International Airport
NAACP:	National Association for the Advancement of Colored People
NAAF:	Naval Auxiliary Air Facility
NAS:	Naval Air Station
NATO:	North African Theater of Operations

NATOUSA:	North African Theater of Operations, United States Army
NBC:	National Broadcasting Company
NCO:	Non-commissioned Officer
NRAB:	Naval Reserve Air Base
NRFEA:	National Retail Farm Equipment Association
OCS:	Officer Candidate School
OES:	Office of Economic Stability
OPD:	Operations Division
OSS:	Office of Strategic Services
OWI:	Office of War Information
PWB:	Psychological Warfare Branch
RA:	Regular Army
RAD:	Rome Air Depot
RME:	Griffiss International Airport
RNVR:	Royal Naval Volunteer Reserve
SOS:	Service of Supply
TLC:	Tank Landing Craft
U.S.:	United States
UMW/UMWA:	United Mine Workers of America
UN:	United Nations
USPS:	United States Postal Service
USSR:	Union of Soviet Socialist Republics
V-Mail:	Victory Mail
WAVES:	Women Accepted for Volunteer Emergency Service
WDGS:	War Department General Staff
WLB:	War Labor Board
WPB:	War Production Board

Steiner/Gillette Family Tree

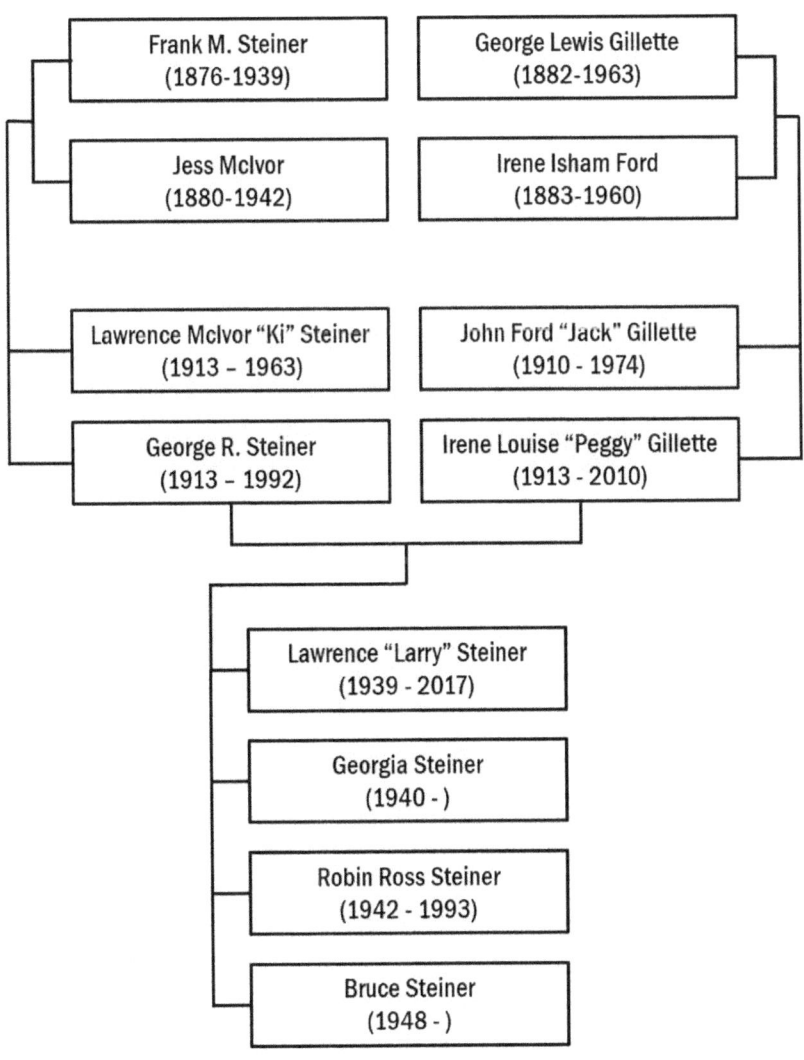

Introduction

In June 1943, three days after Peggy and George's sixth wedding anniversary, George is sent overseas, stationed at the Allied Force Headquarters (AFHQ) in Algiers, Algeria. In Peggy's first letter to her husband, one she slipped into his bag the night before they parted, she writes, "the greatest thing in a person's life is love and I believe the reason that everyone longs more for another's love than any other earthly thing is because it surrounds one with a sense of safety."

Irene "Peggy" Gillette and George Steiner knew each other as children growing up in Minneapolis, Minnesota. Photos of them as youngsters, along with letters and telegrams from their courtship in college, illustrate their unique relationship which culminated in their 1937 marriage at St. Mark's Episcopal Cathedral in Minneapolis. Their married life begins ideally enough, despite inevitable challenges like relocating to New England for George's work with the family business. Larry is born in 1939 and Georgia follows the next year. By then, Reserve Officers' Training Corps (ROTC) graduate 1st Lieutenant George Steiner is already serving stateside but away from his family. In the summer of 1942, George is sent to Key West, Florida with a detachment of 22 men tasked with supplying gasoline to aircraft operating against German submarines in the Atlantic Ocean and the Gulf of Mexico. From there George's service takes him to Kansas, New York, and Washington, D.C.

By the beginning of July 1943 when George arrives in Algiers, Peggy and George's third child, Robin, is seven months old. It has been about two months since the German Army in North Africa surrendered and it will be a matter of days before the Allied invasion of Sicily begins. According to copies of George's military records discovered and shared by a family member, George was working in the G-4 Division at AFHQ as a Supply and Evacuation Staff Officer. In this position George was responsible for the issuing of equipment for provisional and normal units when an amount exceeding regular authorization was required. George also developed procedures for supplying the Brazilian and French forces (operating as part of the U.S. forces) in the Mediterranean. This included the creation of an accounting system to manage the complex lend-lease arrangements and the drafting of paperwork for projects and equipment to be reviewed and approved by the War Department.

While George is in Africa, Peggy spends the summer with her family in Crystal Bay near Wayzata, Minnesota, reminiscing about dates with George when they were young. With George overseas, the couple writes frequently, carefully cultivating the epistolary connection they use to strengthen their relationship while apart. The longing for each other is present in the letters of this volume as Peggy devotes herself to domestic and social obligations and George adapts to life in a new country and culture. Despite the couple's best efforts, the longing is apparent as each recounts memories of experiences shared and reflects on future plans they have been forced to place on pause. Clinging to the belief that the separation will be short (the Allies are in Italy, after all) both write with the hopes of lovers who are focused on a future where they can be reunited. George stoically weathers the separation as he reassures Peggy, "We are always together at least in our thoughts."

Unbeknownst to the couple, the war and George's service will continue. The remainder of their letters will be compiled in the upcoming book, *Darling, Yours Always: The World War II Letters of Peggy and George Steiner, Volume III*.

Editor's Note

Chronology was less of an issue with this compilation as Peggy and George not only dated their V-Mails and letters, but numbered them as well. I have kept their numbers the same as they wrote on the originals, even if they repeated a number. In the few instances where there is no date or number, the postmark date has been included in the heading when possible.

Spelling (in English and French) has been corrected throughout, improving the flow of the letters for the reader. The exception is when either writer purposely misspells words in jest. Grammatical errors have been left as they appear in the original letters unless the sentence meaning is vague or misleading without a correction. The other exception is for periods after certain abbreviations, which I added for easier reading. Sentence fragments are common, especially in V-Mails as Peggy and George run out of space. In certain cases, punctuation has been changed to help the reader, however, for the V-Mails the fragments were usually left as they were originally written. Any words I added for clarification have been included in brackets.

The majority of names in the letters were spelled multiple ways. Names Georgia could confirm have been spelled as she remembers. In instances where the spelling of names could not be verified, the name appears inconsistently spelled as it does in the original letters—with one exception. George spells the last name of Schutz's host family a variety of ways and to make things simpler for the reader, "Devevey" was adopted as the spelling throughout.

Chichi Steiner graciously corrected Peggy and George's French and provided the English translations. French words and phrases have been italicized to make it easier for the reader to skip directly to the English translations in the footnotes.

In accordance with the guidelines of the Chicago Manual of Style and the American Psychological Association, where race is denoted in footnotes "Black" and "White" have been capitalized. While capitalizing "Black" is now widely accepted, "White" has been capitalized in this case to remind the reader that "Whiteness" is not a neutral nor standard way of being. It is a racial construct and using it as a proper noun brings attention to how ideas of race permeate our politics, our societies, our perspectives, and our history. For more on this topic consider Kwame Anthony Appiah's article or Eve L. Ewing's essay, both listed in the bibliography.

Many of the men George writes about achieved a higher rank later in their service. When additional information is included about them in the footnotes, their rank at the time of George's writing is noted as it was not always possible to determine the rank they achieved upon discharge. For people who appear in future letters, biographical information is included only up to the date of the letter in this volume.

Peggy and George frequently express frustration with George's rank. During his stateside service George was recommended by his superiors to attend both the prestigious Command and General Staff School at Fort Leavenworth and the Task Force Officer's Course of the Operations Division of the War Department General Staff in Washington, D.C. Both courses provided specialized training to selected candidates to prepare and qualify them for duty with task

EDITOR'S NOTE

forces and in the highest headquarters. By the time George arrived in Algiers, he was one month shy of completing two full years of service stateside. The reasons surrounding George's lack of promotion are beyond the scope of this book. In short, a reorganization of the U.S. Armed Forces, combined with a change in how promotions were awarded, left many men in positions requiring extra responsibility pursuant to their unique skillset without the accompanying rise in rank.

The Algeria Letters

THE ALGERIA LETTERS

June 1943–June 1944

[Peggy to George]
[Handwritten on personalized stationery][1]

#1

My Darling:

At the moment you read this, I expect you will be flying to your new post which takes you so far away from me and the children who already have missed you so terribly even when we knew you were safe in this country. There is no need to tell you how much we miss you nor how much we all love you. This, my first letter to you while you are overseas is to wish you God speed and tell you that another letter will follow every day until you are back with us again for good, and to let you know that I'll pray for your health and safety every night and Larry will God Bless Daddy in each evening prayer. (Georgia too, if the rascal can be tamed enough before you return.) One thought which helps me a lot when you are away is to think that the greatest thing in a person's life is love and I believe the reason that everyone longs more for another's love than for any other earthly thing is because it surrounds one with a sense of safety. This is not only true when we are together and realize that all our cares become meaningless because we feel secure and happy in each other's arms, but it carries over when we are separated in that nothing can ever take our love from us and we know that at all times the other has a protective influence by forever being near in thoughts and praise in all we do.

Nobody ever need tell me what a marvelous job you are doing and will do as a great leader in this war (not that I'll refuse to listen, of course). You are truly a great man and deserve a full and interesting life in which your family intend to play no small part. Before all this

---

1 George left the United States on June 29, 1943. This letter is from shortly before his departure as its envelope bears the instructions, "Open en route" and was not mailed.

can be begun this horrible separation must be endured, and as you've said we cannot be together so we must make the most of it.

My job is to bring up your three babies to be healthy, happy, well-mannered and perhaps <u>slightly</u> educated before you return. (I also am taking vitamin pills to lose my grey hair so I'll really present a younger wife on your arrival.)

For you, My darling, I've already said I know how excellently you'll do the job before you. Beyond that please concentrate on remaining as nearly as possible your quiet, slow to excite, easy-going self whom I so often have teased. Move quick enough to shoot or find a foxhole, but to all the inevitable horrors and suffering which you must walk among in the course of War, do what you unconsciously would to ease it for all and provide any care available, but don't take it so to heart that you brood over it. Get your sleep. Keep well and then you can do your work best to help those who might suffer if you let yourself become otherwise.

At all times remember I love you and look forward to our future years together with an ecstasy greater than any thing I've known—even my first glimpse at each of our babies which was quite a thrill. God bless you always.

Yours, Peggy

[at top of next page]

<u>Keep this</u> please and write it to me as code. Also the Atlas numbers.
1. I am so glad you have a comfortable house while I'm away.
2. Let's hope that you find the neighbors congenial.
3. Now if the gas ban eases up you won't be too far from our friends.
4. I don't worry about your food rations as the children's books will allow a steak now and then for you and the girls.
5. It will be nice to hear that Dr. Close has found Robin O.K. again.
6. I feel sure he will be fine.

7. I'm glad you have the time to carry on the work for the T. B. sanitarium.
8. However don't wear yourself out with it.
9. If you can arrange it, try to take the children to Mpls.[2] to see their grandparents in -----.

(over)

1. Quarters comfortable
2. Officers congenial
3. Near large modern town of interest.
4. Food good.
5. Medical officers competent—equipment good.
6. Personally in good health
7. Like the work.
8. Getting sufficient sleep
9. Expect to be in present locality until -----.

You can change the meaning of the letter sentences to suit the situation and add adjectives to be more specific. Be sure and do this, dear, as I must know how comfortable you are. Anything you omit I'll understand the opposite meaning is intended.

[George to Peggy]

Tues. June 28

Peg dear:

Spending a couple of hours having a late dinner, talking, and listening to a phonograph. Have been wondering how you made out today with your help problem. I sent Ki[3] a postcard with my A.P.O. number on it. I probably should have called him before I left, but did not have much time.

I forgot to give the bell boy anything in the rush of leaving this

---
2   The abbreviation for Minneapolis, Minnesota.
3   George's twin brother, Lawrence McIvor Steiner, informally known as "Ki."

morning, and those bags were heavy. That bag weighed 56 lbs., not a bad job of packing. So far I cannot think of anything that I forgot to take along.

All my love dear, George

[Peggy to George]
[V-Mail][4]

June 29, 1943

Dearest George.

I just sent you a telegram which I hope you will receive. Perhaps just at this minute. I wanted you to know that everything is under control and will stay that way. The boy at the Western Union desk corrected my spelling of SNAFO to SNAFU which amused me greatly. He was all of fifteen.

Now I am on the train waiting to pull out and you are probably doing the same. I saw you three times after you saw me this morning. First as you turned the corner. Then a cab picked me right up and we followed your cab for about four blocks. Even stopped behind you at the first red light.

This is going to be a very thrilling day for you with all the undesirable features we dislike about it. How I wish I could be tucked in your pocket. I'm going home and [will] explain as much as I can

---

4   V-Mail service, named for the ubiquitous "V for Victory" symbol, was implemented by the United States Postal Service (USPS) in 1942 to reduce the weight and bulk of mail, create space for other cargo, and provide a safer, faster mail service for the U.S. Armed Forces stationed overseas. Letters to and from service members stationed abroad were written on special, combination envelope and letter stationery designed by the Government Printing Office and issued free of charge–capped, however, at two sheets per person per day. The letters were then microfilmed at one of the three massive postal centers in New York, Chicago, and San Francisco. Each sending station kept copies of the V-Mails until the receiving station verified the reels had arrived unscathed. This practice enabled the USPS to claim that no V-Mail was ever lost during the war, at least not on their part (Guise, "Mail Call: V-mail."). The reels of photographed V-Mails were transported by the military via airmail to a V-Mail station overseas where they were then printed and distributed to the recipients. According to the USPS, "150,000 unmicrofilmed [sic] V-Mail letters weighed 1,500 pounds and filled 22 mail sacks." Since approximately 1,600 letters fit on a single roll of film (which reduced the letters to about three percent of their original weight and volume), when microfilmed the 150,000 letters weighed only 45 pounds and filled a single mail sack. V-Mail was an initiative unique to WWII as it was only produced between June 1942 and November 1945. It is estimated during that period over a billion V-Mails were delivered (Historian United States Postal Service, "V-mail.").

about where you are and what you're doing to Larry. Wouldn't he be bragging to his school chums this morning if he were a few years older. Well, here is the first of our many days' letters. God bless you and keep you. Always, Peggy

[George to Peggy]
[Postcard]
[Postmarked June 29, 1943 at 5pm]

Free Soldiers Mail

From: Capt. G.R. Steiner

Peg dear: You will be just about home by now. Looks like a comfortable ride. Ran into Duncan Lee, roomed across from Colby[5] & myself at Yale. All my love, George

[George to Peggy]

July 1,

Peg dear,

Had quite a chat with Duncan Lee on the way over. You probably remember him, he roomed right across the hall from Colby and myself the 2nd year. Scully who roomed with him is now an M.D. in the Army. Duncan won a Rhodes scholarship, and after returning to the states practised law in N.Y. until the war came. Also ran into Maj. Cole who was with us quite a bit last summer.

Mr. Churchill's speech was in this morning's paper.[6] It is worth reading. He points out the confusion and troubles which will come, if our own people and the British do not stick together in working

---

5 Warren Colby, one of George's close friends and former college roommate.
6 Winston Churchill's speech, "We Seek No Profit," was delivered on June 30, 1943 at the Guildhall in London. In the speech, Churchill explains Britain entered the war, "upon a single stupendous impulse at the call of honor" and famously continues, declaring, "we seek no profit, we want no territory or aggrandizement. We expect no reward and we will accept no compromise. It is on that footing that we wish to be judged, first in our own consciences and afterward by posterity" (United Press, "The Text of Prime Minister Churchill's Address."). As George observes, Churchill also lauds the United States, "whose power arouses no fear and whose pre-eminence excites no jealousy in British bosoms" and cautions, "If [the British Commonwealth and the United States] fall apart and wander astray from the lines of their destiny there will be no end or measure to the miseries and confusion which would mark modern civilization" (Ibid.).

toward a decent world after the war. And from his repeated references to Parliament & Congress he shows a respect for representative government that is so noticeably lacking among the leaders of our Government.

Will be glad to reach my destination and get to work.

Love, George

(over)

Might as well write a few more lines. Read your first letter with a very deep, sincere appreciation of the thoughts which you expressed. We are always together at least in our thoughts. I am so pleased with the manner in which you are bringing up our children. Such loving care as they receive backed up by your good, common sense and ability to act quickly on good reasoning will provide them a promising environment in which to develop. As for their hereditary leanings, I guess we will have to hold ourselves responsible too.

After missing a night's sleep on the way over, I found a good, clean, comfortable bed. Shared a room with Howder.[7] Some of the boys took a train over to Edinb[ur]gh, but being short on sleep, and since they would only be there for a few hours I stayed here. Remember the hotel room there. Intend to make my next visit there with you. Heather is not in bloom yet. Did see some larkspur which has memories.

More love, George

[Peggy to George]
[V-Mail]

No. 6
Sat. July 3.

Darling,

Since yesterday morning I've spent my time canning rhubarb and green beans. We shouldn't starve certainly. Last night I finished

---

[7] Major James D. Howder, assigned to the Personnel Division (G-1) in the North African Theater of Operations (NATO)

splicing the movie film and wrote my lecture so everything seems ready for the show. When they can put it on before we go to Minneapolis I cannot imagine. I have so much running through my head as it is to do that I accomplish nothing. Frank is trying to get reservations for us on the 24th and he and Helen[8] may go as far as Chicago with me which would be grand. I haven't seen them since you left, but will try to get in town next Thursday.

Betty Black is coming out on the five o'clock train today to spend the weekend with me. She'll get her fill of tending children I can guarantee.

Larry and Georgia have been pretending the blue chair was a swimming pool all morning and dive onto it from the bench around the tree. Doxie approached and they warned him off with "Watch out you've got water in your nose." Hoping to hear from you soon. Love, Peggy

[George to Peggy]
[V-Mail]

Capt. G. R. Steiner
Hq Allied Forces, G-4 Section
APO 512 New York, N.Y.
July 3, 1943

Darling:

The letters you enclosed in my luggage were sure welcome. There always is that feeling of security about both of us that nothing can ever penetrate. I am glad to know that you and the children have a comfortable home while I am away. Hope you do not have too much trouble fixing up the house and getting moved.

There were a lot of neat, well-kept victory gardens up in Scotland.

---

8   Frank Steiner is George's first cousin. Helen is Frank's wife.

Could not help but remember our visit up there.

We are well taken care of in some billets taken over by the government. A bit crowded for toilets and washing but not bad. Am looking for better quarters and understand they can be gotten without too much trouble. Food is better than I expected. The climate is not bad, not too warm and it cools off nicely during the day. It is eleven so I think I will be getting to bed. Note proper address in upper right corner.[9] Understand this will not go by V-Mail. Love you very much. George

[George to Peggy]
[V-Mail]

July 5, 1943

My darling:

Five of us are sitting around the room talking. One Englishman and four of our group three of whom are going on tomorrow. There are four bedrooms in our house with five cots in each room. I am ready for bed stretched out on my cot writing. The floor is large patterned brown tile and the wall paper is large closely spaced red roses—doesn't that sound smooth. I took a long walk around the town so being thirsty when I came back, we promoted a couple bottles of Mums Champagne ice cold which is not a simple job in this town. Cups and glasses are scarce so we drank out of the bottle. Good bunch of boys. English and Americans can mix well. They are a splendid people and sure deserve respect for the part they have played in this war. Last time I wrote you were going to eat dinner in about an hour. Been thinking about a week ago all day & evening. Ran into Mike Biel who was adjutant of that pursuit squadron Phil

---

9   Each V-Mail features the recipient's address centered at the top of the page and the sender's address placed at the top on the right. For simplicity the addresses have been omitted in the transcriptions. If a writer mentions them, however, they have been included.

Cochran[10] commanded last year. Walked by a fence covered with morning glories today and thought of your garden. I love you so much dear. George

[George to Peggy]

Thursday
July 8, 1943

My darling:

Here is some news which will please you. I just want to sit down and tell you all about what a pleasant place I have found to live. First the people I live with speak practically no English. They are a well-to-do, middle-class French family with three children, one about 18 in the Free French Navy, a little girl about 16, and a boy about 8. They keep a very neat clean apartment and have given me a room comfortably furnished with a couch which makes a good bed, an easy chair, and they have moved a desk in so I can write *ma chère femme*.[11] When I showed them the little pictures I have, they made over *ma belle femme et les jolis petites*.[12]

Oh how I wish you were here. I am having more fun with my French. If I get some evenings off I am going to study French. They run some classes at the Red Cross. Schutz,[13] Helms,[14] and myself went to one tonight. Schutz was out at Leavenworth in the same house

---

10 Philip Cochran (b. 1910, d. 1979) was an officer in the U.S. Army Air Corps who innovated air transport, assault, and combat methods during WWII and was the model for Milt Caniff's comic strip characters Flip Corkin in *Terry and the Pirates* and General Philerie in *Steve Canyon*. Cochran enlisted in 1935 and by the time the United States entered the war, he was a major and training fighter pilots. In 1942, Cochran led a squadron flying support missions in Morocco and Tunisia. He returned to the United States in 1943 and resumed training new pilots—most notably the 99th Fighter Squadron, an all-Black unit of fliers more famously known as the Tuskegee Airmen. Promoted to Lieutenant Colonel, he was then tasked with creating the First Air Commando force which assisted British forces in the invasion of Burma (now Myanmar) in 1944 (for more on this see footnote 214 on page 333). Cochran rose to the rank of colonel before his service ended in 1945. After the war, Cochran returned to his hometown of Erie, Pennsylvania to join his brother's trucking company and involve himself in local charities. A historical marker on State Street abutting the Erie County Veterans Memorial Park in Erie was dedicated to him in 2001.
11 Translated: "my dear wife."
12 Translated: "my beautiful wife and the pretty little ones."
13 Likely Captain John Logan Schutz, initially assigned to the Operations and Training Division (G-3) NATO.
14 Captain Lex C. Helms Jr., initially assigned to the Military Intelligence Division (G-2) NATO.

with me, a good fellow—not one of the crowd of hebrews whom I mentioned when I was out there. Helms is the good looking Capt. who was eating alone near our table at the Stetler[15] in Washington.

Well Schutz lives in the other apartment on the same floor as mine (*le cinquième etage mais nous avons un ascenseur*[16]) elevator if that is how you spell it. Now the *mon[sieur]* in his family (Schutz's) speaks English well and his wife speaks a little. They are both very friendly intelligent people with two children, a baby boy and a little girl about 17. He is the manager of the Cooks Travel office in town and has promised to show us around when we get a ½ day off sometime which I am sure we can arrange. Maj. Ream[17] is also in the same apartment house on the next floor down. There is a nice bath in each apartment with hot and cold running water, tub and shower. We are out on the edge of town; there is a French door opening from my room onto a balcony from where you can see the town spread out far below. A bus (electric) line ends right in front of the apartment and takes us in a very few moments to where we work. Also there is a lot of Army traffic so we can always catch a ride.

They treat us very fine and are very friendly to *les etats—unis* (right?) Madame unpacked my bag putting all my clothes in a bureau, ma[de] my bed, put a vase of flowers on the desk and a dish of fresh plums in ice by my bed. We had a drink of Cognac (Hennessey). I toasted 'la belle France', Madam toasted America, and her husband Victory for the Allies. He fought in the last war and has three wounds.

So now you won't worry about where I am living. Some day you shall meet my good friends. I miss my dear wife and think of you very often my darling.

If you have not sent my duffle bag and bed roll you might put in a couple of sheets and pillow cases if there is room. Also I forgot of

---

15 George probably means the Statler Lounge in Washington, D.C.
16 Translated: "the fifth floor but we have an elevator."
17 Major Edward F. Ream Jr., initially assigned to the G-3 Division NATO.

all things, to mention my book of pictures which I do want. Also you might put in one of those books on bridge.

As for my work I am getting fitted into the picture and am sure that with the unusual and excellent training I have had together with a very sincere desire to contribute all I can, that I can do a really good job. In general the type of men I have met who are working on the staff are intelligent, capable soldiers who are working hard for victory. They are a far cry from the Lewis[18] type of labor racketeers who seem to be so prevalent at home, and the self-styled new deal liberals who are trying to convert our democracy into a one party ~~bauran~~ bureaucy (how do you spell it?) [bureaucracy]. Which reminds me, that little leather covered dictionary in my writing case would come in handy.

If you have already sent all of those things don't worry as I can get along nicely without all of the things I have mentioned here.

The one thing I miss terribly is your presence and companionship. And the one thing I cannot get along without is your love. But I am sure that that is always with me, so far away and still so near.

Tell Larry that there is a nice little boy in the house where I live. Maybe he will meet him some day. He has an electric train too.

Well my darling I must get to bed. It is very late and you are probably just starting to eat out on the porch.

                    My love to you, George

---

18   John L. Lewis was a prominent labor leader who served as president of the United Mine Workers of America (UMW/UMWA) from 1920–1960. He was also a co-founder and the first president of the Congress of Industrial Organizations (CIO). During the war years, while many industries and labor unions adhered to a no-strike policy in support of the war effort, Lewis led over 600,000 mine workers on strike in 1943, closing steel mills and earning the ire of (among others) soldiers, civilians, union bosses, and U.S. President Franklin Roosevelt. In 1943 there were 430 strikes in the coal mining industry alone, more than in any other manufacturing group (Peterson, "Strikes in 1943," 5, 8.). Labor challenges were not unique to coal mining though, and in 1943 there were 3,322 strikes across a variety of other industries. However, unlike the coal mining strikes, many of these other actions were spontaneous stoppages, quickly resolved, and not authorized by unions (Ibid., 1.). Overall, the mining strikes were successful, resulting in wage increases and benefits for the mine workers. Later, Lewis would lead the campaign for the first Federal Coal Mine Safety Act, passed in 1952, which emphasized the prevention of major mining disasters by requiring annual safety inspections of mines with more than 14 employees and the closing of mines if an inspection revealed impending danger. The Coal Act also imposed mandatory safety regulations and penalties on mines that violated them. In 1964, Lewis would be awarded the Presidential Medal of Freedom by President Lyndon B. Johnson for his work with the UMW Welfare and Retirement Fund.

[Peggy to George]
[V-Mail]

No. 8
July 9, Friday

Darling:

Just after dropping your letter down the box at the Savoy last night, Tina phoned that your cablegram had come. You just cannot imagine what a relief it was. "Safe and well" rank with "I love you" in our vocabulary from now on. Frank took us downstairs at the hotel for dinner and I caught the 9:25 out home. If I had slept two seconds longer I would have pulled your trick and been in Stamford. Today Tina leaves for the weekend so I have the children alone with Doxie for three days. Doxie is sick too with his usual ailment. I tried to fix him up a minute ago but to no avail so maybe I'll have to take all the children and deliver him to the 'vet.' It's a rainy day so the kids can play indoors—that requires a little less watching anyhow. They are all well and full of the dickens. Larry just yelled at Tina "Bill is here." Whereupon she left Robin with his pants half off to dash down and tell Bill how much milk we need. Bill wasn't here at all. She went up & told Larry and he said "Oh yes he is. Georgia has him." There was Georgia with the wooden farmer belonging to the play farm animals. She was hugging and kissing Bill. Loads of love. Peggy

[Peggy to George]
[V-Mail]

No. 9
Sat. July 10

Darling.

The children are out doors, the dishes done and Robin's formula made so I can say hello to you before attacking the garden. This being alone with all three is more than I'd care for long. They have been very good though. I just glanced at the paper and I see Sicily was invaded this morning.[19] It does something to my stomach but I suppose I'll get used to it. Your letter written the day you left arrived yesterday. I was so glad to hear from you, but curious as ---- to know where you were. Don't forget any of those details so you can tell me when this is all over. Doxie isn't any better this morning so I fear I'll have to pile all the children in the car and deliver him to Dr. Schofeld.

I had a sweet letter from Teedie[20] yesterday and she did lose the baby. She's fine though but disappointed, naturally. I cannot see why that should happen. Frank says the plant is running smooth as silk and your office looks swell. I can imagine how silly that sounds to you at this moment. Loads of Love. Peggy

[Peggy to George]
[V-Mail]

No. 10
Mon. July 12

Darling.

Tina's back! What a three days I had with three children and the canning. To add insult to injury Bernice & Bill asked me to take their kids for supper and all night so they could go out. Will you please teach me not to be such a sucker. But can you imagine the nerve. Janet was more of a baby than all the rest. She tore the Sunday paper which I hadn't had time to look at into 4" square pieces and covered the whole yard. She was supposed to be looking out for the rest while I got their supper. It was nine o'clock before they all settled down and I could finish my five quarts of beans. Perhaps the neighbors think they are helping me to keep busy and forget my troubles. Johnny Mayer had a three-day pass and I took the children and went over to say hello yesterday. They both wanted to say hello to you in this morning's letter. He looks fine and for one who never touched a gun before army

---

19   The Allied forces launched a combined air and ground assault into Sicily on July 10, 1943. The offensive, called Operation Husky, saw 150,000 ground troops land on Sicily's coast in three days and resulted in the eventual withdrawal of Axis troops back to mainland Europe.

20   The affectionate nickname for Ki's wife, Harriet.

life, is now teaching machine gun and leading 25-mile hikes. Your letter of July 1st came on Saturday and put new life into me. How I wish I could be with you. You may receive this letter about the day we move. It's the 21st. Our new home is lovely. The children are fine and send their own kisses. Love, Peggy

[George to Peggy]
[V-Mail]

July 14, 1943

My darling Peggy:

    First of all I love you very much. I am looking at your picture with Robbie on your lap and Georgia standing next to you in our living room. It is in a neat little picture frame that also has a picture of Larry and Georgia in your old baby carriage out on the lawn. Tell Larry his Teddy Bear is in the picture too. The background is a mirror so I can see that Captain with a pipe in his mouth in between the other pictures. It is that same Captain with a scar on his lip who you have always been so nice to. The other evening Madam Rebillet walked in when I was looking at your picture in that small leather folder. The next night when I came home I found the two pictures in the frame on my desk with a vase of flowers next to it. Very thoughtful.

    Just now Monsieur Rebillet has tuned his radio to an English language broadcast on the day's news. Things are certainly going fine in Sicily. Today of course was a great day for celebration here, Bastille Day. The English made a very nice gesture on July 4, one of their warships fired a 48-gun salute. Considering that it was Independence Day it was very decent of them.

    I have been wondering how you have made out on the help problem. It should not be long now before I get a letter. They say that the mail that was sent to that temporary APO will not reach us as soon as some of the mail addressed to APO 512. Hope you are not overworking on your moving. I woke up in the middle of the night last night and it somehow seemed as if you were thinking of me. If you remember it and were tell me what time it was. I will write another short letter tonight addressing it to Minneapolis. Tell me what you get first as I will send it regular mail. Much love my dear. George

[George to Peggy]

July 14.

To a young lady I love.

Now don't think I am writing two letters to you in one evening just to see which mail is the quickest. Were that the case I could stop right here.

You know I don't often waken in the middle of the night but last night [I] woke up [all] of a sudden to have a very definite feeling that you were thinking of me. Just for fun tell me if you were and what time it was.

How I hated to leave you that morning in front of the Mayflower.[21] It was worse to be parting for a long while, but I knew also that you had a lot of problems to face with the servants and the house, and getting the children out west. The last two years have certainly kept us well apart.

But we have had some happy moments together too. That bicycle ride in the dark over to Hoggson's was fun, breakfast with waffles, Larry, Georgia, Doxie and us on the porch, then the evening we spent alone at home sitting together in our own living room as the twilight faded into darkness, you were in my arms as we talked about our new house and after while we felt it would be so nice to go up to bed. Thinking of pleasant moments—you know one that I thought of the other day and other times too, were those pleasant moments of anticipation and greeting when I used to drive up from New Haven

---

21 Probably the Mayflower Hotel in Washington, D.C.

DARLING, YOURS ALWAYS

for a date when we were in college, and I would wait for you to come down stairs.[22] Somehow after we were married there is still the same thrill of having a date with you my dear. And when this war is over I intend to have a very great monopoly on your time. How you can be such a charming, fascinating young lady and yet be so practical in running a home so well, entertaining our friends, and bringing our children up so beautifully is one of those great mysteries I am afraid I will never fully understand.

You will be glad to know that I have run into a lot of friends. Today Lt. Allbright walked in to say hello. Remember we had dinner with him one night in Key West. He was the boy that was out at Hickman[23] Field the infamous Dec. 7th. I stopped in to ask my way in a little store down town the other day and ran into his 1st sgt., asked him to give Allbright my address.

Also, I saw a couple of boys who had been in our outfit at Manchester as enlisted men and had gone to OCS[24] and are now officers. I will tell you about others as I write, but it is getting late now.

Let me know which mail comes thru the quickest: V-mail or regular mail. I wrote quite small on the V-Mail as I understand they are being sent right through without being photographed. However coming from the states they do photograph them.

Now tell me all about the new house, how you have made out with the girls, and how the moving went.

As for me I am very well, have a good place to live, the food is good, and I am getting into the work so I feel I can be of use. The

---

22 George attended Yale University in New Haven, Connecticut and Peggy attended Mount Holyoke College in South Hadley, Massachusetts.
23 George means Hickam Field, one of the Army's three main air bases on Oahu, Hawaii. During the Japanese attack on Pearl Harbor on December 7, 1941, Hickam was strafed and bombed by the Japanese, killing 121, wounding 274, and rendering only 79 of Hickam's total 231 aircraft usable (Mueller, *Air Force Bases*, 232.). Throughout WWII and during the later Vietnam and Korean wars, Hickam was an important stopover point for heavy and medium bombers that had to be flown to the Pacific theater. It also played a critical role in pilot training and provided support for aircraft transporting troops, supplies, and evacuating wounded to and from sites in the Pacific. When the U.S. Air Force was founded in 1947, Hickam Field was renamed Hickam Air Force Base. In 2010 the Hickam Air Force Base and the Pearl Harbor Naval Base were combined and it is now known as the Joint Base Pearl Harbor-Hickam.
24 Officer Candidate School.

officers I am working with are a good lot, capable and likeable. Chances are I will be here for some time. Take good care of yourself for me specially.

My love dear, George

AF Hq, G-4 Section
APO 512, c/o Postmaster
New York, N.Y.

Best regards to George & Irene[25] and to our friends.

[Peggy to George]
[V-Mail]

No. 11
July 14, Wed.

Darling:

While Tina is getting the children to unpack the car I'll drop you a line. We are about to go over to the house and I told Tina to put the empty sandbox in the back and we'd set it up over there and fill it with sand left over from the porch foundation. Larry got the idea we were moving their toys today and just now when I went out to load our preserves we found the car jammed to the doors with planes, football, fire engine, donkey, steam engine, etc. How they got the fire engine in I'll never know. We are taking our lunch and will have a picnic. How I long to have you join us. The house is lovelier every day. I scrubbed our bathroom yesterday and put your clothes away. It was such fun. I pretend you are doing it all with me and it's much better. Let me know if these letters sent airmail arrive any faster. I can hardly wait for another letter. I'm sure they are on the way. The children are howling to get started so my love for today and every day dear. I love you so much. Peggy

---

25 Peggy's parents, George Lewis Gillette and Irene Isham Ford Gillette.

[Peggy to George]
[V-Mail]

No. 11

Darling!

<u>Two</u> letters arrived yesterday and was I thrilled! I stopped the mail man on the way to the house and felt like a queen with such luck. They were 10 days on the way. Our porch floor is all done and it is a lovely job. The outside painting is nearly finished and inside only the floors are left. Today I have the kitchen shelves to cover and about four hours work in the garden. Yesterday Larry went to Jay Gerle's birthday party at the club all by himself. That is I sent him by taxi from Greenwich with his bathing trunks, life preserver and present and Bernice brought him home. He reports a marvelous time and seems to have behaved himself but lost the new trunks. I hope he isn't going to be like you that way too. It was a strange feeling to turn him loose for the first time. You didn't mention what you wanted sent in the luggage. If I don't hear this week I'd better just send them as is before we go west. All the children are fine and send Kisses. Doxie is at the vet with a cold and has been clipped. You wouldn't know him. He should be more comfortable. More tomorrow. Had a date with you last Monday. Love, Peggy

[George to Peggy]
[V-Mail]

July 15, 1943

Peg dear,

Had my first ½ day off which we get once a week provided nothing intervenes. So I went down to Cooks Travel agency to see my friend the *Chef d'Agence*, M. Lucien Devevey with whom Capt. Schutz is living. He insisted on giving me a free ticket for a tour of the town which was most interesting. They took us into a Mosque, which is usually forbidden to us infidels. The filth and degradation in which many of the natives live is unbelievable. Some of the streets are merely passageways almost dark because of the overhanging upper stories of houses. A person's spirit must be terribly beaten down before they could sink to such depths, and yet they go on living in filth that we would abhor to put our animals in.[26] Tell Doxie that I have not seen many dogs and of course none that could compare with him. Well I had a good dinner downtown at an Army mess then went up to the Red Cross where I ran into Helms. I sat in on a French lesson and parlez-voused for an hour. After that I got a cold lunch [of] deviled eggs, sliced ham and lemonade at the Red Cross then caught a bus which takes me right out in front of

---

26   George's observations lack an awareness of the history of the Algerian-Muslim experience in French Algeria. A century of French colonial rule systematically designed to disenfranchise the Algerian-Muslim population has resulted in the squalid living conditions George witnesses and describes in the above letter. (Note that Algerian Christians and Jews–even those in tribes or rural areas–usually had different experiences with the colonizers.)

        The most recent invasion of Algeria directly preceding that of the French was by the Ottoman Turks who controlled Algeria from 1555 until the French takeover in 1830. Unlike the French, the Turks preferred payments of tribute rather than total occupation. Thus, Algerian chiefs and their tribal societies were usually left intact and with considerable autonomy. "Algerian" is used in contrast to "Euro-Algerian" which indicates inhabitants who were descendants of French colonists and born in French Algeria (White, "Introduction: The Empire of Wine in Algeria.").

        After the French conquest, idealists abounded in France, convinced colonialism in French Algeria would be beneficial to all peoples. Among them was Napoleon III, first president of France, who declared the Algerians would not be subjected to "an impossible and inhumane" total colonialism akin to that of the Indigenous Peoples of North America but that "perfect equality between natives and Europeans" was critical to the advancement of both the Indigenous Peoples and the colonists (Stora, *Algeria: 1830-2000*, 5.) (Ageron, *Modern Algeria*, 38.). Despite high-mindedness in France, the French colonial army and the colonists had other ideas. From 1830-1871 the army terrorized tribes who actively resisted occupation, often utilizing innovative yet suspect methods of warfare. In one example, the army smoked out a thousand tribesmen who had sought refuge in a system of caves after their village had been razed. A member of the French investigation committee surveying the massacre declared the French "have surpassed in barbarity the barbarians we came to civilize" (Stora, *Algeria: 1830-2000*, 5.).

        By 1871 control of Algeria was in the hands of the colonists as the military had subdued the resistance. The French settlers in Algeria advocated "the breakdown and dissolution of the Arab nation" with the goal to "take the tribe to pieces" (Ageron, *Modern Algeria*, 35.). Land dispossession was one of the most effective ways to dismantle the tribes. Before the French rule Algerian property was accessed based on a hierarchy of rights within the tribes. The French quickly dismantled this system, seizing the lands of tribes who had fought against France, public land, and lands pertaining to Muslim religious organizations, then partitioning them into smaller parcels and distributing them to colonists. By 1919 Algerian Muslims had lost 18.5 million acres–obviously of the most arable lands–to the colonial system (Stora, *Algeria: 1830-2000*, 7.). Shared land had provided rural tribes with various safety nets in times of poor harvests or famine. Once the colonists dismembered the system, tribal members were left dependent on moneylenders in times of shortages, especially as Muslims paid twice as many direct taxes as the European colonists at the beginning of the 20th century (Ageron, *Modern Algeria*, 73.). With the sale of land to the colonists, millions of Algerian peasants were displaced–either onto more arid lands where harvests decreased substantially or to the growing slums of the cities (Stora, *Algeria: 1830-2000*, 13.). This emigration from traditional lands further broke tribal bonds and deprived members of potential support networks, leaving them impoverished, likely in debt, and unable to be effectively integrated by the fledgling industrial centers.

        The significance of land dispossession cannot be overstated; however, in addition to the land seizures, the French colonial government also enacted a complicated tax regime specific to the (rural and urban) Muslim population, a special penal code with penalties for offenses "peculiar to the natives," a suppression of Muslim justices and courts, a prohibition of religious instruction, and a closure of many Muslim schools (Ageron, *Modern Algeria*, 69.). The famed political theorist Alexis de Tocqueville summarized the effects of the French colonial policy in Algeria thusly, declaring, "We have, in other words, made Muslim society far more miserable, disorganized, ignorant and barbarous that it ever was before it knew us" (Ibid., 21.).

the apartment. I found a pretty little pink rose in front of your picture. Madam Rebillet poured me a bit of Muscatel and Monsieur et moi talked about skiing only 20 miles from here in winter etc. Mimi age 8 just came in to say, *Bonsoir mon capitaine, voulez-vous venir a voir la lune.*[27] It is bright and beautiful tonight. My love dear. George.

[George to Peggy]
[V-Mail]

16 July, 1943

Peg dear:

    Dinner is finished so I am back up in the office waiting for Maj. Stipp[28] to come back before I leave. It is only about 3 blocks walk down to our mess. Junior Officers to & including Captains eat at one mess, Senior Officers at another. The food is not bad but they have the worst broken dirty native crockery, filthy table tops, and incompetent French waiters that I ever hope to see. They sell wine so it is next to impossible to get water. So long as the food is good you can't complain too much. Still waiting for a letter, read the first one you put in my luggage which is a wonderful way to boost morale which has not been too bad any way. I do appreciate that letter my dear and will live up to all that is expected of me. Stipp is back now so think I will walk home. He is a good gent. Love you tonight. George

[Peggy to George]
[V-Mail]

No. 12
Saturday July 17

Darling.

    Your letter came yesterday telling about your apartment. It made me happier than I have been in two years to know that somebody is taking care of you. If you can think of some little thing Madame would

---

27   Translated: "Good evening, my captain. Would you like to come see the moon."
28   Major George Stipp.

like, I'd like to send it to her. Your french is going to make me very jealous. You'll have to write me that way and keep me in practice. Tell Madame, *Je la remercie chaque jour parce qu'elle nous a fait une belle place chez elle.*[29] Figure that one out if you can. You mentioned the wonderful plums on ice, but what else do you eat? Is it good? This is a beautiful day which I'll spend working in our new kitchen. The house is lovelier every day. I also want to get my spinach, peas, carrots and beets planted so we'll have another crop in September. I have your bags all packed and will take them to the express office this morning. If you want any little things let me know as I can mail small packages. Take good care of yourself each day for me. Also get your Majority. Alf B. is a Capt. now and it burns me up. Larry just brought me a squashed flower to send you. Here it is [doodle]. Yours, Peggy

[George to Peggy]

Sunday P.M.
July 18, 1943

Peg my dear,

    Thought you might be interested in where I am living. Monsieur Rebillet gave me the enclosed picture. It is the building in the center, our apartment is on the top floor shown by arrow, and Schutz lives right next door—there is sort of a little partition between the balconies, but you can look around them. Madame Devevey was just showing Schutz how to hold their baby properly. It is kind of rough they cannot get the food that a baby really should have, very little milk. But what there is they can thank the US for, and they do.

    Madam was just helping me make up my laundry list of *pantalons, chemises, caleçon, serviettes* etc. Monsieur has located a woman who will wash my clothes for a very reasonable price. Most of them are terrible charging soldiers 40¢ for shirts, 50 & 60 for trousers etc. Madam is going to wash my *mouchoi[r]s* because I have had a

---

29   Translated: "I thank her each day because she has made a beautiful place for us in her home."

nasty head cold for the last couple of days, and used up just about all of them.

Strange how you think of things out of the past sometimes with no apparent reason. Remember the day we stopped in on the regatta on our way down to Adele & Fred Miller's wedding. I was reading through some reports in the office when all of a sudden, there I was standing with you just outside the yacht club, at Nina I believe it was. Wish we could be out sailing tonight with a light breeze and a full moon. Time will come again.

I can hear Schutz's voice out there on the balcony talking to the Deveveys about American girls. He is a good fellow, you will meet him some day.

Looking at you holding Robbie there in the picture I would like to pick the little rascal up. Give him a kiss for his daddy.

Schutz just commented on what a nice-looking wife I had and what a cute little daughter. I agree.

I am wondering just where you are now, whether you have moved yet and whether you are in Minneapolis. I know that moving must be an awful job. I'll bet our new house looks pretty fine by now. I hope you have managed all right on the help problem.

I surely am going to be glad to hear from you. But don't let that worry you for by the time you get this I will most certainly have had a letter.

Wish you were in my arms tonight my darling,
                  Yours, George

[Peggy to George]
[V-Mail]

No. 13
Mon. July 19

Darling.

Before I start racing around in circles for another day of moving,

I'll say good morning to you. This is a beautiful cool day with bright sunshine. All three kids are already outdoors to give us elbow room for the washing and packing. They are getting browner every day and look grand. Mother and Dad will get a real thrill out of their grandchildren. Saturday I packed and repacked your duffle at least ten times and finally at the express office I did it again. In the mess I took out one pair of shoes supposedly and got home to find I took out one each of two pair. "What a stupid wife" you'll say and rightly. If you'll write me requesting a pair of shoes I can mail them separately so do it in your next letter and I'll leave them wrapped so Anna can send them. Jim Linen[30] is on his way in a few days for the O.W.I. He has your address so you'll see him shortly. I tried to give him at least one of your shoes but like you 55 lbs. wasn't enough anyway. I hope you don't forget our date tonight at 5. It's such a lovely day I think we'll bicycle to our new house. Your[s] with love. Peggy

[George to Peggy]
[V-Mail]

20 July 43

My darling:

After 3 weeks I still miss you. Well maybe I will get over it soon. You will be out at Minnetonka when you get this. Just thought I might remind you of what a nice ride it is around the block when you are coming back from getting some ice cream in Wayzata some warm evening. Think you might spare the time to do that with me some evening, or maybe just walk down and sit out on the end of the dock? I suppose Irene & George will be playing bridge with the Wilsons. Larry might sleep down in Jack's[31] room, Robbie & Georgia up in the guest room, and you in your own room. Perhaps Larry can help his

---

30   James A. Linen III (b. 1912, d. 1988) served as a psychological warfare specialist for the Office of War Information (OWI) in the Eastern Mediterranean during WWII. After the war, he became the third publisher of *Time* magazine and later the president of its parent company Time, Inc.
31   Peggy's brother, John "Jack" Ford Gillette.

Grandpa move the sprinklers. Hope you can get some good steaks to cook on the grill. But I don't know who will stay at the table for a chat and a second cup of coffee with Irene, at least until I get back. My cold is all gone now, it was a strange time of year for a cold. You might tell Cocky[32] I just happened to think of a very sweet sincere note she wrote me when Mother died. Now I am looking forward to learning all about your trip. Love dear, George

[George to Peggy]
[V-Mail]

22 July 1943

My darling:

There is a very charming young lady whom I have not been able to talk with very successfully, even though my French is improving. She has all the charm and poise of a fine lady together with the charm and gaiety that brighten many lives besides her own. I will have to confess to being deeply in love with her. Perhaps it is best to leave it to your womanly intuition to supply the name. I would give much to spend an evening with her, better yet a lifetime.

Today being my day off I probably should have devoted the above space to what I did. Well I got off about 1:30, had lunch and met Monsieur Rebillet up here. Then we took Mimi (the little boy) and had a look about the city. We took a tram a long ways around thru the city ending up away up at a church on a high hill or little mountain whichever you prefer from which there is a wonderful view of the city below. Then we walked a long ways down to the ocean passing a long line of little girls led by a man who walked along the road singing in French. Just space to [The remainder is cut off as the V-Mail image was not photographed correctly.]

---

32 Catherine "Cocky" Gillette Piper (later Pierson then Knoblauch) was Peggy's favorite cousin growing up. Cocky's mother was Louise Gillette Piper, Peggy's aunt who was married to Harry Cushing Piper Sr.

[Peggy to George]
[V-Mail]

No. 14
July 23. Fri.

Dearest George.

    I am sitting at the table in the dining room of our new house with Larry on my right and Georgia my left & Doxie begging, and looking out our bay window onto a lovely view of terrace and woods. My breakfast is finished except a little coffee but the kids are still buried in french toast. The house is beginning to straighten out but I am leaving most of it to Anna after we leave tomorrow. This morning Doxie and I were in the garden at 6:15 pulling up passé vegetables and planting winter spinach, peas, carrots and beets. These won't be up until we get back so Anna only has the lima beans and tomatoes & corn. Our corn is wonderful. I cannot eat it without wishing to give you at least one bite. Larry just asked me when he could write you another letter. He said he wants to tell you what Kee-Kaw[33] did last night. It seems he was very bad and pulled out Larry's hair and "bopped" (if you please) him on the head so he couldn't comb his hair this morning for the awful bumps. Then he dirtied his teeth so that Larry had to brush and brush to get them clean again. Now Kee-Kaw is in the closet for the day. It looks as if I wrote his letter for him but I feared you might not understand all the writing. Did you get the letter he did write? The workmen are here to do the porch and need some decision or other. Wish you were here. Yours, Peggy

---

33   Kee-Kaw was Larry's stuffed monkey. Georgia remembers helping Larry rescue Kee-Kaw from the incinerator in the basement during this time. The two children hid Kee-Kaw under Larry's mattress after the rescue.

[George to Peggy]
[V-Mail]

24 July 1943

Peg dear,

    By this time you must be out in Minneapolis with the children. Hope Tina or Anna went with you. Have not gotten a letter yet but expect one soon. I think I will probably get mail much quicker once you start using this APO 512 in place of the other one. Was just thinking that 4 weeks ago tonight I arrived up in Greenwich at a late hour to get you out of bed. Next time I get home I will try to arrive at a more convenient hour. However, as I remember I was quite welcome, even if you did not remember it was our anniversary. Everything is going well with me. I am all over a cold I had. I took quite a long walk on the way home tonight. Just about every evening I have quite a chat with Monsieur Rebillet which helps my French along. Miss you very much my dear. Say hello to Larry and Georgia and tell them I have their pictures right in front of me. Much love, George

[George to Peggy]
[V-Mail]

26 July 1943

Peg dear:

    Just got back from downtown. Schutz, Helms and myself ate in one of the down town messes which is a bit cleaner than our own. Then we walked over to the Allied Officers Club to get membership cards, had a beer and read some old magazines. Then we walked over to the Red Cross Officers Club and had a bite to eat at the snack bar which is well crowded. We usually have to bum rides to get back out, but tonight we caught the last trolley-bus.

    Schutz ran into a friend who had seen his girl last Sunday, that is a week ago yesterday. She had gotten several of his letters which I was glad to hear as I figure you must have some of mine by now according to that. Still miss you dear. My love George.

[George to Peggy]
[V-Mail]

28/7/43

My dear Peggy:

This was a very great day for I have received the first letter from you today, it is the 11th one you have written but has no date. It tells about Larry going to a party all by himself. Getting to be quite a fellow, that pleases me. I sure would like to see the house now. If some of those pictures come out well you might send them. Did you ever pick up the ones I left at the drug store in Greenwich. Which reminds me I sure would like a big glass of fresh milk. Can't be had here. These letters will be going regular V-Mail in a few days. I am duty officer so I sleep here in the office tonight. A bit lonely and wish I were with you very much, we can check one month off anyway. I do love you. George.

[Peggy to George]

[#] 17
July 28, 1943
Wed.

Darling,

I've decided to try a few letters on paper this way as yours seem to come faster. Let me know how this comes through.

The lunch party yesterday was a real success. Aunt Louise[34] had

---
34   Louise was Peggy's aunt on her father's side. Georgia remembers, "They had a lake house on Lake Minnetonka where [the children] would be invited for 'tea' on the big screened-in porch overlooking the lake and after some 'proper behavior' [the children] would be released to go out and play and get a ride in the dog cart, pulled by a big dog and handled by the yardman."

Cocky, Debby, Polly, Thelma,[35] Lucy Dayton,[36] Kitty Pillsbury,[37] Anne Snyder,[38] Weezie[39] & Bobby's wife (Ginny Lewis[40]). The Well's house makes a swell club house and the food is fine. Oh yes Marty Howard[41] was there too. She has had no help since Jan. and both her children just had chicken pox and now poison ivy so she looked pretty white and tired. Kitty Pillsbury just had her third boy 2 weeks ago but she looked quite well. Polly is fine and plans to leave Mon. for Fort Worth where Holly meets her. She is leaving the children here until she finds a house. John Pillsbury[42] is in Honolulu now and expects to go on to [the] South Pacific shortly. John Snyder[43] is in Norfolk, VA training for [the] Navy. Anne expects him home on leave shortly. Tut and Ella are in La [Jolla], Calif. where he is teaching for the marines. Weezie Piper just had a serious operation in which her kidney was removed and a stone taken out. After recuperating another two weeks she is joining her husband (Army) in Seattle. They've had a tough time losing the baby and her illness. Bobby's wife is terribly attractive. He has been drafted and she is living with Aunt Louise and Uncle Harry and about runs the house for them. Don Dayton is still home and they have 2 children I think. Thelma has gotten awfully fat and the new baby looks just like the first with blond hair and black eyes. That's all the news I have gleaned so far except that Kay Clark Atwood Elliott gave birth to a boy.

---

35 Thelma was married to Peggy's brother Jack.
36 Lucy Dayton was the wife of Don Dayton, Chief Executive Officer of Dayton's department stores and grandson of the founder of Dayton's Dry Goods Company which is now the Target Corporation.
37 Katherine "Kitty" Pillsbury was the wife of John S. Pillsbury, grandson of Charles Alfred Pillsbury, one of the two brothers who founded the Pillsbury company.
38 Anne Snyder (née Morrison) was married to John Pillsbury Snyder Jr.
39 Louise Piper (later Aldrich) was Cocky's sister.
40 Virginia Lewis Piper was the wife of Harry "Bob" Piper Jr., brother of Louise and Cocky. In 1972 Virginia will be kidnapped from her home and released days later, unharmed, after a $1 million ransom demand is met. Press across the country covered the kidnapping story and the FBI claimed $1 million was the largest ransom ever paid in the United States for a kidnapping victim (Swanson, *Stolen From the Garden*, 80.).
41 Peggy refers to Martha Howard as "Marty" and "Mart" throughout her letters.
42 Kitty's husband, John Sargent Pillsbury Jr., served in the United States Navy during WWII.
43 John Pillsbury Snyder Jr. was the son of John Pillsbury Snyder and Nelle Stevenson, two of the Titanic's first survivors (*Encyclopedia Titanica*, "Nelle Snyder.") (*Encyclopedia Titanica*, "John Pillsbury Snyder.").

Friday night Dad has invited Buzz & Shorty to [the] Mpls. Club for dinner with us before seeing the Aqua follies (some swimming exhibition). So then I'll have more news for you.

Yesterday morning the fishing expedition wasn't very successful. We dug angleworms all right and caught a baby sunfish off the dock before we ever got into the boat, but with Tina & me and the children and three poles we couldn't get another thing afterwards.

Must mail this.

Loads of Love, Peggy

[Peggy to George]

[#]18

Thurs. eve July 29

Dearest George.

I received two letters from you yesterday and one today written the 16 & 19th and not photographed V-Mail. Then the one today was written the 16th also & came photographed. The one of the 19th was on this plain paper so that is the quickest way for you to write me. When you finally start getting my letters, let me know how they come through best too. It worried me that you still hadn't heard by the 19th. I trust it is all different now.

Tina went to Mpls. with Mabel for a day off today so Mom and I have had the children. I took them fishing this morning and we caught several little sunfish and crappies. Of course even the tiniest ones couldn't be thrown away so by the time I finished cleaning the 4-inch ones you could hardly find a piece to eat. We are having them for breakfast tomorrow. Dad and Mom are playing rummy here on the porch as I write. Dad first took us for a row on the lake. Yesterday we took the children to town after the rain stopped intending to let them swim at Minikahda. But it turned out to be Calcutta Golf Day so they chased us off and we had to go to Calhoun Beach and have a picnic. Afterwards we stopped to see the Clows.

Nell was downtown but Marg was there. She was pleased to have us stop. They have bought a very nice duplex apt. and are very happy in it. I took your letter telling about where you are living and read parts of it to her. I was thrilled to get home and have a picture of it. How I hope you can stay there. Especially after reading Time's account of the Sicily campaign tonight.[44] I'm going to try and have that magazine sent to you. I am so relieved to know Madame Rebillet and her husband are taking care of you somewhat. If I could only show my appreciation some way just for the washing of a hankie when you have a cold. The interest means so much. Be sure and learn french so you can teach me. Will say goodnight again. How I wish you could climb in bed with me and listen to the good old Minnetonka bullfrogs tonight, and perhaps give me a kiss now & then.

                      Yours, Peggy

[George to Peggy]
[V-Mail]

                                           30 July 43

Peg dear,

    Received your letter dated July 17 today, that is the second letter I have gotten. Understand our mail will be photographed in [the] next few days, both of your letters have been. Had yesterday afternoon off, so I wrote a couple of letters and took a walk around town. Went to the Allied Officers Club for dinner. It is in one of the down town hotels. It is crowded, mostly British, but clean and a change. I ate with a boy from Philadelphia, U of Penn who would have graduated last year, also [with] an officer in the Yugoslavian Air Force who had an interesting tale of imprisonment in Germany [and] escape to Spain where he was held in a concentration camp. He has really had it

---

44   Colorful descriptions of Operation Husky from the air, land, and sea are found in *Time* magazine, Volume XLII, No. 3 and No. 4.

rough—no news of his family or friends. This war will sure leave a lot of lasting hatred. You might send me some V-Mail paper—it is hard to get here. All my love. George

[Peggy to George]

[#]18
Sat. July 31.

Darling.

Larry and I are both writing you a letter this morning. He is using V-Mail and crayons. I hope it passes the censors. He has drawn all sizes of fish to tell you how many he caught yesterday. I fixed them each a pole out of a stick plus line, cork, sinker, hook and worm. They stood on the dock and pulled them in 2 inches long as fast as I could rebait their hooks. What a thrill they had. Both eyes were just popping. I was afraid they'd fall in with all the excitement.

Last night was the night Dad took us to Mpls. Club with Buzz & Shorty. They both looked grand and wanted to know all about you and said to be sure and give you their love.

I was interrupted here to address Larry's letter and climb a ladder. Dad is putting up a rope swing down where we used to play croquet and he had a ladder leaned up to climb a tall tree. I thought with tennis shoes on and my youth I could stand the altitude easier than I could stand to watch him climb. They'll never know what I went through up there trying to follow Dad's instructions for making a half hitch and not looking at the ground and keeping my knees from shaking me down. Anyway the kids are now helping Dad make the swing board and all are happy. It's so silly to get dizzy up high but I cannot seem to help it.

I saw in the paper this morning that the Air Transport Command is to carry mail overseas now.[45] I surely hope that will get my letters to you more quickly. I know how anxious I got when 10 days passed after your cable and I hadn't heard. Perhaps you've had ten altogether by now.

Robin is beside me here on the porch in his pen. He fusses for me to look at him and then breaks into a smile and puts his arms up to be picked up. How I wish you could satisfy his demands this morning. He's so soft and cuddly.

Yours, Peggy

[Peggy to George]

[#]19
Sunday Aug. 1

Darling.

This has been quite a busy, hot day, but it is ten P.M. now and there is a nice breeze blowing. We are sitting on the porch listening to the radio before going to bed.

Larry and Georgia kept me busy this morning making sand cakes and catching baby frogs. One of the frogs was darker in color than the rest so Larry filled his pail with water from the bird bath and proceeded to bathe the "dirty frog." He was working at it for quite a while and then came up here on the porch carrying a very limp frog and announced, "I washed him and washed him but he's still dirty and sort a sick, I think."

This afternoon Tina dressed them up in blue and white sunsuits. Georgia with an organdie "bow on her janney," which she showed off

---

45 The Air Transport Command (ATC) was created in June 1942 to support the U.S. oversea forces and their allies by unifying civilian and military air transportation options. Combining the Ferry Command (responsible for transporting aircraft around the world) and the Air Service Command (responsible for transferring cargo and personnel), the ATC was divided into divisions based on geographic areas and each section was responsible for coordinating the advancement of supplies, equipment, and personnel for their area. During the North Africa campaign, the ATC's air routes to Africa and the Middle East provided crucial lend-lease supplies to the Allied forces fighting against the German Afrika Corps. The ATC supported each theater and by the war's end, its fleet totaled 3,700 aircraft with 209,000 military and 104,000 civilian personnel (van der Linden, "Air Transport Command and the Airlines During WWII."). Notably, the Ferrying Division of the ATC included the famous Women Airforce Service Pilots who delivered newly-constructed aircraft to training bases and ports of departure.

to everyone. They had a swim later with Tina and me. I think we may have Larry swimming before we are through here. They both love the water. Georgia doesn't seem to care if her head is above or below it. The news is coming over now, and it's looking like a poor bet that Italy will surrender and get the Germans out. The Italian navy looks like it's about to finally go to sea under Nazi seamen.

We just returned from [the] Lafayette Club where we had dinner with the Hornbergs. Chuck & his wife are here visiting from California & Jack's wife is up here from Ottumwa, Iowa where he is in the Navy air service. Both the boys married very attractive girls. Neither have any children so I brought them back here to show off our three despite the hour. Larry and Georgia were hot upstairs and glad to be disturbed and raved over and of course Robin always wants visitors.

Last night I went to a party at the Sparks. Bob & Janet Andrews were there. Bob is working in the Sheriff's office as a policeman for liquor law enforcement. Kinnards were there—both <u>fat</u> especially Betty. The Hangers were there and she is pregnant again. I tried to be especially pleasant to them and was properly snubbed, if you please. They are both very arrogant about his job which seems to be to replace you and Ki to hear him talk. Don't worry dear, I never even expressed an opinion on direct questions and I got plenty of them from Buzz. Evidently they see quite a bit of the Hangers and Roger has told him the most fantastic tales of his position, capabilities, responsibilities and prospects for American Linen. Roger also told me at three different times how wonderful it was that Ki had caught up to you in Army rank as that had been his ambition ever since he entered the service. You'll be glad to know that I even controlled myself on that score and said "Yes, isn't it nice?" Whoever says I'm not self-controlled is crazy.

Another thing that's driving me crazy about Army rank is the question "Is George a major?" Whoever started that story will be quickly poisoned in their sleep if I ever discover them. The first 20 times I was asked out here I carefully explained the whole story. The last 40 times I've screamed "No! He is not." I'd like to add soon—"So help me God—I'll kill the next person who asks me that."

Enough of my petty gripes. But I was stirred up last night with seven couples at a dinner party, plenty of food, gas & too much liquor and every man in civilian clothes & all wives with husbands. I purposely talked war and postwar to try and see what they'd say and nobody did or said a thing except change the subject as fast as possible. This place is far worse than Greenwich. That's not really fair, because it's not true of any other group. The younger married group and all the Pillsbury, Snyder, crowd is split up. Also the defense work and patriotism among older people is all one could hope for.

Dad is going to N.Y.C. tomorrow on a Navy contract to see Mr. Harkrader. He'll be gone a week.

You'll be surprised, I know, to hear I still love you very much darling and miss you more and more each day. I even did a very silly thing and went to Daytons to buy a beautiful pink satin nightie for our second honeymoon. It made me feel good anyway. My alibi was that it was the last one and no more pure silk will be had for many years. I fear even Mother saw through it. It's a very pretty nightie, anyway.

Goodnight sweetheart. Don't forget our date tomorrow night.

Yours, Peggy

[George to Peggy]
[V-Mail]

2 August 1943

Peg darling:

The letter you sent on 19th July arrived on the 31st, not bad. I have been trying to figure how long I should address you at Minnetonka. It is nice and cool up here on the hill in the evening, even after a hot day. Just took a cold shower, put on my pajamas, had a cup of coffee which Madame insisted on fixing for me. They usually do not eat until late, about nine o'clock. I gave her your message which pleased her a lot. Every few days I find a vase with some small flowers next to your picture which is in front of me on my desk here. Gas is rationed so we are limited to one bath with hot water per week, but I take a cold shower about every day. The food is good, we avoid eating any place but our mess. Only items we lack that I miss are milk (fresh, we have condensed) and oranges. So you see we are really well taken care of. They have replaced the crockery in the mess with enameled plates and cups, and have real glasses which are much cleaner than the crockery. Much love, George.

[Peggy to George]
[V-Mail]

No. 20
Mon. Aug. 2.

Dearest George,

The children are in bed for their naps after a very busy morning. We dug angleworms and went out in the boat fishing. This time we caught really good-sized fish and they certainly kept me busy. The screams should have scared the fish right out of the lake. I'd pull one pole in and another would be waiting to be pulled out. We caught 4 big crappies with one angleworm. The children were no more excited than I was. Then we came in and had a swim and played in the water before eating our fish for lunch.

Now I am sitting in the car at the Crystal Bay store while Mom does her marketing and I hope she will bring out a letter from you when she comes. Most of all I hope my next letter will say you have started hearing from me.

There are so many things out here which remind me of good times we had together. Every evening I walk out on the lawn and dock and sit down where we used to sit and think about those happy hours.

Remember old Doxie. He was a good watch dog even then.

I haven't heard from Anna yet but Larry said he had a letter from Kee-Kaw this morning and he told him that Doxie was fine and Anna is getting along very well with the canning. It was nice to know. Yours always. Peggy

[Peggy to George]

#21

Tues. Aug. 3.

Darling.

Robin wore his first pair of shoes this morning and of course they were the same little pair you bought for Larry. He looked just as cute and was just as thrilled. In the playpen he pounded his feet on the bottom, put them in his mouth and untied the laces.

Larry just came in [and] said to write you a big fish that he caught for you. I'll let him do it himself.

As you noticed by the letters, he is getting the idea that letters are written by using the alphabet which was his own thought. He couldn't elaborate on the theory enough to have I G R or A mean anything, but that will come.

Georgia just dropped marbles down the register here in my room. Now that's stopped so I can go on.

Cocky and Carlie[46] came to dinner last night. Also Aunt Grace Cotton. Carlie was very pleasant. I sort of expected the sulky mood when Dad wasn't here but he couldn't have been nicer. He looks fine and certainly had some experiences with the Navy. Now he is raising hogs. They have no help and have 95 pigs. We really should give up all work except farming. When I told him I paid $25.00 for a 60 lb. hog he almost died. Out here they cannot get $8.00 for them. Cocky brought Peggy and Kitty over yesterday afternoon to play and swim with ours and they had a marvelous time. Kitty hung around Cocky like Larry

---

46   Charles Frederick Pierson, Cocky's first husband.

used to do to me but the other three played in the sandbox and then had a swell time in the water. I was asking Carlie how to go about teaching him to swim and he felt another year would be easier when he is 5. They learn easily then. Now he felt he should just splash around and get used to the water. They are both doing that with gusto.

Looks as if New York and harlem are having trouble.[47] The radio tries to imply that the difficulty is not racial.[48] I'm glad we are out here where everything seems so quiet and simple. I am having the most wonderful rest and vacation, but the best part of each day is when I sit down to write you a letter.

Loads of love, Peggy

[Peggy to George]
[V-Mail]

#22
Aug. 4, Wed.

Dearest George

Had a V-mail letter (photograph) written July 20, yesterday. I was sick to know you haven't heard from me yet. As you can see by the number, I have been writing you. The children are all having naps now. We have five here today as Thelma has parked her two. Larry & I went fishing again this morning and had wonderful luck. He pulled in a great big crappie and said "This is for Daddy. We'll

---

47 Late August 1, 1943, a Black soldier intervened as a White police officer detained a Black woman for disorderly conduct inside a hotel. At some point during the altercation, a bullet shot from the police officer's gun grazed the soldier. Rumors spread throughout Harlem that a Black soldier had been killed in front of his mother by a White police officer. Riots followed, fueled by long-standing, dormant discontent over the high cost of living, essential goods and food shortages, rent gouging, job inequity, and racial discrimination in the U.S. Armed Forces. The riots lasted until August 2, resulting in hundreds of arrests, six deaths, and millions of dollars in damage

48 Peggy is correct. News reports at the time declared the Harlem riots to be the acts of hoodlums from other areas. Leaders of local, Black organizations also insisted the riots were not race riots in the sense that Blacks and Whites were not physically fighting each other (as had occurred earlier the same year in Detroit). The majority of Whites involved in the Harlem riots were police officers (again, unlike in Detroit where White citizens were involved in looting and violence). Black leaders in Harlem noted inadequate social and economic conditions, as well as the discrimination Black soldiers were forced to endure in the United States Armed Forces as likely causes of frustration. Today the Harlem riots are considered race riots (riots where racial anger or frustration are seen as primary causes or significant contributing factors to the violence) due to the discriminatory racial policies that led to inequalities and frustrations experienced by the Black residents of Harlem ("Race Bias Denied As Rioting Factor.").

keep it for him so he can eat it when he comes back." Doesn't that sound delicious? Aunt Grace was asking him about you yesterday and he said "My Daddy is in the Army way across the ocean. But he is coming back to live at our new house with me and stay until I am big like he is." I liked your letter with all the reminiscences of this place. Next Monday night I'm going to take a trip around the block and if you've gotten my last letters by now, you'll know I've thought a great deal about you while sitting on the old dock. So far we haven't had a grill picnic but if we can get hamburger, we'll try it soon. I am going to give a mexican party for the children (I mean mexican decorations). Yours, Peggy

[George to Peggy]
[V-Mail]

> Thursday
> 5 Aug. 1943

My dear;

    I just finished a warm bath and feel very comfortable. You might be interested to know that I love you very much. The first thought I had this morning as I woke up was of you. Perhaps I had been dreaming about you all night. I stayed in bed for a few minutes just thinking of you and wishing that I could be waking up with you beside me. So with that start the rest of the day was very pleasant also. At breakfast I had a long chat with a sociable British officer. This afternoon, I went out to the beach with a bunch of officers, two truck loads as a matter of fact. We went out about 1:30 [and] arrived about 2:00. They have a place all fixed up to change, shower afterwards, and serve tea. Remembering the burns you and I got at Glyfada beach I was more careful this time and so have no burns tonight. The water was clean and cool with a beautiful sand beach and quite calm. Spent the afternoon with Lt. Flott, from Chicago, [he] went to Carlton and majored in International Relations, so he knew Spykman[49] at Yale & Schumann on our bookshelf so we had a nice talk. I remember Monday night too. George

[Peggy to George]

[#]24
Aug. 6, Friday

Darling

Our trip to Minneapolis with the children yesterday was a huge success. They saw everybody in American Linen, Miss Finn,[50] Baxter,[51] Jack in [the] elevator,[52] Miss Rose who did Jessie's[53] hair, Pearl, Mr. Benninghoff, Hanger, Tallifer, the man who is hard of hearing, and all the girls throughout. Everyone asked about their Daddy and all were very much pleased. Miss Finn and I talked over the N.W. bank acct. and taxes. Right now there is a balance of $3,412.68 in N.W. and in your F.M.S. Corp. acct. $1,971.64. The latter is not sufficient to buy the tax bond for June 15th and the next dividend is not until Oct. Consequently, I suggested as soon as the rest of the house bills are paid that we transfer enough from the N.W. acct. to buy that. We still owe the Clows a little and also Mr. Hvolbeck. Some of this I can pay from my allowance. I paid for the moving out of my allowance. It was $103.+. I also paid for our tickets to and from Mpls. Miss Finn also suggested that she take the full 20% withholding tax from your F.M.S. salary as each company is deducting exemptions for me and the kids and that will have to be adjusted later anyway as they can only be taken off once. You might write her about this.

---

49   Nicholas John Spykman (b. 1893, d. 1943) was the Sterling Professor of International Relations at Yale University as well as co-founder and first director of the Yale Institute of International Studies.
50   George's secretary, Alice Finn.
51   Jesse Baxter was a nanny for George and Ki. He was also their mother's chauffeur.
52   Georgia remembers Jack as "the man who ran the elevator, keeping the brass all shiny and greeting everyone as they had to take the elevator up to the American Linen Supply offices on the second floor. There were stores at the street level and you went through a granite and marble entrance at street level on the first floor to reach the company offices on the 2nd floor. It was a big deal for [the kids] to go into Minneapolis and visit. Sometimes Jack let us sit on his stool and operate the elevator. He even wore white cotton gloves to keep from making marks on the brass."
53   Jess McIvor Steiner, George's mother.

The final payment has been made this week on your Mother's estate. As soon as your insurance money is paid to you, that is settled. The Knox Ave. house is not re-rented yet. They are hoping to get the Scotts out. They have asked to rent for 6 months more, but of course that's not satisfactory. It sounds hopeful that they might get out and then the Murphys will take it with the idea of buying after a year.

Frank came to town yesterday. They are coming out here for dinner with Dad & Mom & me tonight. They being (Roland Pallock & Frank). Helen didn't come up so he is returning to Chicago tomorrow.

The children behaved beautifully at Estlers for lunch with Mrs. Alworth[54] and the Clows. The lunch was delicious and very enjoyable. Nell had a letter from Teedie saying she'd be up the 20th for a day. Ki doesn't know when he can get leave.

The kids are screaming to go to Crystal Bay and mail this so more tomorrow darling. I miss you so much and love you even more.

      Yours, Peggy

[Peggy to George]
[V-Mail]

                [#]25
               Sat. Aug. 6.

Darling,

Again I am sitting in the car at Crystal Bay while Mom does her marketing and I hope for a letter from you. Yesterday I had two photographed V-letters written July 22 and 24th. It certainly was grand to get them. I love to know the things you do and particularly what you think about and how you are feeling. I told Larry and Georgia about your trip with the little boy on the tram and they both want you to take them instead. They want to know if you have gotten

---

54 Margaret Alworth was the wife of Duluth businessman and philanthropist Marshall W. Alworth and daughter-in-law of mining and real estate tycoon Marshall H. Alworth. In 1949, Marshall W. and Margaret established the Marshall H. and Nellie Alworth Memorial Fund in honor of Marshall's parents. The Alworth fund provides scholarships to high school seniors from northern Minnesota who will study math or science in college. Marshall W. also funded the construction of the Alworth Planetarium at the University of Minnesota Duluth.

another little boy while you are away. I assured them that you only borrowed one. Frank and Roland Pollock seemed to enjoy the evening and so did we all. Daddy made a martini which we had on the porch while Larry and Georgia entertained in their pajamas. We just talked after dinner mostly on postwar free trade. I am just ignorant enough, I guess, to believe that it is a good thing. They felt it would cause a terrific depression here. Perhaps it would for a while but I think everything would seek its own level and so would labor. Goods would flow in here cheaper so why should we have to maintain such high wages. The standard of living would not be lowered. Yours, Peggy

[George to Peggy]
[V-Mail]

Sat. 7 Aug. 1943

Dear Peggy,
    My printing in the address doesn't look so good tonight, guess I am getting sleepy. There is an annoying habit here of everyone coming back up to the office after dinner, but then there is not much else to do of an evening anyway. I have gotten 4 of your letters, but never did figure out what arrangements you made with the girls. Hope you tell me well ahead of time when you return east so I will know where to write. Would like to be out there at the lake with you. Guess I will go on up the hill to my "home." Miss you very much my dear. With love, George

[George to Peggy]
[V-Mail]

Sunday 8 Aug. 1943

My darling,
    Just got out of bed, so I thought I would tell you how much I miss you before I get dressed. Don't believe there is ever a morning when

I wake that you are not the first thought I have, a nice way to wake especially when I shall find you really there. It is probably because I always enjoyed so much the intimacy of those few moments in the morning, and the evening too at bed time, when we could talk and do just as it pleased us without being disturbed. That is of course if the children did not think of something or wake up. It would be fun to pry you out of bed, put on a swim suit and try the water before breakfast. I suppose you are doing that often now. The clock seems to have kept right on going while I have been writing so I will have to hurry now. Wish its hands would go like a windmill for the next year. Here I have wasted a lot of paper when I could have just said I love you and miss you very much. George.

[George to Peggy]

No. 1
Sunday
Aug. 8, 1943

My Peggy,

    Last evening I was comfortable in a deck chair on the balcony just outside my room, taxing my memory to name some of the constellations. I am wrong, it was the night before last, and here with something important to tell you I wrote two letters with no mention of it. Perhaps that will arouse your womanly curiosity. At any rate, as I was saying, I was on the balcony Friday evening when I saw two falling stars one right after the other, so of course I made two wishes, one being that my best girl might make any wish she wanted and have it come true. So there you are. Now probably one of those stars represented each of the 'great dictators' which should make them extra potent wishing stars.

    I received the letter you wrote the 1st Monday you were in Minneapolis, so will number my letters as you request beginning with this one. Sure wish we were sitting out on the dock together tonight.

Perhaps we could even take a swim out to the Gluek's float and climb up on the tower. I remember doing that with you once. Wish you had the little x-boat there to sail.

You might tell Larry about my little friend Mimi. I showed him how to make some animals out of pipe cleaners tonight. When I came out from my shower I found a *cheval* or a *chien* I have not quite decided which, standing on my desk along with a fierce looking serpent. Mimi has a sling shot which he was trying out on the balcony tonight but the *lune* and the *étoiles* were *trop loin*. They give us a ration of candy, chewing gum, cigarettes, etc. so I brought Mimi some candy and chewing gum tonight which pleased him very much. He very nicely took part of the candy to his sister. He is a nice little boy. Tell Larry also I hope he is learning a lot of nursery rhymes for me, because I want to hear them when I come home.

Hope you received the picture of this apartment which I sent you some time ago.

That is strange that you should have awakened at that particular time. Somehow those things seem to be more than just a coincidence.

Maj. Stipp, who is [in] charge of the section I am in, is a good gent and a capable officer, reserve of course. He commanded a battalion of artillery through the Tunisian campaign seeing considerable action. He was an engineer for a power company in Indiana, has a nice looking wife and children. Speaking of promotion, I may have gotten a bad break on this transfer, but he has been in grade for 2½ years with an excellent record so at least I have company.

I am not managing very well without you my dear, guess I am a bit in love maybe.

All yours, George.

[George to Peggy]

No. 2
Monday
9 Aug. 43

Peg dear,

Well I am all ready for bed. I suppose you are lying out on the lawn getting some sun in one of those swim suits that I always look at more than once. Glad to hear the lake is so high again.

Course I know you are thinking of me about now. I wish I were there too. There are a lot of things I would like to do with you in Minneapolis. I will be glad to hear about our friends out there. Of course I have been over every little minute detail of the lake house and grounds since I have known you were there. I suppose you have taken the boat across the bay to play golf with your Daddy. And you probably sliced the first one right up alongside of the club house off the 1st tee. Well if I were there now I am sure that the 4th hole would find me in Hornberg's back yard.

Went down to the Red Cross to a French class right after dinner but found the teacher to be one we don't get much from so returned with Schutz, walked all the way back up the hill from town, about 40 minutes hike up about a 45° slope. Found Ream and Sparks[55] (also junior G men from the "Pantygone") along the way and persuaded them to play bridge for a while which we did across the hall in Devevey's apartment. Came back here to find some talisman roses & small pink flowers by your picture. Also a bottle of rum & a glass so I took a drink to your very good health. I do miss you and love you so much my dear.

George

---

55   Murray E. Sparks, assigned to the G-4 Section NATO.

[Peggy to George]

[#]26
Monday Aug. 9

Darling,

Dad's just left for work and we have all finished breakfast but Georgia. As usual she's still at it. Larry has his new "jeep" here on the floor of the porch while I write to you. He wants to know if your own airplane will take this letter across the ocean to your house. How nice it will be when he knows that "your house" and "our house" are one and the same.

We had a nice weekend. Saturday night the Harry Doerrs came over and we played cut in bridge. I mostly knitted. I have finished the yellow suit for Robin and it looks very cute. Now I am going to make myself some underwear. Mine all went to pieces just when there is nothing left in silk to buy.

Yesterday Jack came out with little Georgie.[56] They try to have him with our children so he can learn a few things he is so backward. I could cry over the little fellow. He's six months older than Georgia and you'd think he was a year younger. He is much smaller, doesn't say a word, still wets his pants and sits on his Mother or Grandma's lap all the time. When they aren't around, Larry gets him to play occasionally. I wish I could take him back to Greenwich for a couple months and I know he'd be O.K. But I'd probably lose Tina and it's an awful responsibility if he should get sick. It's pathetic to watch either Jack or Thelma try to discipline him. They should never have had children.

There are so many things I'd like to tell you of how I miss you and look forward to our reunion, but it's so hard to write those things knowing other people are to read them too. After six years of married life it seems as if we should have some privacy. Anyway, you know how much I love you and miss seeing you and feeling you around me

---

56   Georgie is Jack and Thelma's eldest child.

so these things don't really have to be written. It is nice to have them repeated at least once a day though.

We had a terrific thunder storm last night which the children are still talking about. Georgia is just asking her doll if the thunder woke her up too. The sun is coming out though this morning so I'm going to dress and help Mom wash. Then we'll all drive to Wayzata and mail this. Saw the Pipers yesterday. Uncle Harry thinks we should put Georgia in the movies.

Loads of Love, Peggy

[Peggy to George]
[V-Mail]

[#]27
Tues. Aug. 10.

Dearest George

You cannot guess what I am going to do. Tomorrow I am taking the morning train to Duluth to spend Wed. & Thurs. with Mrs. Alworth. She is having a party tomorrow night so it may not be too bad!

This is a rainy day and the children are raising the devil indoors. Mabel and Tina are trying to do the ironing with them at their feet. Mother and I are going to Mpls. to do some errands and stay for dinner. Dad is coming in and we are taking the Clows for dinner at the Minikahda Club. Then I am going back to spend the night with them and do some planning on the drapes for the house. Also the Duluth train leaves so early in the morning, that it's too hard to get in from the lake.

Yesterday I received a photo V-letter written July 24 telling of Schutz's girl getting letters. At least I'm glad you know I've gotten word from you. In another week if you haven't heard still I'll try and cable you through the Red Cross. Georgia just stopped to give you a big hug and kiss on this letter. It ought to strangle you from all the grunting she went through. Yours, Peggy

[George to Peggy]

[#]3
Wednesday
11 Aug. 1943

My dearest,

Really I should be getting into bed right now. You see I started to write just three letters. I had gotten home by 7:30 which is a very early hour to get away, but just about the time I got my paper out of the drawer Monsieur R. came in with a great deal of chatter so I got to *parlent avec lui*,[57] whereupon Madame brought out a tray with coffee and cups and a bottle of liquor. I get quite a kick out of talking to him, [and] well, we ended up talking about labor unions, strikes, and means of improving labor conditions. Well it seems that our good friends the juifs[58] are the agitator racketeers among the french syndicates the same as in our own unions,[59] [and] he referred also to Premier Blum[60]

---

57 Translated: "talk with him"
58 Translated: "Jews"
59 While some American Jews participated in labor demonstrations and were union members and organizers, it is disingenuous to imply that they were the sole or main "agitators" among the U.S. labor unions (see footnote 18, page 19, for example). Similarly, it is misleading to claim on those grounds alone that their work was dishonest, fraudulent, and frequently relied on intimidation to succeed–as the use of "racketeer" indicates. A closer look at how Jews were portrayed in the media in both France and the United States as well as a deeper examination into the history of Jewish labor unions might reveal what helped shape these perspectives. Unfortunately, that is outside the scope of this book.
60 At one time the "most hated man in France," Léon Blum (b. 1872, d. 1950) was the country's first Socialist prime minister and the first person of Jewish heritage to hold the office (Judt, *The Burden of Responsibility*, 30.). As a Socialist government, Blum's Popular Front was committed to improving workers' situations throughout the country. From June 1936 to June 1937, the length of time the Popular Front remained in power, Blum's government achieved numerous gains for workers, including but not limited to, prohibiting sanctions against strikers, an increase by 20% for average wages, unemployment insurance, a forty-hour work week, and two weeks of paid vacation each year for workers.
    To the extreme concern of French colonists in Algeria, the Popular Front empathized with the disenfranchised Algerian Muslims. In 1936 Blum co-sponsored the Blum-Viollette bill, proposing an extension of political rights (including the right to vote) to qualified Algerian Muslims (initially 21,000 Muslim academics, professionals, and military service members) (Stora, *Algeria 1830-2000*, 18.). Said rights would then gradually extend to the Muslim masses. Most importantly, Algerian Muslims would not be required to abandon their status as Muslims in order to access these rights reserved for French citizens. (Previously both Algerian Muslims and Jews were required to renounce their identity as Muslims and Jews in order to become French citizens. This was fixed in 1870 for Algerian Jews but Algerian Muslims will have to wait until March 1944 for the same rights as French citizens.) The Blum-Viollette bill earned Blum the contempt of French settlers in Algeria. There was such an outcry among colonists in the government, the bill was rejected by the Senate and never brought before the Chamber of Deputies.
    Critics of Blum's government erroneously claimed the Popular Front was responsible for France's defeat by Nazi Germany and these critics capitalized on Blum's Jewish background to fuel "a vast wave of anti-Semitism" that engulfed France and bled into her colonies (Birnbaum, Leon Blum, 98.). In September 1940, Blum was arrested and imprisoned (along with other officials of the former Popular Front) and Marshal Pétain's Vichy government took Blum to trial in February 1942 for allegedly betraying the duties of his office. Blum defended himself so eloquently and effectively that the Nazis "discouraged Vichy from continuing the trial for fear that Blum's courtroom

with all his jewish cabinet[61] as the very center of the rotten core of the prewar french government. I still contend that there must be a few good ones some place.

The colored picture arrived today in your letter of July 28th. I am very pleased with it but would of course preferred one with you in it. We had fun that day. That is really a very good picture. Thanks a lot. I wonder if you got the one of the apt. I live in. I never have gotten any of the letters sent to APO 4004. I was glad to hear all about our Mpls. friends. Sure wish I was with you. Miss you so much my dear and love you, well a little any way.

George.

[Peggy to George]
[V-Mail]

#28
Aug. 12, Thurs.

Darling,

I've had a lovely time up here in Duluth except for my usual emptiness without you to enjoy beautiful places with me. The party here last night included Ade and Lib Howard but no other people from Minneapolis. We had a delicious dinner and I won at poker. This morning I had a long visit with Mr. A. He is a very lovable person and most interesting. When I have more space I want to tell you his ideas on settling this mess in our own government and labor. We went to

---

achievement–turning the tables and assigning responsibility for the French tragedy to his accusers–would have disastrous public consequences" (Judt, *The Burden of Responsibility*, 34.). In March of 1943, Blum was deported to the concentration camp at Buchenwald. Blum survived Buchenwald and later imprisonment at Dachau. He was liberated by Allied troops and returned to France in 1945.

61 While this book is not the place to address the origins, mutations, and perpetuation of Euro-Algerian and French anti-semitism, clarifications on Monsieur Rebillet's comments are required. Unlike his predecessors, Léon Blum chose to govern with a small cabinet of fellow members from the coalition (which included the French Communist and the Radical-Socialist Republican parties in addition to Blum's own French Section of the Workers' International). Religious or ethnic background was not a determining factor as to who could participate. As an example, Blum's cabinet leader André Blumel was of a Jewish background, but Roger Salengro, the Minister of the Interior, and Édouard Daladier, the Minister of National Defense, were not. Blum also made a point to include women in government positions at a time when women in France did not even have the right to vote. Irène Joliot-Curie (daughter of Nobel Prize winners Pierre and Marie Curie and not of Jewish origin) served as Undersecretary of State for Scientific Research and was one of three women to head departments in the Popular Front (Birnbaum, *Leon Blum*, 101.).

the country club and I enjoyed three sets of good tennis—doubles. We had lunch there and came back for the 'siesta.' A Mrs. Mitchell came for cocktails and then the Alworths and I went to the town club for a delicious lobster dinner. Now we have just returned from an hour's drive along the lakeshore after dinner. There is a lovely moon on the water tonight and I cannot help wondering if you have a moon too tonight on the water and are wishing all the things that I am. This is such a lonesome life even among the extreme luxuries of this household without you, dear. It must be so much worse living the way you are without old friends, or children around. I cannot even think about the awful nights you must spend, but I'll do all I can to make it all up to you when this horrible war is over. Yours always, Peggy

[George to Peggy]
[V-Mail]

No. 4
Friday 13 Aug. 1943

Peg dear,

Things were going rather slow this afternoon so I pulled out one of the 4 V-mail sheets, which is our weekly ration and managed to get the address on it when along comes some work. So I have had dinner now and am back up in the office. Yesterday was my day off so I went out to the beach with Maj. Little and Lt. McIntyre. It wasn't so good as last week, as the water was very dirty and there were a lot of flies, so we stayed on the beach for a short time then went back up to dress and get some tea. We got off the truck down town, went to a movie the Red Cross put on, then had dinner at one of the down town messes. When I got back up to the apartment Schutz, Sparks, and Ream wanted to play Monopoly so we did for about an hour with M. Devevey. Then I went over to bed and wished you were with me until I fell asleep, but woke up this morning wishing the same thing. Yours, George

[George to Peggy]

[#]5
Friday
13 August 1943

My darling Peggy:

Note the date. I am being real foolish, writing you two letters on the same day. I walked up the hill early tonight [and] took my weekly warm bath. Came out to find some fresh pink flowers in a little silver vase next to a picture of a very charming young lady whom I adore. Also a tray with hot coffee and a bit of rum to go with it.

Larry's letter arrived today. You thank him, tell him I am trying real hard to read it, that I think it is one of the new nursery rhymes he is learning for me about the little boy who went fishing. Don't know of any such myself. Hope you do.

Guess since I have told you all the news already tonight I will have to tell you a little of a story about a girl who has come to be such a part of me. Remember when you came to our prep school prom there was a youngster who kissed you under a tree in the moonlight. After that I never did learn my French very well. You see that tree was just outside the room we had our French classes in. Of course when I looked out that way, I just could not keep my mind *sur le français*. Then between week ends at college, perhaps a Thanksgiving dinner at the Whale Inn, the party-filled Christmas holidays, with always a date on New Year's eve, then summer vacations with dances at Woodhill, Lafayette and Minikahda, a house party up at Thunder Lake, or sometimes just an evening talking out on the dock, or a movie at Wayzata, we came to know each other so well. So different in temperament, we found ourselves so alike in the way we wanted to live, to think, to work, and to be considerate of other people.

Remember a starlit evening on a terrace in a strange land, a bottle of champagne, soft waltz music, a blanket over our knees, and a beautiful city spread out far below. That night and many others we talked of what we wanted to give and take from life, and so always you strengthened in me my desire to be a fine, decent, truly great man who should have your love and respect. Then what can I say for the pride and joy you have given me with Larry, Georgia, and now Robbie. There is the deep happiness of knowing that we live on in them. Nowhere is there a more beautifully kept home, such carefully looked after children, nor such a charming hostess to entertain friends.

There are thoughts too of the good meals you cooked for me with the happy evenings that followed in a funny little apartment in the wrong part of town. Larry looked so comfortable tucked into my bed roll.

You came a long ways to see me last summer and I hated so to see you leave. Then there was a queer little hotel room we stayed in when you surprised me by bringing Larry up to see me at Rome.[62] With Larry's bed right at the foot of ours we had to be so careful not to wake him. There were happy moments we shared in each other's arms that night too. I am looking forward to other moments, whole evenings like that.

It was fun having a picnic lunch out on the lawn of a beautiful home that is our own. Or perhaps you recall riding a bicycle over a very dark country road, with a kiss when we stopped to rest, then to a walk in the moonlight along the edge of our lawn, and next evening talking in our living room as the twilight gradually left us sitting together in the dark, then you thought it would be nice to go up to bed, and I don't remember saying no.

So when I just say at the bottom of a letter 'I love you dear' those are a few of the thoughts that go along.

I do dislike to have such a nice story interrupted, but in the coming

---

62 Rome, New York was the site of the headquarters of the Army Air Force's Air Service Command established on February 1, 1942. Until it was renamed the Griffiss Air Force Base in 1948 it had 12 different names, among which was the Rome Air Depot Control Area Command, its name while George was there. When referenced further, it will be called the Rome Air Depot (RAD) for simplicity. During the war, RAD's main mission was to provide aircraft engine maintenance and repair as well as to train air depot groups in aircraft engine maintenance (Mueller, *Air Force Bases*, 208.). Its airfields now comprise the civilian Griffiss International Airport.

years we shall add many more happy chapters to it my dear. So, for me, do take good care of yourself. And on Monday evenings you might guess I will have thoughts like these and of many more to come.

Yours, George.

[Peggy to George]

#29

Sat. Aug. 14.

Darling

My trip down from Duluth was very pleasant. There is a nice train both ways with a parlor car. I read a book by J.B. Priestley called "Blackout in Gretley." It was sent to you after you left by Mr. Howe— minister at Presbyterian Church here. It is a counter-espionage story and very good. Dad met me at the Nicollet after his Rotary luncheon and we drove over to the U. of M. to see the new union building which he helped to build. It's a mammoth affair for recreational activities, social functions and has a cafeteria. It really is lovely. The entire campus is in uniform this summer. It is some Army training center.[63]

The children were glad to see me when I got home. It's such a thrill always to see their little faces light up. They had all been good but Tina became very disagreeable as soon as I left. It looks like there will have to be a change. I'd like to keep her through the winter if she doesn't become too unbearable as I think by next spring girls may be sick of defense work, and therefore easier to obtain for housework.

I am dressed in riding clothes now about to go to Woodhill with Mr. Henry Doerr for my first ride since Steppy[64] left. This afternoon I'm taking the children to a horseshow—hunter trials. They'll get a

---

63   In the spring of 1943, the University of Minnesota became one of over two hundred universities in the United States to host an Army Specialized Training Program (ASTP), originally designed to provide training in advanced engineering. As the war continued and the need for specially-trained personnel in the U.S. Armed Forces grew, the ASTP program expanded to include training in psychology, medicine, dentistry, and area and language studies in German and Japanese. These additional areas were realized at the University of Minnesota in the summer of 1943, around the same time Peggy and her father visited campus (Kress, *A History of Military Training at the University of Minnesota 1869-1969*, 19, 20.).

64   Stepson was Peggy's horse. In May 1942 Peggy sent "Steppy" to her friend Cecil.

kick out of it I know. I'll write you all about it tomorrow.

My love darling and do tell me if the Allied Officers Club is in a hotel that makes a saint out of you. Marg. Clow wants to know.

Yours, Peggy.

[Peggy to George] #30

Sunday Aug. 15.

Darling,

This is one more day gone of our separation. It has been a lonely one as usual at heart but I've been pretty busy. Mother had one of her dizzy spells and has been in bed and since little Georgie was here for the weekend I've been looking after him. Between rain showers Dad gave the children a grill picnic this noon of hamburger, corn, scalloped potatoes and ice cream. We had the three of them sitting on the floor of the sand house eating off one of the benches to keep them out of the rain. The[y] looked awfully cute. After their naps I put all three on the back seat of the row boat and rowed along the shore up to [the] bay to the channel. They loved it. Georgia is taking Georgie under her motherly wing and it's too funny. She sat in the boat holding one of his hands and with her other arm about his neck she comforted his fears and asked him if he were enjoying the boat ride. Not being able to talk, if he gave anything but a protesting squeal she was thrilled to death and certain that he was having the time of his life.

When we returned Baxter and his wife came to call. He said Larry looks and acts exactly as you did when he first started to work for your family. They thought Georgia perfectly beautiful and Robin was as cute as always. He looks fine and his wife is very nice. I was barefoot changing Robin's pants when they walked in. I showed them the picture of your apartment and gave them what news I could.

I was able to send you a carton of V-mail with your request for it, but so far I have no request for your other pair of shoes. Don't forget to mention them.

Yesterday I had a very nice ride with Mr. Doerr. The scenery made up for the horse. She was willing but had no fun in her. We rode over as far as the Wolsfeld picnic grounds which brought back the memory of a picnic there with you and a full moon. We had the full moon last night too, but it was very uninviting. In the afternoon I took the children to a hunter horseshow held on the property of Locust Hills Club. They seemed to enjoy it and loved to watch the horses jump. Mr. Kingsley was there and we had quite a chat. He asked me to write and ask you if the 40,— owed you by Jess could be transferred to your father's estate so that they could close the other one. All he needs is a written agreement from you, but he'd like it as soon as possible. I'll also put that in a V-letter as it may reach you quicker.

Last night I dressed up for you in my old gold-colored dinner dress and was very gay. I went to a cocktail party at Cocky and Carlie's given for John Snyder. He's a navy ensign on leave on his way to Santiago Calif. Tuesday. They had Dexter Andrews (Louise Partridge), Phil Littles, Ginny Bell (Sam's wife), Kitty Pillsbury, Chuck Pillsbury (Navy flier on shore leave from Norfolk for 4 days),[65] Jane Pillsbury Rysor[66] (husband Army Lt. in Tenn. on maneuvers),[67] Lucy & Don Dayton, Monie & Earl Savage, Bob and Mart Howard. We went on to Woodhill Club for a dutch treat dinner dance which was loads of fun. Bee and George Crosby[68] were also with us. I danced

---

65   Charles "Chuck" Alfred Pillsbury (b. 1917, d. 1943). Chuck is the son of John Sargent Pillsbury (b. 1878, d. 1968) and grandson of Charles Alfred Pillsbury (b. 1842, d. 1899), one of the two brothers who founded the Pillsbury Company. Only several months after this reunion of friends, on November 21, 1943, Chuck will be declared Missing in Action when he fails to return from a combat air patrol over Kangu Hill in Papua New Guinea. Chuck was officially declared dead on February 8, 1946 but it was not until 1968 that the crash site of his Corsair was discovered and his remains were found, identified, and transported to Minnesota for burial.

66   Jane Pillsbury Resor was Chuck's sister.

67   Jane's husband Stanley Rogers Resor (b. 1917, d. 2012), who would later become the 9th U.S. Secretary of the Army serving from July 1965 to June 1971. A Lieutenant Colonel by WWII's end, he was awarded a Silver Star, Bronze Star, and Purple Heart for his service.

68   Beatrice Goodrich Wells and her husband George Christian Crosby. George was from the famous milling family that made up the Washburn-Crosby Co. which later became General Mills. His brother, Thomas Manville Crosby, was married to Ella Sturgis Pillsbury, sister of Jane and Chuck.

THE ALGERIA LETTERS

with Chuck Pillsbury, Bob Howard, Harry Belden & Bob Howard and had long chats with Bee Crosby, George Dayton (Dottie's older brother), Barbara McFarlane (p[e]roxide blond & tight). She and Warren were visiting the Hawleys for the weekend. Uncle Harry was worse than usual as far as being drunk and obnoxious. I wish he'd get some husband on him good one time. There was quite a crowd of Navy fliers from Wold C. field[69] out there. They had a cute system for getting liquor. Members had their own bottles labeled and set on a table behind the bartender. The boys picked out the liquor they wanted—asked for a drink from Mr. so and sos bottle. Then signed Mr. so and sos name for the set-up. When the old birds arrived for their bottles, many were empty. They not only gave the liquor but paid for the set-up. Good enough for them—says I—

I talked to all the people I mentioned above at least once during the evening and they all wanted to hear about you and asked to be remembered when I wrote today. Those who were particularly solicitous were John Snyder, Bob, Earl Savage, Monie, Cocky, Dexter and Harry Belden.

I told you I wanted to tell you some time of Mr. Alworth's plan to eliminate bad politicians and labor racketeers so as long as I've started another page I'll do it now. He felt that everyone fundamentally is selfish and capitalists are no exception. But his idea is that if a great industry employing several thousand workers would start dividing profits with labor our troubles could be solved. He thought capital should provide first—that it receive a fair percentage

---

69 Originally called Wold-Chamberlain Field, it is now the Minneapolis-St. Paul International Airport (MSP). The United States Navy has had a Naval Reserve Air Base (NRAB) at MSP since 1928. In 1941 the NRAB was expanded into a Naval Air Station (NAS) to provide primary flight training for participants in the Navy's V-5 cadet program. George Herbert Walker Bush, who would later become the 41st president of the United States, was one of the program's graduates. In 1943, as the demand for more pilot training increased, Fleming Field, a Naval Auxiliary Air Facility (NAAF) was established in South St. Paul. MSP became the A-Base, as the area west of MSP was Area 'A' of the flight training and Fleming Field became the B-base. In 2003 the A-Base area at MSP was redesignated a joint reserve air station as its facilities are multi-use (Scharch, "E.L. Scharch USNR."). It is currently the home of Minnesota's only Air Force Reserve unit, the 934th Airlift Wing nicknamed the "Global Vikings," whose mission is to provide airlift, airdrop, and combat support both stateside and abroad in support of the Air Force (United States Air Force, "Minneapolis-St Paul Air Reserve Station.").

return on its money and set up necessary reserves to run the business, and then set up a wage for [a] good standard of living for labor plus reserves for unemployment, old age and sickness. After that labor should be treated as a partner and divide excess profits by 50% between them. Of course, it seems to me it would have to be a pretty profitable business to be able to do this and pay the present taxes. However, I didn't pretend to know enough to argue on the subject.

You'll never get through reading this letter if I don't stop now.

I do want to tell you something which has helped me over several of these sleepless periods, nights, lately before I close though. It is concentrating on praying. Not only does it sort of pass the anxieties to another's stronger shoulders, but praying brings to mind always the many things we have to be thankful for. This always eases the other cares. It seems to be just as relaxing as a few tears and far more constructive. Our love seems to fit into those times too so intimately that I often wonder whether I am praying to God or chatting with you like I have so many times in those dark hours. Both have the same effect but I must confess the best is to snuggle up to you, really, and talk it all over.

My love as always, Peggy

[George to Peggy]
[V-Mail]

16 Aug. 43 Monday

Peg dear,

Got another letter from you today marked No. 20, so you see some mailed later came thru faster. You cannot tell which is quicker V-Mail or Air Mail as one time it is one and the next time the other. I am back up in the office after dinner and things being a bit slow, a poker game is getting started. As for myself I am a bit tired so think

I will go up early. It is Monday night anyway, thing is the difference in time makes it rather hard to figure where you might be, and what you might be doing. I was not quite sure when you planned to return to Conn., but figured this ought to arrive about the time you do. I have not seen anything of Jim Linen, perhaps he went somewhere else. I got some more shoes over here; so I will write you if I should need those others you mentioned later. Would sure like to be in the new house with you. I will be thinking about you tonight. All my love dear. George

[Peggy to George]
[V-Mail]

#31
Tues. Aug. 17

Darling

We had a swell date last night. Didn't we? About dusk we drove around the block and it was just the same as ever. Not even a new house there. Then we went to the movies in Wayzata to see "Five Graves to Cairo." It was a war picture but pretty good. We took Irene and George along. I didn't think you would mind. When we got out of the movie wasn't the moon beautiful? A perfect full moon over Lake Minnetonka. It would have been fun if we had a sailboat.

Now I am at breakfast with Dad hoping to finish this so he can mail it. The Clows and Miss Finn came out for lunch yesterday. The weather was a bit chilly, but they enjoyed the children and we had a nice visit. Teedie is expected Friday for a day and Ki a week later on leave. I hope to see him Sun. the 28th before I leave for Greenwich on the 31st. I want to go up to the house with him and see if it is agreeable to take a couch out of the amusement room. The Clows say it would be as the Scotts don't use the room. Loads of Love.
Peggy

[George to Peggy]
[Postmarked August 18, 1943]

#7

My darling:

This morning when I was walking down the hall, the nicest English Sgt. stopped, a very likeable sort indeed for he had a V-letter from No. 22, and yesterday I got No. 20 so the No. 21 ought to be along soon. Sounds like you are having a nice visit with Irene and George. You and Larry are certainly getting to be real fishermen. Hope you got enough meat for a grill picnic.

Here a few things you might send. A couple of boxes of kleenex, laundry is a problem, so that saves handkerchiefs. One of those books on contract bridge with the problems to work out. A jar of Nox[zem]a which would help out the sun burn.

There is a daily paper here which has an extra good Saturday edition. It is the "Stars & Stripes." It is a G.I. publication, very well written considering the difficulties under which it is put out. I am having the Saturday edition sent to you, think it will interest you. The "Stars & Stripes" was published in France during the last war, and most of the staff later became quite prominent in different branches of the publication business.[70]

This letter has been interrupted several times by Madame or Monsieur coming in for a chat with me. The last subject was special dishes and good places to eat. I inquired about escargots, he loves them, but she thinks they are *trés sale*.

Guess I will be climbing into bed and thinking about you until I go to sleep. Hope you took a ride around the "block" and tell me what you thought of. I love you very much dear and miss your companionship so much.

My love to you dear, George

---

70   George is correct. Private Harold W. Ross was the managing editor of *Stars and Stripes* in 1918 when it was popular in the trenches of France. He later became a cofounder and editor of the *New Yorker* magazine. In addition, contributing writers to *Stars and Stripes* like Sergeant Alexander Woollcott and Lieutenant Grantland Rice went on to become a well-known literary critic and a celebrated sports writer, respectively.

[Peggy to George] #32

Wednes. Aug. 18

Darling

Larry and Georgia have just written you letter[s] and now gave me this paper and pencil to write you too. I tried to use a pen but Larry insists you can read it more better if I write with this.

We had a nice day yesterday. Mom & I took the children to Mpls. I took Larry & Georgia to see Dr. Rodda and he was very pleased. They are in good health and he sent you his very best. After that visit we went to Minikahda for a swim. The children were playing in the wading pool while I took a turn in the big pool. First thing I saw was Georgia hanging onto the ladder swinging her feet in the deep water. She's a terror. We had lunch there and they both ate so much we were sure they would burst—soup, celery, bread stick, raw carrots, white fish, corn, tomato, <u>cold slaw</u>, tartar sauce, sweet roll, chocolate sundae, cookies, milk. Georgia's stomach stuck out so far her dress was two inches shorter in front. We did some errands downtown. In fact, I bought myself a blue wool (navy) suit with a red & white silk (plaid) blouse. It's awfully good looking. I'm going to put it away to dress up when you come home.

We also called at Mrs. Price's to see Kay and her baby. Kay was playing golf but we saw Danny. He's 2 yrs. old. Keep your eyes open for Webb. He's gone in that direction.

Yours darling, always, Peggy

[Peggy to George]
[V-Mail]

Aug. 19, Thurs.

Darling

This is a cold windy day but the sun is out and I'm about to walk Larry, Georgia, Georgie and push Robin to Crystal Bay while Tina gets the bus. It is her day off. The children love to walk up there and play in the school yard while Robin and I go to the grocery store and do Irene's marketing and look for letters from you.

Yesterday afternoon I took Larry & Georgia over to Mr. Kingsley's for supper. They had a tour of the pig pen, cow yard, chicken coop and saw nine horses and two had babies. They really were almost as excited as I was. One of the colts was Faustania's. Mr. Kingsley had several things to tell me. I don't know how many you already know. I assume you heard about Ki and Osterberg's difficulties. That is all straightened out thanks to Mr. Kingsley. However, Mr. K. let drop that Ki never paid him anything for this service and then put the whole Aviation business in Hangar's hands who Mr. K. feels has many of Osterberg's tendencies and lacks his brains. This is none of our affair. I'm glad we have no part of that enterprise but you might warn Ki that he might get his fingers burned again. Also—about Baxter I advise you to stop giving him any payment to supplement Am. Linen. Benninghof is not satisfied as he takes time off for Knox Ave. work. He is nice but very lazy. Love, Peggy

[George to Peggy]

#8
Saturday
21 Aug. 43

Peg dear:

They finally have put me in a room with bars on the window, but it is not what you might suppose. You see one of those African bugs caught up with me, giving me a sore throat which I took up the hill to have painted with iodine. But the doctor took my temperature; result, me in a hospital bed looking out through barred windows. I came in Wednesday night after dinner and am—

Sunday evening

Can't remember just exactly what I was going to say above when

I was interrupted, but I _am_ very much in love with you. At the dash above the doctor visited me. I told him I was all well, but being a skeptical fellow, he would not let me have my trousers until I went to the Colonel and got permission to leave. It was just kind of a grip that made you feel kind of mean, but it is all fixed up now. They led me into a double room and who did I find but Capt. Rogers another officer from G-4. I had a lot of work yesterday and had to work late so did not have a chance to write. Just ate one of the biggest and most delicious peaches I ever saw. Will write more tomorrow. Left the hospital before noon Sat.

      My love, George.

[George to Peggy]
[V-Mail]

              No. 9
            23 Aug. 43 Mon.

My darling Peggy:

 Now can you remember a few of the things I may be thinking of when I tell you I love you very much. Here is it just eleven o'clock Monday night. I wonder just where you are now, what you are doing and what you are thinking. I am pleased to hear about the pretty nightie, you can be sure you will find me prone to give you a lot of attention when you wear it. Do you remember when we stayed in Utica one night how you took advantage of me while I was trying to help you with your nightie. Tell me if you remember. Wish I could be out at the lake with you. Thank you for the way you handled the Hangers, it never does harm to be nice to people. Evidently, he thinks it would be smart to cause trouble between you and Ki and Teedie. Surprised to hear about Andrews. Thanks for taking the kids into the plant and having the Clows to lunch. Peg how do you manage to be such a perfect wife. Always doing something to please me and succeeding 100%. I am well. Love you very very much. George

[George to Peggy]
[V-Mail]

No. 10
23 Aug. 43 Tues.

My dear,

    Here I am duty officer for G-4 tonight so I spend the night here. Thought I would get quite a few letters written but Col. Bolon came in to talk for awhile and got to talking of the last war and how he had happened to stay in the Army. I envy him a bit; he is just over here for a few months from Washington. Then the boy that came in to set up my bed seemed a bit down so I had to talk to him for a while to cheer him up a bit. I did not have any way to notify my "family" where I was while I was in the hospital, Schutz was off on a trip, so when I got up to the apartment they were practically worried to death, had called the headquarters, and seemed very pleased to get me back. Capt. Shoebridge[71] one of our group from Washington got well into this last affair and has returned for a short while with many interesting stories. Wondered if you were in Greenwich thinking of me yesterday afternoon at five when I was writing you. Got Larry's letter. All well now. My love dear. George

[Peggy to George]

#33
Monday Aug. 23.

Darling

    We have all had a wonderful weekend. Even little Robin learned to stand up holding on to his playpen which thrilled him to pieces. He is so cute now. I hope you received the pictures I sent you by now. He looks just like that. Larry and Georgia are also creating quite a sensation out here. Everyone thinks they are so good looking. In fact I've been asked several times why we don't have ten when they are all such beauties. Sometimes I wish we did have a fourth coming now

---

71   Captain Benjamin B. Shewbridge assigned to the G-2 section NATO.

with you away. In fact if the help situation were easier I believe I would like it. Don't worry though, we <u>aren't</u>.

Saturday night Mom and Dad had a grill picnic for me. There were no steaks, of course, but we had hamburgers, wienies, corn, au gratin potatoes, [and] apple pie a la mode, after several of Dad's martinis. Buzz and Shorty, Mart and Bob, Cocky and Carlie, and Kitty Pillsbury came. Aunt Jess Wilcox was here with Mom and Dad. Uncle Ralph was out fishing somewhere. As usual everyone wanted to know what news I'd had from you. They all sent their love and Buzz said he had written to you that same day, I believe. We played bridge and poker after dinner. It was much more fun than Greenwich 'cause we couldn't lose more than $3.00 no matter how bad one was at it. There are lots of things out here which won't make me feel a bit badly to come back to after the war if business requires you here.

Yesterday we were up fairly early and Dad rowed Larry and me across the lake for nine holes of golf. Larry was fascinated watching us and he trudged along like an old man who had done it all his life. Each time I groaned over a lousy shot he wanted to run ahead and pick it out of the trap or wherever the ball happened to roll. Between us we could play a good game, I think.

After the naps I took Larry and Georgia over to Cocky and Carlie's for a hay ride. Carlie had gone out in the woods and <u>whittled</u> a new wagon tongue just for the occasion. He should have been a front-line pioneer.

Here Larry came down ready for breakfast and he wanted to tell you about the hay ride himself. I'll go have breakfast with them before finishing this.

The hay ride was a huge success. Barbara and [illegible] brought Corty and Ansie. So with Kitty and Peggy, Cocky & Carlie and Harry Belden there was quite a crowd. The M^{ac}Farlanes and Harry had to bring their whiskey along which I didn't approve of for a children's party, but I guess they were too young to notice. All six children

stood up in front watching the horses' hooves trot along and I drove most of the way. They were the cutest sight you could imagine. We took sandwiches along for them and stopped along the way for their supper.

Dad, Mom, Jack & I (Thelma is in Greenwood) went to Minikahda for dinner afterwards. I saw a cousin of Barbara Miller's there who is flying your way very soon and will look you up. You may not be too thrilled to see him but he can give you first-hand information on how healthy and fat I am after a month in Mpls. We watched the swimming awhile and then went to call on Barbara [and] Arnie. They appear fine, but nobody ever sees them. That's the first time I have even.

Loads of Love as usual, Peggy.

[Peggy to George]
[V-Mail]

#34
Tues. Aug. 24

Darling

Larry and I are about to go out and fix the yard for a children's party. We are having 16 children and 11 Mothers here today. I'll tell you all about it tomorrow. Yesterday I took Larry, Georgia and Tina for a rowboat picnic. You should have been with us. I rowed them up into Stubbs Bay where we fished and then walked all over the property that you and I once looked around with an idea of maybe building there. Do you remember the high hill overlooking the lake? Larry and Georgia clambered up that pretending they were climbing a mountain. We had our picnic in the boat and the mosquitoes drove us off.

On our date last night we went fishing about five o'clock. The fish weren't biting very well but I enjoyed your company as usual. You fell asleep on me I believe about seven so I rowed you back and had dinner. What time did you go to sleep? I received your letter telling me about your thoughts on Lafayette golf course. I must tell you my first drive went precisely where you predicted. Yours with love, Peggy.

[George to Peggy]

#10
Wednesday evening
25 Aug. 1943

Peg my dear,

Just had quite a chat with Monsieur. He told me a joke about the Pentagon which was in the *locale* french paper. It was about the pregnant woman who approaches a guard to tell him she was about to have a baby. He told her she should never have come into the bldg. in that condition whereupon she answers that she was not pregnant when she came in.

I walked up tonight guess I told you it is about 30 minutes' walk at a sharp grade up. Stopped in the hospital on the way up to see Lt. McIntyre who has a sinus infection, left him his candy ration, a letter from his wife, and some cable blanks to wire his wife on their 1st wedding anniversary. It was kind of a dark walk by the time I got up here.

Thank Georgia for her well wishes. Tell them both I miss them very much and would like to play with them and tuck them into bed at night. I think that is fine the way Larry can swing. Please, <u>please</u> don't climb up on things like you did to fix that swing. I know just how you feel, I have felt that way, a desire to jump. So just stay away from high places. When I come back that will no longer bother you, just wait and see. I will explain my theory on it some time.

I am wondering what that new nightie looks like or rather what you will look like in it, rather a pleasant speculation. Hope it is just a bit naughty for our honeymoon. Do I need to say I miss you very much? Shall we have dinner served in our room some evenings kind of late and just never bother going any place in particular. Maybe it will be down at the Old Homestead, or the Lodge at Sun Valley, or Lake Louise, just so you are with me in my arms I won't care where it is really.

        My love dear, George.

[Peggy to George]
[V-Mail]

#34
Wed. Aug. 25

Darling

    The children's party was a huge success. Everyone seemed to have a good time with a minimum of tears, breakage and fights. Buzz brought Shorty and their two and Barbara M^{ac}Farlane and her two from town. He fished during the party without any luck. He wouldn't be satisfied with worms and sunfish, but tried only frogs for bass. Lucy Dayton came with Neddy (3 yrs.), Cocky and her two, Mrs. Brooks and Michael Hollern, Kitty Pillsbury and her boys Jack (4) Don (2), Betty Kinnard and her adopted girl Sally (3), and Martha and her two girls. They played in the sand box and used the rope swing. Then we gave them lunch on the lawn and finally a rowboat ride. By the time they left I was worn out but it was fun just the same. Larry and Georgia both were nice to all their guests and behaved very well.

    Today we have all been lazy. I sewed on some underwear I'm making myself and Mom made a cute pink dress for Georgia. The big excitement was a letter from you #4 mailed Aug. 13, the day I came back from Duluth. You seem to have made many good friends already. Pretty soon you better start writing to me in french. I'll have to work to keep up to you. I'm anxious to hear if you have received your duffle bag and what you'd like for Christmas. I still haven't been able to get your shoes off. We are all out on the porch with a martini & wishes. Peggy.

[George to Peggy]
[V-Mail]

No. 11
26 Aug. 43 Thursday

My dear Peggy,

Today has been very pleasant. Right this moment I am looking at your picture with Robbie sitting in your lap, his cute little hands in yours, while Georgia stands beside with a happy little smile, and you have that proud look that says 'they are ours my dear.' And Larry is in the other three pictures. There are some pretty little pink flowers in a small vase next to the pictures. Had a nice talk this morning with the barber who had been manager of a good sized Piggly Wiggly grocery, an intelligent boy, and incidentally got a very good haircut. Had good company at lunch. Went out swimming about 1:30. The day was perfect just a little breeze, a clear sky, and the water, calm and just the right temperature. Got dressed about 4:30 and had some coffee and graham crackers. Went to a movie at 6:00 by myself then went over to the Red Cross for a French lesson at 7:30; a WAAC[72] was the only other student so we got in a lot of conversation for an hour. Afterwards I took the Frenchman who teaches us into the snack bar to eat. He speaks practically no English so we continued to *parler*.

---

72   The Women's Army Auxiliary Corps (WAAC) was created in May 1942 to work alongside the U.S. Army (but not as a fully integrated or equal part) so that women could fill various essential service and communications jobs enabling more men to fight overseas. On July 1, 1943, the WAAC was converted to active-duty service and renamed the Women's Army Corps (WAC). Women serving in the WAC were now entitled to the same benefits and privileges as their male colleagues. By the end of WWII, over 150,000 American women had served in the WAAC and WAC in a wide variety of positions. Their responsibilities ranged from manning aircraft warning stations to issuing weapons and processing soldiers to working as cryptographers, parachute riggers, mail sorters, equipment field testers, and even as crew members aboard B-17 training flights. A handful of women were also involved in the Manhattan Project (Hammond, The Women's Army Corps, 3, 4, 12, 13.). From this point on, George's spelling of "WAAC" has been corrected to "WAC" by the editor.

He was very pleased to eat there at the Red Cross. Caught a ride up the hill in an Army truck. Had a chat with the Rebillets over a cup of coffee and here I am ready for bed, thinking how pretty you will be in that new nightie when I let you wear it the second night I am home. So you say 'but the first night' and then blush a little. Yours, George

[Peggy to George]
[V-Mail]

#35
Friday Aug. 27

Darling.

There isn't much news this morning. Yesterday was a very rainy day and I did little but sit and play with the children as Tina was off. Anne Dalrymple Hull came over with her little boy who is about a year and a half. Her husband is skipper on [a] D.E.[73] boat now. He was the one who used to see Moon Hanan occasionally. Last night we had our threesome at rummy and went to bed early. I just wrote a note to your Aunt Helen sending snapshots of the children for them and the Matthews.

It seems as if with two months behind us now of this horrible separation I should be getting used to it but somehow I seem to miss you more and more and now am so anxious to get back to our lovely new house and get it all ready for you. Larry is here swinging on my knee begging to send you some kisses so of course I'll have to let him. Mom and I are going to Mpls. with Mart Howard in a little while so I'll have more news for you tomorrow. All my love dear, Peggy

---

73   A Destroyer Escort (DE) warship was used primarily in convoy escort duties to defend against aircraft and detect, pursue, and attack submarines.

[Peggy to George]
[V-Mail]

#35
SAT. Aug. 28.

Dearest George

Larry, Georgia and I are sitting in the Wayzata barber shop waiting to get their hair cut. It is a lovely cool morning and we look out the window to see the cars go by and have just watched the Empire Builder go through on its way to the coast. Beyond the tracks is the lake with just enough wind to be good sailing. There are two x-boats in sight and one chris-craft.

Yesterday Mart and I had lunch with Mom at [the] Mpls. Club and I bought Larry's winter clothes which consist of a new wool suit just like the one Mrs. Alworth gave him except this one is blue. Then I got him two pairs of overalls and two cotton striped knit shirts to go with them. In the afternoon Mart and I went to Minikahda and played three sets of tennis. I won each one which surprised us both I think. Then we went to Barbara & Arnie's for dinner. They cooked hamburgers outdoors and had a rice salad, coffee and cake. We had a good visit and a very nice time. Barbara seemed the same as ever. We had fun looking at Arnie's old scrap books. She had a picture of us at a Junior League party. I had on a red crepe dress with white ruffle around the neck and you look about fourteen. Do you remember? Bob picked us up after his drill with [the] State guard at the Armory and brought us home. Ki and Clows are coming for dinner tonight. Love, Peggy

[Peggy to George]

#36
Sun. Aug. 29

Darling,

This has been a very nice weekend and my last here with the family. After the haircut expedition in Wayzata yesterday we came home to find Dad all ready for fishing. He had put new hooks and lines on the children's willow twig poles and dug enough angleworms for a month. The four of us fished all afternoon and had 4 tiny sunfish to show for it. This was terribly disappointing as it was Grandpa's first trip with us and also the first time we didn't catch too many to use almost.

I kept the children up to see Ki and primed them to make a big fuss over him. They nearly smothered the poor guy. Georgia was upside down in his lap and Larry climbing on his back. He seemed to love it and didn't mind getting a very snappy uniform all mussed up. He looks fine and certainly acts more like a General than a Captain (that will come next I suppose). The Clows came out too and I got Jack to bring a projector from the office to show them the last pictures we took of you and the children and the house.

This morning, Sunday, I went in to meet them all at Knox Ave. to look over the house. It doesn't look like it used to in that several pieces of furniture are changed about and lamps moved etc., but on the whole they are pretty neat tenants. Ki was a little upset to find the furnace going this hot day but I suggested it might heat hot water—Seems silly but I can't imagine what else—Also he found the freezer running but badly wrapped and falling apart. That I think is more Baxter's fault. The house itself though is clean and not abused. I believe the Scotts have re-leased for another year which is a bit disappointing as the Kingsley Murphy's really might have bought it if they could have rented this year. I suppose the option has to hold though. Anyway, after seeing how vacancy has completely wrecked the Rand house, we are lucky to have it cared for. That place even had hoodlums living in it last winter who set up a stove and burned the woodwork and doors for heat.

I took Larry in with me so Ki had a chance to see him again. Then we called on the Howards and M^{ac}Farlanes Sr. before coming back to the lake.

Anna writes that Doxie would keep running up to Bowdens and the old house so she sent him to the 'vets.' I'll bet he'll be glad to see us Thurs. She also said the painters never came back to finish work after I left. It makes me so mad I could kill that man. I've wired him to be through by Wednes. or else.

Mother is not going back with us but will come down later and stay for Christmas. I didn't want a Christmas in that house until you could be there but it's too difficult and expensive to try and travel back here again this year. Ki said Teedie might be able to come down for a week in Nov. while he takes a few Generals out shooting. I would love to have her.

If you were home tonight I'd climb in your lap and promise you anything and work you to death for a mink coat. Aren't you glad you are far away? Dad is giving Mom one for Christmas and we are going in to Schlampps tomorrow to pick out the skins. He has enough left at prewar prices to make one other coat. I considered to buy it monthly myself out of my allowance, but I have so much yet to get for the house that I don't dare get signed up any more. Also, the girls are taking quite a bit more of it each month as well as food prices and kids' clothes. I'm doing nicely so I figured I better let well enough alone. Anyway, that's one thing I've wanted so long that it would be much more fun to wait and have you give it to me.

Ki leaves Tues. morning for a week at Thunder Lake. Teedie is meeting him there. How I wish we and ours could go too. We will not [be] too far off, I know.

Dad's just gone into the kitchen to make Sunday night supper. Does that sound familiar. I'm going to miss Mom and Dad terribly the next few weeks so don't get upset over some lonely letters. You'll have several I can promise you. But I wouldn't give up my independence in our new house for anything.

Your letters haven't mentioned hearing from me lately or maybe they aren't interesting enough to comment on. See, I'm fishing. I also love you very much and would love to have you join me for a sandwich and climb into bed.

       Yours as always, Peggy

[George to Peggy]
[V-Mail]

               No. 12
            Monday evening 30 Aug.

Peg dear:

 Guess from your last letter written two weeks ago, that you are either on your way back or about to leave. The mail seems to come thru pretty good now. Maj. Howder called me yesterday (you met him in the Sales Store, Washington) said he had been checking on our baggage, gave me the check no. of mine and boat it arrives on so it will be coming through all right. Walked up the hill tonight stopping in the hospital to give Mac Intire his mail and talk with him. He has stomach ulcers and a bad sinus infection. An orderly had just carried out the written instructions of the doctor to give Mac an enema and the Col. in the room with Mac a glass of Milk, but had made a mistake and reversed the order of things, so you see the Medical Corps operates on Normal Army procedures. Had my usual chat with the "family." Love you very much and wish I were with you. George.

[George to Peggy]
[V-Mail]

               No. 13
            Tues. 31 Aug. 1943

My dear,

 Mimi just brought me a small silver plate with ½ doz. still warm "petite gateaus" which his mother had baked. They are good. But I sure would like to sit down to one of Anna's dinners. From your last letter I gather that you will be leaving Mpls. today, I suppose on the evening train. I sure would like to have been out there with you. I have thought of so many places in and about Mpls. since you have been out there. It must be strange to walk into 1941 to find someone else living there. Hope the trip goes well, but the children must be a handful. Thanks for the attention you showed the Clows and Miss Finn. Wish I could pick up Robbie right now, I am afraid he is going to be so big when I return. Give Larry and Georgia a kiss from me and tell them I miss them and think about them each day. I was thinking about you last night my dear, you were probably having dinner out at Crystal Bay. Hope you saw Ki and Teedie before you left. They are very fortunate to get up to the lake together. Well two months are past in this place now. I am busy so time goes quite fast, but I do miss you so very very much. All my love, George

[Peggy to George]
[V-Mail]

#36
Aug. 31, Tuesday

Darling,

    Our trunk has gone and the suitcases are ready and we leave tonight at 10:45 for Chicago arriving Greenwich Thursday morning. Robin is so active now I'm afraid we are in for a struggle with him. Mart Howard is coming up this afternoon to give the children a ride in the motor boat and Kay Bull is coming for a visit too. I have seen everyone I wanted to after she comes today and am rested up and ready to go back to work on the house. I sort of have the feeling that as soon as I can get everything in order there you will be home to look it over. Anna forwarded three nice letters of yours yesterday. What a thrill that was. I've reread the one reviewing the highlights of our school days and married life several times already and know I'll wear it out along with many others. Last night we had a swell date.

I have gotten so I find myself unconsciously looking at my watch Monday evenings on the stroke of five. At that time yesterday I was driving through Wayzata on my way out from town having been in to see Georgia's new pastel at Miss Baxters. It's very good. I also went with Mom to pick out a beautiful mink coat. Dad may give me one too or part of one. Is that O.K. with you? Then we sat on the porch rejoicing in the first cool breeze of the day. Dad made a daiquiri which we all drank to you. Preston Covey[74] is stationed there in [the] Navy. Love, Peggy

[George to Peggy]
[V-Mail]

No. 14
3 Sept. 43 Friday

Peg dear,

Guess I am getting to be a regular drunkard. I have had a drink two nights in a row. It is about a quarter to nine and Maj. Stipp produced a bottle of Scotch proposing a drink so I have said to the devil with any more work tonight, just write you a letter and go home. Too much work to take my half day off yesterday but I did not work after dinner. Started to go down to a French lesson but ran into Schutz and Helms who talked me into going to the Red Cross Movie which was "His Woman Friday," not a bad picture. The movie house has a rolling ceiling just like that hotel in Sofia. We walked all the way back up to our apartment, so I thought I needed a short drink out of that bottle we bought in Washington, still half full, so I drank to our early reunion. Love you very much. George

---

74   Preston was the husband of Nancy Covey, sister of architect Karl Humphrey.

[Peggy to George]
[V-Mail]

#37
Sept. 3, 1943

Darling

    I am nearly beside myself worrying about what happened to you between Mon. the sixteenth and a week from that day. I've read and reread your last letters several times for any possible clue after arriving home today and reading about you not being able to inform your "family" of being in the hospital. Please tell me what was wrong, and how you are. Also were you and Schutz together that week? You promised to always tell me if you were sick. Another thing which bothers me is that eleven of my letters, one from F.G., Ki, Uncle George, Gertrude, Uncle Art and P[indecipherable]res written to the 4004 address were all back here today. I'll readdress them all just so you can read them but it's a shame they didn't get through. Two also came for Lt. Chas R. Smythe which I'll readdress the same way. We all arrived safely this noon after a not too bad trip. Yesterday we spent in Chicago with Helen and it was very pleasant. It was hard to say goodbye to the family, but I must say our own house looks awfully good to me. Somehow I feel closer to you here than in Minn., by more than 1400 miles too. When Mart came over Tues. afternoon we took the kids boat riding and saw the old [Minnetonka] Yacht Club burn to the ground in 45 minutes. Kay Bull came later. Webb is co-pilot on flying fortress. Left the country four weeks ago. More tomorrow. Love & Kisses. Peggy

[Peggy to George]
[V-Mail]

#38
Sept. 3, 43 Friday

Darling,

    This is sure to be a surprise to you, especially when you see how few mistakes I (whoops) am going to make.[75] I still cannot think of much except your being in the hospital, but I might as well forget it and pray for an explanation in the morning's mail. We are pretty well back in the groove here today except that Georgia developed a cold from the air-conditioning on the train, I believe. Needless to say it has not slowed her down any as yet. She and Larry helped me rake and put grass seed in the spot by the new porch where the flagstone was removed to make the porch floor tonight. I'll try to describe the house to you a little. Tonight I will do the little sitting room where I shall hibernate until you come home. My desk is centered on the long wall to the left as you enter. In the corner opposite the door is my rose-colored easy chair with the round table next to it that used to support the radio in our room. On it is the blue-based lamp with the white shade that was on the table between our beds. In exactly the same position as the sink we removed from the lavatory is our little consol[e] table which held piano music with the small eagle mirror from the dining room over it. Upon this is your typewriter and here I sit and will sit each evening after you are asleep, to send you a letter on my love, thoughts, and doings of each day we are apart. Now it is difficult to look up and see the girl who loves you so very much, but as I get better at this I'll try to watch her through a whole letter. A boy I mention [indecipherable] the Navy as assistant to [indecipherable][76] More next time. LOVE, P.

---

75   Peggy has typed this V-Mail message on her typewriter. In the original, Peggy has tried to type a capital "I" over the "i" she first typed.

76   The large "V-MAIL" logo at the bottom of the film has obscured two parts of Peggy's sentence.

[George to Peggy] [#]15
4 Sept.

Peg dear

Je suis heureux parce que j'ai rêvé de tes trois lettres aujourd'hui, une avec les trois photos de nos enfants. Donnes chacun d'entre eux un baiser pour moi, et gardes-un pour toi-même. Pendant que je me promenais de mon bureau à ici, je pensais à toi. Tu vois que tu me manques tout le temps, et je voudrais que tu sois ici avec moi. Un jour peut-être nous visiterons ensemble cet endroit.[77]

You must have had a very pleasant visit in Duluth. That is a beautiful home of the Alworths. Ki and I were up there for a house party one summer and they really gave us a good time.

I was interested in Mr. Alworth's ideas. It is worth thinking about. Trouble is though that half of a 5% profit margin does not add much to wages which probably average around 30% or more of sales.

We talk a good deal at mess about the importance of a stable economic structure after the war and all agree that one of the big problems is a fair distribution of the total "world income" which is really the annual production of consumer goods and services. It is interesting to discuss this with some of the English boys who seem to have done more thinking on this from a practical standpoint than ourselves.

One thing you can send me that would be very useful would be one of those sharpeners for a double-edged razor. If you can find an "Allegro" I remember that is a good one. Also some razor blades, Schick injector if you can find any which I doubt, or any double-edged blade preferably a Gillette "blue blade."

Glad you had such a nice visit with the Clows. Thank you for the attention you showed them. I assure you that I was very happy to

---

[77] Translated: "I am happy because I dreamt about your three letters today, one with the three photos of our children. Give each one of them a kiss for me, and keep one for yourself. While I was walking from my office to here, I thought about you. You see that I miss you all the time, and I would like you to be here with me. One day perhaps, we will visit this place together."

learn of the good use the Veuve Vrai was put to. I do remember that dinner at Morton Hempstead, I believe it was. Marg certainly has a good memory for names. You can usually depend on what she says.

Good night my dear, I miss you very much.

My love, George

[George to Peggy]
[V-Mail]

No. 15
Monday 6/9/43

Peg dear;

You will be surprised at who I had dinner with. Remember Lt. Allbright who had the Sig. detachment[78] at Meacham Field[79] last summer. His supply officer came in the other day wanting authority to draw some stuff so I told him to have Allbright give me a ring. He got married shortly before leaving the states to a girl he had known all his life; she is teaching school down in Louisiana now. He has picked up French quickly and speaks very well. We ate down at the Allied Officers Club which was very crowded and not too good a meal, but I enjoyed the visit. He is a smart boy and good company. I never have heard anything from Jim Linen, I wonder if he went some

---

[78] In a letter George wrote to the Key West Art and Historical Society in 1991, he details Lt. Albright and the Signal Radio Intelligence Company's setup, writing:

> In one of the rooms they had a dozen men scanning the radio frequencies used by the subs to communicate with Bremen. When they spotted a frequency in use they passed it to several direction finding sets they had posted up [of] the keys, then plotted the fix on a big wall map. The coordinates of the fix were then radioed to planes in the air. (George R. Steiner to the Key West Art & Historical Society, January 9, 1991.)

> George goes on to wryly note that in Africa he ran into Albright who, despite being fluent in Japanese, had been assigned to cover German radio chatter. (The correct spelling of Albright's surname has not been confirmed.)

[79] In the summer of 1942 George was stationed in Key West, Florida in command of an Air Force unit tasked with developing and operating an emergency airfield at Meacham Field (now the Key West International Airport). In addition to emergency services and supplies, George's unit also provided fuel for military planes. The ability to refuel in Key West was crucial in the battle against German submarines in the Gulf of Mexico and the Atlantic Ocean. Several weeks into the assignment, George's unit had the thrill of supplying Colonel W.C. Dolan's unit. Dolan's task force arrived with "a dozen specially equipped twin engine B-18s...They were the first American planes equipped with airborne radar, made by the British. Their mission was to spot and attack enemy submarines at night while they were running their diesels on the surface to recharge their batteries" (George R. Steiner to the Key West Art & Historical Society, January 9, 1991.). George's military records list his job at this time as "Unit Commander Air Force Service Detachment" and note that he supervised 75 servicemen. In brief, separate biographies decades later, Peggy and George both write that there were 22 service members under George's command and the unit's sole task was to make refueling possible.

place else. The pictures of the children arrived pleasing me very much. My but Larry has grown, he sure looks fine. I like that picture of him on the swing. He is getting to be quite a boy. Got a nice letter from Irene also.

My love dear, George

[Peggy to George]
[V-Mail]

#39
Tues. A.M. Sept. 7

Darling

The three of us are eating breakfast on the porch at our new table and chairs. From where I am sitting at one end I look out on the driveway just at the edge of the cedar hedge. Larry is at my left with his back to the living room door eating toast and Doxie begging a bite. Georgia is on my right with her back to the end of the porch eating cantaloupe. They both want me to leave space for them to write you too. It is very hot here and we all have slight colds from the train air conditioning, I believe. Nothing much but a nuisance. Yesterday besides the washing I covered the ironing board, started sorting nails for my work bench, canned nine quarts of pears and finished at five in time to shower and get dressed for our date. I put on that old navy cotton dress with the white lace trimming as it was cool. We sat on the porch and played with the children and then ate out here—broiled tomatoes from the garden, cabbage, creamed duck on toast and orange marmalade whip for dessert. The meal put you to sleep but I sat out there and read "30 Seconds Over Tokyo" before turning in. Very good. Will ride this to the box on the bike.
Love, Peggy

[Peggy to George]
[V-Mail]

#39
Wed. Sept. 8

Darling George

    Oh Boy! Have I got a cold this morning. It's a good thing you can't see this nose you like to tease me about. I'm making up for all the colds I didn't have last winter. The kids fortunately only had theirs for a day and are fine. Betty Bowden is arriving in a few minutes with her little girl to spend the day. I phoned her early to warn her about my cold but she couldn't be scared off.

    Betty Hite, Marg Adams and Marg's Mother came over last night for dinner and bridge. Marg's mother and I won every rubber. After cocktails in the living room I left a bowl of potato chips and a plate of cracker canapés on the coffee table as we went in to dinner. We heard a crunching noise and I dashed into the living room to find Doxie's head buried in the potato chip bowl. He had already finished the crackers. George Hite is coming home on leave Friday after finishing OCS. Betty hasn't seen him since April so it's quite a reunion. She is having a party at her Mothers on Sat. and Izzie & I are going [to] a dinner at the club a week from tomorrow night. How I wish you were here, but then I am always saying that. Love, Peggy

[Peggy to George]

#40
Thursday Sept. 9, 1943

Dearest George

    My cold is better this morning, but I certainly am a queer looking individual as I look at myself in the mirror here. Tina is off today so I have a mask on to try and prevent giving this to Robin.

    There is a definite feeling of autumn in the air this morning and my thoughts turn to Steppy. I believe days like this were when we used to enjoy each other the very most. Larry was just talking at breakfast about the barn you are going to build up by Momie's garden when you come home, and how we are all going to have ponies and horses according to our size. Do you remember the day we took him over there and talked about that. He mentions it at least once a week.

Yesterday Betty Bowden did come up with the child but I felt too lousy to enjoy the visit much and sent her home about three. Nan Miller came after I got into bed and she sat with me while we listened to the news of Italy's surrender over the radio. That came as a welcome surprise, but I can't see how that will make much difference in getting the Germans out of there if they don't want to go. It no doubt will save some lives, however. You never gave me the vaguest notion of your work. Surely there is some part of it that you could write. My imagination runs wild trying to imagine what you may be doing behind the scenes of all the exciting headlines from that theatre. What notables have you met? Who have you seen that I know? A letter from Dale Bigham says you met one of the Healy boys. Which one? You see I'm so curious to have a picture in my mind of the life you are living. It must be very thrilling. I have a very good idea of the Rebillet family, and am so happy that you have such thoughtful people to live with at this time. I would love to see a picture of them all. Can you think of something little Mimi or Madame or Monsieur would like "*pour Noel?*" I must send your Christmas box soon, I understand. Your french is progressing to a point where I know I shall be very envious of your ability. I wish you would write me a letter in french and I will try to answer it.

Larry and Georgia are hanging on the typewriter table here watching every punch I make and offering suggestions which don't seem to help my effort very much.

I have some pictures of the children to enclose which were taken the last week out at Mothers. The day of the children's party was very dull and mother's old camera doesn't do too well on such occasions which was a disappointment as I wanted to give you a good idea of what our friends' kids all look like. If you will take the party pictures as I number them and place them on this sheet, I'll try to fix it so you can tell who they belong to.[80] Loads of Love. Peggy

[George to Peggy]
[V-Mail]

No. 16
10/9/43 Friday

Peg dear:

Had a real surprise when three of your V-mail letters from Mpls. arrived all together today. That is a nice piece of property on the lake. It should make a nice place for a home up on that ridge with water on both sides, must look even better with the high water this year. So I was right about where your drive would go off of the first tee. To be honest I cannot tell just when I went to sleep that night. Tell Larry and Georgia that I am glad to hear they treated their guests so well. I am looking forward to hearing that you got back to Greenwich. If any of the pictures of the house came out well I should like to have one. I imagine you will have much to tell me about the house. I am glad to know you are living in such a nice home. *Ce soir Madame a préparé des bonnes Crêpes Suzette. Je suis arrivé à sept heures du soir et Monsieur et moi avons parlé de la guerre. Nous sommes heureux d'entendre les événements qui arrivent ces jours. Tu me manques tout le temps, ma chère.*[81] If I stay around a while I may learn a bit of this French but I do not get much time for it. My love dear. George

---

80 At the bottom of this letter Peggy wrote numbers arranged to match the position of children in two photographs so that if George held the photos beneath the numbers, he could match a child to a number. In the margins Peggy listed the child's name next to its number. In the first photo there were 14 children and in the second there were seven (likely why Peggy made a separate list for everyone rather than writing on the back of the photo)
81 Translated: "This evening Madame made some good Crêpes Suzettes. I arrived at seven o'clock in the evening and Monsieur and I talked about the war. We are happy to hear about the events which are happening these days. I miss you all the time, my dear."

[Peggy to George]
[V-Mail]

#40

Friday Sept. 10

My dearest George

I am sitting for breakfast in our lovely new dining room writing you between comments on "hurry up and finish your cereal, Georgia" [and] "Larry don't feed Doxie at the table as the food drops on our new rug before he catches it." Does that sound familiar to you. I am aiming at getting all these remarks over with so that our breakfast will be peaceful by the time you are home. I suppose then I'll be at it with Robin by then.

There hasn't been a letter from you for five days now. Perhaps you have spoiled me so that I begin worrying after two days now. I prayed for a letter last night so we'll see what comes today. With the news from Italy I've been worrying that you may have taken a trip shortly after your last letter. It's terrible what an imagination I have isn't it?

It has turned quite cold here now. The house is getting into shape. I cleaned the garage after dark last night. Anna and I had to push your car out as the battery is dead. I don't know how I'll get it to Mr. Wamback. I'd like to sell that car if I didn't need the gas ration. It doesn't run too well and I need the space in the garage for bikes and children's toys. What would you think of it if they do let up on the gasoline? Am going to the village now. Hurrak the milkman just gave us 2 lbs. of butter. First since Mpls. Love, Peggy

[Peggy to George]
[V-Mail]

#41

Sat. April 11, 1943

Darling,

My prayers weren't answered yesterday. No letter again. But it's sort of like picking up bridge hands. As each new day comes I'm sure it will bring word from you. It's so silly I suppose to get upset as there no doubt will be times when you can't write. Then so many girls don't hear for months so I shouldn't complain. It is only that you have spoiled me so up to now. This morning I am down at Marg. Adams waiting for the movers. Braman has graduated from Quonsett and is to be stationed at Naragansett for another course of 3 months. They have a house up there with another couple. Such luck! All their things are going to storage so I am here to help list things as they go into barrels. I went to the Hoggsons for dinner last night and played bridge. Mrs. Dick Croft (Greenwich) was there and I found she has been writing to her husband, a major, at the same address as yours except for the G-4. Now he is with the Amgot[82] in Sicily. The children are fine and so am I. We are still busy canning. Apple jelly and peaches yesterday. If I finish here in time I am going to play golf with Helen Gorton. Love, Peggy

[George to Peggy]
[V-Mail]

No. 17
12 Sept. 1943

My dear:

Last night we had quite a dinner. Madam Devevy fixed up a real meal for Capt. Schutz, Majors Ream, Sparks, Howder, and myself, all "Junior G-men." There was steak, some really good soup, rabbit meat, vegetables, melon, and several wines including champagne with the proper size wine glass lined up for each wine, a nice <u>white</u> <u>linen</u> table cloth, nice dishes and glassware and real silver. Maj. Howder told the boys what an attractive wife I have. We sat around the table most of the evening talking and drinking. They are a good bunch of boys, making it an interesting and pleasant evening. There was the usual amount of beefing, all of us having taken a real beating on promotion.

---

82   Allied Military Government for Occupied Territories.

Each one of them had convinced the CGs of their outfits that they were really good, had done the same with the faculty at C&GS,[83] and also with OPD[84] in Washington including Marshall,[85] and now they have the job of convincing to do all over again. Guess we will make out all right though. It is a beautiful moonlight night. Miss you dear George

[George to Peggy]
[V-Mail]

No. 18
13 Sept. 43 Monday

Peg dear,

Can't tell you how pleased I am with the pictures you sent from Mpls. Mentioned them before when I received them about a week ago, but I have kept them since, taking them out to look at like a miser with his treasures. Larry and Georgia look just the way I want them to look. Larry has such a confident poise standing on the swing. When I look at Robbie's happy face I would just love to pick him up. Of course you might have put one in of yourself. Wonder what you are doing back in Greenwich now. It is 10^{30} here and I just got home. I suppose you might be sitting out on the terrace knitting, watching Larry fish in the brook, and thinking about me. My love dear, George

[Peggy to George]

#42
Monday, 6:50 PM. Sept. 13, 1943

Darling,

We have had a very nice date since five o'clock. Don't you think? After doing the washing this morning and spending the rest of the day in the basement and garage cleaning up after the summer's

---

83 Command and General Staff College in Fort Leavenworth, Kansas—usually abbreviated CGSC.
84 The Operations Division of the War Department General Staff (OPD WDGS).
85 George Catlett Marshall (b. 1880, d. 1959) was the United States Army Chief of Staff and General of the Army from 1939-1945. Tasked with expanding and running the U.S. Armed Forces, Marshall provided strategic direction on a global scale and saw that the U.S. Armed Forces received the supplies necessary for their endeavors. Serving as Secretary of State from 1947-1949, Marshall will design the post-war European economic support plan, named the Marshall Plan, and in 1953 he will be awarded the Nobel Prize for his work reviving the European economy.

workmen, it was good to get a shower and dress up for you. As soon as I was dressed I took your two letters which came today and sat on the couch in the living room and we had a glass of sherry. That was the first drink I have had alone since you left, but since we were really having a date I alibied myself over it easily. The children were eating while we sipped and then Anna said that dinner was ready. After just re-reading your letter I told her how you said you would like to sit down to one of her meals. This was a good one too. We had creamed dried beef on toast, baked potato, fried summer squash, and lemon meringue pie with coffee.

This has just been followed by a rough house with Larry and Georgia and now they are on their way to bed having given such big hugs and kisses to be relayed on to you that my hair is all mussed up and I barely have my breath as yet. A while back I wrote you a description of this little room and now I think you ought to know how the living room is settled. We'll begin by entering through the first door as you come in from the drive. Over the mantle is the Carl Rawson painting and the greens of the picture are beautiful against the pink walls. On either end of the mantle are the meissen figures Jessie gave me flanked on the ends by the pair of rose glass vases. The brass in the fireplace is shined to perfection and to the left side is our couch and to the right is the love seat at right angles to the wall. In front of the couch is the coffee table you mended. On the end of the couch nearest the fireplace and consequently next to it is the square table with the shelf below and the photograph book on it. The same lamp is on the table (that with the glass balls). Across the fireplace from this table is the record holder table with the same kind of lamp on it. This of course is at the end of the love seat. At the other end is the magazine rack and across from this at the other end of the couch is the little divided table with the handle that Helen and Frank gave us. Now, let's see, as you look towards the bay window the piano is in the right corner with the key board facing the window. In the opposite corner is the radio and that inside aerial has been fixed so it works fine. On the wall opposite the fireplace is the large living room table with one of the other pair of lamps, the silver horse bookends, ash trays, etc. on it. In the left far corner from where you entered is the round table with the prism lamp that was on your dresser and the two little white man and lady figurines. In the left near corner is the plant table and our first chair. Oh yes, your green chair is up by the radio. We need a tall secretary in that room and the Clows suggested that the blue painted one from your mother's room would be nice someday.

    The party for George Hite was very nice Saturday. I saw him first at the club at noon. He had his gold bar and was about to play golf with Pete, Bill Wellington and Bowden. I had just come in after nine holes with Helen Gorton. It had been a perfect day to play, a bright blue sky, temperature about 75 and a slight breeze. The day made up for what the golf lacked which was plenty. I wore that black and white net dress to the party with a black lace scarf mother gave me on my head and carried my silver fox as it got chilly in the evening. I drove myself in the blue car and wished so much for a date with you. I had many compliments on the turnout and knew you would have enjoyed that. The party was at Betty's family's and the guests were Bowdens, Bouscarens, Hites, Foshays, Gates, Adams, Izzy (having a baby in Feb.), Audrey Platt, Wellingtons. We played bridge and poker. I only lost 50 cents at Bouscaren's table which is an achievement as he took plenty from everyone else. I drove myself home at 2:30. Yesterday morning was too nice to sleep so with Anna off I helped Tina get the children's breakfast, did the dishes, finished canning the peaches which were too green Fri., made peach ice cream and then we put Robin in the carriage and all took a walk down North street. We had as nice a day as Sat. and came home with all our pockets full of black walnuts which we picked up on the road. There were three big trees full of them. At noon I took Larry and went up to Nan Miller's for lunch and tennis. Larry had a good time with her girls and I enjoyed the tennis. For supper last night Nan came back here and the Gortons brought a steak and came over. We had cocktails to you and then I made a vegetable salad and johnny cake while Bob cooked the steak. It was very pleasant and they left early after trying out our fireplace for the first time. It works perfectly. Now you're caught up on my hourly activity since my last letter from Marg. Adams on Sat. morning. I honestly think you know an awful lot more of my daily doings from these letters than you would ever know if you were home. This way you have to listen to me, or at least I think you do. Doxie just came in to curl up at the foot of my red chair and sends his love to you.

Tomorrow Mr. Hvolbeck is sending a man up to clean the sceptic tank. It's not a very pleasant subject but he said you had mentioned it to him and I thought you would like to know it is being done. Also, I talked to Wally Hoggson today and we are getting 4200 gals. of fuel oil for this house. It is much more than I'll use, but comforting to know we can have that much. We only had 2900 gals. for that sieve last winter so you see the difference and the space was the same. Wally also said he thought I could surely get a B-ration for one car, so I called Bob Crawford to ask him to see what he could do about selling the Olds. I happened to call when Frank Mihelich and Ben Siedel were in town so I spoke to them both and invited them out for dinner on Wed. I don't believe they can make it though. Ben said everything is fine at home and that he had enjoyed so much a letter from you not long ago.

I haven't told you that when I finally got your letter telling the reason for your being hospitalized it was the happiest moment of my life. That came ten days after the one you had written the following day when you got back to your "family." In that case v-mail was much faster. Usually it doesn't make any difference.

I am enclosing a letter received this morning from Miss Finn so you can keep track of what I am asked to do with your signature. Of course I am doing plenty with it on my own which you'll never find out about, I hope. Are you worried?

I must end our date. You've been asleep for hours now, I've been at this an hour and a half. That shows you the speed of my mind and this typewriter. Quite a combination…. Hope you are having pleasant dreams, dear.

    Good night, My dearest with all my love, Peggy

[Peggy to George]
[V-Mail]

#43

[Wed]. Sept. 15

Darling,

Again we are all at our breakfast table. I am finished except for a half cup of coffee and the children, besides dropping pieces of toast for Doxie, are eating apple sauce made from our trees. As Doxie begged just now Larry noticed some white fur on his stomach. Here is what followed: Momie: "Yes, Doxie's getting old and grey like me." Georgia: "I'm getting old too like you." Larry: "Momie is not getting old." Georgia: "Yes she is" etc., etc.

Last night I had dinner at Mary Wards with Elsa Domerick Slocum (Walt, husband, is with the Sea Bees in New Guinea.) [and] Izzy Lewis (Jack is shuttling over near you). You might inquire at an armed guard center for his Liberty boat. We went to Mary's to discuss places for showing the Stony Wold[86] movie but we didn't get very far. What with [the] new bond drive, community chest and taxes, nobody wants to give to a private charity. Let me know if this letter comes through as fast as other V-mail. It's the first time I haven't put 6¢ on it. Larry is here to write too. I can't put him off any longer. Hugs & Kisses. Peggy. This tell[s] you how Larry rides his bike with me on mine to the mail box.[87]

---

86 Stony Wold was a charitable sanatorium located on Lake Kushaqua in upstate New York. It was founded by Elizabeth Newcomb to provide disadvantaged women suffering from tuberculosis a tranquil, encouraging environment in which to convalesce.

87 Peggy is explaining Larry's scribbles at the bottom of the V-Mail. The V-Mail image is blurry and the scribbles have not been included.

[George to Peggy]
[V-Mail]

No. 19
16 Sept. 1943

My dear,

    The last letter you wrote in Minneapolis before leaving for the east arrived yesterday. Guess I started writing to you in Greenwich too soon. Glad you liked my letter going back over some of the happier moments we have had, I enjoyed writing it. Thank you for sending pictures of the children to the aunts. I am sure they will be very much appreciated. I just got some pictures printed which I will send you, one of me which you probably won't like because I have a cigar in my mouth. One is of Schutz, another of Maj. Allen[88] (one of our group from OPD who is in my section), all taken in our office. I took quite a few of Helms with a good-sized mustache, which (the picture) he wanted to send home. Had dinner with him tonight and he had shaved [it] off and now looks more human. Went across the hall and had quite a chat with Capt. Schutz to pass the evening. You might send me some Hershey bars plain and with nuts, any kind of chocolate bar in fact. He had some from home and they tasted good. Am well and miss you dear. George

[Peggy to George]
[V-Mail]

#44
Fri. Sept. 17

Darling,

    This is a dull morning and I am about to drive Tina and Helen Gorton into N.Y.C. in the Oldsmobile. I believe Bob Crawford is going to get us $1200 for it. I do hope you approve as it is such a load of responsibility off my mind. I spent yesterday morning cleaning all

---

88   Major Irvin L. Allen. Like George, Allen was initially assigned to the G-3 Section NATO and reassigned to G-4 shortly after arriving in Algiers.

the upholstery and washing the outside. It shines like a new car even the chromium. Yesterday I also had great fun climbing the apple tree and picking apples. We have 2½ bushels now of beautiful macintosh apples put away for the winter. After that job I was so filthy it took me two hours to clean up for Izzy and my party at the club for the Hites. It turned out very well. We had Bowdens, Bouscarens, Hites, Gortons, Wellingtons, King Tudington, [and] Pete Peters. I played bridge afterwards. Also had a poker game. It will be nice when I can really give a party and enjoy it again. I always feel so guilty having any fun with you over in that stinking mess. Anyway it would never be fun without you here, but it seems necessary to make the effort occasionally anyhow. One thing I've been meaning to tell you for months is about Larry wearing an old Army identification button of yours. He has it on nearly every day and proudly shows it off to all comers. It's such a bad picture of you it embarrasses me with people who don't know you. It makes no difference to him. P.

[Peggy to George]
[V-Mail]

#45
Sept. 18, Sat.

Mon cher George,

Votre lettre en français était si excellente que j'ai peur de t'écrire. Après quelques semaines avec le dictionnaire peut-être tu pourras me comprendre.[89] Right now I have neither the time or the dictionary, and the children are fighting as Larry complains that Georgia is pointing her gun at him. You seem to have done a good job on that lesson already. He asked me the other day if you were in the war because some soldiers were naughty and pointed their guns at people?

I am so glad that you saw Lt. Allbright, and that he is married. I remember him very well and know you enjoyed seeing him. Mrs.

---

89   Translated: "My dear George, Your letter in French was so excellent that I am afraid to write you. After several weeks with the dictionary maybe you will be able to understand me."

Bigelow just phoned to say in the *Times* this morning there is an account of the first landing party on Salamaua[90] [that] was made under the leadership of Lt. Myrus Folsom,[91] who is her nephew. She was very thrilled naturally. I am going over there for dinner tomorrow. Yesterday I drove the Oldsmobile to the plant and found Ben Seidel there. We visited for a while and he left. Bob went over the car with me, and I asked how he was fixed for a car. It seems his has gone 50,000 miles and is in bad shape. I figured what you would do in the situation and told him to give me whatever he could get for his own car, and whatever part of the difference in the sale values of the two cars which he felt he could afford. You'll lose out by about 200.00, but that would have been your decision. Wouldn't it? Anyway, I'm really the one that loses as I was going to use the money for my coat. Poor you. What a wife you left behind. I love you. P

[George to Peggy]
[V-Mail]

No. 20
19 Sept. 1943

Peg dear:

Day before yesterday a lot of the V-Mail that had been addressed to that temporary APO came in, so I received 19 letters in one day. That is better than Lt. Cronin did though, he got the first letter his wife wrote him one year later. I got the first letter you wrote in this bunch. Also I found out that you had managed to keep the girls with you. Am certainly glad they are staying. It is nice to realize that you have nice decent people in the house with you. True that is a mighty high wage to pay, but when you consider it in light of the general wage level I guess you cannot do much better. Glad to hear that George Hite got his commission, give him my congratulations when you see

---

90 Salamaua, Papua New Guinea, site of the Salamaua-Lae campaign which saw troops from the United States and Australia capture two critical Japanese bases
91 As Peggy notes, an article in the *New York Times* credits 1st Lt. Myron Folsom and his reconnaissance patrol as the first American unit to set foot in Salamaua ("Foe Slipped Away as Salamaua Fell.").

him. Thank Larry for the nice letters he has written. Also just heard you were back in Greenwich safely. Had most of the pictures which I mentioned taken by my friends to send home, but will send the one of myself. Love, George

[George to Peggy]

Sept. 19

Peg dear,

Here are a few pictures [that] might be of interest to you. Wanted to send some of my friends, but they convinced me that their own families would be more interested in them than you would.

So I will give you my own impression of some of them.

Schutz to begin with is starting to get bald, freckles taking the place of hair above his forehead. He has a straight nose [and] rather a frank, open face that takes on a rather quizzical expression while he listens, turning to a thoughtful look before he speaks as he usually has thought about what he is going to say before he speaks, and like myself not having too ready a memory wants to be sure he is right, and he usually is. Having been Gen. Patch's[92] aide for a year, he has developed a good deal of tact for saying the right thing in the right way at the proper time. His ideas are for a good part original, his line of thought very logical but not quibbling. He is one of those people who look carefully before they leap, but then puts a good deal of follow thru into what he is doing. He has a mischief sense of humor so it often pays to think twice about what he means. He is a little over

---

92   General Alexander "Sandy" Patch (b. 1889, d. 1945) was a WWI veteran who has the distinction of being the only American general to command large forces in three theaters during WWII. Initially assigned to defend New Caledonia and surrounding islands in the event of an attack by the Japanese, in January 1943 Patch and his Americal Division relieved the overwhelmed 1st Marine Division on Guadalcanal. Within a couple of months, the campaign ended with the Japanese routed. Patch received two Distinguished Service Medals for "exceptionally meritorious services in a position of great responsibility" (Wyant, *Sandy Patch*, 56.). In spring 1944, Patch was made head of the Seventh Army and was tasked with planning the invasion of southern France (Operation Dragoon). The Seventh Army under Patch would notably liberate Marseilles, Lyon, and Toulon before pushing farther into Europe and eventually capturing, among other cities, Nuremberg and Munich. Despite Patch's renown as a tactician and reputation as a "soldier's soldier" who made every effort to spare the lives of his men, Patch remains one of the least well-known military leaders of WWII (Ibid., 2.) (Associated Press, "Gen. Patch Dies of Pneumonia at 55.").

medium height, a bit toward the wiry side, and has a light complexion. His uniform is always neat, but he likes to get comfortable in his quarters. With ambition to get ahead backed up by confidence and good common sense he ought to do all right for himself. Incidentally he has a high sense of moral right and wrong. Of course in my opinion he is just a good for nothing lout like Colby.

Now Maj. Allen who works in the same section and room with me makes a lot of people sore at him at first by being bossy, outspoken, and critical. He is angular, fairly tall, and has a freckled face with brown hair not too carefully combed. Having studied law his line of thought is logical, and questioning. He is rather abrupt and quick making mistakes which he is usually able to either explain or correct. Under the surface he really tries to help people being quite effective in doing so. Once you know him you like him. He also was a general's aide for 6 months and after that G-1 of a division for about a year. He graduated from college as a mining engineer, got his law degree at night school while working in the mines and then got himself a good job with Liberty Mutual Insurance Co. in Boston.[93]

That will be all for right now, but I will continue in another letter. Both of the above were with me in George Marshall's training class, or whatever it was we are still wondering.[94]

You probably won't love me at all when you see this picture of me smoking a cigar so why should I say anything nice about you.

Can't tell [you] how good it is to get your letters, nor how much I wish I were in that new house with you my dear.

                      With my love, George

---

93   Allen graduated from the University of Kentucky in 1929 with a BS in engineering. His graduate studies included Northeastern University Law School and Business Administration at George Washington University.

94   George is referring to the Task Force Officer's Course for the OPD WDGS that he attended in the spring of 1943. ccording to George's military records, the Task Force Officer's Course was three months of specific training given to select graduates of the CGSC in order to better qualify them for staff duty in higher headquarters and task forces.

[Peggy to George]

#46
Sun. Sept. 19, 1943   7:00 P.M.

P.S. I must tell you Robin weighs 22lbs. which is three more than Georgia did at a year. He cut two teeth on Fri. and stood alone today. Guess we'll have to have another. ?

Darling;

I have just settled our three for the night, put on my bathrobe, pulled the coffee table over to the green couch, lit a fire, and am ready for our weekend chat. Doxie is lying on the floor directly in front of me and all we lack in comfort is your presence and that is plenty to us both. George and Betty Hite stopped [by] late this afternoon to see the house and George in uniform nearly ended all conversation after he was spotted by your daughter and Doxie. Larry wasn't fooled any.

Yesterday after we all walked to the mail box with your letter which has gotten to be a ritual at 9:00 a.m. weekdays and Sat. Larry helped me pick the rest of the green tomatoes as we fear Jack Frost any night now. We were discussing his arrival at length when Larry came out with, "Oh, Momie, Jack Frost can't paint the windows—The screens are still on. He couldn't reach them." Anyway we did pick all the tomatoes and then I proceeded to try and finish the rack for the vegetables that you started to help me with last June. I ended up putting the posts on the inside and cutting the trays to fit. I was just thinking how well I was getting along having finished the standard and one tray when I ran out of lumber. The workmen had used up all the rest. They also helped themselves to my little camera which I had put in the closet downstairs. Last night I sorted out all our ski clothes with many nostalgic sighs I must admit, and packed them in labeled boxes and moth balls for a better day to come. I did get a chuckle out of a pair of sugar plum dice which fell out of a pocket of that Bavarian jacket. Do you remember the occasion for those? I went to bed just after the children last night and read all the magazines of the week. You can imagine my surprise to come across the enclosed article on A.F.GHQ. in *Time*.[95] It answers many questions I have wondered about so often. Obviously, you could have told me lots of things you didn't. I thought until reading this that the location of A.F.GHQ. was a secret matter. Let me know when your edition of *Time* starts to arrive and I'll stop sending clippings from it.

While I was in town on Fri. I forgot to tell you I had the bridge book sent, kleenex, double edge swedish steel razors (50) and the only sharpener recommended. It looks like a piece of bakelite and you just rub the razor on the rough part and smooth it off on the other. It can't go out of order like the others. I didn't send the noxzema. You will find some in your duffle bag when it arrives. Let me know as these items get to you. If I send you periodically movies of the children do you think they would go through and would you have a way of showing them?

I had a very nice time at lunch today with Mrs. Bigelow. That place is so beautiful, it is always such a joy just to walk in. Of course a house without children always gives a daintier, fresher, quieter atmosphere, which I particularly appreciated today with Tina on her vacation and Anna at church all morning. Too, that butler of hers is something out of this world for elegance.

I stopped in to say hello to Fred Cuthbertson the other day and find he has gone into the service. He is training at Princeton.

Sometimes as tonight, sitting here in front of the fire and missing

---

95 The functions of the Allied Force Headquarters (AFHQ) are explained in great detail in the September 13, 1943 edition of *Time*. For example, one learns that the AFHQ was made up of 1,100 officers and 15,000 enlisted men on over "2,000 pieces of Algiers real estate." Each Army unit's leadership and purpose are also described in the article giving the reader an idea of the enormity and complexity of the Allied mission. George's G-4 group is responsible for "handling the incredibly complicated British-American supply job." The officers in G-4 operate at times like soothsayers, working three months ahead of battle schedules in order to ensure personnel and supplies can be organized as planned. According to *Time*, "at least once [the Allies] vetoed an invasion plan because the supplies could not be promised in time." General Dwight D. Eisenhower himself lauded the contributions of his "unbloodied workers" when he said to them, "the job is a hard and thankless one. You will not go down in the pages of history. But we have shown…that the Allies can fight under one command and as one nation" ("World Battlefronts.").

you so very much, I try to imagine what it will be like to have you home again and not have to look forward to another one of those hideous partings of which we have had so many in the past two and a half years. When I can imagine it at all, it seems as if the joy would be too great to take and keep one's sanity, and then I think if this is so difficult for me to imagine when I still have the children and surroundings the same as we have always known, how much more difficult it must be for you in a strange land with new friends and new work. You must just think each night that there are three of us here and soon four who pray for just this one thing to come true, and before long too. We all love you and miss so you very very much. Peggy

[George to Peggy]
[V-Mail]

No. 22
Monday eve 20 Sept. 43

My dearest Peggy:

Wrote you a regular air mail letter last night with a picture of me, forgot to number it, but number should have been 21. Tonight I am duty officer. Things are pretty quiet. It has been hot today and is still but there is a breeze coming in off the bay so I think I will step out on a little porch adjoining the room here when I finish writing and think about what you might be doing now. They set up a regular cot for us to try and sleep on right in the room here. Your V-Mail letter written Sept. 10 arrived this morning, that is really good service. My baggage ought to arrive one of these days. I will try to check on it tomorrow. I sure am anxious to see our new house with all the furniture moved in and everything fixed up. How did the porch come out? Now don't worry about sending me anything for Christmas dear. I am looking at a ring you gave me thinking of how you put in on my finger. I wish I were with you my dear. There is taps so good nite my dear. Yours, George

[George to Peggy]
[V-Mail]

No. 23
Tues. 21 Sept. 43

My darling:

    Wrote you last night so I really should not spoil you by starting to write every night, but I have just been thinking about you as I walked up the hill—what good company you are, how much I enjoy being with you, how beautifully you take care of our home, even how pretty you will look in that nightie you wrote me about. I am happy to know how thrilled you are with Robin and to hear all the compliments our friends had for our children. I have their pictures out here on the desk and they sure are cute, handsome, healthy, intelligent looking children. They must keep you busy now. And even then you say you would not mind having one more. From one of your last letters written at breakfast on the porch I could see the picture you drew very clearly and wished I were part of it. It was a warm walk up the hill tonight, so I pulled out the bottle of bourbon we bought in Washington and had the last drink left in it to our happy reunion at an early date. The package of V-Mail you sent arrived, so I filled my pen with the black ink which is supposed to show up better and which I found in the package. Madame just brought me a glass of grape juice which she had crushed from fresh grapes. It is good. Love you so very much my dear. Yours, George

[Peggy to George]
[V-Mail]

#46
Sept. 21

Darling:

    This is going to be a difficult letter to write, I fear. I have left Robin on the toidey, put Georgia out of doors. She is already hollering that she wants to lick the stamp and take this to the box. Larry is in bed for one more day, but is feeling fine. He woke up with a temperature of 104 degrees yesterday morning, and scared me to pieces. Dr. Close came out and found only a sore throat to account for it. I told him he must have picked it up by telepathy from you. That of course thrilled Larry and he held it over Georgia's head all day. She is so afraid she won't get it and I'm afraid she will.

    I had to take her and go to the village for a nose drop prescription and the marketing yesterday, but otherwise I worked here all day as I am today. You just can't imagine how many things there are to do. For proof I bought four books on Friday that I am dying to get at and last night I mended the kid's winter clothes until midnight. I'm glad as you know to keep busy, so don't worry about it. I am trying to get a <u>good</u> man for the outdoor work. I haven't even been able to get the firewood in yet. That I cannot do myself. Mr. Hvolbeck is going to send someone when his work lets up to trim the trees and dig out the brook. Wally Hoggson stopped to call on me about 3:30 yesterday afternoon as I was trying to get some grapes ready for grape juice, take care of Larry and watch the other two out the window. (Anna was up taking her afternoon nap.) I naturally was a sight not to be seen, but he stayed just visiting until nearly five when I had to bathe the kids. It was nice of him to come but ---. He did give some good ideas about the trees though, by suggesting what ones should come out to give the good ones sun. He also made an excellent suggestion to move one of those nice pines down at the drying yard up to the back door to screen off the milk bottles and boxes that are always there.

    I am buying a 5 thousand war bond this week. This is the first one as I have needed the cash up to now for the house. Miss Finn said to ask you to please sign and send back the insurance company's power of attorney for that $31.—monthly check as they won't accept my signature indefinitely.

    I've made one trip up now to praise Robin and to put him back to bed for his morning nap. Now Georgia is really ready to go she says, and Larry says he is through cooking with the dishes and wants his army—so please excuse me for today. We had a date last night but I am afraid I bored you with domestic issues and my everlasting sewing. Anyway I did enjoy knowing you were thinking of me.

    I love you very very much, my dear. Peggy

[Peggy to George]
[V-Mail]

#47
Wed. Sept. 22.

Darling

    We are all down at the breakfast table and I am looking across at your arm chair thinking how wonderful you are going to look sitting there framed in the bay window (probably with the morning paper covering you and the window) and Doxie begging your toast. This is a cloudy day but we are all dressed in our overalls to build a compost pile for next year's crop of vegetables and see what we can do with firewood on the wheel barrow. Larry is really a big help. He runs errands and many little things for me. Last night I fixed the boom on his sailboat which you and I had both promised to do since it arrived two years ago. He figured out all the stays and sail ropes and now he works it like a master. I also made a key board last night so we have all our thousands of keys hung up in a good place. Needless to say I don't know what half of them belong to. At least they are out of my desk. I started one of my new books last night. "A Tree Grows in Brooklyn." Rather a squalid setting so far, but it is very well written. Bob Crawford called to say he could trade his car in for $900.00 and pay $100.00 himself so he gets a good car and we still get a good price for the Olds. Both kids are fighting to lick this. You can guess what a ritual we have. Love, Peggy

[George to Peggy]
[V-Mail]

No. 24
Thursday 23 Sept. 1943

Dearest Peggy:

Had the day off today at least this afternoon. It was a nice sunny day after several days of rain, so I took my camera and walked around the town looking for some good pictures. There are plenty of subjects. A lot of them do not like to have their picture taken though so you have to be a bit careful to get it when they are not looking or at least quickly before they can spoil the picture. One was an old Arab letter writer sitting on the sidewalk in a quiet little square, his back against a building, his writing material spread out on a small rug in front of him. There are many of the Arab women in the streets with their white shawls covering their head and a veil across their face so that only their eyes peer out. Many or rather most of the Arab men wear red caps, long white gowns that look like a very dirty night gown, others wear jackets that are patched to a point where they look ridiculous. The town itself is interesting, part rather modern wide streets lined with trees much like Paris streets, then there are streets with arcades built out over the sidewalks like Havana, and then narrow dirty little streets that wind into the remote dark alley ways of the native quarter.[96] Could use filter for the Leica, a roll of color if possible and several of plus-x and panoramic-x. Miss you and love you dear. George

---

96 The Arab quarter of Algerian cities was called the "Village Nègre," literally the "Negro Village." In a memoir, one Algerian Jew writes regarding Algerian independence:

> All peoples desire liberty and all will eventually win it. Only privilege fosters lies. If the friends and family around us refused to open their eyes to this plain truth, it was on account of the comfortable homes, the businesses, the little advantages of being French, while the Algerian masses endured poverty, ignorance, and servitude. People used the familiar *tu* with Arabs, showing them no respect. They were penned up in the *Village Negre*. Shorn of all dignity, they formed the underclass of their own beautiful country. (Guénoun, *A Semite*, 71.)

[Peggy to George]
[V-Mail]

[#]48.
Thurs. Sept. 23

My dearest George

This morning besides two companions at the table I also have two under the table, Doxie and Robin. The latter I am watching carefully on our new rug as he is without his underpinnings. I spent a very boring evening last night. I had to sell doughnuts and cider at the Flower Show at the YMCA from 6-10. A very nice girl came to help at 7:30. She has three children and lives alone up on Round Hill Rd—5 miles further out than we are. Her husband is at Fort Phillips in Kansas.[97] I took all three children to call on our neighbors at the end of the lane and arrived at the same awful moment as they called on me. — Moving day. They are going to N.Y.C. for the winter and then coming back to a small house they just bought in Greenwich. They just rented this. I asked them about getting the road plowed in winter and they weren't very helpful. It seems the only other family living on the lane are also moving to N.Y. next week and even with all three houses occupied they had great difficulty. I am getting busy right away at this 'cause I don't care to shovel from the house to No. St. myself. The children are all on the floor crawling & yelling with Robin now. Must go. Love, Peggy

[George to Peggy]
[V-Mail]

No. 25
Friday 24 Sept.

Peg dear

Now I would like to know just what you were thinking about when you wrote me on Sat. 11 Sept. and dated it <u>April</u> 11, 1943. Sorry you

---

97 Peggy probably means Camp Phillips near Salina, Kansas. From 1942-1945 the camp was used as an Army training base providing recruits with instruction in small arms, artillery, bayonets, grenades, and bombing as well as anti-aircraft, anti-tank, and chemical weapons. The Smolan satellite prisoner of war internment camp was also part of the Camp Phillips complex (Kansas Department of Health and Environment, "Kansas Department of Health and Environment Bureau of Environmental Remediation Identified Sites List Information.").

are worried about mail. I don't think I have let you down that badly, but you can be sure even though I write you quite regularly that there will be times when there are bound to be rather lengthy delays. So don't worry about me, if you don't happen to hear from me for a while. Meant to answer you before about that fur coat, how about letting that be my christmas present to you? If I run into Croft I will say hello. Say the Colby's baby must be just about due, be sure to let me know about that. Sorry to hear about Teedie. I had to come back up here tonight for a while at the office and missed a good laugh [as] Helms had to give a lecture to a bunch of WACs on the whys and wherefores of the G-2 section. I really regret not being present to help him. My love, George.

[Peggy to George]
[V-Mail]

#49
Friday Sept. 24

Darling

Again at the breakfast table waiting for the kids to finish their poached eggs on toast. It's a crisp sunny fall day and we are all going to Greenwich to do the marketing. That is quite an event in our lives now. It happens twice a week. Otherwise, we keep pretty busy here at home fixing things for your return. Yesterday Larry started following me upstairs for the umpteenth time and I asked him to wait outside for me. He said "But I can't Momie. I have to come with you 'cause I promised Daddy I'd take good care of you until he comes home." What could I say? Bernice deposited Anne here yesterday morning and Chloe came out with her four and we all had a picnic lunch on the front terrace. I'm going to miss Chloe. She's such a swell person and they leave for Chicago Oct. 1st for good. They have rented a house out there although Pete has been warned that he'll be drafted very soon.[98]

---

98   It is unclear from the letter why Pete believes he will be drafted soon but there are several possible explanations. It is likely that Pete, assumed to be of draft age, was originally deferred for service because he met a criterion for deferral. The most probable criteria were because of his occupational status (his job was important to national security or a crucial component of the "arsenal of democracy") or because he had dependents (in Pete's case, a wife and children).

Your daughter has cleared the whole breakfast with the prospect of licking this letter as a reward. Each morning there is a fight over who licks it, who puts the stamp on, and who carries it to the mailbox. So you see there is more to this epistle than meets the eye. With the distraction goodness knows not much meets the eye. We all love you and that's what it's all about anyway. Peggy

[Peggy to George]
[V-Mail]

#50
Sept. 25, 1943, Sat.

Dearest George

This has become a daily breakfast letter. It is sort of fun to talk to you over our coffee with the children's silly prattle going in one ear and out the other. I ended up going to Greenwich alone yesterday. Mrs. Pearson who lives in that huge white house next to the parkway sent her seven-year-old son Scott over to play with Larry. He was very well behaved and sweet to the youngsters and had such a good time. I asked him to stay for picnic lunch. I let Anna off for just the afternoon and evening since Tina is away so I had all four for the afternoon. The boys made airplanes with some pieces of wood, nails, & hammers I gave them. Georgia hung on like fly paper. I could hear Scott suggesting to Larry that they get rid of her. But Larry would have none of it. In the end Scott was riding her piggy back and loving

---

Before 1943, the emphasis had been on protecting the home—thus fathers and husbands were to be drafted only after single, childless men had gone first. Even some military men advocated for a dependency deferral in order to keep families intact (Blum, *Drafted or Deferred*, 57.). However, by 1943 the U.S. Armed Forces were experiencing a severe shortage of manpower and in April the men who previously qualified for dependency deferrals were reclassified based primarily on the type of dependents they had (Ibid., 59.). An attempt was made to entice fathers to seek employment within agencies necessary to the war effort by allowing the fathers to continue with a deferred status if they did so. Fathers had until September 15, 1943 to obtain said job or they could lose their deferral status and be drafted as soon as possible. The reclassification did little to free up manpower and the idea of drafting the previously deferred fathers was reconsidered seriously.

In December, Congress will pass Public Law 197, which (among other things) will provision non-fathers to be drafted before fathers. President Roosevelt, concerned about public opinion, will decline to veto the bill (Ibid., 61.). In deferring fathers in favor of single men, even single men crucial to the war effort (e.g., those working in aircraft assembly plants, etc.) will be drafted. This will exacerbate the already serious problem of factory-worker shortages especially among skilled or specialized workers in the shipbuilding and aircraft production industries.

it. I finally had to send him home at supper time. Unfortunately, they move to town next week too. I'm sorry as he'd be good for Larry. As I was getting supper last night, I called up to the kids to hurry. The answer came back "Hush it, Momie. Georgia's talking to Daddy on the telephone." I wish I could have recorded the conversation. They both talked then came this gibberish down the stairs. "That's Daddy talking french, Momie." Then they came down with you for supper. Larry sat you down, gave you supper and talked to you all through the meal. When they said their prayers, he said, "when I say 'God bless Daddy,' that's so God will take care of Daddy and bring him home to us to stay all day when the war is over." Joe & Penn Bridge came over last night. They sold their ranch and are waiting for the draft. Peggy

[George to Peggy]
[V-Mail]

No. 26
26 Sept. 43 Sunday

Peg dear:

    Good evening. I am very well thank you. All my work is cleared with nothing hanging over until tomorrow which is a nice position to be in. So for once I did not even go back up to the office, but walked up home from mess. They have set the clock back one hour though so when I got up here at eight o'clock it was quite dark. I have the water running now for my one warm bath per week. It has been a very cool, clear, pleasant day. I walked down to breakfast this morning with an English officer, and had a pleasant chat. Being Sunday there were many French men and their women folk pedaling up the hill on single and tandem bikes. It is a ½ hour walk and they pedal all the way. If you want that coat please get it as my Christmas present to you. I should have left the "if" out of that. Wish I were there to be persuaded. My love dear. George

[Peggy to George]

#51
Mon. p.m. 8:25

Darling.

    I've been thinking about you for such a nice long time tonight and it's so wonderful to know you are doing the same. I have thought of so many things that I wish we could do and realize you probably are enjoying the same thoughts. I have quite a bit of news for you tonight, so I'll pretend you are sitting right here beside me on the couch and I'll tell you all that's gone on since my letter Sat. morning.

    That day was hectic for both Anna and myself. Besides the house, cooking and children, she tried to can applesauce. In the midst the pressure cooker broke and the entire kitchen was applesauce. That took her about three hours to clean up. I reglued and painted the four green porch chairs for the third-floor room. They came out fine without a mishap, but when I went to pick up Robin after his nap he also had done a paint job and his was anything but fine. By the time I had bathed him three times, washed his bed, mattress and all his clothes and bedclothes I had a two-hour job. Needless to say I was reminded of our first experience of that kind in Forest Hills when Larry pulled it and Koch had just come up to call. Sat. night I went over to get Mrs. Bigelow and brought her back to a very nice dinner of Anna's. She is very good company. I took her home early as she is afraid to be out after dark. Anyway I was ready for bed.

    Then yesterday I really had a busy day. About a week ago I offered to take two officers any Sun. who wanted to spend the day in the country. A woman called me from N.Y. on Fri. and asked me to do it this week. I thought with Tina off I never could manage it, but then I remembered how much I like to think of how nice the Rebillets are to you so I decided I could take them to the club. I met them on the 11:24 and they were just as sweet boys as you could ever meet. John Tyack[99]

---

99   It is possible the last name is "Tyacke" instead of "Tyack."

is from Greenwich, England, just outside of London. He had to write a letter to his Mother with this Greenwich postmark on before he left. He is about 34, married, with a 7 months old boy. He is a navy officer of rank like our ensign. He is a navigator and expects to go out of here on a new ship, comparable to our D.E. In civilian life he is in a bank. Allan Lunn,[100] is about 25 in appearance, blond and pink cheeked. He is not married. He is from Newcastle and is of the same rank and job as John. His hobby is playing the cello. They both love good music and know too much about it for my company. First we played golf and it was such a gorgeous day that the game was just an excuse to be out of doors. They both used your clubs, but were pretty bad golfers. Then we met the Gortons for [a] buffet lunch. After that all they wanted to do was see the children. Of course that made me mad. When John saw Robin, he was so thrilled to get a hold of a baby the same age as his that he never put him down all the rest of the afternoon. We all took a tramp through the woods and he carried Robin, Allan had Georgia, and I Larry. We went along the bridle path to where it turns at the reservoir and came back. This you will love. As we came in Anna was waiting for Robin and John asked if he could please "bath" him. Of course I was delighted, and he had the time of his life and did a marvelous job, diaper and all. Only having seen his own baby for four days I don't see how he gained all the experience. Of course then Georgia insisted in Allan bathing her which I thought would embarrass a bachelor to death, but he wasn't anything but flattered and likewise did a good job. By this time the Gortons were here and I showed them all our wedding movies taken in England. They seemed to enjoy them a lot. We all went up to Nan Miller's for a party supper she had. It was very nice, but except for the Hoggsons, Grays, and Bridges, I didn't know anyone and the boys didn't drink so we came back here early. The Gortons and Hoggsons also came. I tried to play some records the boys wanted to hear but there were too many

---

100   Allan George Ramsay Lunn (b. 1921) was born in Newcastle and served in the Royal Navy during WWII.

people. John had been trying to find a teddy bear for his boy and as there are no more made he was very disappointed. Connie came over today with a brand new one that her boy had never played with. I am going to N.Y. tomorrow and will leave it at the Barbizon where they are all put up in hopes he will get it before they leave. Incidentally, they had never been to this country before and now had docked in Halifax and come down to N.Y. by train two days ago. From all this you can gather that I enjoyed doing a little something as much as they seemed to like coming out.

I am getting so sleepy I guess I'll have to stop if I expect to get up and go to N.Y. tomorrow. I did an enormous washing today and was ironing until I sat down to write this.

I miss you so much darling, and I guess that's why I loved doing for those British boys yesterday. I could watch them and imagine someone giving you the same respite from war and a glimpse of home life over there.

Yours always—Peggy

[George to Peggy]

Sept. 28

My darling Peggy:

Received your letter v-mail today sent the 15th Sept. in which you asked if a letter V-Mail with an air mail stamp would arrive any sooner. I do not see why it should, because I believe the V-Mail is processed in New York. If you were a good ways away from the point where they process the mail I suppose it would save a few days with an air mail stamp within the country but once it has been photographed it makes no difference at all.

With the clock set back an hour it sure gets dark early. I did not get through until 9:30 so it was rather a dark half hour walk up the hill. There are so many G.I. vehicles running all over the place that none of us that live up here have any trouble in hitch hiking any hour of the day or night. There certainly is flagrant misuse of government transportation, but it helps us out when we want a ride. Officially we are not allowed any transportation, which burns me a bit when I see the French crowding the streets with vehicles and gasoline for which I am paying a devil of [a] lot more than my share.

I was glad to hear that the Scotts were taking good care of 1941. Did you get the furniture from there you wanted?

Peg I mentioned it before, but some of these letters may stray, so once more I would like to have you get that coat as a Christmas present from me. You might as well get it right away and have the use of it all winter.

As for trying to send me anything for Christmas don't worry about that because you know how we have to consider every item we take with us when we pack to move about. The only thing that I can use is some chocolate bars.

Believe I asked you once before to send me the best one of that odd pair of shoes. If I need the other one I will let you know later or if you sent both already that is all right, as I will need them sometime. My duffle bag and bed roll should be catching up soon.

Went down town last night with Capt. Rogers to see Adol[phe] Menjou[101] in person. There was quite a crowd. The show was not too bad, but it was pouring rain when we got out so we went over to the Red Cross and got a bite to eat at their snack bar, and by the time we left there it had stopped raining so we walked back up to Headquarters from where I caught a ride up here.

Your letters have been arriving quite regular every day or so, and are always eagerly read, which you know without being told and I love

---

101 Adolphe Menjou (b. 1890, d. 1963) was an American actor known for his iconic, elegant "Menjou mustache" and debonair demeanor. Frequently listed as one of the ten best-dressed men in the world, Menjou originally found success in Hollywood silent films, often playing suave lovers or villains. Menjou served in WWI in an ambulance unit in France and in WWII he entertained troops overseas. During the latter, the OWI utilized Menjou's multilingualism to issue broadcasts in French, German, Italian, Spanish, and Russian. After the war Menjou will continue acting to great success (he appeared in 200 films over the course of his lifetime). However, his accomplishments are perhaps overshadowed by his eagerness to testify before the House Committee on Un-American Activities in 1947 and provide the names of people in Hollywood he alleged to be Communists.

you very, very much, and miss you all the time, and think about you a lot more than I should which you also know without being told. In fact I would like more than anything in the world to have you in my arms right this moment, and I do remember often, right this moment too how much fun it is to kiss you and to, —well I will tell you the rest some other time. I was thinking of you all last evening too, but right now I am going to go to bed.

My love dear, George

[Peggy to George]
[V-Mail]

#52
[Tues]. Sept. 28

Darling,

    I'll have to rush to get myself and the kids down to the mail box in time this morning. We just had a kicking, biting fight under the table over who was to lick your stamp on the letter today. Larry [won] and the other is sulking with her lip out a mile. The breakfast conversation has been about our barn and the horses again. Larry suggests that when you come home you can pretend to be the farmer "and take care of the horses." Georgia says that when she gets to be a big girl she is going "across da ochun and bring Daddy home." I told her you would come to us first. "Then," says she, "when Daddy goes to the station again I'll tell him, No, Daddy you can't do that."

    My trip to N.Y.C. was successful. I did the children's winter clothes, preordered myself a suit from Twyeforte (your birthday-Christmas present to me) met Crawford and settled the car. He has it. I have one grand. Arson Knapp and wife are at Savoy. I called on them with Crawford and invited her out for a day if she cares to come. Must hurry to mail this. Thanks a million for your picture that came yesterday. Love, Peggy

THE ALGERIA LETTERS

[Peggy to George]
[V-Mail]

#53
Sept. 29, [Wed.]

Dearest George,

I was afraid I'd miss the mailman this morning so I brought this and the children down here to the box and I'm waiting for him. It's really cold today so we won't tarry long.

All day yesterday I spent painting the vegetable bin. It is finished now and really looks nice. Then Frank, [the] gardener, arrived and cut most of the tall weed in front by the drive so that looks much better. I bought a brush scythe the other day and did quite a bit myself. It reminded me of the day up at Thunder Lake that we cut a vista through to the back bay. I wish we could cut out one through to the reservoir. I also painted a new ladder (extension) that I bought for the man I hope will come someday to fix the trees.

Last night Pinky Boussevain came for dinner and we talked about Freddy[102] all evening. She's so pathetic but very brave. We ended up having a brandy from your glasses & bottle—the first time they've been used since you christened them.

My fingers are getting cold and the children make me nervous throwing stones on North Street for Doxie. So with love for today, and every day. Peggy

---

102 Frederick W. Boissevain was Pinky's husband. In 1904, "Freddy" was born to a Dutch father in Batavia when it was part of the Dutch East-Indies (now Jakarta, Indonesia). A landscape architect and gardener, Freddy assisted his aunt (famed poet Edna St. Vincent Millay) and his uncle (Eugen Boissevain) with their design and development of Steepletop (now the home of the Edna St. Vincent Millay Society). As a child, Georgia was told that Freddy was killed in combat by the Nazis. Additional research, however, suggests otherwise. One source claims that Freddy, after gaining his U.S. citizenship in 1942, served with the OWI and was accidentally killed in June 1943 while on an overseas assignment (Beagan, "Frederick W. Boissevain."). Freddy's son "Fitsy" was one of Larry's friends.

[George to Peggy]
[V-Mail]

No. 28
30 Sept. 43 Thurs.

My dear,

Wrote you a letter yesterday air mail and did not number it, should have been #27. I have written out a series of numbers up to 120 in the back of my note book and cross [off a number] each time I write. Wonder where I will be when I line out number 120. Had a nice letter from Col. Smith.[103] He said that "by accident" he got talking to a cute looking WAC in the post hospital at Fort Dix. Turned out she used to do your hair in the beauty parlor in Greenwich. He sent you his regards and best wishes. I sure am proud to hear what a brave boy Larry was when he got his tetanus shot. From the picture he drew he must have gotten a vivid impression of the needle. Give him a kiss for me, and tell him I am sorry it hurt him, but I am very proud of him and glad to know he has had the shot so he can't get lockjaw. Then you will no doubt have to explain all about lockjaw. I do enjoy your letters very much dear. Just heard Madam *dit à Monsieur "J'ai froid. Voulez-vous coucher avec moi."*[104] Wish I could hear you say that, to me of course. I would at least consider the matter. I love you so very much dear. George

[George to Peggy]

#29
Friday 1 Oct. 43

My Peggy,

Today had a big red circle around it on the calendar. You may not have noticed it, but you see I received three letters from you today; one V-letter dated Sept. 21, one air mail with some wonderful pictures dated Sept. 9, and a nice long letter about our living room, a party for

---
103 Colonel Milton J. Smith, assigned to the Air Service Command headquarters in Rome, New York with George in 1943.
104 Just heard Madam say to Monsieur, "I'm cold. Do you want to sleep with me?"

Lt. Hite, etc. dated Mon. evening Sept. 13, letters no. 46, 40 and 42 respectfully.

So just now I have drawn out a diagram of the living room to put everything in just as you told me. I think I have a good picture of it. What about the rug though? Also tell me how the porch is built and how it worked out. It all sounds like a mighty pleasant arrangement. I don't know just what kind of curtains to hang up over the windows for my mental picture though.

I like the pictures of you with Larry and Georgia. Madam was very impressed with you [and] said *"Elle est très chic, élégante comme une Parisienne." Et Monsieur a dit "Je sais pourquoi vous désirez retourner tout le temps, ooh là law, elle est une belle femme, et votre fils est comme son père, un brave garçon."*[105]

Of course I showed the pictures to everybody around the office with a great deal of pride and got very complimentary remarks. Robbie looks so happy, cute, and plump. He sure has grown. Trouble is when I look at the picture of my pretty wife here on the desk before me tonight I would like so much to take her in my arms, kiss that cute little mouth, and tell her how much I love her. Which reminds me that I would like to know just how our bedroom and dressing room are arranged. Those pictures taken out on the lawn remind me too of some beautiful star lit evenings we spent out there talking and planning with your hand warm in mine with so many dreams of days to come.

I can't tell you so very much about my work. It is the common understanding here, just as it was in the War Dept., that when we leave the office we do not discuss our work even with the other officers. In general, as you can gather from the G-4 section in my address, our work is concerned with supply matters in this theatre. For additional information see *Time Magazine* Sept. 13.

---

105 Translated: "She is very chic, elegant like a Parisian." And Monsieur said "I know why you want to go back all the time, wow, she is a beautiful woman, and your son is like his father, a good [or brave] boy."

Maj. Stipp, who is in charge of our particular part of the work, is in the same room with Maj. Allen and myself. You would like him. He is a couple of years older than me, dark brown hair, rather a broad, ruddy face with an earnest expression. I was just thinking today how his wife would like to see the pleased intent look in his face as he read a long letter from her today. He had an executive engineering job with a power company in Indiana. He listens carefully to what you say, and usually doesn't start talking until he is pretty sure of what he is saying. He does not work all on theory either as he commanded a battalion of armored artillery during the fight in Tunisia and has been through a lot of rough spots. He is practical and efficient yet generous and likeable.

The three of us work together very well, keep busy, and turn out a lot of work. The fact that there is much to be done is something to be thankful for, as the days do pass fast. There is a good deal of kidding between us with the usual amount of razing about "Are you going to let me take care of all of this or are you just going to read those letters from home for half the day."

There is a French woman who comes in to clean the office every morning, interrupting all work for about 15 minutes as she sweeps and swishes around while we practice our French words on her which usually brings some good laughs. They are good boys who put their heart into their work, and turn out careful well-finished jobs.

My dear how I would like to be home with you tonight. I will be thinking of you as I go to sleep, I love you so very much.

Yours, George.

[Peggy to George]

[#]54
Fri. Oct. 1.

Darling:

This is a really rainy day. The kind it is so much fun to sort of curl up indoors in and do all the things you never get around to on nice days. The children are up in the third floor room for the first time with their barnyard and greyhound bus having a wonderful time. I can barely hear the noise so now I am happier than ever that we finished that room. Robin is on the toidey and is about to go back to bed for his morning nap. I am still in my bathrobe and expect to dress directly and do all sorts of these things I just mentioned— mending, painting the third floor radiator, spraying all your clothes with moth killer, put[ting] away my summer clothes. Anna is going off on the early bus today and as Tina won't be back until Sun. from her vacation. I'll be here alone which I also enjoy once in a while. If you could only drop in right now what a really cozy day we would have. There are loads of things I could suggest for you to do too, but I promise I wouldn't say a word. You could putter to your heart's content, and I'd love it.

    Yesterday I spent the morning with the brush scythe and got a lot of the front cleaned out among the trees next to the wall on the left as you drive into the house. In the winter I am going to have several of the trees in the clothes drying yard moved to the end of the drive to cover up the road from the house. I also moved a lot of fireplace wood yesterday onto the back porch here with Larry's help. He really brought a lot of kindling in with his little wheelbarrow and stacked it up. I know you will be glad to hear that I got a man through the Gortons for one day every two weeks. It's not much but it will help.

    Last night I went up to the Bowden's to a party for Chloe and Pete. They leave today for Chicago. Incidentally, I took the meat loaf and an apple pie for the dessert. Bernice is a scream.

    Izzie lost her baby Mon. It was a boy too, which is what they both wanted so much. I haven't seen her yet.

               Loads of love, dear. Peggy

[Peggy to George] #54

Sat. Oct. 2

Darling,

My cozy day indoors proved to be pretty strenuous yesterday. I did the mending and enjoyed the children, and ended up with Nan Miller and the Bridges for dinner. There wasn't a thing in the icebox so we had canned tomato soup, canned asparagus salad, dried beef on baked potatoes, and gingerbread for dessert. We played Frank Steiner's game of dirty eights, as I was too sleepy for bridge.

The children played in the third floor all day and had Robin up there too. They are so sweet to him and entertain him so nicely that I only went up once in the morning and not at all in the afternoon. When I took Robin down for his bath I asked them to start picking up which they did and then brought all the toys down and put them away. In another year with them in school part of the day and Robin trained I can manage for a while at least if I find myself without any help. Larry is really very good about taking responsibility when I ask him to.

I love to think also about you wearing that ring and remember the fun I had giving it to you. I wish we could repeat the procedure at least once a day. Does that make you think of the story you told me once about the window shade.

The White Ensign Club called me again yesterday and said the British boys had been in three times to say what a good time they had out here. They sent me a lovely box of candy and letter. The woman said they didn't want to seem forward and call me themselves but they had arranged their duty so they were free from this noon to tomorrow night and could she see if I would take them. Of course I agreed and now I am wondering what Greenwich will say if I have two strange men in the house overnight. YOU may hear about it way over there. I am taking the kids to Greenwich for the errands and lunch. Then we will meet them on the 1:34. My love now and I'll tell you all about it Mon. Guess we'll play golf in the rain....Peggy

[George to Peggy]
[V-Mail]

No. 30

3 Oct. 43 Sunday

Peggy Dear: See Sept. 13 Time Magazine for an article on AFHQ.

Have the water running for a warm bath, so I will probably finish this when I am through getting clean. I figure a letter is about half written anyway when I have filled out the heading. A bit tired tonight, had to drive out about 75 miles east of here and back today, spent about four hours out there. Now ~~Ball~~ that I have finished my bath I find a glass of muscatel on my desk, *c'est bon*. Drove out today with Capt. Ballard in our ordnance section[106] and an English officer in the Military Govt. section who had spent the last 15 years in different British overseas garrisons, rather an interesting fellow. The car we drove was a good symbol of allied cooperation, the body and chassis made in England powered with a Ford V-8. But seriously I am sold on the necessity of something stronger than just "cooperation" between the U.S. and English govts. after the war. Ballard's wife and children incidentally are living in N.Y. The ordnance sections I have worked with on different staffs have been good, they always seem to get some of the best officers. I sure would like to be with you right this minute my dear. George

[Peggy to George]

[#]55

Mon. Oct. 4-6:30 P.M.

Darling;

Both children are sitting here on the couch beside me. We have a

---

106 The Ordnance Corps is the part of the U.S. Army's logistics system, responsible for managing, testing, and supplying weapons, ammunition, and related equipment.

grate fire, and the radio is on. They have promised to go right up to bed if I let them watch me for a few minutes. The weather has turned quite chilly now, but so far we have had no frost. I still have several dahlias blooming from the bulbs you helped me to plant. They are of every color and very pretty as well as having the ability to remind me always of the fun we had putting them in.

The weekend with the British boys was very pleasant. The children and I met them as I wrote you. We came directly home and I got them some lunch. We went over to the club with the kids along for a little tennis. Again I was sorry to beat them. They are awfully good sports about it but I could see they were a little embarrassed to both lose. I don't see why either as I surely worked for each game. Anna gave us a nice dinner of lobster first, leg of lamb, potatoes, green beans, peaches and cookies. After dinner we spent the entire evening until midnight listening to the records. The youngest one, 22, Allan Lunn, who I told you was a cellist really seems to know exactly what instrument comes next through the whole of Tannhauser. What pleasure one could get out of such talent is even difficult to imagine. Sun. they came down for breakfast with toys for each of the children—books for Larry and Georgia and a little wooden rabbit for Robin. We all had waffles which they had never seen before and Larry ate more than either of them although they did very well and claimed they liked the dish. We all walked to the mailbox for the paper and then sat around on the lawn playing with the children all morning which seemed to remind me that you preferred that occupation to most any other. In the afternoon I took them to the Bridge's for a cocktail party and I must say for the notion most Americans have of the reserved and cold unsociability of the British these two don't measure up very well. They did not drink except to hold a glass, and they didn't know a soul, but by the time we left they had made a point of speaking a few words with almost everyone there and knew the names. For supper I made them macaroni and cheese which was something they hadn't had for two years and seemed to enjoy. A caller of Anna's took them to the train about ten. I sent in my ice skates as I am going in on Thurs. to go to Madison Square rink and skate with them. From all the conversation I gather they both excel as fancy skaters so there will be a good chance for them to make me look like a monkey. They expect to get their orders soon after that. I shall be sorry not to see them after that as they have been very refreshing and stimulating after the stagnant conversation and entertainment of the few 4-fs[107] or whatever the men are that still are seen around Greenwich. Perhaps the next ones I am asked to take will be just as well-mannered and interesting. The one feeling that seems so invariable among these boys as well as those fighting in our own services is that this war must be the last one and that details are difficult to work out but an international police force is the primary requirement. It's too bad that all men from 18 to 40 can't see a bit of combat in this war as long as it has to be fought and maybe some of the troublemakers and war profiteers would change their ideas and we'd all know what we are fighting for. It will always bother me that the boys that see the worst of the fighting seem to be the ones that bear ill will to no one and ask a very small place in the sun in which to raise their families and earn their daily bread.

One thing too which requires a great deal of my thought now and which I feel myself inadequate to answer properly are Larry's questions about the war. He seems to think a good deal about what you are doing, and asks such questions as: "Do good soldiers shoot bad soldiers? Then why are they good? Is Daddy a good soldier? Do you like war? Then why do you let Daddy go? Why are Germans bad? If some are good why do they stay with the bad ones?" Perhaps the answers are obvious to you now, but I still am unconvinced on several accounts so you will enlighten two puzzled souls if you will

---

107   A 4F classification means that a person was determined unfit for military service for physical, mental or moral reasons and was rejected.

tell me how you want him to feel on the subject. Georgia announced at breakfast this morning that she would go to the next war and you and Larry could stay home and take care of Robin and me. I honestly believe she could take care of the enemy in short order too. She really has us in hysterics most of the time. She has an answer for everything. Yesterday morning I told her to put her overalls on. She refused in no uncertain terms although she has worn them every morning for months. "NO, Momie. I want to put on my pink dress to look bery pretty for the boys." Added to that she came downstairs in the dress and before I had a chance to tell the story to Allan and John, she went up and asked them if they thought she looked pretty.

I must end this. First I want to say that Ki phoned me last night about 1 A.M. It frightened me to death but he had waited since 7 for the call to go through. He called mainly to settle about your Mother's furs which worked out satisfactorily for all. Teedie has the martin jacket and also wanted one of the sables. That is perfectly o.k. as I am too short to wear four anyway. The rest of the stuff Miss Finn will dispose of the best she can. Oh yes, we each got a white coat too. He said to send you his best of course and they are both fine. There didn't seem to be much news otherwise. He still thinks he may be moved in a month or two.

A letter from Mom today gave distressing news of Kay Bull. The day after she was over with Danny she got up at night to go to the bathroom and fainted and hemorrhaged for hours before Mrs. Bull found her. She was in the hospital for days before they knew if she would live or not. She is practically O.K. now. It was due to an ectopic pregnancy which burst the tube and became infected.

Again goodnight, Darling. We've had a nice date here by the fire. The children are in bed. Now what shall we do?

                Yours always—Peggy

[George to Peggy]

#31
Oct. 5, Tues.

Peggy dear:

    First of all I love you very much. It is such a long time since we said good bye. At least that much time of our separation is passed. Tonight I would like so much to have your good company for the evening and all the love of you in my arms. I often speculate on just how we would spend an evening together letting my imagination roam through our conversation before our fire place with a cocktail or two perhaps, the pleasure of sharing a dinner alone with you. Somehow we have captured such a rare art of thoroughly enjoying each other's company. Sometimes I think of how much fun it will be to take you out where there is good music to dance. I have you all dressed up so fresh and charming in a gown you have worn just for me to admire, so graceful and pretty for me to be proud of. Then again we have dinner at home together and go in to sit in the living room before the fire, play backgammon, and kiss you when you sit beside me and think maybe we should go upstairs. I think of every little detail as we get ready for bed, how dainty and sweet you look in a nightie, and how you tease me knowing all the time which bed I will get into. Those moments are worth remembering and looking forward to once more. So you see it is not a very happy prospect for me to be getting along without you. But then there are always the happy times to look forward to when we will be together again. Well I must get to bed and you will not have to try hard to know just what I will be thinking of as I fall asleep tonight. I wish so much we were together dear.

                      My love, George

[George to Peggy]
[V-Mail]

No. 32
6 Oct.

My dear:

Good morning. I just finished breakfast and walked up the hill to the office thru the rain. It was a bit too wet to walk so I rode the trolley bus down the hill from [**blacked out by censor**][108] to breakfast. Wrote you a letter last night, but I guess you will take time to read this one too. I love you just as much as I did last night. I received your letter with the clippings from Time on the Hq. Strange to say I had just mailed a letter to you mentioning that article which I had seen in a copy one of the officers receives. If I had written as much information in a letter I would have been in plenty of trouble and you would not have gotten the letter. [**Three lines blacked out by censor.**] I would like to have Time sent to me over here. They print it in a reduced size, less adv[ertising] for overseas mailing. None of the editorial wording is eliminated just the actual size of the magazine. They call it the pony edition, the rate is $3.50 per year. Time, 330 East 22nd Street, Chicago 16, Illinois. You mentioned this before but I thought perhaps you might need a request from me. My love, George

[George to Peggy]
[V-Mail]

No. 33
7 Oct. Thurs.

Peg dear

This was my day off, but there is not much point to taking time off as there is practically nothing you can do around here. We cannot use any transportation. It is too cold to go out swimming now and the rainy season has started. So I spent most the morning around

---

108 Since V-Mails were fed through a Recordak machine that microfilmed them, censors could not cut out words and phrases the way they did with regular letters. Instead, so as not to create constant paper jams, censors blacked out sensitive sections of the original V-Mails before feeding them through the Recordak.

the headquarters, went downtown along in the afternoon, ran into Rodgers in the Army Sales store, went over to one of the hotels to get a glass of wine and talk awhile then came back up for supper. Think I will walk out to Cronin's apartment for a while, there are three or four officers living together there who have gotten an apartment for themselves. He is sitting over across the desk from me writing a letter to his wife also. They have a baby which he has never seen. He was up in Ireland and England before coming here last fall. Wish I were home tonight. Good night dear. Yours, George

[Peggy to George]
[V-Mail]

[#]57
Thurs. Oct. 7

Dearest George

Right now I am sitting on a bench in the Greenwich station waiting for Marjorie Peters and the 10:06 train. I have the green suit on which we got in Wales and just had Charlie, here, shine my alligator shoes. I don't look very citified but as I told you I am going to skate this afternoon so that is the reason. This is another beautiful fall day. Larry and I worked out of doors all day yesterday. We had five enormous bonfires to burn the long weeds cut down last week from Oakley Lane to the house. You should have seen me using the pitch fork and Larry filling a bushel basket and trudging along. He really is learning to work and not quit on me every few minutes. Georgia climbed at best half way up the apple tree while all of this went on below.

Last night I went to Mary Wards for dinner and we went through the Stony Wold lecture and movie. It's pretty good now and tomorrow is the big day. I don't see how we can possibly hope to make what we need for our patient, though.

This is an awful scribble but I just wanted to say hello as usual and tell you I still love you this morning. Love, Peggy

[Peggy to George]
[V-Mail]

[#]58
Oct. 9 Fri.

Darling,

    My day in N.Y.C. was quite eventful. I had a nice chat going in on the train with Marjorie. We don't have much in common any more, but she can be very interesting if she gets talking about Guatemala and the people and life down there. I did several errands in the morning. I finally managed to get you some leica film by certifying that it was going overseas. I also have located plain hershey bars. They don't advise sending anything with nuts in it as they get bad. I also have scavenged Greenwich for the ingredients for a plum pudding. I have them here and will make the things today. I hope one will reach you all right. About three I went up to the Savoy and visited with Mrs. Bigelow until time to meet the boys. They took me skating for a couple of hours. One was excellent—the other like I am. I tried the waltz once and spilled John good. We stayed watching mostly as my poor shins got tired. They took me to a place on 58th for dinner. It was very nice. I'll remember it for us sometime. I caught the 10 o'clock express home. They may be leaving today, but if not I invited them out for the club dance tomorrow night. I am going to try and get Pinky Boissevain to go with us. I hope she will. I have two very "jammy" faces hanging over this letter—each to lick half of the seal. Loads of love—X. Peggy

[George to Peggy]
[V-Mail]

No. 34
9 Oct. Sat.

Dear Peggy:

    Who should walk into the office this morning, but Dick Bosord. He seems to have turned out to be rather a decent chap. The army has certainly taken a lot of weight off of him. Said he had rather a good trip over, never even got sea sick. He ought to be well qualified for his job in military government with his Harvard law training, but I am glad that I have not had the misfortune to fall into such a lot as that misorganization seems to be. Had a nice visit with him, envying him very much of having seen you so recently. He says young Bob Doerr is in the same group with him, hope I see him too. Went down to see James Hilton's "Random Harvest" tonight which is very well done by Ronald Colman.[109] Capt. Rogers went with me and we were very glad to run into Schutz on the way out of the show as he had promoted a jeep for the evening which was more than welcome as it was raining this evening. Received a very nice long letter from your Dad today and enjoyed one from you telling of your hospitality to the English officers. Think that was a mighty nice thing to do. Peg, honest I love you so very much, wish I were going to bed with you, my dear. George.

[Peggy to George]
[V-Mail]

#59
Oct. 9 Sat.

Dearest George

Cannot find my pen this morning and I have to rush this. Anna is off for the weekend and I have last night's dishes to do, plum puddings to make and Frank is already here and I want him to clean the eaves today. Our Stony Wold movie-tea was a disappointment. We didn't have a third enough people. Those who did come were very enthusiastic but couldn't donate all we need. While I was at that affair John & Allan (navy boys) arrived and took the bus out here. When I drove in the drive they had Larry and Georgia piggy-back and were

---

109 Ronald Colman (b. 1891, d. 1958) was a British-born WWI veteran and Hollywood film star. Colman was successful in both silent and sound films over the course of his 40-year career. He will receive his third Oscar nomination for *Random Harvest* (a film based on James Hilton's novel of the same name) but it will not be until 1948 that he will win an Oscar for Best Actor in a film (*A Double Life*). Known for his suave, debonair elegance and distinct voice, Colman will also find success in television and radio.

racing around the yard. Marjorie & Pinky came for a cocktail and then I cooked dinner. We had roast chicken, mashed potatoes, gravy, corn on cob, peas and cake and coffee. They received a phone call about 8:00 to return to N.Y.C. and leave for Boston. I was sorry to say goodbye. They are nice boys. They have your address and hope to go to that area sometime. Yours, Peggy

[Peggy to George]
[Typed on plain paper]

#60
Sun. Oct. 10

Darling,

    Usually I have the pleasure of writing this letter during our date on Mon. nights, but being home alone tonight with a gratefire, I'm going to push it up one night this week. Also tomorrow night our date will be going to the rodeo at Madison Square Garden with the Bridges. It will bring back the many years we have really had a date for that event. I'll write you all about how different it was without you. Yesterday I worked hard all day. Anna was off, as I told you, so I had the regular work to do plus Tina's as she had one of her grouchy days and did little but pout and pick on the kids. I've given up reforming her and will put up with it as long as possible and then just kick her out one day when it gets unbearable. Her boyfriend has cooled off and gone back to an ex-wife so I try to excuse things for a while on that score. Don't worry about it. I don't.

    I am enclosing some pictures which the British boys took a week ago today. Having had my camera stolen, I have to rely on others for pictures to send to you. Last night after making 32 pounds of plum pudding, cleaning the garage, and washing the car besides the other work, I persuaded Pinky it was high time she go to the club for a party. So I dressed myself up in that red silk jersey and chiffon dinner dress and we stepped out. We went to the Peters for cocktails and ran into the usual fast, drinking crowd which always makes me feel so inhibited and miserable. I hadn't been there in so long I hoped they might have changed. Then we went to the club for dinner and dancing. We had a good group at the table and it was fun, considering. Jack Lewis was there having just returned from Sicily, Tunis, Bizerte, Malta, etc. He was sorry not to have been able to get nearer to you. Maybe, another time. I danced with several people and was the first to go home and at that it was 2:30. Even Pinky stayed and rode home with the Lewises. I took Tina to church at Banksville this a.m. and stopped at the Bowdens with the kids. They were still asleep and never called me until three to say they were just having breakfast and that they got home at 6:30. I couldn't do it with you for support even.

When I left, Pete Peters asked if I would drop him home last night. Of course I was glad to—particularly because he hadn't talked to anyone all evening and was obviously not enjoying himself. I tried to be cheerful taking him home, but it was wasted. I'm expecting a crack up in that household anytime. It seems so simple to avoid it if they would both swallow a little pride and be decent to one another. However I wouldn't breathe a word of it except to you after the spot I found myself in before, when I used to see so much of them.

Today I spent hours packing a Christmas box for you and one for the Rebillets. (They are both addressed to you, but the perfectly square one is a plum pudding and some hersheys for them.) I wrapped each silly little thing for you in Xmas wrappings but I suppose by the time the censor has gone through everything, it won't look very festive. Anyhow I had such fun doing it for you, and you'll know how much love comes from each of us in every stick of gum.

Wally, Connie, and Wally's mother and the children stopped in for a drink late this afternoon. It was a bit hectic as our children were just starting baths and supper, but we were all glad to see them.

The hounds and hunters raced right down our path from the garden yesterday. It was very exciting, especially for old Doxie who felt it his duty to protect the place, but didn't feel quite up to tackling single-handed that yelping mob. A fox actually ran across Oakley Lane but he outsmarted them. That reminds me about the story of the bitch in heat who wouldn't be left behind one hunting morning. She broke away and joined the hounds and went along. When a bystander asked how the hunt was progressing, the answer came that the last report had the fox running fifth.

I haven't thanked you for your marvelous offer for Christmas. It makes me feel very cheap after planning on using the money from the Olds.

Love. P

[George to Peggy]
[V-Mail]

No. 35
Monday even. 11/10/43

My dear Peggy,

Wonder what you are doing right now besides thinking about me. It is rather late for me to be up but I worked until 11, so here it is 12:15. I am ready for bed, just thought I would tell you I was thinking about you and love you very much before I climb into bed. It is a beautiful clear moon[lit] night. I do wish you were with me. After missing you so much I am afraid I will spoil you when I return, aren't you worried about that. Last night I played bridge with Maj. Simons,[110] Col. Bolan and Lt. Col. Libby,[111] who did not play too well nor me either but we had a lot of fun. Did not get to bed until one which is unusual as I get to bed quite early now days. Must be about 7 there now so I suppose you have finished dinner and may be writing me too. I will be thinking of you when I go to sleep, dear and just wishing. All my love, George

---

110 Likely Webster L. Simons, a veteran of WWI and colonel by WWII's end.
111 Donald Maxwell Libby, also a veteran of WWI.

[Peggy to George]
[V-Mail]

#61
Tues. Oct. 12

Dearest George,

    Here I am at the breakfast table again, although I had every intention of sleeping a while this morning. I had carefully closed both doors to the hall last night. But I heard them quietly open, followed by much whispering—then incoherent little songs started coming from two sources. I had to peek then and this brought two flying figures onto my bed. So—I am up. Perhaps I'll go back a few minutes when I finish this. I'll have to tell you what I did yesterday now. As usual Mon. a.m. was dedicated to doing the washing. When I had that hung out I grabbed a sandwich, dressed, did my Greenwich shopping, caught the 2:42 for N.Y.C. After a fitting on my suit and several errands I met the Bridges and a Mrs. Snowden at Trouville for a cocktail. We had dinner and went to the Rodeo. They knew people riding in it which made it very exciting. The rodeo was the same as ever, but I missed not going with you. We joined a cowboy party in a bar afterwards. There was even a <u>2 year</u> old daughter of one along. I finally excused myself and caught the 12:55. I hope it wasn't rude but I'd had enough. Dottie Beck phoned from N.Y.C. Sun. P.M. Love, Peggy

[George to Peggy]
[V-Mail]

No. 36
13 Oct. 43, Wed.

My dear Peggy:

    The weather has been perfect the last couple of days. Fairly cool and clear. Last night and tonight too there has been a bright full moon. Tonight I walked up the hill alone in the moonlight. Last night Schutz walked up with me. When we got up here he came over to have a drink of wine with me and we talked things over for quite a while. He is good company, hope you meet him some day. Only trouble is he thinks he may want to stay in the army after the war is over. Tonight I stopped in at Stipp's apartment, had a drink and chatted for a while. He is a good gent. You kind of get to feel as if you know some of these fellow's wives especially Stipp and Allen as I work with them all day and they usually have some little remark or story to tell when they get a letter. Mrs. Stipp wrote today about having knitted a neat pocket on a sweater to find when she got to the top that she had put the pocket on the back. Had a letter from Gertrude. Will you see if you have a picture of the children to send to her. I love this one of you on the lawn at the lake with Georgia and Larry. I look at it every nite and wish. My love dear, George

[Peggy to George]
[V-Mail]

#62
Wed. Oct. 13.

Darling,

Again at the breakfast table, but the outdoor coloring is falling off now. We have had two frosts now and a wind which makes our woods look as if the old winter is coming soon. Yesterday morning I took a saw and rope and fixed a swing for the children up where we put the white bench by the vegetable garden. Don't worry I didn't have to climb high as I did in Mpls. Then Larry and I explored that back field up there again for the barn to come when you get home. I took the brush scythe and we cut a path to the spot we chose and today if I have the energy we are cutting the place where we want the barn. My man never showed up. I guess that was to be expected. No one does these days. I had lunch at Elsa Dommerick Slocum's yesterday. Walt is in New Guinea & she lives at her Mother's. It is one of the old places in town and really beautiful. The grounds are unbelievable. I think much prettier than Mrs. Bigelow's although they do not have the view. Elsa is a new acquaintance that is not of the type here we are not too keen on. I know you will like her. Miss Finn wants to know the amount of your government salary at present for tax purposes. My love, Peggy

[George to Peggy]

Capt. GR Steiner
APO 512, AFHq G-4
c/o PM New York.

#37
Thursday
14 Oct. 43

My darling Peggy:

Now last night I wrote you a V-Mail letter, but you won't object if I write you again, even if all I have done in between letters is sleep and think about you.

You see I have the day off, so I am just taking my time about getting dressed. I suppose you might be interested in some of the material details of living here.

Maybe that fine little diagram of the apartment will help. I am sitting here at the desk looking toward the french doors which open out on the balcony. My bed is over to my left. They make it up for me every day. It is one of those studio couches and makes a good bed. There are some long curtains, which are thin enough to see thru, with flower patterns sewn onto them, hanging from the ceiling to the floor in front of the french doors, then there is a rolling shutter on the outside which can be cranked up and down from the inside. I imagine Larry would really appreciate that. Practically every window on every house in town has such a shutter.

Right in front of the french doors is a table with a big square glass bowl of goldfish about 12 of them. I have been trying to get Mimi to name them but it is too hard to tell them apart he thinks. Anyway you can tell Larry they never have to worry about keeping their faces clean. Too much talk about that and you may end up with some goldfish to take care of yourself. But that would not be near so much trouble to look after as you will have when you get one husband back. You see I am back to engaging in that favorite sport of Isaac Walton's.

Well to go on the window panes still have cross patches of gummed paper on them to keep them from breaking from bomb blasts. That gives sort of a sorrowful expression to windows all over town. Off to my right is a big comfortable leather arm chair, with a small table next to it supporting a big jar with some sort of a plant that looks like a juvenile rubber tree. In fact I told Mimi if they took good care of it there was a chance it might grow some Wrigleys chewing gum.

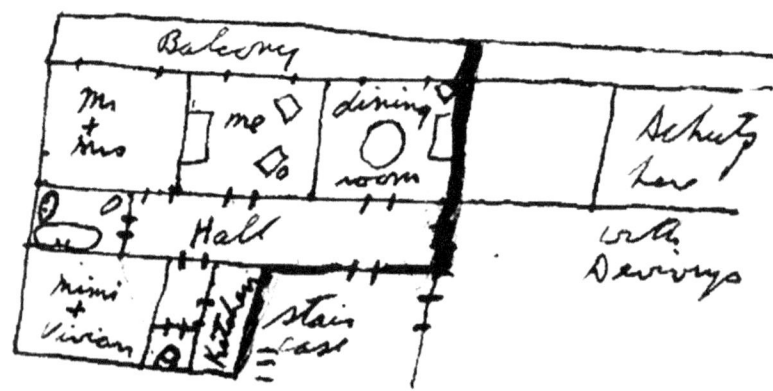

Well that just about finishes up the room except for a table behind me kind of like a boule table but inlaid with wood of different colors and ivory instead of brass and shell. The floor is tile of brown and white squares covered with a nice rug with some oriental pattern, none of it being dyed, but woven from natural colored hair of different colored sheep. There are a couple of lights which they are kind of proud of. One is a bronze figure of a woman lying face down with her hands stretched forward to support a blue glass ball with a light inside.

The other is glass quarter moon *comme ça* with a bulb inside it. The man in the moon does look a little more happy than I have drawn him.

Of course then there is me sitting here in my blue pajamas with a finger right on the picture of the man in the moon to keep this sheet of paper from sliding around on the glass top of the desk. And of course there is a gold wedding ring on that finger which I believe you gave to me. In fact I even remember right where you gave it to me, and wish very much that we were both right there this moment.

I should not forget to tell you either that while I was in shaving, Madame brought a tray of coffee, toast, and believe it or not some butter, to place it on a small table beside my desk. It tasted good. And that is really how you came to get this letter, as I decided that with that much to eat I would write you a letter rather than rush off to breakfast.

Now I will get dressed and go down to the headquarters. We always report in on our day off usually [to] find there is something that should be done, so what the day usually ends up with is the privilege of coming in late in the morning. But there is not much else to do so what's the difference.

<u>Ki has asked me to ask you if you would send some of my letters</u> along so he could keep track of me, adding "if they are not too personal." Guess this one ought to fall under that heading, so far at least. Well I just won't include any of those nasty remarks I usually make about Ki and Teedie.

Madam just came in again *pour chercher mes chaussettes parce qu'ils ont des trous qu'elle va raccommoder.*[112]

My love dear, George.

---

112 Translated: "to look for my socks because they have holes that she will mend."

[Peggy to George]
[V-Mail]

#63
Oct. 14, Thurs.

Darling,

Well from the looks of my hands you'd know I cut space for the barn and then some yesterday. Finishing that the children wanted to walk down to the reservoir from up by the barn site. The grass was so high we decided to make a path and now have a nifty one which connects with the bridle path close to the pine trees by the reservoir. I just happened to cut in the right direction and ended at a break in the stone wall. We climbed down to the water and Doxie took a swim. About 10 min. after we returned, the Greenwich Water Co. inspector came and I was sure he'd seen Dox in the water. He only wanted to know about our sewage drain. In the afternoon I fixed up a pantry cupboard for silver so it won't tarnish as easily and then pruned some shrubs. Last night I pasted snapshots. I put all your Army shots in one book. So that was yesterday—one more day gone of our period of separation. At least I keep busy which is the main thing. Most of it helps improve this place for your homecoming. Have you heard? The Queen Bee is a gentle soul. She doesn't practice birth control. And that's the reason, if you please, there are so many sons of B's.
Love, Peggy

[Peggy to George]
[V-Mail]

[#]64
Fri. Oct. 15,

Darling,

This is a foggy morning and the children are all excited because they can play in the third floor today. Tina is going off and Anna and I are preparing for 13 for dinner tonight. Hoggsons, Bridges, Frays, Bowdens, Wards, Pinky, Helen Mayer and myself. I had letters from

Boston yesterday from the British officers. One may come back this weekend, but the other has gone. Yesterday, Connie and I played golf and had lunch at the club. It was a beautiful day. Larry as usual is waiting to lick the stamp and Georgia the envelope. I really wish you would write the children once a week. You don't realize how they talk about you each day and beg to write letters, lick stamps, and be the first to open the mailbox each morning. I pretend some of your letters are theirs and make up the contents to pacify them. The only trouble is they take them to bed and refuse to let me have them back. Most anything you want to tell them will be easily understood. It would be a real thrill I can promise you. My interpretations are too rushed to be very interesting. I'll write you all about the party tomorrow. Called Mom last night. Dad's away and she's fine. Love, Peggy

[George to Peggy]

Capt. GR Steiner
AFHq G-4 Sec.
APO 512, New York

#38
Oct. 16, 1943
Saturday evening

Good evening my darling. Two very nice letters arrived from you today. One written Oct. 7 V-mail, the other typed on Sunday Sept. 5, Georgia's birthday. You see what happened I believe was that the air mail letter came by boat. When they have the space they send the air mail by plane otherwise by water. However, the V-Mail almost always comes by air. I always like to get the air mail letters especially well because they are a little longer and then I get a certain satisfaction out of just knowing you have touched them with your own hands. I enjoy your letters so much my dear, I read them very eagerly first then bring them home here to go over them more slowly to consider each word and thought like a drink of fine old wine. I don't know what I would do without them. It is swell of you to write so often, and I do appreciate it.

There is an English boy and an American who act as messengers for us, bringing in papers and cables for us to work on and also pick up our mail which usually comes in twice a day. They come in for a lot of good natured rebukes when they return with only work for us or perhaps with mail for two of us and none for the other. They always seem pleased when they do have mail for us and you can usually tell whether or not they have by one look at their face when they come in the room.

If you do have any written notice concerning my baggage you might copy it off onto a V-mail and send it along as I have not located it yet.

Thursday evening we had quite a time. Schutz got ahold of a jeep and Sparks, Helms and myself took a long ride away up on top of a mountain to a little restaurant where we got two wonderfully well prepared omelettes for dinner, some good wine, excellent cake for dessert and coffee.

There were pictures of some excellent ski slopes and there is a ski lodge up there. It was nice to get up in the mountain air among the pines and it was a beautiful clear moon[lit] night. There was a crowd of nice looking British and American naval officers up there who were celebrating the engagement of an attractive English girl to one of the British officers. She was the only girl present and blushed very prettily at the toasts. There was much singing accompanied by a mouth organ. One of the British officers sang a lot of the popular American college songs. It had the atmosphere reminiscent of an evening in the mountains after a day's skiing. It was a very pleasant change.

I have been wondering if you have received copies of the Saturday edition of Stars and Stripes, our Army paper. I wrote up a subscription for you about a month back. It is very well gotten up coming out daily with an extra size Saturday edition. The daily editions are not supposed to be mailed.

I met a Capt. Adams from Mpls. who runs the Adams Construction Co. in peace time. It is fun to meet someone from home. Healey (Red Cross) drops in every once in a while to say hello and leaves us some magazines now and then. He has left me several Mpls. papers. One had a picture of Johnny Hartman in a swimsuit of course showing some sailors how to inflate their trousers and sea bags to make life preservers.[113]

I had a nice note from Buzz. One also from Ki quite long telling all about his visit to Mpls. and Thunder Lake.

Others seem to share my good opinion of Schutz. He has been personally requested by the CG of one of the divisions over here and also by a high-ranking officer in the War Dept. in Washington, but his section chief here wants to keep him which is just as well for him. It does give him a good build up. All of the boys in our group are doing quite well and we manage to help each other now and then.

I do miss you so much my dear Peggy and you are always in my thoughts and before too long I hope you will be in my arms again.

With my love, George.

[George to Peggy]
[V-Mail]

No. 39
17 Oct. 1943 Sunday

Peg dear,

You know when I start to write you a letter, the picture of you receiving it is often in my mind. Here the V-Mail letter is waiting for you in the mail box on top of its post, perhaps with some bills, a magazine and a letter from Irene all stuffed in with it. While you come down the lane with Larry and Georgia hiking along you are not sure just what you will find. It will be kind of cold when you get this one so you probably have on a polo coat. I hope you are real careful crossing

---

113   This article appeared on page 24 in the *Star Tribune* on July 11, 1943.

the highway to get the mail and real careful going back. Now you have got the mail and maybe even open this to read before you walk back. If you do—you can pretend I am walking back with you, or driving over to Greenwich in the car maybe. Daddy says hello to Larry and Georgia and sends a kiss to each of them and one for Momie too. I meant to tell you last night that the name of the naval officer you mentioned in connection with Hewitt got blurred in the V-Mail so I could not make it out. Are mine legible enough or should I write larger? The article clippings and the post card came through all right. I am duty officer tonight. I love you dear. George.

[George to Peggy]
[Typed V-Mail]

No. 40
18 Oct. 1943

Dear Peggy:

You see I did not have any intention of writing you but there was a little portable typewriter sitting here, so I thought I would see if I could still find the right keys. Looks as if you were becoming quite an expert with very few mistakes. How many fingers do you use? At the rate I am going here I am going to be minus a couple wrapped up among these keys, if I am not careful. Major Allen has been trying it out, as I can see from a paper on my desk entitled travel orders directing that Capt. Steiner visit a WAC organization for the purpose of an inspection which I will not take up in detail. It is in connection with some correspondence which we have with one of their outfits, so maybe I will take them up on it. We are just about ready to go down to eat dinner. The liquor ration is just about non-existent,[114] but we did get ahold of a bottle of Gordons gin which we have used to make a very excellent concoction when mixed with some local produce.

---

114 Officers in the U.S. Army were allotted a ration of two bottles of liquor a month. Enlisted men, however, were not issued a liquor ration, resulting in questionable yet innovative methods for procuring alcohol. Many enlisted men created their own elixirs often containing V-1 flying bomb fluid or antifreeze when no alcohol was available (DePastino, *Bill Mauldin*, 161.).

Spent rather an uneventful night as duty officer, and think I will see if I can get ahold of someone to go down to a movie tonight. When we first got here it used to be quite light for a long time after supper, now however it is dark when we walk out. They have fixed our mess hall up a bit, but it could still stand a lot more fixing. Someone had quite a sense of color when they chose black oil cloth table covers. The food is not too bad at least before they start cooking on it in the kitchen. We have a bunch of old French girls for waiters. They are slow getting what you want and slower yet understanding what you are trying to tell them. The place has the usual atmosphere of any institution run by the government. There is no real effort to improve conditions, just good enough to get by, and then if anything is wrong just hire a lot more people. I have been down trying to find my baggage and sent a cable back to the P of E to try and trace it. I think it must be over here by now. You said there was something in it that would surprise me, I have been wondering what it is. The evenings have been getting a bit chilly so that field jacket will come in handy. I don't think we will be going into woolens very soon though. Sure am going to be mighty glad to get out of this deal and be able to live my life the way you and I want to rather than the way some joker at the top of the military machine decided it should be done. Can't see why anyone ever chooses that as a regular life, unless they are so completely devoid of brains and initiative that they prefer to be told where they will live, what they will wear, and where, when and how they will make every move in their life. Say hello to Larry and Georgia. Next letter will be a little better than this. Sure do miss you right at this point. It always seems to be worse right at the present anyway. Seeing that this is Monday night perhaps I will write you later after dinner when I get up home if that will be all right with you. If I want to get in to get some of that food I will have to hurry now. I have wanted to send you some kind of a present from here, but there is nothing I can find that isn't just so much junk, the war has pretty well cleaned thin[g]s out. My love dear, George

[Peggy to George]
[V-Mail]

#65
Mon. Oct. 18

Dearest George

    I couldn't get a letter off Sat. morning and I am saving the air mail to write tonight so I'll just say good morning now. I've had a very strenuous weekend. One of the British boys came down from Boston during the party Friday night and stayed until the fast bus last night. Here Larry put a big hug and kiss X The party seemed to be enjoyed by everyone but me. It was the first I have attempted since you left and it fell pretty flat for me. In fact I couldn't stay awake past midnight which broke up a poker game and bridge game and they all went home. Sat. morning your letters 30 & 32 came and you surely were right about "<u>Time</u>" knowing more than you can say. The next four lines after telling me that were blacked out with no question about it. That's the first time too. I'm sorry I mentioned it. The children are after the first lick of this envelope already. I do want to say that after thinking I had done Crawford such a good turn he called me 10 days after receiving the Olds. to say the transmission was gone. I hope he can get the part. He has been without a car for a couple of weeks now. Very interested about Ballard's wive<u>s</u> & children. Love, Peggy

[Peggy to George]

#66
Mon. Oct. 18, 1943

Darling,

    Curled up here on the couch, with Doxie chewing an old envelope up and listening to "Blondie" on the radio, and a lot of writing to do to you is our date tonight. It has been nearly of a year since we've had to confine all our dates to 'blind' ones and I don't like them very well yet. I must say I never thought I could look forward to writing letters the way I seem to now. It's sort of an evening conversation which has to satisfy us both on paper.

My v-mail letter this morning started you on the weekend's doings, so I'll continue. Saturday Allan (RNVR)[115] slept until ten which was a treat for him and allowed me to help get the house in order from the party and get the children outdoors. It wasn't a nice day which added to my difficulties in entertaining. The rain had come down all night and started again about noon. By the time the children were up from their naps it had cleaned enough so we took them for a long walk through the woods and back home on North Street. We didn't do anything that night but play records and go to Greenwich to bowl and have a chocolate soda. I really wanted a coca cola, but thinking about you and our after the movies' sodas I had to have one for you. It was good too—chocolate ice cream & all. Sunday we took all the children in the car and drove Anna to Banksville to church. That was a beautiful morning and the foliage was still quite nice so for the first time in 2 years we took a ride to Bedford. The children were as thrilled as I was. Allan seemed to enjoy it too. He thought the village was very lovely. Seemed particularly fascinated by our little white country churches. Sun. afternoon, to make up for a guilty conscience for the morning drive, we rode the bicycles down the parkway and over to the club. Played nine holes of golf and rode back over Clapboard Ridge Road. It really wasn't too bad, but 10 years difference in age certainly showed up on the last few miles. My legs nearly gave out. The children greeted us as we came in the yard with "Ride us now, Momie." That was the last straw. We did play with them, though, until they went to bed. Then I proceeded to write the rules and teach Allan poker, gin rummy, backgammon, and craps. He took the last bus and I was worn out. I enjoyed the boys but am going to take a rest for a few weeks now.

The usual proceedings have gone on today such as Monday's washing, cleaning etc. Tina & I took all three to Dr. Close this

---

115 The Royal Naval Volunteer Reserve.

afternoon while Robin had a shot. His last for whooping cough. Tomorrow Larry will probably want to write you about it. Doxie caught an enormous rat in the garage this morning. It had nearly devoured one of my squash from the vegetable rack. I hope he hasn't any friends or family to bother us now.

Had a letter from Ki this morning which I'll enclose. Also I'll send a couple of letters from these British boys so you'll know something about them. I hope I still have them.

You should get quite a few Christmas packages. Besides mine, Connie phoned for your address and sent one. Also Marge & Pete Peters. If some of your friends aren't so lucky you can open my box and pass some things on. Each package inside is wrapped for Xmas too. The films are wrapped two together and the razors in gold paper. The rest are things that others could use. The round one plum pudding & rest mostly candy. Naturally, I'd rather you had it, but knowing your generous nature I thought I could make it easier for you to know what to share without opening each.

The edition of "Stars & Stripes" did arrive at last. I've been very interested reading it. I must say you aren't lacking for daily headlines.

Tinkle Brainard just phoned to invite me for dinner Sat. night. So now I'm dated up Thurs. with Pinky & a 75 year old dutchman (Bee Hekma's father). He's a wonderful old gentleman who was a good friend of Freddie's. He asked Pinky for dinner & told her to bring two friends for bridge. Friday I'm going to the Gortons. Moon Hanan is in this country so he and Anne will be there. Also the Bowdens I believe. Doesn't that sound gay? Frank Hekma also got back to this country on leave after 18 months overseas. I don't see how she stood it so long. Kindly arrange it so I won't have to.

Well darling, I'm sure you have gone to sleep by now. Our Mon. date is over again. This is a very cold night and I wish having Madame's feelings could bring me the same results. We will always have winter nights after you come home to stay. I love you so very much dear. This love of ours really makes these months of separation easier for us than many others who have to worry about what they'll find different in each other when it's over. Don't you think so too?

Always, Peggy

[George to Peggy]
[V-Mail]

No. 40
21/10/43 Thursday

Peggy dear.

    Here it is my day off again, a very bright sunny day. I stopped up here to the office and found two letters from you, one from Gertrude and one from Frank Mihelich. So that was worthwhile. Now I might as well drop you a note. Monsieur Rebillet is sick. He will probably have to be operated on for ulcers of the stomach, at least that is how I understand. From what some of the army medics have to say about French medical practices they are rather primitive. Believe I will take a walk up the hill to a park where they say there is a tennis club with some possibilities of arranging to play. There is not much to do on a day off here. But it is kind of nice to know you don't have to work.
Love, George

[Peggy to George]
[V-Mail]

#68
Oct. 21, Thurs.

Darling,

    This could probably be the longest letter yet to you, as I am now seated in the high school auditorium with number 146 in my lap waiting until 3:30 when the teachers start issuing A gas book renewals. Bernice and Helen Gorton are also waiting here so at least I have company. My day yesterday was fine until I drove back into the garage at dusk and saw a huge tree lying in the yard. Mr. Hvolbeck had sent a man to help clean up our trees and take out a few. He was supposed to trim yesterday but got a notion to cut some down as he had another to help him. He cut the wrong tree of course and I haven't gotten over it yet. It was a white hickory and right on the lawn so roots have to be dug out too. It's going to be two days' work for two men at $8.00 per man besides loss of the tree. The man has told Hvolbeck that I told him to cut it which is his word against mine. I sure wish you were here to handle it. I know I'll lose out. In the end I'll probably do all the pruning as well as the rest of the outdoor work. Excuse the griping but the prices labor gets for either doing nothing or worse than nothing these days makes me sick. Crawford phoned and he has gotten the Olds. fixed and was only charged for the labor. Well the girls send their love and of course I do as always. Peggy

[Peggy to George]
[V-Mail]

#70
Sat. Oct. 23

Darling.

The children are outside already watching Frank. He is digging flower beds next to our property line back from the circle. I bought a lot of tulip bulbs and am trying to get peonies to go in there too. I also have 100 jonquil or daffodil bulbs which I am putting on the little hill across the break which you will look at each morning from the breakfast table. That is—if you can put the paper down long enough. Oh just to see the pipe smoke curling up from behind that paper would be enough for me. It's nearly four months today since we parted. Just think—in fifteen years we've never gone that long without seeing one another. How much longer must we wait. My only consolation is in getting this place in perfect order for your homecoming. Then all you'll need to do according to Larry is pretend to be a farmer and build the barn. I worked outside all day yesterday morning and stack[ed] nearly a half cord of wood in the cellar. It isn't as hard as I used to think. Then I pruned one dog wood tree and several bushes. By next summer this place should look quite differently.

Tonight I am going to Tinkle Brainard's for dinner. I enjoy her but don't know the other guests very well. The Ellis's and Peggy (Ex) Sherwood and King Ludington are going. Tomorrow Pinky and her children are coming out for the day.

Yours, Peggy

[George to Peggy]
[V-Mail]

No. 41
Oct. 24 Sunday

Wrote Larry & Georgia an air mail tonight.

Well my darling I am comfortable here this evening in my wool dressing gown and wool slippers GA gave to me. Guess who I would like to have here this evening and just how we could pass the time. I don't think we would be too bored. I miss your love and good company so much my dear, but your letters brighten me up so much. I like the way you write about what you do as it all rings such a familiar note to the girl I love. I can almost join you at the breakfast, where our letter talk is intruded upon just as our conversation is by little faces with butter and crumbs on them and a big brown beast who most surely is not retiring. I wonder if some of my V-letters are hard to read, Ki's are, but yours come through fine. Let me know will you. I was surprised yesterday when Bob Doerr called me up. He is an officer in Military Government. He was downtown at the Red Cross and was just going through so I did not have a chance to see him, but may later as he is not too far from here. Love you dear. George

[Peggy to George]
[V-Mail]

#71
Mon. Oct. 2[5]

Dearest George

Another Monday morning and I am about to start the washing. I have poison ivy on my left hand so I'll have to try and keep that out of the water. This hasn't been a very exciting weekend although I've been busy. I went to Tinkle's Friday night and when that broke up early I stopped in at the Peter's party for a couple of hours getting to bed about 2:30 after a dull evening. Saturday all the children and Tina accompanied me to Greenwich and we did the usual shopping. I spent the afternoon in the basement staining your cupboard and painting. Sat. night I sat home and enjoyed knitting on Georgia's sweater. Yesterday I had Pinky and her children for the day. Anna was off so I cooked fried chicken, peas, potatoes, gravy, cranberry sauce and jelly roll. The kids all ate here with us and that was fun. Pinky and I took a long walk after dinner and talked about Freddie, mostly. Last night Izzie Lewis had a cocktail party for Jack. He's about to leave again. After this I went to the Gorton's for supper and that was the most pleasant part of the weekend. Annie Hanan and <u>Moon</u> were there. I hadn't met him before. He's swell. We talked about what a swell guy Rob Peake[116] is. Date tonight. Peggy

[George to Peggy]
[V-Mail]

No. 42
25 Oct. 43 Monday

My dear Peggy.

Here it is another Monday night again. I suppose all the rest of our lives Monday night will have a special significance for us. I do

---

116   Frederick Robinson "Robbie" Peake was one of George's closest friends and also a Yale graduate. Georgia believes her brother Robin was named after him.

wish we could start spending them together again. I suppose you are writing me tonight also. I have just finished writing 'Ki,' cousin Frank, Stanley Brock, and Col. Smith. I am not sure I mentioned it before, but several nights ago Schutz, Sparks, Allen, Helms and myself went to a nice little hotel a ways out of town to have a delicious dinner with the best of wines, excellent service and even napkins. You have to make reservations about a week ahead. It was such a good deal we decided to try it again tomorrow night. So we have found two really good places to eat this one and the one away up on the mountain I told you about two weeks ago. The only difficulty is to get transportation. Had a letter from Dick yesterday. Would sure like to be with you right now. It is eleven and I still have to walk up the hill so I will be thinking of you my dear. Yours, George

[Peggy to George]

#72

Monday 7:30 P.M.

P.S. I have all your letters thru #26. #27 (the air mail you forgot to number) hasn't come—neither have 29, 31, or 36. (Today 35 & 37 came—the last took only 10 days.) How are mine coming?

Dearest George

I am listening to a broadcast from Algiers and having a date with you all at once. Doxie is lying beside me here on the couch and the old banjo clock is ticking off the time. (It keeps perfect time now.) The children have just knelt beside me here to say their prayers and are now tucked away for another night. I had quite a discussion with them tonight. It went something like this

Momie: "It's just seven o'clock. Do you know that Daddy is thinking about us right this minute?"
Georgia: "Why?"

Larry: "Maybe he's thinking how glad he'll be to see us."
M: "I'll bet that is just what he is thinking."
G: "When Daddy sees me he's going to hug and kiss [me] so hard and say I have missed you so much, Georgia."
L: "He's going to say that to me too."
Momie: "Won't we be happy to see Daddy, too, when the war's over and he gets back to us?"
Larry: "Yes. But Momie, don't forget to always say God Bless Daddy in your prayers, will you?"
M: "Of course not. Why?"
L: "Katie and Fitsy 'must-a-got' cause the bad soldier got their Daddy and he's dead and won't come home."
M: "Katie and Fitsy didn't forget their prayers."
L: "Then their Momie 'must-a-got' hers."
M: "No she didn't."
L: "Then why is their Daddy dead?"
M: "I don't know. Sometimes God [doesn't] take care of every Daddy even when he is asked to every night."
L: "Does God forget?"
M: "No, but war means that lots of Daddys are killed."
L: "Why are there wars, then?"
M: "<u>I don't know</u>?"

<u>Please</u> answer his questions if you can. After this he wasn't at all sure that you were still all right. They both wanted to know if I was sure some bad soldier hadn't shot you. I tried to assure them. Finally, I read both your letters to them that arrived today. One was about your apt. & the Rebillets. I explained the diagram etc. and they were satisfied. Larry had everything explained to himself when he went to bed. He said "Momie, I know what happened. Daddy saw the bad soldier shooting at Fitsy's Daddy and he called to him to come where he was, but Fitsy's Daddy didn't hear him so he got shot. But Daddy

runs real fast when he sees a bad soldier so you don't need to worry. God takes good care of him"—My sides nearly split at the last idea of you running, but he was so serious and happy with his explanation that I kept my face straight somehow.

Our threatened railroad strikes[117] and 40,000 coal miners on strike[118] have gotten me to such a state of rage that I can hardly look at the papers or hear the radio. How I hope the boys overseas come home and beat all these guys to a pulp and take their jobs away from them. It's so humiliating to have such incompetence at home when you are all doing so well every place else in the world.

Be sure and let me know when you receive your duffle bag and also when the Time magazine starts to arrive. I have had two issues of Stars & Stripes now.

I'll drop Ki & Teedie a line and forward your letter. I hate to let one go, even, as I'm afraid they'll forget to send it back. Besides I've only read it 4 times.

---

[117] The majority of strikes and work stoppages in 1943 were directly related to issues surrounding employee wages. In the above case, railroad employees were frustrated their wages had not been increased to match the rise in the cost of living (Peterson, "Strikes in 1943," 29.). An 8-cent raise had been approved by President Roosevelt in August but was overridden by the director of the Office of Economic Stabilization (OES) and never put into effect. In response, the railroad unions threatened to issue strike ballots to their members, allowing for the possibility of a future national strike, which would paralyze not only the war industry but non-military transportation and freight across the country (Stark, "Labor Unrest Mounts Over Wage-Price Policy.").

[118] As noted in footnote 18 (page 19), there were 430 strikes in the coal-mining industry in 1943. In addition to the hundreds of smaller, local stoppages, there were four nation-wide stoppages in response to two disputes between mine employees (represented by the UMW) and mine operators. At the center of each dispute was the expiration of the miners' two contracts and the UMW's demands for, among other items, a basic-wage rise to match the increase everyone had experienced in the cost of living (especially of food products) as the war and rationing continued (Peterson, "Strikes in 1943," 29, 30.). No settlement was reached and the cases were directed to the War Labor Board (WLB). The WLB was originally created to settle disputes when unions and operators of national industries reached an impasse but after Executive Order No. 9250, which saw the creation of the OES in October 1942, the WLB found itself with the power to control wages and salaries. Consequently, adjustments to salaries and wages almost always had to be approved by the WLB before changes could be implemented.

Nationwide stoppages had already occurred on May 1, June 1, and June 21 of 1943. As a result of the May strike, the mines were seized by the Secretary of the Interior and remained government property until the end of August when they were transitioned back to private ownership. Despite this precedent, by mid-October the WLB will still refuse to approve the latest two contract options the UMW and the mine operators submitted, citing the wage increase as the reason for the denials. Widespread stoppages will ensue during October and the fourth nationwide strike will begin on November 1. Mines again will be taken over by the Secretary of the Interior but it would not be until May of 1944 that the WLB would approve a contract (Ibid., 30-32.).

It is not clear where Peggy read or heard "40,000" and this number has not been verified. However, she is correct in that tens of thousands of miners across the United States were striking during this time (Associated Press, "Coal Strikes Imperil War Pace.").

Must say goodnight. You have been asleep at least three hours by now. What I'd give to just turn over and look at that dear face right now. I have a pretty nearly perfect picture of just how you look in your room. I can even guess how you are lying—flat on your back with your left hand outside the covers across your chest and your right bent at the elbow with the palm up to and resting near your head. Since you've taken up Isaac Walton's habit, you are probably snoring too. <u>Now</u> will that cure you?

         Peggy

[Peggy to George]
[V-Mail]

                  #72
              Oct. 2[7], Wed.

Darling

 Again I look upon two smiling jam covered faces and bibs plus a [drooling], begging dog as I say good morning to you. The rain outdoors isn't nearly as pleasant today. It has rained for two days and Monday's wash is still dripping on the line. Today I am going to N.Y.C. to finish several errands and get Dad some cigars for his birthday. Just think. He'll be 61 next Friday. How I hate to contemplate their ages. We've just seen the list of exchange prisoners from Jap[anese] territory coming on the Gripsholm.[119] We were so sure Ford[120] would be among them but he is not. Poor Aunt Mary. Mom had bought her a ticket to N.Y.C. to meet him. They were so sure he'd come. I had a busy day painting yesterday. I have to help Santy Claus this year and

---

119 The MS Gripsholm was a Swedish ocean liner with the distinction of being the first ship built for transatlantic express service powered by diesel instead of steam (Miller, *Mercy Ships*, 99.). Initially a passenger ship used for back-and-forth travel across the Atlantic, from 1942-1946 the United States chartered it to make exchanges and repatriations. The ship carried Japanese and German nationals to exchange points at neutral ports where American, Canadian, and Latin American citizens were brought aboard. Peggy is referring to the Gripsholm's second, and last voyage during WWII, which returned to New York in late October 1943.

120 H. Ford Wilkins was Peggy's cousin. Peggy's mother took care of Ford when he was a baby and he and Peggy were close. Ford was working in the Philippines as a *New York Times* and Columbia Broadcasting System (CBS) correspondent and as the editor of the *Manila Bulletin*. He was taken prisoner when the Japanese captured Manila in January 1942.

repainted the sled, bike, fire engine etc. as he just cannot make new ones until the war's over. Everything that breaks or wears out Larry comes out with, "Oh oh Momie, and we can't get another one until the war's over and Daddy gets home." Yours always, Peggy

[Peggy to George]
[V-Mail]

#73

Oct. 2[8], Thurs.

My dearest

Again at breakfast and a dark rainy day outside. The children are a bit irritated with all this bad weather, but they roller skate and ride their bicycles in the basement and really have quite a good time. Now that the furnace is on most of the day it is lovely down there and a wonderful big floor to ride on. I had lunch with Mrs. Alworth at the Savoy yesterday plus an Atlanta friend of hers and daughter. It was very pleasant. They asked me to go to "Harriet" (Helen Hayes play)[121] but I had a final fitting at Twyeffortes. Therein lies a funny story. T. didn't expect me yesterday and as I walked in I heard a woman say, "Yes, I'll take a suit if you'll make me that beautiful blouse." Answer— Yes we'll be glad to for $35.00. The fitter seemed embarrassed as I came in but it took a minute before I caught on. It seems he was selling a copy of a blouse I had him make me from one I had. The original I bought in Mpls. and he asked to copy it for me for $10.00. I was so dumb I didn't know that he just wanted to get the pattern. I really don't care with the few good clothes I have, but it was a sneaky trick and I had fun telling him so. All our love. Peggy

---

121   *Harriet* is a play by Florence Ryerson and Colin Clements about the life of Harriet Beecher Stowe. Renowned actress and "First Lady of American Theater" Helen Hayes (b. 1900, d. 1993) played the titular character.

[Peggy to George]
[V-Mail]

#74
Friday, Oct. 29

Darling George,

    Speaking of red-letter days, yesterday was mine and Larry's. We received <u>six</u> letters from you. Three airmails and 2 V-letters for me and an airmail with a picture of some goats for Larry. We were both thrilled needless to say. He just squealed over it, and both he and Georgia kissed the kisses you sent them and hugged the letter until it was a bit disheveled. I'll have to write Marty Howard for the name of that fellow with Hewitt. It was a boy from Blake younger than ourselves but she thought you might remember him. Please tell me if you have trouble after reading these. Yours are fine, but I noticed you are using blacker ink. After one of your letters of yesterday concerning the shoes was read, I immediately took the shoes over and mailed them. You had not asked for them before. I am sorry your luggage hasn't arrived. It must be very inconvenient. I'll go up in our files this morning and copy that receipt. Larry says he must have the rest of this space. Yours and again I love you very much. Peggy.

[George to Peggy]

Capt. GR Steiner
AFHq G-4 Sec
APO 512 c/o PM New York
[30] Oct. Sat.

My darling:

    Came back up to the office after dinner tonight to write some letters and found Allen had the same idea. So he is pounding his out on a typewriter while I am using pen & ink. Incidentally, the better I know him, the more I like him and respect his ability to think clearly and get things done. He kind of provoked me at first, but he is O.K.

I have a bit of time to catch up on as I have not written you since Wednesday. Thursday was my day off, but there was not much to do. Saw a movie late in the afternoon. Went down to the Red Cross for rather a late breakfast and actually had toast which we do not get in the mess. Played bridge in the evening, Allen and I showing Col. Bolan and Maj. Simons some of the finer points of the game.

Friday morning Bob Doerr, Capt. in the Military Govt. Sec. came in. You remember him—red-haired, freckled and a very likeable boy with a merry twinkle in his eye. We had dinner together last night which I enjoyed very much, not the food but the conversation. He is a smart boy, interesting and likeable. We went down to a movie then over to the Red Cross snack bar. There was a halloween dance on with pumpkin faces lit with candles, pretty girls, music and all.

Doerr is in the Medical supply part of Mil. Govt. and ought to be very well qualified for that work as he has had military training at V.M.I. and been in the drug business.

Yesterday afternoon I went out to the Q.M. depot and finally located my baggage. I found it had been out there for nearly a month and I had been within a few yards from it on several previous visits for other purposes. I was very pleased to find the contents of one of those fleece lined boots all in good shape. I think I shall keep that for Christmas. It was good to get that picture album out too. Of course I thought of you while I unpacked things.

I think you were right about my dreams; I can't quite remember if that was the night I woke up though. I will blame it on you anyway. I am a bit disappointed in having your desires limited to giving me that ring only once a day. Maybe we can have a lot of rainy mornings though. I hope we do, because then I won't even have to think of an excuse. Just to think about it makes me wish you were very close to me right now.

But I better start on my way up the hill as it is about twenty minutes' walk. I love you ever so much dear.

Yours, George.

[George to Peggy]
[V-Mail]

No. 43
31 Oct. 1943 Sunday

Peggy dear,

Well I wonder just what you are doing on a Sunday afternoon. Whatever it is I wish I were there to share it with you. I finished dinner and came back up to the office to write a letter. I wrote you air mail last night that I had finally located my luggage but you may get this first. I sure enjoy your letters dear. They all get read over several times. After being a captain for nearly two years they have made me a captain again with a date of rank[122] going back to last Wednesday from which date I will have to have at least six months in grade before I am even eligible for promotion to Major. That is a swell slap in the face after a perfect record of "Superior" from each commander I have had, C&GS School, with a personal recommendation from Gen. Marshall, not to mention previous recommendations for promotion. That is the result of being transferred from Air Force to Ground Force.[123] My love dear. George

---

122   Date of rank is the date an officer's service begins at their current rank and is an important factor determining when an officer is eligible for a promotion.
123   As a reserve officer, George was a member of the Field Artillery (FA), part of the Ground Force. However, when he was assigned to active duty it was within the Army of the United States Air Corps: AUS (AC) (Ulio, *Special Orders No. 172.*). Restructuring of the Air Corps in 1941 and 1942 resulted in the creation of the Army Air Force (AAF), equally as autonomous as the Army Ground Force. It is possible these restructurings affected George's assignments and promotion prospects but it is more likely that either his attendance at CGSC or OPD WDGS resulted in his promotion problems as the WDGS was initially "purely a ground staff" and George would have been transferred (Nelson, *National Security and the General Staff,* 395.). The difference between captain and major can be understood as a difference in benefits related to status. Captain is the highest rank of the junior officers whereas major is the lowest rank of the senior officers. Being in the company of senior officers (generals, lieutenant colonels, etc.) meant that usually majors would enjoy better quality amenities and services than captains. Regardless, each of George's promotions in AUS were temporary and six months after the war ended, he reverted to his original status as first lieutenant, FA. His honorable discharge certificate issued in 1953, however, lists both his permanent status in the reserves and his temporary, expired status during his active duty as a member of the AUS.

[Peggy to George]

#76
Halloween night—Sun.
7:00 P.M.

Dearest George

    How I wish you could have watched us here since about 5:30 until now. We've had a real halloween party. I brought two pumpkins back from the club party last night. We made jack-o-lanterns with candles inside and all. Then I bought a black cat mask for Georgia and a horse mask for Larry. Georgia dressed up in the Indian costume and Larry in the cowboy suit. Mr. Wamback furnished ice cream for supper and then we played in the living room until dark. Both girls are out but I left Robin long enough to walk down to North St. with them and scare a few cars. There was a slim sliver of a moon and I had their imaginations working so hard that they were sure they saw a witch riding her broomstick across it on the way home. They really looked cute all dressed up carrying pumpkins nearly their own size. I offered to play the witch but they were afraid I might not find my way back from the moon. Georgia said, "I don't want you to go, Momie, and I don't think Daddy would want you to either. He wants to keep you to get married." Someday we'll have to tell her that. Now they are all in bed exhausted.

    Last night there was a Halloween barn dance at the club. I wore a white blouse and pinafore and looked nearly six years old. But everyone else was about the same. The Terbells had a cocktail party first. I asked Marj. and Pete to pick me up thinking I'd make myself stay up after midnight for once if I didn't have my own car. It was a mistake. Marjorie found herself another guy at the cocktail party and when I asked her if she was ready to go to the club, she announced that she was going with another guy. I evidently looked surprised so she loudly asked if I were afraid to go along with Pete alone? At the party I had a fine time and never saw them again until Pete asked if I was ready to go home. Again Marj. didn't come and he was very tight, but I didn't dare cross him enough to insist on driving. We arrived O.K. and unthinkingly I asked him to come in. That meant a nightcap. This was followed by a weepy story of what a mess he was making of his life. He kept complaining that all the good friends he ever had are in uniform. I've been wondering for months why he didn't enlist so I asked him. The answer was he's trying to keep jobs for his boys from the office when they come back. Sounded pretty lame to me and I could see it didn't satisfy him so I made no comment. I just told him that I was sure everything would work out O.K. if he and Marjorie could talk things over and give up a lot of pride to recapture companionship. Here he wept on my shoulder and said it was no use. They hadn't talked on any personal subject for over a year. He wasn't a very impressive portrait of a man at this point and I was in deeper than I wanted to be as you can imagine. I told him I'd be glad to help any way I could but that I thought he might get more experienced advice from some men friends. He again said they were all in uniform so I suggested his father. He's 70 years old, says Pete. Here I offered the thought that a prayer never hurt any and if it was sincere and followed by a conscientious effort on the part of [the] person things were certain to be worked out. I felt like a hypocrite talking of praying to a drunk but I was hoping it might penetrate a little. After a bit of a struggle which I'm sure he regrets today I got him out of the house. He's pathetic to say the least—A slacker and knows it—A loving husband with a wayward wife and everyone knows that—added to this he knows Hodgey is not getting what he should in Mother love and has become an uncontrollable and a lonely, bad little boy. I hate to write you all this sort of thing, but I want you to always know my mistakes as well as achievements if there are any. This incident is regrettable only in so far as Pete will be so chagrinned upon sobering up that he probably will never want to see me anywhere again and that will be difficult to avoid. If I'd had any drinks I might pretend I couldn't remember it either.

I have our diary of our wedding trip here and the stack of pictures you enlarged. I am going to label them and put the ones together which haven't been finished. That will take most of my evenings this week.

P.S. Speak of the devil. Pete just phoned and very cleverly asked if he got me home safely. Then apologized for what he knew must have been bad driving. That was all. So that makes it easy. He doesn't remember coming in as far as I know.

      Loads of Love, Peggy

[George to Peggy]
[V-Mail]
                  No. 44

Peg dear,

Just finished breakfast and walked up the hill to the office. We are in wools now which is a bit more comfortable as it does get cool here. Ate breakfast with Lt. Hayes who was up at Rome with me. He went down to the local opera here last night which bore the title of "Three Musketeers in a Convenant,"[124] guess it was good for nothing except some laughs. Breakfast is usually quite a pleasant meal here as I usually get in early enough to sit around for a second cup of coffee, read the paper and talk to any sociable soul that happens along. Some of the English officers are very good company once you get acquainted. One never ending source of humor is the antics of many little men who have in the haste of war been given power and rank that they enjoy but know not how to use. The deflation after the war will be even more amusing. My love, George.

---

124 *Les Mousquetaires au Couvent (The Musketeers at the Convent)* was an operetta by Louis Varney. It debuted in Paris in 1880.

[George to Peggy]
[V-Mail]

No. 45
1 Nov. 43 Monday eve

My dear Peggy:

Your thoughts right this minute would be worth a franc to me or perhaps even two francs. Maybe I will get them in a week or so all free by mail though. As much as I would like to kiss you right now it would be a little while before you would have a chance to talk, and then there is one thing in particular that I would want you to say. It is twelve o'clock so I suppose you are eating dinner by now. I wish I were too with a whole evening to look forward to, with you in my arms. I have had that book of photos open looking at my pretty wife. That is a good bunch of pictures[.] Larry and Georgia look so cute and I just hate to think of having little Robbie all grown out of his babyhood by the time I get home. You know I am pretty proud of my family. I have been showing those pictures all around getting very nice comments in both french and English. Peg have you ever gotten weekly copies of "Stars and Stripes." I paid for a subscription to be sent to you so would like to hear if you get [it]. Wish I could take you where I am going right now, my love [This V-Mail was poorly photographed and the remainder of the message is cut off.]

[George to Peggy]

Capt. Steiner
AF HQ G-4 SEC, APO 512
New York, N.Y.
Tuesday, 2 November

Dear Peggy:

I have just finished writing a letter to Larry and one to Georgia, both of which will no doubt take endless explaining on your part as to just exactly what an Arab is and why do Kings have castles, [and] why do they put ditches around them with water in them. So why don't you just forward the toughest questions to me for a proper answer. I am sure that we can get very much [involved] in that way.

It seems like we have been separated for an awful long time now, but I guess we can be sure that there will [be] a [great] deal more time pass[ed] before we get back to the States again. Maybe I will be an old man with a long white beard. I will shave it off when I get home though. Well as long as I started telling stories tonight I might tell you one of my own little productions put together in a frantic effort to get a laugh out of a couple of glum chums who had not received any mail.

It is of a highly classified nature, in fact is it so secret (sh) that I have not even told the high command. You see we have been confronted with a very difficult problem of giving a name to a new group of sea going french females which Franklin's good friend Mrs. Hobby would call the FFNAC. But we thought that would be too alphabetical a name, and being allergic to alphabetical names, and at the same time feeling that this group should have a real salty nautical name like our own dear Waves and Spars, we decided to call these french girls the Oars. In addition we have given them the slogan "Don't lay down on the Oars." Orders have been issued that only Captains are to mount on the poop deck. I have been seriously considering requesting the Navy to have Colby sent over here to take command of this unit.

Well after that I don't suppose you will read any further anyway so I will just quit and go home.

Yours, George

[Peggy to George]
[V-Mail]

#77
Nov. 2, Tuesday

Darling,

We had a fine date yesterday—all day and night. I had one of M[r.] Hvolbeck's men here damming up our brook and digging it out in spots, so I kept thinking how much more fun it would be if you were here to do it yourself. There still will be plenty to do when you come. He's just made a pool to the left of the first little culvert under the garden path. I am going to plant tulips, daffodils, iris and lily-of-the-valley around it. Then I dug up some ground for my garden and really wished you were there to lend a hand as well as your company. After a shower and baths for the children we sat here in the living room looking at Schwartz's catalogue (Santy Claus's book) and tried to decide what we wanted most for Christmas. Larry picked out a wooden train and tracks that can be put together to go under bridges etc. also an electric stove he wants. Georgia will be satisfied with nothing short of the whole book. Already Santy Claus is in the prayers each night. How I wish you could be with us this year! And every day—every year. The coat you so sweetly want to give me has been ordered and I am so thrilled I can hardly tell you. Many many thanks. As usual you are too good to me. Last night I sat and knitted listening to Winston Burdette[125] and wondering if you ever met him. Then I went to bed and dreamt very bad dreams about you so you see we had a quite a long date. Peggy

[Peggy to George]
[V-Mail]

#88
Nov. 3, 1943. Wed.

Dearest George

This is a lovely crisp November day. All the leaves have left the woods and from this breakfast table I look out onto the black trunks of the trees standing above the bronze underbrush as the sun comes into it. Also this morning I can see our new pool and the little waterfalls

---

125 Winston Burdett (b. 1913, d. 1993) was a journalist for CBS during WWII. His broadcasts included coverage of the Axis retreat in North Africa and the Allied invasion of Sicily.
  After the war he will become a European correspondent for CBS based in Rome. Notably, in 1955 he will testify before the Senate Internal Security Subcommittee that from 1937-1942 he was a member of the Communist Party and during several of those years he spied intermittently for the Soviet Union (USSR). During his testimony he also will provide a list of other known Communist party members in the 1930s which will result in over thirty subpoenas. (Levy, "Buffalo Native Winston Burdett, 40-year CBS Veteran, Dies at 79.").

as the water overflows the stone dam. Then there is Joe out there in the middle of it all cutting wood. He finally came today after my waiting for nearly two months. Now I have four men coming here and altogether I can't get a week's work in two out of them. But it does help and if I can keep them coming through the winter I should have most of the necessary things done by spring. Yesterday was uneventful except for a trip to Greenwich. Marketing gets to be more of a chore each week. Food prices are terrific. If Robin were only a year older I'd certainly be doing my own work. I pay wages to Anna & Tina who do half the work they should and glower at me all the time. [It] just isn't worth it with board and room & clothes thrown in. Sorry to bellyache but I do have to once in a while as you remember. I've got my blue denim pants on and will work with Joe this morning. Love, Peggy

[Peggy to George]
[V-Mail]

#79

Thurs. Nov. 4

Darling,

We are sitting as usual at breakfast. This morning we are discussing the fact that it is Grandpa's birthday. I asked Georgia how old she thought he was. "He's two-six old. Me give him a kiss." Yesterday I ended up with two men here. So our Christmas present to the children is nearly finished and the daffodils are planted. Incidentally Santy Claus is fixing the strip of ground off the back circle of the drive opposite the garage as a play-yard. The place has been dug up now ready for grass seed in the spring and Mr. Hvolbeck is helping Santy make a jungle-gym, ladder, swing stand etc. It is something they need since I've postponed school another year. It will be about $200.00 before I finish but it's not much more than we'd spend at Schwartz on a lot of little things and then we've improved the property and given them something to use for years. I trust you approve. I phoned Esabel last night and got a cold reception and lecture as usual for neglecting her. I don't know why I bothered to call. Anyway she sent you her love. Yours, Peggy

[George to Peggy]
[V-Mail]

No. 46
5 Nov. 1943 Friday

My dear:

Wednesday night Allen and I went to the Special Service show "Hey Rookie"[126] which starred Sgt. Sterling Holloway.[127] It was put on at the Algiers Opera House[128] and was really excellent. There was a series of about 25 vaudeville type acts each of which was well put on including the usual tumbling acts, songs, gag acts, rope tricks, and a male "chorus" that was really funny. I got a laugh out of one off-stage remark made by a lieutenant sitting near us. Another officer called his attention to a rather senile looking general who was squiring a cute looking little blonde WAC, remarking what a wonderful relationship existed between such old boys and their WAC secretaries on a platonic basis. The reply was, "Yeah, well it's probably just play for her, and just tonic for the old fella." Well I guess I will be on my way up the hill [as] it is getting a bit late. Sure wish we could get this war over with. Almost forgot. I received the razor blades today for which many thanks. My love dear. George

---

126 *Hey Rookie* was a travelling U.S. Army show produced by soldiers at Fort MacArthur during WWII. The show was a parody of Army life, designed to boost morale. By the end of its run, it had raised $250,000 dollars toward the construction of a swimming pool. The pool was closed in the 1990s but renovated and reopened in 2016. Called the "Hey Rookie Pool," it is open to the public in its original location in San Pedro, CA.
127 Sterling Holloway (b. 1905, d. 1992) was a comic actor known for his distinct, high-pitched voice. He enlisted in the U.S. Army in 1942 and served with the Special Services. In addition to future success in radio programs, television shows, and films, Holloway would famously provide voices for over a dozen Disney projects, including the voice of Winnie the Pooh.
128 George is referring to the original Algiers Opera House, also known as the Théâtre National Algérien Mahieddine Bachtarzi.

[Peggy to George]
[V-Mail]

#80
Nov. 5, 1943 Fri.

Dearest George,

The mailman brought a typewritten letter from you yesterday and a letter from Grandpa saying he will be here for the weekend with us. I have already planned a party for tomorrow night even though it is Anna's weekend off, but when I heard he was coming I asked her to please stay in. The answer "No, I won't. I have my plans too, you know." So —— I'm meeting Dad about eight tonight under the clock at [the] Biltmore to spend the evening in town. Then tomorrow we have a date for lunch and golf at the club and somehow in between I must get a dinner ready for a party of ten. I'll let you know how I get on. Here's who is coming. Brainards, Hanans, Buckhauts and Brasnahans (friends of Kay and Webbs from Omaha who have moved down here). As you see it's not the same old gang but I've told you how fed up I am with that crowd and after my experience with Pete I have gotten busy to see people that really do interest me and have more to offer than the glass in their hand. I must get dressed and be off to Greenwich for the marketing. The children want to go too of course and Larry needs a haircut, pending Grandpa's arrival. Loads of Love. Peggy

[George to Peggy]
[V-Mail]

No. 47
7/11/43 Sunday

Dear Peggy,

Received your letter just now saying that you had gotten six letters] [from me all on the same day. Sorry not to have them spread out a bit more, but guess it cannot be helped. It means quite a wait between letters that. The same bunching happens here, but not often. Now if the ration board had a say in it they would probably have you read them one a day when they arrive like that. I don't think you did that though. Now I will tell you what the brackets in the first sentence are about. I started to write you a real quick letter before going to dinner away back last night, but I got rudely interrupted by Stipp and Allen who wanted to go see "Five Graves to Cairo" after dinner and we only had an hour to eat and get downtown. Well we made it and it was a pretty fair show too, at least we found out how Rommel really got chased out of Egypt, Hollywood version. Well it is getting late so I will be on my way up the hill. Thinking of you tonight dear, George.

[Peggy to George]

#81
Monday, Nov. 8, 1943

Darling,

It seems ages since I wrote you last Fri. morning, but with Dad here until this afternoon and Anna off I have had my busy time. Incidentally, that letter was #80. I think I forgot to number it. Now to get you caught up on the doings since then. I didn't get to N.Y.C. to meet Dad on Fri. night as he wired me from Wash. [Washington, D.C.] that he would get in too late to do anything, so I went on to dinner with Pinky and two of her friends — Betty Williams and Mrs. Seymore. The first is an unmarried girl about 38 in the real-estate business, and the other a canadian married to a fighting Frenchman. We have started a once a week meeting of odd women interested in talking over current issues and discussing postwar plans. This was the first time and we had planned to go to the library to hear the father of one girl talk on post-war England. We arrived too late to get a seat and couldn't hear from the stairs so ended up in the movies. I hope the next attempt will be more successful. It should be quite a group as Pinky and Mrs. Seymore are definitely very "pink."[129] I left the movie early to pick Dad up on the ten o'clock express. He looked fine even though he had just survived a

---

129   Leaning to the left politically.

personal spanking from W.P.B.[130] It seems a month ago W.P.B. officials met with farm machinery manufacturers and dealers in Chicago and painted a rosy picture of the large amount of steel to be made available for production of farm machinery in the next year. Dad was tired of hearing all the promises and no follow through so after two days of this, he got up and told the dealers that he didn't think they would get one piece more than they had last year. That already four months of the fiscal year had gone by and not an ounce of steel had been received yet for this program.[131] Well, the Ass. Press and Internat. News service ran his little impromptu speech and he's gotten hell from Wash. All the manufacturers were glad he'd had the nerve to tell the truth, but they were also glad it was he and not themselves who had the noose around his neck. The climax was that he was called to Wash. Fri. for an executive meeting with Batcheller[132] who Dad says would even criticize the All Mighty. Dad stuck to his guns and said the promises they had been given only provided a hunting license for the material. Then

---

130   Established in early 1942 by Executive Order 9024, The War Production Board (WPB) was the government agency assigned to supervise private manufacturers' wartime production. Peggy's father, George L. Gillette, was the vice-president and general sales manager at the Minneapolis-Moline Power Implement Company, a prominent midwestern farm machinery company. In December 1942, he was appointed the chairman of the WPB Farm Machinery and Equipment Division.

131   As Peggy writes, her father was present at a meeting between WPB officials and members of the National Retail Farm Equipment Association (NRFEA) held on October 13th in Chicago, Illinois. Several months prior, the WPB had announced their authorization of the production of farm machinery at 80% of the output of 1940, including a steel allotment of 900,000 tons for farm machinery, assuring the public the allotment would increase production. This optimistic declaration was decried by Mr. Gillette (an unscheduled speaker at the event in Chicago) who felt the well-publicized claim misled the public and misrepresented the most important issue: it was not that companies' outputs were restricted by lower allotments, rather the problem was that raw materials were in such short supply manufacturers could not acquire them in the first place, regardless of how much they were allowed to have. For example, the WPB had authorized production of 40% of the output of 1940 for 1943, but only about 20% reached the fields in time (Associated Press, "Farm Tool Supply for '44 to Increase.").

   Mr. Gillette denounced the notion that higher allotments would automatically result in higher production levels, responding that unless the raw materials were supplied in advance, little would be done to advance the output of farm machinery. He declared the supply situation for manufacturers so dire that fewer machines would be produced than the previous year and he implored his fellow NRFEA members to inform the Truman Committee (a bipartisan special committee formed to correct problems in war manufacturing) that production was and would continue to break down because the materials that manufacturers needed to increase production were not available for purchase, despite the allotments allowing them higher quotas. He explained to the WPB representatives that dealers would unfairly "bear the brunt of farm equipment program misinformation when they try to explain to customers why machines supposedly in production cannot be delivered" ("Urges Senate Inquiry of Farm Equipment Output Hike Delay.").

132   Hiland G. Batcheller (b. 1885, d. 1961) served as the director of the WPB steel division and then later as the WPB vice chairman. He resigned his vice chairman position in 1943 but was reappointed in September 1944. Before 1942 and again, after the war's end in 1945, Batcheller was the president of Allegheny-Ludlow Steel Corporation and later became the board chairman.

he pointed out that AA[133] priorities on 99.99% of a machine and no priority for the last .01% which might be a machined tiny part was still no machine at all. This was good for getting Mpls.-Moline the dis[c]s for harrows that have been finished [for] months.[134]

We sat up quite late talking after I had showed him every square inch of our house and we had wakened the children for a kiss. He just loves the place. Saturday was lovely and we walked over the grounds and down the road to see the Clifford place. At noon we went to the club and met Helen Gorton and her mother and stepfather for lunch. After that we had a father-daughter nine hole golf game. I was so

---

133   "AA" refers to the priority or preference rating assigned to contractors by the WPB. The system of priority rating was formally initiated in July of 1941 to ensure that high-priority military industries (tank and shipbuilding, for example) had access to the raw materials and components needed for manufacturing before less-important civilian industries (e.g., the automotive industry). The farm machinery and equipment industry was classified as a "civilian industry" during the war, giving it a lower priority rating than a "defense industry." Despite it receiving the highest civilian priority rating of B-1 for new machinery (it received a temporary defense rating of A-10 for materials needed for maintenance and repair), the high food quota demands pressed upon farmers, the inability to get the much-needed farm machinery to market, and the lagging production on the contracted war items showed the priority rating to be inadequate. The B-1 rating was temporarily raised to the A level (first to A-3, then A-2, and finally, in April 1942, to A-1-a).

The higher the priority rating, the more diverse the products the company could manufacture and the higher their allotment of raw materials and components. Since each uprating was temporary, the farm machinery manufacturers, distributors, and customers constantly had to protest and appeal the existing permanent priority rating and petition their elected officials for a higher one.

In late 1942 farm machinery was granted a temporary priority rating of AA-1 (all permanent AA ratings were reserved for the U.S. Armed Forces) for the first quarter of 1943. The priority rating was not permanently uprated nor was it uprated uniformly across the industry and its products because the military was concerned about civilian industries holding a priority rating equal to their own because of the competition for limited resources (steel especially). Any change in the output of the defense programs could dramatically affect lend-lease arrangements and the armed forces' own progress as they prepared to advance into Europe (McAleer, *Farm Machinery and Equipment Policies of the War Production Board and Predecessor Agencies*, 155.). The different priority ratings of farm machinery products within the same industry caused much consternation among manufacturers. For example, deliveries of materials for repaired parts were rated AA-2X (for urgent nonmilitary items), higher than the delivery of materials for new machinery which was only AA-3 (Ibid., 76).

Based on Peggy's words the reader can understand her father's frustration with the priority rating system as follows: Using Mr. Gillette's example, a higher priority AA rating on harrows only meant that manufacturers were allowed to produce more of them than other less-vital equipment and that it was more likely they would receive the materials needed for their manufacturing. A lower rating on the component parts (discs in this case) meant that manufacturers could build as many harrows as their quota allowed, but because discs were rated of lower importance, they were not being manufactured in high enough quantities to meet demand, thus the harrows would sit unfinished on Minneapolis-Moline assembly lines for an indeterminate period of time.

By 1944 farm machinery was ranked as the fourth most important war production program by a WPB official, outranked only by military programs for landing craft, high octane gasoline, and military trucks (Ibid., 146.). Despite this recognition of the industry's significant role in the war effort, subsequent requests for AA-1 ratings in 1944 will be denied.

134   Minneapolis-Moline, while among the leading farm machinery and tractor companies in the United States, was a small company when compared to others in the farm equipment industry and their volume of business (Ibid., 184.). It was common for smaller companies dealing with the priority rating system to struggle more with the logistics of receiving their allotted amounts of raw materials than with ordering them (Ibid., 134). These transportation difficulties often resulted in longer waits for their orders to be filled.

terrible that although Dad was the best, we still lost 8 down playing low ball-low total. My mind was on the dinner party I had to get home and cook.

The party was a success. I had chicken and noodles, peas, grapefruit and alligator pear salad, rolls, cranberry sauce, cake and coffee. I had it on the buffet so they could help themselves and then we all sat down at the table. It was good too, if I do say so. Anna's so lazy about cooking for me that I was about convinced that the trouble was with the food we get now. It isn't at all. She just doesn't bother to look at the cookbook anymore. We had two tables of bridge and one of poker as the Gortons and Helen's parents joined us after dinner. When they all left Dad and I did the dishes and cleaned up. How we all wished you could have been here. I will say having Dad gave me a purpose this time so it didn't bore me as much as the other party I had a couple of weeks ago. Sunday we spent here with the children. We took them and Scott Pearson, who came over to play with Larry, for a walk down the bridle path in the morning, and then Dad cooked hamburgers, potatoes and peas on the rocks behind our new pool for their lunch. I took some pictures of the picnic which I will send next week. In the afternoon Dad cleaned up the yard and burned a lot of brush. He did more to improve the place in one afternoon than all these men have done in a month. The kids loved the bon-fires too and were quite a help. I fixed Dad and me a drink after he had finished rough-housing with the kids and they had gone up to bed. Then I made scrambled eggs, toast, cranberry sauce and milk and cake and brought it in in front of the fireplace. Can you picture that scene? It surely brought back many happy memories to me. Then Dad read the enclosed article to me and wanted me to read him some of your letters. I got them all out and read all the parts that I thought would interest him. We played a bit of rummy, listened to the news and went to bed.

This morning was rainy and Dad had lunch date with Mr. Harkrader so I went along. I got all dressed up in my new Twyefforte suit, new hat and Jessie's neckpiece. I'm so thrilled to have those furs and they look really smooth on me. I'll have to get Tina to snap my picture in that outfit for you. Conceited, am I not? We met at the Biltmore and had whiskey sours in the cocktail room where we have sat so many times. Then we had lunch in the room just off of it where the music is. I took the 3:30 train back and Dad was to go about an hour later. It surely raised my spirits to have him here just those two days and a half. If anything should happen to them before you get back, I don't believe I could take it. No use to cross that bridge now though.

Dad says that Jack is slated for the draft in Jan. He hasn't told Mother so if you write, don't mention it. He also is very worried about their new baby, Robin's age. It seems he is as large as Robin, but doesn't even sit up yet. I only tried to say he was a little slow and dispel his anxiety, but I could see it bothers him considerably. Poor Dad.

I told the children tonight that you and I were having a date via the typewriter and what messages could I send for them. Larry said, Tell Daddy I didn't have time to write him tonight but I will do it in the morning. Tell him Grandpa was here and that I was a good boy for him (you) and that Robbie is just fine. Georgia said, Tell Daddy I was good too, and send him 6,7,8,9, kisses and ---- (grunt) hugs. I told them that you had sent them a letter airmail and that it should be here any day now. They can hardly wait for morning to go to the box. Heaven help us if it comes by boat. I've been trying to figure out when you said you are all comfy in the dressing gown and slippers G.A. gave you, if that means you finally have received the luggage. I believe you only had the tan gown I gave you in the bag you took.

I must wind this up and get at my bills. I know you are asleep now and I trust having sweet dreams. I love you so much my Dearest.

                      Yours, Peggy

P.S. Please tell me how to release the right margin on this damn contraption. It stops right in the middle of the page and I have to release it on every line. This has gone on for months and I've practically had the thing apart trying to fix it. P.

[handwritten at the bottom of the page]

P.S. On reading this over I made it sound like Dad felt Batcheller dared criticize him because he would even criticize the All. M. What he meant was that B. was so self-satisfied that he could improve on the All Mighty according to Dad's impression.
P.P.S. Your V-mail comes through fine (You can see I just reread today's letter).

[George to Peggy]
[V-Mail]

No. 48
Tues. Evening 9 Nov. 43

My dear Peggy:

Here I am all clean after a warm bath, but I am a bit chilly even with my wool dressing gown, and those wool slippers feel pretty good too. Wish you were here so when I finished writing this letter I could climb into a warm bed. Maybe I would not bother to finish a letter then. As a matter of truth when I woke up this morning I was awful disappointed to find you were not with me. That book of Culbertson's arrived today for which thank you very much. I have been sitting here looking through it for a while this evening. I pulled out those pictures you sent me, taken at Minnetonka this summer. That is a cute bonnet Georgia has on. I like your smile 'cause I think you were thinking about me when you had that one taken with Georgia on your lap and Larry standing next to you. Larry looks like he was looking after you two girls. I was surprised when you wrote they were roller skating in the basement. Love you so much. George

[George to Peggy]
[V-Mail]

No. 49
10 Nov. 43 Wednesday

My dear Peggy:

Looks like I am missing a lot of birthday parties. Ask Larry what he would think about having a roast turkey with a candle on it instead of a birthday cake for Robbie. I remember what Larry did to his first birthday cake down in Miami. But I got a piece of it anyway. I was thinking this morning of the breakfast we had in the Mayflower before I left. Strange how all the details stick. Sounds like everybody was pretty optimistic in the states right now. Hope they are right. I suppose something could break any time. Received that razor sharpener from Abercrombie & Fitch today. I will try it out tonight and let you know how it works. Got the start of a cold so I think that ought to be a good excuse to open the bottle of bourbon. I miss your good company and your love so much dear. George

[Peggy to George]
[V-Mail]

#82
Nov. 10, Wed.

Dearest George

Larry and I are both writing to you and Georgia is talking as usual with a mouth full of toast and jam and Doxie begging it from her. It is a sunny cold day after many rainy ones (2). Yesterday I stood four hours at the Masonic Temple selling chances for the Woman's Exchange Christmas Sale. It was more work than a full day cutting brush I decided. The afternoon I spent on my check book. For the first time I couldn't agree with the bank without hours of refiguring. It's O.K. now. Then I wrote Cocky, Chloe and Jean each a letter and had a rough house with the kids. You should have seen it. I was on my hands and knees in the living room with both of them on my back.

Doxie was barking and trying hard to get in the fun too without much encouragement. Then suddenly he bit me on the fanny and I jumped so fast both kids rolled off on Doxie and knocked him down. It must have been a sight. Went to Marjie & Pete's for dinner. Just three of us. Very pleasant. Peggy

[George to Peggy]

#50
Capt. G.R. Steiner, AF Hq G-4 Sec
APO 512, c/o PM. New York
Thursday 11 Nov. 1943.

My darling;

Here I am night duty officer again. I don't mind it, rather like it as a matter of fact, because it is [a] good place to write some letters, and read a bit and they set up a cot so it is not a bad place to sleep. And the chances are pretty good now that you will not be awakened during the night.

Allen just came in to say good night, he has been down the hall in our room typing some letters. We just fixed up a job on Maj. Simons. I found some papers on his desk which should not have been left out, so we took the papers and left a letter requesting a reply by indorsement as to the causes of such negligence. He seems to be coming out on the wrong end of things today.

This afternoon he walked into our bathroom to find there was hot water available, so he mentions the fact, then starts back to his room, which has no bath, to get his soap and towel. When he returned all set to take a bath, Stipp was [al]ready in the tub. You see we have to have our fun. I'll bet Larry would think it was funny anyway.

Makes me think, I wish I could help you wash your back. It would take a lot of concentration to keep from wandering off the job. Do you think you will need any help like that when I get home?

Now there you go again just leading me on, you should not [be]

having me thinking those things when you are so far off. I wouldn't mind a kiss, right now though, or two or even three and then a lot more.

Had the day off today but did not really do much of anything. It was wet and cold all day. I went downtown to try to buy some wool shirts as I have only one but they are still sold out. If you could send two or three I could use them. There should be a couple of good ones from last winter 15½ neck 33 sleeve.

I have gotten a good cold in the head now, but everyone has had one. It will be gone by the time you receive this.

Your nice long letter of Oct. 18 arrived today. I was interested to read the letter from Lt. Tyak. I am glad you gave them such a good time.

Think I will get some sleep—good night dear.

Love, George

[Peggy to George]
[V-Mail]

#83
Nov. 11, 1943. Thurs.

Darling

Our breakfast conversation so far this morning. Larry – "Santy Claus came and got in bed with me last night and said, 'What do you want Larry?' I said, 'I want something to draw on with lots of Indians and horses Santy Claus'" – pause – "Momie, I know Santy Claus didn't really come. Couldn't I call him up this morning on your real telephone and tell him so he will know?" Can you beat that? Do you suppose at this tender age I'm going to have him doubting Santy?

I went to N.Y.C. yesterday and had lunch at the Savoy with Mrs. Alworth. Then she took me to see "Early To Bed."[135] It had a very

---

135 *Early to Bed* debuted in June 1943. Renowned jazz pianist and entertainer Thomas Wright "Fats" Waller composed the score making *Early to Bed* the first Broadway musical for a non-Black cast arranged by a Black man (Blue, "Fats Waller.").

bawdy background being set in a house of ill fame in Martinique, but the place was taken for an A1 girls' boarding school by certain important personages and made a very funny play. The music was good too. I came home right afterwards and the Bridges were on the phone as I walked in so they came over for a ham sandwich and salad with me and had a visit. Penn is surely a lot of fun.

Love to you, Peggy

[Peggy to George]
[V-Mail]

#84
Fri. Nov. 12, 1943

Darling.

    I wish you could see Larry's face right now. He found an envelope on the telephone stand and as usual wanted to know what was in it. Fortunately, it was some tiny gum drops that Bernice sent to the kids last night, so I told him I didn't know what was inside. However, his name was on the outside and Santy Claus' stamp on the back. His eyes nearly popped and when he found the candy it was marvelous. He is still dancing around singing, "Candy, candy from Santy Claus." Now he is trying to count them all. Tina just came in to say that Georgia started outdoors with her blue denim overalls, heavy navy pullover and a cap over one eye so she said to Anna, "Look at our Pistol Packin' Momma." Whereupon Georgia at the top of her lungs marched on out singing, "Lay that pistol down, Babe. Lay that pistol down." She's the most comical child you can imagine. Every expression is funny. I had dinner up with Bill and Bernice last night. It was Bernice's birthday and she got a very nice dinner and Bill opened a bottle of champagne. We had a very pleasant evening. Had a bit of snow yesterday. Clear & cold today. Peggy

[George to Peggy]
[V-Mail]

Saturday 13 Nov. 43

My dear Peggy,

You know that is a very possessive form of "my" that I use in that phrase. It is satisfying to feel how very much you do belong to me. And I am just selfish enough to be glad to know that it makes you a little unhappy to have me away. Nothing has the interest and importance over here, that exist for all sorts of small events when we are together. Your letters are very interesting, they reproduce well on V-mail, [and] I have no trouble reading them. The darker ink you noticed is from the bottle that was enclosed in the package of V-mail forms you mailed to me. Glad to hear that you are receiving the Stars and Stripes. The boys who get that out deserve a lot of credit. There is a regular daily edition also, every day except Sunday. I have been sharpening a bunch of blades tonight and will try one out in the morning. Peg, I love you so very much. Yours, George.

[Peggy to George]
[V-Mail]

#85
Sat. Nov. 13, 1943

Dearest George

First of all I want to make you a post box for Maggie Seymore. She is a new friend of mine who is married to a fighting frenchman. She hasn't seen him for almost two years and only hears from him about once in 3 months. He went 9 months without hearing from her. Last night we figured out this system. She cannot write V-mail to him so she is writing to you and you could forward it I hope to:

Enseigne de Vaisseau
Michel Seymour Tripier

Forces Navales France Libre[136]
Levant

In Greenwich they told her Levant was not sufficient so she said she added Syria[137] as a guess. You may need that too. I hope you can help her. She has two little girls and is working 48 hours a week in a defense plant to support them. Letters mean just as much to those left behind. I spent all day yesterday working outside with a man. We cleaned and burned all the brush in front of the house to the first wall going towards the garden. It looks much better. Had dinner at Pinky's with her & Maggie. Read "Our Time for Greatness."[138] Peggy

[Peggy to George]

#86
Nov. 15, 1943
Mon. 2 P.M.

Dearest George,

If we could really be having our Mon. date right now I wouldn't be a bit good company. You see I picked up the mail on the way here to the hairdresser and just read about your promotion to Captain. Now I am under the dryer and will start my Mon. evening Air Mail early on the strength of my wrath at the moment. No Sir, I wouldn't be a bit good to you. Not even a kiss for consolation. I am more furious than I have been on the numerous other occasions when after doing all the

---

136 The Free French forces were aligned with Charles de Gaulle's government-in-exile and opposed to the Vichy regime's collaboration with the Nazis. As their name suggests, they fought alongside the Allied forces during WWII for a free France.

137 Following WWI, the League of Nations designated Syria and Lebanon French mandates—ultimately destined for independence, according to the terms of the authorization. In June 1941 the Allies (comprised mainly of troops from the British Commonwealth along with Free French forces) invaded Syria and Lebanon from British-controlled Palestine, ousting the Vichy government and depriving German aircraft of a convenient refueling option near North Africa. Tripier appears to have served among the Free French forces and was likely part of the joint British-French force occupying Syria and Lebanon after the Vichy regime was removed.

138 *A Time for Greatness*, by Herbert Agar, seeks to encourage Americans that greatness is within reach only if they have the moral courage to rise to meet it. Agar argues that in order for Americans to achieve this greatness, they must recapture their spiritual dignity and the inwardness of their religious traditions, strive for "creative conservatism" in business and labor, and cherish their civil liberties (Stout, "The Time And Its Opportunity.").

hardest jobs the best, and desserts are passed around, you come home empty handed. I thought you had learned enough bitter lessons on that score already and would learn to be on your good behavior with the right guys even if it does go against your opinion of the old sap whoever he is. But I see you haven't. At least you might have refused the damn thing and still had a decent date of rank. Personally, I wish I were there to raise hell. It's maybe too late to accomplish anything, but I sure could raise hell and cut that six months to six days.[139] Damn it, dear, you've got to fight a few battles for <u>yourself</u> these days and all through life. There just aren't enough people like you to always be fighting for the other guy. We're going to need plenty of them to fight [for] the peace but right now if you won't do it for yourself, do it for Larry and me. Get really mad for once. I am sick of your rank too. It was bad enough in Mpls. but now all of Greenwich that's been in a year is a Major of some description.

    Now I feel better—just like I'd really had a good fight with you. Perhaps the date will improve from here in.

    We had more snow yesterday and the children were so unhappy because it refused to stick to the grass. I was just as glad to see it go as winter seems so long these years with you away and no skiing trips or vacations or cozy evenings by the fire.

    Saturday I spent digging out our brook for about 20 more feet. It's hard work even with Larry's help. From the looks of me today, I got into the poison ivy again. It's hard to distinguish now when there are no leaves on it. I hope to get the brook widened and deepened both before the spring comes in hopes that the low land in front of the house will drain better. It really needs a lot of fill, but at $2.50 a square yard I don't believe that will be done very soon. That night Jessie Bedford came up for dinner with me and Larry and Georgia ate at the

---

139 George was first promoted to a rank of captain on June 29, 1942. Peggy argues that George should have fought for recognition of that earlier date so that he would already have served his six months as a captain and would be overdue at this point for a promotion to major. By accepting the second promotion as captain, effective October 25, 1943, George will have to serve an additional six months before he will become eligible to move up to the rank of major.

table with us. They even had spareribs and loved them.

Sunday I went to Joe and Penn Bridge's for cocktails and dinner at noon. We had a swell new drink called Southern Comfort. It's a cross between whiskey and brandy. They poured it over a canned peach in a champagne glass, added crushed ice and I had three. Really I can recommend them except I was so thirsty all the rest of the day I couldn't get enough ice water. I got home about five and played with the kids. Robin is so cute. He has gotten that "Taylor-tot" going just as fast as Larry used to maneuver in it. We are always just catching him at the brink of those two steps to the front door. He waves bye-bye, plays patty-cake, covers his eyes and plays peek[-a-boo] and Larry and Georgia are determined that he is going to walk soon for Santy Claus. They each take a hand and command him to walk between them. When he drags on his tummy he is severely reprimanded for not putting forth the proper effort. Here I ran out of ink in my nice fountain pen so must carry on with the beauty parlor's offering. It's not too bad but will probably be difficult to read on the other side.

At home I have several enclosures for this letter so won't mail it in the village now. I must put in one of Larry's letters. Each morning for a week he has come down stairs with a letter all sealed in an envelope reading for either you or Santy Claus. This morning it was both. I am closely watched if I ride the bike to the mail box and if I come to the village I am reminded just what slot it belongs in at the post office about ten times. (They are always air mail.) He spent all this morning while I was doing the wash & the girls the cleaning in his room with Georgia, Robin and the telephone. He had Santy Claus on the wire and was relaying all of Georgia's and his own desires and their interpretation of Robin's wants to Santy. It went on by the hour. He insisted on having the door closed but I peeked in a couple of times. He was sitting leisurely in one of the little chairs next to their table with his legs crossed and a blasé, distant look in his eye with the phone on the table and the talking-listening part to his head. It was a real picture of the smart executive.

I must be nearly dry (I mean my hair) so will close and get my marketing done. You should be about finishing your dinner now.

Well now I am home. Just received a box of hersheys from Allan Lunn (British boy). I'll send them on to you.

Now it is my dinner time and we are having a nice date. I would kiss you and I do love you, but I also meant every word of the explosion.

We girls are having our discussion group at Pinky's tonight, so must run and change my clothes.

You must know that Larry just came down for supper. I tried to explain about Army rank to him. He said nothing until I got all through then said "Daddy's a Captain but I guess he'll be a 'cornelus' someday."

Yours always. Peggy.

[Peggy to George]
[V-Mail]

#87
Nov. 17, Wed.

Dearest George,

This is a sunny cold day with ice on the pond above our little dam. There is great excitement as Joe, our once in two week gardener, is here to dig next year's victory garden and cut some wood. Also Mr. Hvolbeck and two men are taking the awning off the porch and the screens down. Also the storm doors or windows are going up.

Yesterday I spent the day listening to the Herald Tribune Forum over the radio. They are having a two day conference on "Pioneering for Peace."[140] The paper is publishing the speeches so I'll mail you

---

140   The two-day, four-session forum was entitled, "Pioneering for a Civilized World."

some of them. In the midst of a speech by Dr. Walter Judd on China[141] at about 2:30 Mrs. Alworth called to see where I was. I'd forgotten I had invited her to go to lunch with me in N.Y.C. Frankly, I thought it was today but you can imagine how far I got with that alibi.

Last night Dad called to find out if I had poison ivy. I surely do but I guess nothing compared to him. I fear he won't be as anxious to work outside for us next time. I must mail this and see how things are going outside. Love X Peggy

[Peggy to George]
[V-Mail]

#88
Nov. 17, Thurs.

Darling,

What I wouldn't give to have you here this morning. These numerous men I have coming here to clean up outdoors have gotten to fighting. Frank went to the place Joe works Tuesday and told him not to come here again— that he, Frank could give me all the time I needed and wanted to be here. All this after he never even showed up last week for his three hours. He's here this morning and I can't decide, as usual, what to do — fire him or try and straighten it out. Life would be so much simpler if I never needed any help.

The children are outside watching Frank. Larry heard the conversation yesterday with Joe and announced this a.m. that he'd tell Frank not to come anymore. In another few years I could let him take over. Robin is screaming sitting on the toidey. He stays there most of the morning but is still stubborn.

There is not much news. Mr. Hvolbeck is here again today fixing storm windows so we are all busy. I took screens off yesterday

---

141   Dr. Walter Henry Judd (b. 1898, d. 1994) was a medical missionary in China before being elected to the U.S. House of Representatives (Minnesota). In 1938, after negotiating his release from the Japanese-controlled Chinese city of Fenchow, Dr. Judd returned to the U.S. and spent two years travelling the country, cautioning Americans not to ignore Japanese expansionism in China and voicing disapproval of American shipments of raw materials to Japan that could be used for munitions. Once an elected representative in 1942, Dr. Judd rose to further prominence as an opponent of Chinese Communism.

downstairs. All ready for winter and believe me it is here. All my love, Peggy

[Peggy to George]
[V-Mail]

#89
Nov. 18, Fri.

Dearest George,

    Another day gone by without you and each is worse than the last. I did get through the gardener trouble yesterday though. Frank agrees to give me more time and not bother Joe anymore. He also informed that he wasn't working at all Jan. or Feb. His hands get too cold outdoors. This is the first year he hasn't begged summer customers to give him some kind of work to carry through winter months. Now he has so much money he is vacationing; probably Florida. Had a telegram from Colby this morning. They have an eight lb. girl, Betsy, born last Monday. You must write him. They are still at Fairfax. Tell him you aren't surprised to see he started off with one of the weaker sex.

    Mother should be down in a little over a week now. She surely will look good to me. She needs a rest too having been nurse, cook, cleaning woman to Thelma & Jack for weeks. The children received your letters yesterday and you'd think they had a gold mine. Neither would let the other see theirs for fear it might be torn. Loads of love, Peggy

[Peggy to George]
[V-Mail]

#90
Sat. Nov. 20

Dearest George,

    Right now I am sitting in the morning session of the 4th Report Conference of the Commission to Study Organization of

Peace.[142] I had to leave so early I couldn't get my letter written to you. Pinky is going to meet me here later. I am taking notes today to make a report on this to our little group on Monday night. It is my week to have the girls for supper and supply the topic of discussion. I told Larry where I was going today and said several men were going to talk about what we are going to do to make a nice world for little boys and girls after the war is over. He said he had talked to you on the telephone early this morning and you said that the war is almost over and you will be home two weeks next Sunday. And that you won't ever leave us again and someday you'll take all of us to see where you have been but you won't let anyone shoot at us. Such a busy little mind he has.

So far this first speaker has emphasized mostly the necessity of completely disarming the Nazis and Japs and building ourselves an international air force. More tomorrow. All yours, Peggy

[George to Peggy]

[#]50
Capt. G.R. Steiner
AF Hq G-4 Sec APO 512
c/o PM New York N.Y.
22 November 1943

My darling:

Another Monday evening. Just ten to eleven here, wish I knew exactly what the time difference was, but it must be five or six there. Went down to a movie with Schutz. It was an English picture "Squadron Leader X," not too good but it passed the evening.

It may not show that way in the school books, but I am convinced tonight that certain parts of North Africa are definitely well within the

---

142 The Commission to Study the Organization of Peace was founded in 1943 with the purpose of promoting the creation of the United Nations. The fourth report, published in November 1943, was titled "Fundamentals of the International Organization" and discussed ways to create a United Nations that would not fall victim to the same pitfalls as the failed League of Nations.

Artic circle. If I should run into a few Eskimos and polar bears on the way down the hill in the morning I will not be surprised to find them taking the place of the usual arabs and goats.

Usually I go right to bed when I get up here at night now just to keep warm. Result is I do not come up until fairly late. Forgot my pen as you will note. If I should ever lose it I don't know how I could continue in the war effort. Also I am not sure this letter should not be 51 in place of 50.

Schutz and I are going to try to get an apartment, maybe one other officer. This is quite aways from downtown, it is high enough so it is cooler, and living in someone else's home has its drawbacks.

M. Rebillet has not been operated [on] but evidently is not too well off, they are not sure whether it is ulcers or cancer. It is very difficult to get photo supplies for x-rays, *medecin* is scarce, and the foods he should have are to be had only on the black market. Wish I could help him, as he is a good sort.

I love you my dear and find it not easy at all to get along without you. Wish you were in my arms right now. I hope by next Thanksgiving we will be doing just what I am thinking of now. Is it a date?

Must tell you about the third farce in my military rank. After all the proper paper work had been gone thru promoting Lt. Steiner FA-Res (Capt. AUS-AC) to Capt. AUS, a cable came back from Washington saying, you can't do that, we did it first, officer was promoted to Capt. AUS in June of 42. It would have been thoughtful of them to let me know about [it]. When you tie the whole story in you sure get a laugh, if I had just minded my own business, not gone to C & G S School, not gone thru all that high powered training under Gen. Marshall, I would now be a Major since last December and probably a Lt. Colonel, comfortably fixed with ASC[143] for the duration.

---

143   It is likely George means the Air Service Command (ASC). George served in the Army Air Corps and was stationed at various stateside ASC headquarters and command centers before being transferred overseas after completion of the Task Force Officer's Course.

Incidentally our loud mouthed Jewish friend, Blume,[144] is a Lt. Col.

You can probably guess that Schutz and I have been beefing a bit, but then we are glad we had the experience, even though we are both without promotions which are long overdue.

Guess I will go to bed and stop worrying about the sorry state of affairs[.] I just wish that when Marshall called us [in to] say goodbye, that I had known what I do now.

Now you guess just what I will be thinking about you when I get into bed.

Love you very much, George

[Peggy to George]

#91

Tues. a.m.

Dearest George,

I couldn't write you on our date last night as the discussion group was here for supper and I tried to report on the conference Sat. Several times I was interrupted by memories of a date we had a year ago last night, the Monday before Robin was born. The wonderful dinner at Mirliton of pea & turtle soup, wine and the stewed oranges. Then you took me to the hospital. I can remember so well the taxi ride over through the blocks of east side tenements and then arriving at the hospital. You stayed and we talked mostly of how we hoped the baby would arrive the next day. Then you left and as usual that vacant feeling returned which has become so familiar to me the last 2½ years. Now it is sort of a permanent part of my personality. A year ago today I had by now downed the largest glass of castor oil ever offered one individual and the waiting started. By night we were pretty discouraged and all set for Thanksgiving together when the little fellow appeared. How thrilled I was through the fog of ether to see your surprised face when you came in to find he was already here.

---

144 Along with George, Major Irving Blume was assigned to the ASC headquarters at RAD in January 1943.

So tomorrow Robin is one year old, but right now he is racing around me in Larry's tailor tot wearing Larry's old blue flannel bathrobe and looking exactly as he did in just the same outfit in our colored movie of him Christmas of 1939 at Knox Ave.

So much for this week's memories. The conference was very interesting. I will send you some of the literature. We finished about 5:30 and went to the Biltmore for a cocktail. Then up to Michel's for dinner. We sat upstairs at the same table you and [I] had one night. Took an 8:20 train home and went right to bed exhausted.

Sunday morning Tina, the children & I took Doxie to the vet again. This time he has an infected ear. Poor old boy hated to be left so it nearly killed me, but we can get him tomorrow. When he's well he seems like a puppy, but not well he is just a miserable old hound. Tina went to church while we were over there and I took the children down to see Mary Ward's kids. Hers were in quarantine for mumps so I let ours play on their beach in the sun and they loved it. Larry was quite fascinated when I told him you were across that water. I don't believe it seemed so far after that. He told all the children that his Daddy was over there as his finger wandered vaguely across the horizon.

I went to the Grays for a cocktail late in the afternoon and met the son and daughter-in-law of Mrs. Blake—Peary Curtis's Aunt that has that convent looking house across from the stable. He was drunk but interested to hear of someone knowing Peary.

Yesterday was work day—washing, marketing etc. and the girls last night. Today I am going to N.Y. for Christmas shopping & spend[ing] the night with Mrs. Alworth.

      Loads of Love, Peggy

[Peggy to George]
[V-Mail]

#92
Nov. 24, 1943.

Dearest George,

I am at Margaret Alworth's desk and we are talking about what a wonderful, sweet husband I have. You are in my mind and heart each minute these days with the memories of last year at this time, even in this very building, so vividly in mind. I just phoned Carmen Chandler for a bit of news and to see if she would come for lunch. She came for the phone with two children hollering so we couldn't say much. Marne is still around with a six months deferment and they have two children, both boys. The Happels have moved to Garden City and have a boy if you remember. Hank expects to be drafted soon. She hadn't heard from the Von Amerongens.

At Schwartz toy shop yesterday I found the most wonderful Christmas present for you to give Larry. It's not going to be a Santy Claus gift but one from Daddy. You really should see it to appreciate it. I'll take a picture and send that. Now that you are really curious I'll say I found a pair of skis his size with a real harness, ski boots identical to ours and poles. You cannot imagine how cute they are. He will no doubt draw you pictures by the score. My love dear as always. Peggy

[Peggy to George]
[V-Mail]

#93
Nov. 26, 1943 Fri.

Dearest George,

We had a lovely Thanksgiving even though I couldn't get any Army or Navy boys for the occasion. I tried St. Albans Naval Hospital on Long Island, the Officers Club of N.Y.C., the White Ensign Club and the Coast Guard at Captains Island. Everyone had to "work as usual" I guess. The Peters came up though and brought Hodgey. We did have a turkey despite the shortage and some plum pudding I had made when I made yours. Incidentally, if the ingredients are available tell Madame Rebillet, the recipe for the pudding sauce is as follows: Mix 2 tablespoons of butter with one cup of powdered sugar. Add 1 egg well beaten & stir until smooth. Add ¾ cup of whipped cream. Flavor with 2-3 tablespoons of brandy. Canned milk will whip so that could be substituted for the cream. I know nothing of powdered eggs but imagine that could also be used in place of a fresh one if the amount could be measured. I wish you could have seen the children eat—two helpings of turkey and pudding. We toasted you in burgundy and it helped remove the resentment I had for watching Pete carve the first turkey in our new home. We took a walk with the children in the afternoon. This is a lovely clear day and the children are already outside. Robin is one year old today. What I wouldn't give for a cablegram? Yours, Peggy

[George to Peggy]
[V-Mail]

No. 52

27/11/43 Saturday

My dear Peggy:

Big news tonight is that we have hot water so Pop (Maj. Simons) is in taking a bath. He is an engineer who did all of his fighting in the last war, so he is back here in the headquarters with all the rest of us arm-chair-borne infantry men. He takes quite a ride from all of us, but is good natured about it. It has warmed up a bit and not quite so much rain the last few days. I received two Christmas boxes from you yesterday, a box of candy [from] Aunt Gertrude, and a box from the Am. Linen Co. in Milwaukee, plus one from Art & Helen and a box with some soap, magazines etc. from Wally & Connie. Quite a haul. Last night Allen and Stipp came back from mess with a few drinks of wine to cheer them up so we had a few drinks of the bourbon you sent and spent quite an evening kidding and opening packages. Of course I have not opened my Christmas presents. I love you dear, George.

[George to Peggy]

Capt. G.R. Steiner AFHq
G-4 Sec APO 512, c/o PM New York
Nov. 28, Sunday.

My darling:

Just finished a bath so I feel comfortable and clean. M. Rebillet is feeling better now, the doctor took some x-rays and says he only has bad ulcers of the stomach. He got his radio fixed so we have had a good program of American music from the Army Station here.

Received your letter with the pictures of the dining room at home and that Christmas party. They both brought back many pleasant memories. I thought of F.M.[145] sitting in his leather chair at breakfast talking to us. I think of him and Jessie often. Sure would like to have a chat with them now. I kind of feel as if they are still looking after me some times.

[George to Peggy]
[V-Mail]

No. 53
Monday evening 29/11/43

My darling:

Sure I am thinking about you this evening, trying to picture just where I am going to meet you and how you will look when I return. Think I can see rather a happy smile among other scenes. Your Father sent me the very welcome news today that he and Irene were going to be with you over Christmas in Greenwich. Ask them to make a similar date for the first Christmas I am home. That little razor sharpener you

---

145   George's father, Frank M. Steiner.

sent works swell; it doesn't take long to use and gives a very sharp edge. Thank you. I have gotten letters written tonight thanking Ben Siedel, Roland Pollock, the Hoggsons, Ki and Teedie, the Wallaces and Karbergs for Christmas packages. I ate half of one of your hershey bars just now too. Sounds like [the] Peters were in a bad way, hope they patch things up. Wish so much that I was home with you tonight my dear. My love, George

[Peggy to George]
[V-Mail]

#95
Nov. 29, Mon.

Dearest George,

 This is a really exciting breakfast. Besides our usual group and a beautiful sunny morning, Grandma is with us. She is so thrilled with the house and children that it adds to the pleasure of having her. The house showed off fine too. I even had managed to get the brass door knobs polished and they shine like gold. I used up some precious gasoline and drove all three children to Harmon yesterday morning to meet Mother. She looks grand and sends her best love to you. We had a lovely drive back with her as the day was sunny and the kids were so thrilled to have a drive. Needless to say, we were too. Anna had a nice dinner for us when we arrived. Then we took a walk after the naps and Connie & Wally Hoggson dropped in for a drink. Mother has her mink coat and it is gorgeous. Mine should be here any day now. My knees just got weak trying hers on. I have never seen such a beautiful coat before anywhere. I must get dressed now and do the washing. The table has been deserted. We have two chicks with colds today. Robin & Georgia. Yours, Peggy

[Peggy to George]
[V-Mail]

#96
Wed. Dec. 1, 1943

Dearest George,

    We've had children with colds for two days and I missed writing you yesterday. They haven't felt very badly, but we had to keep them in bed. They are all well again this morning. Mother and I haven't done much but talk since she arrived. Monday night our girls' group met at Betty Phelps, the crippled girl, for dinner and more arguing about the Peace discussions I went to. Mother seemed to enjoy it. Tuesday, last night, we played ping pong in our basement—believe it or not. I made a cover of pressed wood to go over our iron porch table which has been put in the cellar for the winter. It is pretty wobbly but works fine if you don't lean on it. Mom's very good too. After that we put on aprons and helped Santy Claus repaint old toys. We did a magnificent job on the red fire engine with red enamel and aluminum paint. Also the old horse for Robin and even rejuvenated the old wheel barrow making it red, white & blue. Tonight Connie and Wally are coming for dinner. Mom sends her love and I wish I could have a few hours at least to show you how much I send. Yours, Peggy

[George to Peggy]
[V-Mail]

3/12/43 Friday

Peg dear:

    You will be surprised to hear that we went down to see that old classic "The Drunkard" complete with red checkered table tops, candle light, beer, and even tomatoes to throw at the actors, especially that foul and loathsome villain. Stipp, Little, Cronin and myself went down. I had phoned in the afternoon to get a table, but the woman who took my call was a volunteer worker who got things crossed up, so when we arrived we were told "no reservation," but we hung around and finally got seated right behind Howder who had dated an attractive English girl. So we insisted on introductions and ended up by moving up to join them. When it was over we even offered to escort them home through the dark streets, but Howder didn't seem to care for our company so we let them go. That made a pleasant evening especially with free beer. Howder, another officer and myself got hauled up somehow to sing Sweet Adeline which with my fine ear for music you can imagine was a success. Lot of fun anyway. My love dear. George

[Peggy to George]
[V-Mail]

#98
Dec. 4, Saturday

Darling.

Mom and I went to N.Y.C. yesterday and wore ourselves down being gay. We wore our mink coats for the first time and felt so dressed up we hardly dared to move. They are so beautiful and I cannot tell you in a letter how thrilled I am to have such a lovely coat. Someday I will try to tell you though. We met Carmen for lunch and she looked wonderfully well. I had almost forgotten what a swell girl she is. Marne and she may join me on a ski weekend in February. (Maybe I'll take Larry on his skis you are giving him for Christmas. I have nearly finished the heavy wool socks for him.) We had dinner last night with Mrs. Alworth at the Savoy. She is always so peppy and so much fun. Our eyes nearly dropped out when she produced a ukulele and her spectacles and music and showed us what she'd been learning. You cannot imagine a funnier sight. (Robin is so cute now. He patty-cakes, plays peek by covering his ears instead of his eyes, waves bye-bye and eats anything in sight.) A long letter soon. Yours, Peggy

[George to Peggy]

[#]56
Capt. G.R. Steiner
AFHq G-4 Sec APO 512
c/o PM New York N.Y.
5 December 1943

My darling Peggy:

If Larry gets as big of thrill out of "my" Christmas present to him as I got reading about it, I will be very pleased. You sure do build up Daddy's stock with our kids. It flatters me as well as pleases me because I figure it must just be a reflection of your own feelings. And your good opinion is my one most prized possession. To keep it well shined up is one of my principal incentives. Most of the things I do are held up before the mirror of your opinion to see if they look all right, with the result a good many times being a change, so I can look again with a satisfied smile saying "Yes I think Peggy would pass on that." So when I check myself that way, it gives me confidence and satisfaction in what I do. Of course I am not always pleased with the picture I see, leading me to grumble a bit at the necessity of exerting myself to rub off the tarnish. There is always my ruinous habit of wanting to put off doing some work which I know should be finished off at once. You know well my ingenuity of thought in proposing perfect arguments in favor of procrastinating especially when some unpleasant situation must be ironed out. Anyway, you see you are mighty close inside me my dear, kind of a part of me that is always ready to prompt me and then lend a helping hand. Then when I become conscious of your presence with me it always leads to cheerful thoughts for you are quite an originator of happiness and goodness.

You see I am just fumbling around in my mind to say I love you, need you, and appreciate your love so very much my dear. Will you kind of think of these feelings when you pin on some flowers I have asked to have sent to you for Christmas day, and remember how much I would like to take you in my arms, to hold you while I told you all this and much more.

Now to turn to a bit of news, as you must know what goes on. My good friend Schutz is in a direful predicament. Someone stole his jeep. He was up here today to get some helpful advice from us "professional" supply people. Allen, Stipp, Sparks and myself offered our best which at times was more fun for us than it was for him. We were very ready to tell him the value and to offer helpful suggestions such as referring him by date and number to circulars stating that losers of G.I. transportation were held responsible unless they had thoroughly demobilized the vehicle in addition to locking it. He had the rotor which he had removed from the distributor, but we were shocked to learn that he had not removed any of the wheels nor even chained the vehicle to a tree. You can see we helped him a lot. Incidentally, this theft of GI vehicles is of surprising frequency with very few recoveries.

I don't believe I have told you the funny story Allen's wife wrote. She and a number of others whose husbands are overseas instituted a friendly and thoughtful practise of dropping in to call upon the wives of officers who had newly departed for overseas.

On one occasion they went to call upon such a wife whom they did not know very well to cheer her up a bit and see if she would spend an evening with them. She met them at the door of her home in a negligee and asked them in rather reluctantly.

On the hall table they noticed an officer's cap and upon walking into the living room they found a captain's blouse on the davenport. Since her husband was a lieutenant, they figured some else was already helping her to forget her loss. Some of the boys laugh when Allen tells them the story and then [they begin] to look a bit concerned. I just laugh.

I was duty officer last night. Allen and Sparks came back after dinner to take Col. Bolan and myself over the rocks at bridge. Of course we just held bad cards. Allen is on duty tonight so I guess I will go in to say good night, before I go up the hill to bed.

From what he mentions and reads to us of his wife's letters she sounds like an interesting likeable person. I should like to meet her. Some day perhaps we shall all have dinner together.

He is a funny sort. Anyone would have a rough time trying to impose upon him yet he came in about half an hour early to relieve me so I could go down to breakfast this morning. He has had to dig in hard to get his law education and get a start in the world so he is gruff and sarcastic, still under it all he is considerate and helpful in an unobvious way. Freckled face, straight nosed, blunt-spoken with a keen mind and a good sense of humor, I think I should miss the guy if we go different ways.

Peg I want you in my arms so very much. I am afraid I am awfully in love with you. Do you wear a pretty nightie for our Monday dates? End of the page or I would tell you my thoughts.

George

[Peggy to George]

#99
1943
Dec. 5, Sunday P.M.

My Dearest George,

Well, I have lots of news for you tonight. Yesterday Ki called me from New York. He and Harriet had just arrived at the Savoy. He was in to attend some meeting to be held here tomorrow and may stay until Tues. They are having a gay time seeing shows and doing the town like we will when you get home. Mrs. Alworth and they came out on the 12:25 today and saw us all, had dinner, and admired our house. Georgia clung to Ki like a debutante and he loved it. He played with them all the time he was here and even brought them out some presents which they loved. I do hope they can have a baby soon. He seems to have become pretty keen on the subject. Did you ever think Ki would be interested in anything so commonplace as a baby? They both looked fine and were very keen on the house. I was disappointed that the curtains haven't come yet. Helen Steiner is in town too, but she couldn't make it today. Her son-in-law is back from Vladivostok and being reassigned to Santo Domingo. Her daughter is going with him and they leave in a few days. What a break? On the phone Helen said Frank had dislocated his shoulder badly out shooting by trying to hold an outboard motor onto a rowboat when it started to get away from him. He still has it in a sling. I haven't seen Frank. You know Helen's stories. Chances are the next time I hear it, the duck will have dislocated its shoulder trying to pull Frank into the boat.

After I returned them to the to the train I came home to find Jessie Bedford here with Mussey Ballard and all their children which consists of Jessie's two and Wendy Ballard. I got your letter out in which you mentioned Bill Ballard. She said he is a Major now, but only heard that through his Mother as she has never written since he went overseas.

I just listen[ed] to Drew Pearson[146] and the news. He is enraged as everyone should be at the refusal of the senate to allow soldiers to vote.[147] Already they must be afraid of you boys. He says they are

---

146   Journalist Andrew Pearson (b. 1897, d. 1969) had a radio show on the National Broadcasting Company (NBC) radio station called "Drew Pearson Comments" from 1941-1953.

147   The Soldier Voting Act of 1942 declared that anyone serving in the U.S. Armed Forces was entitled to vote in federal elections. In reality, however, it was not implemented in an effective, timely enough manner to allow for the majority of overseas service members to participate. Some estimate that only 28,000 service members out of four million were actually able to vote in the 1942 election (National WWII Museum, "The Soldier Voting Act and Absentee Ballots in World War II.").

In anticipation of the 1944 election, efforts to streamline and standardize absentee soldier voting were proposed in the Green-Lucas Service Men's Absentee Voting Bill. Opponents of the bill were less against the idea of soldiers absentee voting and more concerned by what they perceived was the federal government's overreach into states' rights by creating a centralized absentee voting system. Of particular interest to many of the opponents was the notion that if the federal government consolidated the absentee voting process, states would no longer be able to enforce a poll tax (traditionally used by Southern states to disenfranchise their Black voters).

The bill was revised repeatedly before finally failing to come up for a vote. Instead, a substitute compromise was passed on December 4, 1943 awarding states the power to decide how to handle absentee voting for their service-member residents. Unsurprisingly, all 13 Democratic representatives of poll-tax states voted in favor of the compromise (Trussell, "Soldier-Vote Bill Shifted By Senate To Let States Rule.").

willing to vote that you all go overseas to fight and die, but you can't vote in the democracy you are fighting for. He suggests that everyone pick out one of the senators and write to him. I'm going to do it.

Alph Beane is on leave for a week and he also called a few minutes ago with Jeane and his Mother. Jeane had on a new mink coat too but it is not nearly as beautiful as mine. Alph was so annoyed over the lousy break you've had on rank that he couldn't talk of much else. He claimed it was the fault of some incompetent adjutant whose job it was to take care of such matters when an officer was changed from the USA to overseas duty. I'm going to have lunch with Jeane next Tues. in N.Y.C. She surely looked good to me. She is always so sunny and smiling.

The girls are acting worse each day it seems. They promised to stay through the winter if I gave them the raise. However they seem to do less work each day and become increasing insolent and disagreeable as if to force me to fire them. I will too as soon as I can see a ray of hope of getting most anything else.

The Patton incident[148] has certainly raised a ----- over here. It is finally dying down now, but we've had it hashed and rehashed for nearly two weeks in every paper and each radio program. Personally

---

As a result of the compromise, Congress recommended the states review their existing absentee voting legislation and make appropriate updates. Opponents to the compromise rightfully feared many states were not interested in making official changes to improve soldiers' access to absentee ballots. Perhaps most importantly, under state supervision the enforcement of personal registration requirements to vote (also traditionally used to disenfranchise voters of color and including the poll tax), which had been eliminated under the 1942 bill, would now be waived or implemented as the state chose.

148 In two separate incidents in August 1943, U.S. Army Lieutenant General George Patton slapped and threatened two service members languishing in Sicilian evacuation hospitals. Patton believed the servicemen were shirking their duties at the front, however, today it is widely accepted that both men were suffering from shell shock which did not receive the same recognition in the 1940s as it might now (Lovelace, *Slap Heard around the World*, 81-82.). The first man assaulted, 26-year-old Private Charles Kuhl, wrote about the incident in a letter to his family. Kuhl was suffering not only from what was diagnosed at the time as psychoneurosis, but a high fever and malaria. Patton slapped him and threw him out of the hospital, infamously kicking him in the rear. Patton went further the next time, threatening the second man, Private Paul Bennett, with his pistol while declaring he ought to shoot Bennett himself (Ibid., 88.). Bennet, diagnosed with dehydration and combat fatigue, had begun to cry while Patton spoke with him, which had infuriated the Lieutenant General. Both incidents were immediately reported to Eisenhower who ordered Patton to apologize to the men and sought to suppress stories of the incident from reaching the press (Ibid., 89.). Newscaster Drew Pearson broke the story about Kuhl's assault on November 21, 1943. Known for his brash behavior but deemed essential to the war effort, Patton was never formally disciplined (Ibid., 83, 84.).

I think it's a shame it ever got out at all. Eisenhower[149] had covered it two months ago. That is one drawback of our free press.

I am so sorry to hear that you are suffering from the cold. If there is anything I can send you, please write for it as they accept packages easily with a request. I do hope you and Schutz can find an apartment closer to the HDQ.

If you requested a film of the children and had some way to see it over there, I could send you a new colored one. Perhaps this isn't practical. But it is an idea anyway. They are so cute now and movies are so much better than the snapshots.

We miss you so much, my darling, and I've gotten so that I'm not quite fair in judging girls who still have their husbands and are kicking because they are reclassified as 1A.[150] This has just happened to Bill Bowden. Pete is still roaming the country—now goose shooting in South Carolina. I cannot figure that out. Could he be doing some secret work with radio that would exempt him?

Tomorrow night on our date we will have it at 10:00 o'clock your time. From Stars and Stripes I figure with your change in time that we are then five o'clock here.

Dad is coming down Xmas eve to stay until the 30th when Mom will go back with him. I am so happy always to have them with me, but the sooner the holidays are over the better I will like it. The way we use to feel about Christmas is so completely gone with you away and the war in all our hearts that except for the thrill to the children I'd like to let it go by unnoticed. We will have peace on earth and good will to men again someday and then the gay parties and beautiful carols and decorations will gladden our souls and mean more for the ordeals we have had to obtain them once more. Then we must keep the world that way.

---

149 Dwight D. Eisenhower (b. 1890, d. 1969). As a lieutenant colonel in 1942 Eisenhower headed Operation Torch, the Allied invasion of North Africa. In the summer of 1943, as a full general, Eisenhower then directed the amphibious landings of Allied forces in Sicily and mainland Italy.
150 A 1A draft classification meant the man in question was considered available and fit for military service.

I have mailed you some literature on these peace studies I have been so interested in. After you read the papers you will notice they stress the necessity of periodic councils of Allied peace planners. Tonight Drew Pearson predicted that that will be one of the announcements tomorrow when we finally get the report on the Tehran conference.[151]

Ford did not come on the Gripsholm.

That about covers the news from here. Don't forget our dates are Mon. 10:00 your time. The children will usually be sitting here on the couch with me. If you could just see their little faces when they get your letters, you would write every day. The story of the little Arab was wonderful. I can't believe you just thought that up. I did have lots of questions, but we ended up with a discussion of deserts which seemed tremendously interesting to them both. It must be a child's idea of paradise to find a place where there are sand piles as far as they could see.

My love and kisses as usual. How I wish I could give you the real thing. Someday—someday etc. etc. etc. If I'm not living on memories, then it's always "someday"...

Yours. Peggy

[Peggy to George]
[V-Mail]

#99B:

Wed. Dec. 8, 1943

Dearest George

There is great excitement here this morning as Dexter Ford[152] is back for a while and then reports to Dallas for Naval Air Cadet

---

151 The Tehran Conference took place between November 28 and December 1, 1943. U.S. President Franklin Roosevelt, British Prime Minister Winston Churchill, and Soviet Premier Joseph Stalin met at the Soviet Embassy in Tehran, Iran to discuss opening a second front in western Europe. The three leaders had dissenting points of view regarding plans for post-war Germany and Poland, the Soviet Union's proposed borders, and a post-war international organization but they did agree to guarantee Iran's independence when the war had concluded (as an Axis-aligned country Iran had been occupied by British and Soviet forces).
152 One of Peggy's cousins on her mother's side.

training. As usual Georgia and Larry are very excited to see a man. Larry controls himself but Georgia makes no attempt to hide her emotions. She clings to him and cannot even talk—just keeps muttering—uh uh uh. I asked her what I'm going to do if at sixteen she grabs every man she sees around the legs and mutters only uhs and ohs. She answered "I don't know." You better hurry home and make a normal girl out of your three year old daughter. I took Mom, Dexter, Ruth Black, Mrs. Bigelow and her sister and Harriet (Teedie) to [the] Savoy bar for cocktails. I had a visit with Ki before we went in but he couldn't join us. You'll be glad to know I impressed him in my furs and Twyeffort suit. That's quite an achievement. I took the rest except Teedie and Ruth to [the] Yale Club for dinner and then Dexter and I went to "Rosalinda." Mom went back to the hotel with Mrs. Bigelow. We got home pretty late. I also had a nice time at Jeane Beane's lunch yesterday. She is so sweet. I have a package of wool shirts ready to mail you. We'll take the children over now to send them. Yours, Peggy

[Peggy to George]
[V-Mail]

#100
Dec. 9, 1943 Thurs.

Dearest George,

Dexter is about to catch the morning bus and then he goes up to Middleville. He isn't down for breakfast yet and only has twenty minutes but I guess he'll make it. We didn't find much excitement besides the children yesterday. Georgia gave him quite a rush as I told you. Then we rode the bicycles up to Wambacks for air in the tires and last night we had a ping pong tournament. As the ball dashed under the wood pile a fat mouse ran out and we chased the poor thing until I swung at it with the ping pong paddle and actually hit him. Then we gave the old fire engine a final coat of paint and turned in. I had a letter from you yesterday telling about your Thanksgiving. I'm glad the bourbon was on hand. Send me a request for more and I'll see what I can do. Must get Dex to the bus. My love darling. I've sent your shirts—hope they keep you warm. Peggy

[George to Peggy]
[V-Mail]

9/12/43 Thursday

Peg dear,

 Here it is my day off so I have just been lazy this morning. I have not left the apartment and it is noon. You see I found a copy of Treasure Island or rather *L'Il du Tresor* so I was looking up some of our old friends. I am going to have some fun someday introducing Long John Silver, Ben Gunn, Dr. Livesey and the rest to Larry, Georgia, and I suppose Robin too. It is a cool day here, but clear. Think I will take a walk this afternoon then see if I can find someone to go to a show tonight. There is not a great deal to do with time off, especially since we do not have any transportation. It seems rather ridiculous too because all the other sections with the exception of G-4 have vehicles practically on a basis of 1 each per officer. Schutz found his jeep incidentally, it was stolen from in front of the Red Cross, and run till out of gas. Miss you dear, George

[George to Peggy]
[V-Mail]

No. 58
9/12/43 Thursday

My darling:

 Good evening. When I went up to the headquarters at noon today the mail orderly came staggering into our room with a pile of packages. Allen and Stipp beamed at the sight of them until the whole load was left on my desk with one small meagre letter for Allen none for Stipp and four for me. So you can just think of me sitting over at my desk in the debris of many packages, my mouth full of chewing gum, candy, and fruit cake, counting my razor blades and soap while I read my letters and make nasty faces at Allen and Stipp. If the fruit cake gets too stale before I finish it or if there is some of the candy I don't like, I will consider letting them have a bit of it. Tonight Schutz, Helms, and myself went down to see a show at the Red Cross, arriving about 20 minutes early to get seats. There was a band concert in the same theatre preceding the movie and most everyone at the concert stayed for the movie, so we walked back up to our apartment without seeing a show. Good night my dear. Yours, George

[Peggy to George]
[V-Mail]

#101
Dec. 11, Sat.

Darling,

This is really a good old freezing morning. The sun is out but a strong north wind is blowing. Yesterday I spent with Frank (gardener) and two of Mr. Hvolbeck's men and a truck over at Armonk getting some bushes and small pines for planting around the house and in the woods. We dug up a nice spruce for a[n] Xmas tree and Frank is down [in the] cellar now fixing a box to plant it in until after the holidays. Larry and Georgia are so excited about Santa Claus that they talk of very little else. Right now they are each writing him a final appeal and also you are to be scribbled to this a.m. Robin is still in his high chair eating bacon. He is so wise now you wouldn't believe it. How right you were when you said he seemed ahead of the others at his age. He even says "Bye-Bye"—"Mama" and "num-num" already. Mother took us all to the Women's Exchange for lunch yesterday and the kids were so thrilled and behaved so well. Even the table manners were fine. We had quite a few compliments. Yours, Peggy

[Peggy to George]
[V-Mail]

#102
Dec. 13, Mon.

Dearest George,

We have some snow on the ground this morning and the kids are thrilled to death. It isn't even enough to cover the grass, but they don't care. Sat. Mom and I enjoyed the theatre very much. We saw Helen Hayes in "Harriet" (Beecher Stowe) and Paul Robeson[153] in "Othello." They both were excellent. We had Jesse Bedford with us in the evening and I took them to [the] Yale Club for dinner. It was very nice and they serve the least expensive meal in town now. Yesterday we were home with the children all day. Ginny Street phoned me and came to call with a Greenwich friend and the friend's year old baby daughter. Gordie is on Atlantic convoy duty now but gets in to N.Y.C. about every two months. She looks fine and I'll see her in town some day. There were too many children to do much visiting yesterday. Last night I left Mom for a few hours and went to the Grays for supper. It was very nice. Joe Bridge is inducted Thurs. so it was a farewell to him. Don't forget at five tonight. Yours, Peggy

---

153 Paul Robeson (b. 1898, d. 1976) was an athlete, human and civil rights activist, singer, and actor. Well-known for his stirring performances (especially that of "Ol' Man River"), he achieved international fame playing the titular character in Othello in London. After lengthy tours performing various roles across Europe, he returned to New York City to play Othello on Broadway, becoming the first Black actor to perform as Othello with a supporting, non-Black cast (Whitman, "Paul Robeson Dead at 77."). Later in his life, Robeson's quest for racial justice and an expansion of civil rights often found him performing for and interacting with prominent labor unions, leading to accusations that he was a member of the Communist party (an accusation he privately denied). Although out of favor in the United States for a time, internationally he remained celebrated for his artistry and devotion to human rights advocacy. India's former prime minister, Jawaharlal Nehru, once described Robeson as, "one of the greatest artists of our generation [who] reminds us that art and human dignity are above differences of race, nationality and color" (Ibid., 30.).

[George to Peggy]

[#]59
Capt. G.R. Steiner
AF Hq G-4 Sec
APO 512, c/o PM New York
13 December

My darling:

Guess I will have to mend my ways about writing to you. Think it has been three or four days since I last wrote. I have just finished supper and come back up to the office.

It is Monday night so of course I have you in my thoughts a little more than usual if that be possible. You would be surprised at all the places you have been with me since I left the states. But my image making is not a very satisfactory substitute for your own reality. Still it helps to remember how you walk and how you talk, vivacious, so full of life and interest, and so pretty.

Peg I love to see you all dressed in a lovely evening gown when I know the principal reason is to please me. And it does. I would like to see you in your new coat, even wouldn't mind helping you get in it on our way to the show. I keep trying to think of how long it will be until you are in my arms again but it seems so far away. It is easy to remember how white and even your teeth are when you smile, just how your nose has that cute dip in it that I like to run my finger down, because you pretend to be provoked. You see I wish very much you were with me tonight. - - - - - At this point [the dashes] Allen came back from dinner and has been bothering me with conversation for about an hour. You know, kind of like Colby and I might talk along, sort of an enjoyable pastime about how we ought to settle things up after the war, how we would like to live, about people we have known, just a rambling interesting talk. Well you will surely meet him when the war is over. Don't know why I should go to the trouble of introducing you to such an ornery, freckle faced guy who argues with me though.

Last night Allen and I gave Maj. Sparks and Col. Bolan a lesson at bridge. The night before last I played with an English boy and we gave Hayes and a Scotch officer a good trimming. Hayes was up at Rome with me.

Work has let up a little the last few days, but there is still enough to keep us busy. Heyduck[154] and Adcock[155] are not "Empire builders" so our section is small and as a whole is as efficient as a staff section can be expected to be. I don't need to tell you what the result is of rapid growth, lack of time to investigate actual needs coupled with self seeking, unscrupulous, loud mouthed people who are to be found in any group always ready to build themselves up regardless of the damage done to the war effort or other people involved in it. You find this type here also setting up needless offices then over staffing them in order to build up an important looking position for themselves. I suppose it is inevitable, sometimes even amusing. So far I have no particular like nor dislike for the two men heading up this section, but I do have an honest respect for their intelligence, experience and conscientious application to the job before them.

Had a very nice letter from George Doerr Sr. today. I was surprised to learn that Father and Mother had been here once. Somehow I never remember hearing them mention it. I am glad to have found that out.

Well my darling this has turned into a strange rambling sort of a letter. Guess I had better start my walk up the hill, thinking of you all the way along and finally wishing so much when I get into bed that you were there with me.

Tell Larry and Georgia that I sent them my love and [a] couple of big kisses. And I do like to hear of Robin's adventures in this big world. You gave me quite a picture of the two of them teaching him to walk.

Good night my darling, George

---

154   Colonel Lawrence E. Heyduck (b. 1893, d. 1970).
155   Major General Clarence Lionel Adcock (b. 1895, d. 1967) helped plan the Allied invasion of North Africa and served as a senior supply officer on Dwight D. Eisenhower's staff for the Algerian and Italian campaigns.

[George to Peggy]
[Handwritten on U.S. Army Air Force stationery]

#60
Capt. G.R. Steiner
APO 512 AFHq G-4 Sec
c/o PM New York N.Y.
14/12/43

My darling Peggy:

Here I have your V-letter of Dec. 2 on the desk before me. That is pretty good time. Wish I could get home that quickly. Sorry to hear you have a family cold. How is the heating situation? Does the furnace work well, the house seem well insulated, and the ration board allow you enough oil?

This is some stationery that Frank and Helen sent to me in a Christmas package which I had much fun opening. I wanted to have some flowers sent to Mamie and Helen on Christmas day. I don't know for sure where they will be. If they stop through New York will you send them some flowers from you and me.

I hope my arrangements to have some flowers for you to wear for me will work out. What about letting me pin on your corsage next New Years eve? And be sure to have some mistletoe too. Of course this year I don't want you to have even a little piece of it in the house. I surely would like to take you in my arms tonight. Then I would take you upstairs, undress you, lay you in our bed, and then—well I would go brush my teeth, of course wouldn't I.

Anyway, don't forget you have a date with me on New Years eve and I will be thinking of you my dear, wishing many good things for you in 1944. Guess I will have something on you there too, for a while at least I will be a whole year ahead of you.

You might tell Larry that I have a piece of clover right here on my desk that I picked out on the lawn at the other house this summer. Tell him I will bring it home to show to him some time.

I am afraid that I am going to be mighty envious of you Christmas morning. My love dear to the girl I am so very fond of, good night.

Yours always, George

[Peggy to George] #102

Tues. Dec. 14

My Darling,

Tonight, I am in a state of worry as Mother has come down with the "flu" bug that everyone is having and I fear that Christmas will find us all in bed. The bug is very contagious, but not as virulent as that of the last war. As of this moment, however, there is no indication that the kids are coming down with anything.

Our date last night was a trifle interrupted as Mom was in bed and at five the children went up for their baths, and insisted on seeing her. We had a glass of sherry together afterwards, though, and visited about Sun Valley, and even Key West. What a day it will be when we can start in on a new set of experiences and leave the old ones for a while.

You and Allen and Stipp have surely stretched that bottle of bourbon. I am only serving rum in the house now as that is all we can buy, but there are a few bottles of good gin, scotch, and bourbon which I have put away for you and would love to send you now if I could. I am glad so many of your Xmas boxes arrived o.k. It won't seem much like a holiday but at least you know a lot of people are thinking about you and wish you were here. We expect Dad on Xmas eve.

I am having quite a bit done around the brook directly in front of the house. If you remember, last spring most of that ground was swampy and the brook seemed to flow all over. I got a good price on some fill and am having the lowest spots filled in and the bed of the brook dug lower. The little pond above the dam is frozen solid and is almost smooth enough to skate on. That is for the children—a bit small for us. When Santa brings their skates, I am going to flood it and they can practice every day. It won't take more than one load of water like we wheeled to the vegetable garden this spring to flood the whole thing. The storm windows are all on and we are warm as can be, with the exception of the attic playroom. I have to have a larger radiator put in there and that one put in the hall to fix that up properly. The curtains are going to be hung the end of this week and so when I take pictures for you on Christmas we should look pretty well finished.

We hear so much now about Marshall going over to be Commander-in-Chief of the western invasion and Eisenhower coming here to do his job that in spite of all common sense I find myself wondering if that might bring you back. It is too much to look forward to the end of the war—even the european phase of it before seeing you again. It all progresses so slowly nowadays, if at all.

Maggy Seymour has asked me if you have received and forwarded any letters to her husband as yet. When you do, let me know and comment on your opinion as to the chances of such reaching the destination so I will have something to tell her.

Poor Doxie is at the "vets" nearly every week lately either with cankers in his ears or a tied up intestinal tract. It looks as if he is cracking up. However, when he is well, he is a[s] much a playful pup as ever. Right now, it is his ear again, but I have been nursing it myself this time and it hasn't gotten any worse in the last few days so maybe he won't have to go this time.

I took Robin to see Dr. Close this afternoon for his regular examination, and the poor old bachelor made such a fuss over him that I almost told him he should have three or four of his own. The kids certainly love that man and adore to go even if they know he will give them an injection. Today Robin weighed 24 ½ lbs. and was 30 ins. tall. Isn't that quite a contrast to a year ago. I just looked up in Larry's baby book for your comparison, and on Larry's first birthday in Miami, he weighed 24 lbs. and 7 ounces. Isn't that amazing that they should be so close. They look and act a lot alike too, but Robin is much livelier, even more so than Georgia which frightens me when I can't manage her. She surely has made a man out of Larry, though. After Scot (7yrs.) was here the other day, Larry said, "Momie, Scot hit me hard up on the path and I didn't cry and I hit him back just as hard as he hit me." I was so glad and told him so, which probably isn't ethical, but I don't care. He won't be the kind to ever pick a fight any more than you were, so I don't have to worry about that. I'll never say that to Georgia or Robin, though.

The girls are down in the cellar playing ping pong on the table I made. They don't sound very good, but I guess they are having a good time. As Xmas gets near their dispositions seem to improve. I went to an agency in town last week to put my name in for after the holidays. They just laughed at me. Said I'd have to pay at least 50 dollars more to get anyone which was doubtful, and then they wouldn't do half the work I was asking of them. In fact just to mention three pre-school children to one nurse in the household would make them uninterested regardless of wages.

I must write Colby and Ki tonight so I'll end this now.

My love to you Darling and may you not be too unhappy on Christmas Day. We'll have a drink to you about 6:30 your time and it will be that you will be safely home with us next Christmas.

All My Love. Peggy

[George to Peggy]
[Handwritten on U.S. Army Air Force stationery]

#61
Capt. G.R. Steiner
AFHq G-4 Sec APO 512
c/o PM New York N.Y.
15 December 1943

Dearest Peggy:

Just been wondering where I would be December 15, 1944. Hope it will be with you, and it probably will be. If you will remember the date and remind me, I will take you out to dinner, take you to a show, then go somewhere for dancing and a drink, then help you into your nightie and promise not to fall asleep right away. Think you can remember? Anyway that is what I would like to be doing tonight instead of sitting up here in the office writing a letter and smoking a pipe.

It is my day off tomorrow, so I have been finishing off a few odds and ends so Stipp or Allen won't get stuck with them tomorrow after I had started them.

That was my reason given for not going down to a movie, but the principal reason was I kind of wanted to write you tonight. So if you read real carefully between the lines you might find something about how I love you written all through the letter.

The ring you gave me is always on my finger where you put it that night, remember? It is really a magic ring, bright and handsome. All I have to do is look at it or if it is dark rub my finger over sort of like Aladdin's lamp, then all sorts of happy events, humorous situations, and pleasant memories come rushing up just like a real vision. Right now it brings out a very dear face close to mine with lips I love to kiss, and then there is a rather reproachful looking brown face between two out-stretched brown paws a bit jealous of all the attention you get when I hold you in my arms. Give him a pat on the head and tell him I will be home to see him one of these days, and tell him I won't forget to toss him a few bits of bacon from my breakfast plate either.

Darling, I don't remember if I told you that I received those two pictures you sent me of the dining room at home and the Christmas party. I wonder if I was foolish enough to drive you right straight home. I wouldn't be that foolish tonight. Thank you for the pictures, one reminded [me] of course of F. M. sitting in his red leather chair at the breakfast table with his watch laying there before him but not paying a bit of attention to the time as he talked to us. Gee but I miss him and Jessie.

Take good care of yourself for me my dear and before you know it you will find yourself right in my arms where you belong.

With my love, yours, George

[George to Peggy]
[V-Mail]

No. 62

Dear Peggy:

Had rather a good day off yesterday, took a long walk which I just wrote Georgia about. I didn't tell her how much I would have liked to have you along. I walked by an old time fort but it had barbed wire around it so I could not get in to look around and was so annoyed. There was an old Frenchman with a white full beard, carrying an old muzzle loading, double-barreled shot gun, and about 14 birds hanging from little leather thongs. They looked like prairie chicken. I [had] gotten talking to him and he said what with the shortage of meat and rationing he just went out once a week and brought back a nice bunch of birds for his wife and himself. Yours, George

[George to Peggy]

[#]63
Capt. G.R. Steiner
AFHq G-4 Sec APO 512
c/o PM New York, N.Y.
18 December 1943

Hello Peg,

How might you be doing this evening? Trouble is it is still afternoon there. A week before Christmas. Must be making a lot of preparations for Christmas. Hope you managed to get a Christmas tree. Of course you won't be able to do a very good job of decorating it without my help or should I say supervision. I think some of those decorations I got that first Christmas we spent in Forest Hills will probably be on the tree.

You wouldn't ever guess what I was thinking about walking up the hill in the star light tonight. Do you remember a beautiful church all filled with throngs of our friends, candle light, larkspur, bridal music, pretty bridesmaids, [and] a bunch of good for nothing ushers. Never will forget what a nice kiss you gave me in front of all those people too. You were so beautiful in your bridal gown, it is a shame I can only have you dressed like that once. But then there are a lot of other pretty clothes which I am sure you will be wearing for me.

Peggy this isn't much fun living along without you. Guess it must get a bit lonely for you. When it does remember I love you so much, and sure as anything I will be back there for you to tease one of these days. Why is it that you get so much amusement out of contemplating me in awkward circumstances I don't know. I do seem to get into them, though.

Hope you are over your cold and all well. Do take good care of yourself for me.

Peggy I adore you and while I can't be with you your letters are so very welcome. So many times during a day things are brightened up by thoughts of you.

      Yours dear, George

[George to Peggy]
[Typed V-Mail]

            No. 64
        Sunday, 19 December 1943

Dearest Peggy,

  Thought I would see if I could still type for a change. I would write this way more often, but cannot always get ahold of a machine. Noticed that you have stopped using one. Your writing is very legible on the V-mail so it does not matter.

  As usual I am wondering what you might be doing at this point a way back home. Whatever it is I would like to be participating even if you did put me to work. After I went to bed last night, I walked all through our house trying to picture just how everything looks. That dining room must be pleasant with those big windows looking out over the lawn. I was just thinking that with butter so short maybe there would not even be any waffles on Sunday morning. That little sitting room down stairs must have worked out nicely as a place for you to read and write when you are alone. Of course now with George and Irene there you probably use the living room. I would sure like to see young Robin scooting himself around on that kiddie car. How did the rooms come out for the girls? I have not got much of any idea of how you arranged our bedroom and dressing room, how about a description. Seems as if the beds must be to the left as you step into the room, with you sleeping in the one nearest the door, is that right? It must look a lot different outside now with all the leaves gone. Is anyone living in the nearest house, and do you see any of our neighbors?

You would get a laugh out of Schutz; he is really the wolf. He always has some girl on the line. Last week he got his boss to let him go up to an officer's rest camp for a few days. But before setting the date he made careful enquires to make sure that there would be some of the nurses going up at the same time. Then not happening to have met them, he arranges with the car dispatcher to have them put in the same car with himself and Capt. Helms. Well, by the time they arrived at the camp he had everything well in hand and all dated up to prevent any competition. He claims that he never dated a girl in high school, but he sure is making up for lost time now.

For once I am getting just about all the oranges that I can eat. There are baskets of them on the table at every meal. You see them growing all around here. Hope that they are getting some of them shipped up to England as that is one thing they have not had up there for several years now. Had a letter from Col. Smith saying that Peairs is up there now.

Maj. Stipp is now Lt. Colonel which is the first promotion that has been put thru in the G-4 section since I have been here and for some time before that I understand. That is the first one he has gotten since he went on active duty, and was very well deserved. He was with one of the first American outfits to land in [the] U.K., then came down here on the landings last fall, and commanded a battalion of armored artillery in the Tunisian campaign. He has been trying to get my promotion put through but after the deals I have had I will believe it when I see it. The last cable from the War Dept re[garding] my status was that I had been promoted to Capt. AUS in June of 1942 of which I had never been informed, so now they are forwarding copies of the special order covering that promotion which are necessary to establish my time in grade for promotion to major. That makes three separate times that I have now been officially promoted to Captain, some deal. Col. Smith had copies of all the correspondence sent to me on the recommendation for a majority initiated in February '42.

That was returned once for errors in spelling, once for wrong serial number, finally canceled due to transfer.

My love dear, George

[George to Peggy]

#65
Capt. G.R. Steiner
AF Hq G-4 Sec APO 512
c/o PM New York N.Y.
Monday
Dec. 20, 1943

My dearest Peggy:

Just got up here to my room and it is 11^{30}. Had to catch up on a bit of work this evening. But of course this being Monday night I have had you with me more than usual. Got too lazy to walk up the hill tonight so I caught a ride. That is never any trouble; there is so much traffic in fact that I have never had to wait more than five minutes for a ride. I presume that of course all the riding around at such hours is in connection with official duties.

The box with my shoes arrived today. Thank you very much. I will be glad to have them walking around Greenwich again. I sure will be glad to put on a white shirt and get away from all this hocus pocus.

Capt. Schutz, Maj. Ream and I are planning on getting a little feed together, look up a few drinks if possible and see if we can't celebrate Christmas eve a bit. Nell & Marg sent me a copy of Dickens' "Christmas Carol" which I am enjoying all over again. Darling I love you so very much. Miss you a little bit too.

My love dear, George

[Peggy to George]
[V-Mail]

#103
Dec. 20, Mon.

Dearest George,

    This week has made me realize how much I depend on writing you a morning letter to keep my morale for the rest of the day. You can bet the flu has hit pretty hard to deprive me of this pleasure for five days now. I am up and dressed this a.m. and we are all on the mend but still weak with coughs and Robin has diarrhea. Two men came out yesterday, Sunday, to hang the drapes and they really look lovely. Our room has draw drapes to the floor of a yellow background with sort of green vines and darker yellow [flowers]. Won't we be cozy in the evenings when the children are finally tucked in bed and we pull the cords and close ourselves in from the rest of the world? I'm trying to get enough film so I can take pictures of each room and send them to you. It would be so much better than any description I can write you. The weather stays cold which I hope will bring snow before Saturday. Larry and Georgia are sure Santy is waiting for snow before he can come. It would be a great disappointment not to have any snow I'm afraid. So many people have called lately to ask about you. Marg Adams, Connie & Wally, Eleanor & Jack Gray, Helen Meyers, etc., etc. They all receive the only news I have which is you are well but cold and we miss you very much. They ask me to send you their best when I write. We are all sending love too. Peggy

[Peggy to George]
[V-Mail]

#104
Dec. 21, Tues

Darling,

    We are a little stronger this morning. The children seem fine but turn white when they get out of bed so they are staying down another day. Mom and I were supposed to go to N.Y.C. this morning but have put it off another day. There are two men here putting another radiator in the third floor hoping to get it warm enough up there so we can use it. Marj. M^{ac}Cagney phoned me last night and we had a nice chat. I haven't talked to her for two years. She's such a sweet person. She is living in Brooklyn with her Aunt and taking care of her 2 year old daughter, Nancy. Mac is assigned to a Navy air squadron somewhere in the pacific. He's been gone since March. I have been thinking all night that if the girls continue to do less and less work I might let them go and approach Marj. on bringing her baby and coming to live with me. She's the only person that I have ever thought of who I believe would fit in with both me and the children. What would you think? It would save a lot of money, be company evenings, and the work wouldn't be what I'm doing myself now. Robin had Mom and me up pacing the floor with him all last night. Fever and nausea. Tina never budged. All my love, Peggy

[Peggy to George]
[V-Mail]

#105
Dec. 22, Wed.

Dearest George,

    Mother and I are waiting on the noon local to start back to Greenwich. We finally acquired enough strength this morning to get the ten o'clock express in to finish our Christmas errands and now go back out. I bought Dad a nice sweater from us, Robin a crib blanket which he badly needs, Mom a purse and nightie and the rest of your family I already wrote you. Yesterday all three children enjoyed a visit from Dr. Close. They seemed better from just seeing him except Robin. The flu went to his ear and we gave him sulfa-diazine all day yesterday. His fever broke about midnight and he's much better today. If it stays normal until tonight we can stop the drug. Why do we always have sickness at Christmas time? I expect they'll all be well by Saturday. Larry was outdoors a little while this morning and I believe Georgia can get out of bed this afternoon. We had lunch at the Biltmore and it made me feel so lonesome for you and the good times we used to have this time of year. The cocktail lounge has an enormous tree in the center of it and the room was filled with boys in their uniforms and their girls. I guess they know how lucky they are to be together, but I wanted to go up and tell them just to be sure they weren't wasting a minute of it. The Tripp florist called me to stop on my way home today. I'll tell you what I find. Yours, Peggy

[Peggy to George]
[V-Mail]

#105
Dec. 23, Thurs.

Darling,

I have someone very dear to us on either side of me here on the couch and we are each writing you a letter. They have stacks of letters all over the house which haven't been mailed as Momie is saving stamps and I guess the censors' patience. But today I have promised that these will be mailed. So you will have lots to read. They are each carrying your Christmas card around with them and have passed out kisses from them to everyone in the house. They always take hugs and kisses off all of your letters to me so now they are being generous with their own letters. The date of changing help here has finally arrived without any incident except by accident.

I didn't tell you but about two weeks ago Anna had a convulsion one morning which resembled an epileptic fit. I sent her to the Dr. afterwards but she had no history of previous attacks so we tried to forget it. However last night she and Tina went to Greenwich and she had another in the drug store. I feel sorry for her but I can never leave her alone with the children again. The spell itself is so dreadful to watch and so frightening that I don't ever want to have it on my mind that I'll see her in another if I keep her around. The children have finished their letters. All yours. Peggy

[Peggy to George]
[V-Mail]

#106
Dec. 24, Friday

Dearest George.

    A beautiful poinsettia plant I have here this morning from my darling husband who is so thoughtful of me even at the great distance which now separates us in miles only. And this afternoon I am to get a corsage too. I'll wear it trimming the tree tonight and all day tomorrow. Thank you, dear. We aren't to have any snow for Christmas I guess. The sun is out bright and it is nearly below zero this morning. We are all feeling all right but have coughs, but they don't bother any. We are expecting Dad any minute. His train is about getting into N.Y.C. now and so he'll be right out. Also we may have two Australian naval officers for the night and tomorrow. I'll give them our room as I can sleep in the third floor now. I put a cot up there this week. The radiators are fixed too so it keeps nice and warm. It will help to give some boys a good time even though I cannot hope someone is doing the same for you. The children's eyes are literally dancing this morning. How I wish you could see them! Mr. Hvolbeck has come to put in the play yard so now we must keep all eyes indoors. I'll be thinking of you dear every minute and will get some pictures. Love, Peggy

[George to Peggy]
[Handwritten on U.S. Army Air Force stationery]

Censored by Capt. Steiner

> Capt. G.R.Steiner
> AF Hq G-4 Sec APO 512
> c/o PM New York N.Y.
> 25 December 1943

Merry Christmas my dear,

    Been thinking of you all day in the happy surroundings of Christmas cheer. It is a big day for Larry and Georgia I am sure. I have been wondering just where you put the tree. I have looked at my watch many times saying, now Peggy is waking up to get dressed, now packages are being opened, breakfast, paper wrappings all over, lights and decorations on the tree. Gee I sure would like to have watched the kids with their packages. You probably are wearing the corsage I sent you. I'll bet George got our silver bowl out to mix up some good cheer. I think those skis for Larry were a wonderful idea.

    Last night was really a celebration with many woeful sights around today and no great deal of work turned out for Uncle Sam.

    It is six fifteen now so I am going down to get some turkey then see a movie with Allen, Schutz, and Ream. Will write more tonight in another letter. Love you so much my darling.

> Yours, George

[George to Peggy]
[Handwritten on U.S. Army Air Forces stationery]

Capt. GR Steiner, AFHq G-4
APO 512 c/o PM New York N.Y.

Censored by Capt. Steiner

Sunday
26 Dec. 1943

Dear Mrs. Steiner:

This will inform you that your husband has survived a most rigorous Christmas celebration. Fully intended to write you again yesterday, but never got to it.

Christmas eve Col. Donahue[156] and Maj. Little had a party for the G-4 section up at their villa. There are about fifteen of us in the section all of whom were present. That party started at 7^{30} so we could hear the President's speech[157] at 8^{00}. They are really a swell bunch, so we had a really good time, had some excellent whiskey, talked, and sang songs, [and] talked of Christmas at home. I was thinking of you during the President's speech thinking you were probably listening to it back in Greenwich. What time was it there incidentally? Everybody got feeling pretty good, but nothing

---

156   Colonel Joseph J. Donahue.
157   On December 24, 1943 Roosevelt delivered "Fireside Chat 27: On the Tehran and Cairo Conferences." In the speech, Roosevelt informs his listeners that there are over 3.8 million service members serving overseas and hints at the impending expansion of the war saying that by July of next year there will be five million. He expresses certainty that peace on earth will be realized and ensured, "though the cost may be high and time may be long."

An update then follows on the Cairo and Tehran conferences. Roosevelt and Churchill were joined at the conferences by Chiang Kai-Shek and Joseph Stalin, respectively. Referring to both leaders as "unconquerable men," Roosevelt explains that in addition to military matters, plans for the future were discussed, including the importance of disarming Japan and Germany. With regards to the Cairo Conference Roosevelt claims, "Today we and the Republic of China are closer together than ever before in deep friendship and in unity of purpose." Similarly, in summing up the Tehran Conference he declares, "I can say even today that I do not think any insoluble differences will arise among Russia, Great Britain and the United States." Ironically, he recognizes the need for self-determination for nations in the "Far East" but remains mute on the controversial topic of Poland's postwar borders.

Roosevelt also takes the opportunity to announce the appointment of Eisenhower to lead the combined Allied attack on Germany. Roosevelt again stresses the importance of the Allies remaining united and explains, "The doctrine that the strong shall dominate the weak is the doctrine of our enemies–and we reject it." Addressing the isolationists at home Roosevelt calls them "cheerful idiots" who truly believe "that there would be no more war for us, if everybody in America would only return into their homes and lock their front doors behind them." Peace must be defended and it is unrealistic to be unprepared to keep it by force.

A recording and transcript of this speech can be found by visiting millercenter.org and searching for the chat title or number.

unbecoming of an officer or a gentleman. Little got out a book of songs and we sang some of the most beautiful Christmas carols along with such fine old numbers as On the Road to Mandalay, There's a Tavern in the Town etc. Along about 11 I wandered out on the terrace to look up into a clear star lit sky to say Merry Christmas to Jessie and F.M., and tell them I am doing my best to live like they told me I should. Then there were the three stars up there that I have picked out especially for Larry, Georgia and Robbie. They are off to the east in a vertical row, first Larry on top, then Georgia and Robbie's is the bottom one.

Well Stipp and I took a couple of colonels home about 11^{30}, then went to a dance for a while. Ran into Maj. Schrect down there who was out at C&GS School with me, also Hayes, (from Rome) and two English officers I play bridge and eat with often, Price and Callahan, so we all walked a few blocks down to attend a catholic midnight service. Everybody was full of goodwill and good cheer so it really made you feel what a wonderful day Christmas is. After the service we went back to the dance for about an hour, had a few drinks and started home along about 2 AM in a British vehicle. The driver was not doing too well as he had evidently been given a drink here and another there, so after he had just about wrecked us we put him in the back seat and I did the driving.

When I finally got home I had a very pleasant surprise awaiting on my desk. My leather book of photos was open to the picture of my dear wife with those three grand kids, and lying on the other side of the book was a beautiful corsage of dainty little flowers, together with the enclosed note [a Christmas card from the Rebillets].

Well Christmas morning I got down on time somehow and felt fine. We managed to get quite a bit of work out between Allen and I, but Stipp and along with numerous others was feeling just horrible. The spirit of Christmas was very prevalent, with many pleasant greetings and visits. Schutz came up for quite a chat along in the afternoon. We had a couple of drinks before supper which was the main meal of the day complete with turkey and all. After dinner Schutz [and] Capt. Boger, with whom I had supper, went to see a movie—"Flesh and Fantasy" along with Ream and Allen who we met at the movie. On the way over to the movie we were walking up a very black street in the rain when I remembered something, so I told Schutz if he could turn on his flashlight I could probably produce a Christmas present right out of my pocket. He did so sure enough there was a package of hershey bars all wrapped in Christmas paper with a couple of little kittens for stickers which you had put on. So we each enjoyed a chocolate bar, thanks to you and it tasted very good.

After the show we stopped up at Ream's apartment for a snack. He lives in the same apt. as Schutz and I, a couple of floors below us, with the Bells a very nice old French couple who set the table very nicely for us with some fruit cake, sliced oranges in wine, nuts, and excellent wine. After that they came along with us upstairs to the Devevey's apt. where Schutz lives. They had crêpes suzettes, more wine, radio music, and a bunch of neighbors. I finally got to bed about one o'clock.

I wrapped a bunch of packages for the Rebillets and gave them a lot of the packages different people sent me. They were very pleased; especially little Mimie who really danced for joy. You tell Larry he was very pleased with the Hershey bars from Larry. They gave me a very nice bottle of brandy. I managed to get down by a quarter to eight this morning, but it was a struggle. Evidently most of the other sections did not work yesterday so as a result there was very little work sent into us today fortunately. Along about three thirty we were all cleared up so Sparks came in and he and I played Allen and Stipp a couple of games of cribbage.

So I have had dinner now and come back to write you, and now I am going home to bed. Here is hoping that by next Christmas we will be together. My love darling, George

[Peggy to George]
[V-Mail]

[#]106
Dec. 27, 1943

Dearest George,

    Our date tonight started a few minutes after five with a daiquiri in the living room made of rum you brought from Cuba. Mom and Dad joined us and Larry and Georgia were whipping around in their bathrobes. Larry had a Christmas commando helmet on his head and a wooden tommy gun in his arms from which he obtained a terrific noise. Doxie hid under the piano. Our date consequently wasn't exactly peaceful and alone but there was plenty of good cheer. Dinner followed with ducks and pheasants from Minneapolis. They certainly were marvelous but I won't tell you too much about that. A rummy game has just been finished and Dad won. Now we are alone listening to the radio and I have dressed especially to please you and my feet are very cold. The radio is on a subject which is a bit jolting to this line of thought but perhaps conducive to more apt ideas and considerations right now. It is Eisenhower's new appointment.[158] I am very excited about this naturally and can hardly wait to know how this will affect you. It surely is a great compliment to the men under him as well as to himself. That sort of superiority cannot be obtained by individual effort. I'll write an airmail on the children's X-mas. My corsage was lovely and I adored wearing it. I love you. P.

[Peggy to George]
[V-Mail]

#107
Dec. 29, 1943

Darling,

    We really have cold weather here now. The rhododendron leaves

---

158   On December 24, 1943 Eisenhower was appointed the Supreme Allied Commander of the Allied Expeditionary Force. In this post he will stay overseas and plan the invasion of Germany while General Marshall would remain in Washington, D.C., as chief of staff–an arrangement that satisfied officials in D.C. and service members abroad.

are curled tight this morning and our little pond is frozen clear to the bottom. Dad and I are about to continue a job we started yesterday of cutting the weeds and burning the brush up on the hill where we are going to let you build a barn some day. Dad also put a cable on that crooked larch tree to straighten it yesterday. If he would just retire and live with us here for a few months, this place would look fine. Last night we cooked some more of the ducks and pheasants Dad brought down and had the Blacks over—also Corp. Wayne MacFarlane[159] who is working in N.Y.C. in "strategic services." Then I asked Eleanor Grey and Penn Bridge. The pond in front of the big house next to us here is the most perfect ice skating rink you can imagine. I've given Larry and Georgia one lesson since Christmas and we may have another today. Dad put your skates on and he is really good. What fun we we'll have there when you are home. Yours, Peggy

[George to Peggy]
[V-Mail]

30 Dec. 1943

My darling:

I am just about all wrote out. It is my day off so I have been writing a lot of letters. One of them to Larry and Georgia was a lot of fun. Tell me what they say about my story on the elephant. Does Larry still call the beast an ephelant. Gee how I would like to see you all right now. Robin must be a lot of fun now. I am pretty proud to hear that he is beginning to talk already. A lot of letters came all together the last few days, so I am beginning to get caught up. Sorry to hear that Ford was not on the Gripsholm. I will always be thinking of you particularly at ten PM my time on Mondays.

     My love dear, George

---

[159] At the time of Peggy's letter, Wayne H. MacFarlane was the assistant superintendent of Minneapolis-Moline while Wayne's father was the president and general manger. During WWII Wayne volunteered for the U.S. Army and served in the Office of Strategic Services (OSS). The OSS was the first centralized intelligence agency in the United States and an important precursor to the Central Intelligence Agency (CIA).

[Peggy to George]
[V-Mail]

#108
Dec. 30, Thurs.

Darling,

    Your cablegram arrived yesterday while Dad and I were cutting brush. Larry came running up the path calling "Momie, Momie there is a cablegram from Daddy—run fast." I was sure he couldn't be fooling because he wouldn't have known the word cablegram. I certainly got to the house in a hurry. It was just what I wanted to hear. "All well." Thanks so much for adding those words to the seasons greeting. Today Dad and Mom leave so it will be pretty lonely for a few days until I get used to my solitude again. We are taking the morning express to N.Y.C. and having a visit with Aunt Mamie & Uncle George before Dad's train goes. They came into town Tues. a.m. and are leaving for Florida on Sun. Aunt Mamie is fine but as usual says G.A. is only fair. They aren't going to try and come out [but] I don't blame them. It is quite a trip. If there weren't so much sickness around I'd take the children in to see them. But the effort would be too great to add risking a sick spell again. I'm staying in to see Marg McCagney a little while then having dinner with Ann Hanan before I come back. My love. Peggy

[Peggy to George]
[V-Mail]

#109
Dec. 31, 1943 Fri.

Darling,

    Well tonight of all nights we should be having a date. When I put on your flowers I'll think of you looking so handsome in your tux and smelling so good when you put your arms around me and pin on the gardenias. Then at midnight I'll think of you kissing me Happy New Year and I'll give a little prayer that this will be a Better New Year for us and all the rest of the wives, husbands, and boys who are separated now. Uncle George and Aunt Mamie looked fine yesterday. Dad took them and Marg McCagney to [the] Biltmore for lunch. Uncle G. told a long story of how he has finally been recognized as a General. It seems your friend Capt. Hestad[160] sent him a Xmas card from China or India addressed to General Steiner. He was very pleased Marg had heard from Mac somewhere around New Georgia Is[land] I believe. He said he hoped to be home in July. The Navy is better than the Army on getting men home after a year or so out of the USA. Instead of poison ivy I sent Dad home this time with a very sore eye. A branch slapped across his eye ball while we were cutting brush. It really looked badly when they left. Mom cried over leaving me with the help situation so bad here, but it doesn't really worry me. How happy most of Europe's mothers would be just to have food and heat for their children. I still have Tina. Peggy

[Peggy to George]

#110
Sunday Jan. 2, 1944

Darling,

Well it's a week past Christmas but I'll have to tell you all about it. Dad came Christmas eve although we expected him before lunch. The Commodore Vanderbilt from Chicago was nine hours late. At the same time in the late afternoon I took Larry & Georgia over to meet a British Navy sub-lieut. who we were taking as a poor substitute for you. After the excitement of bringing home the Britisher and having Georgia embarrass him to death with hugs and kisses and Grandpa following a few minutes later by cab and many more hugs and kisses for him, we all had a steak dinner and talked about Santy. The children's eyes were popping out of their heads and we had to clean out the fireplace to the last ash which I have been saving all fall

---

160 Captain George H. Hestad, assigned to a G-4 Division stationed in the Asiatic Theater.

so Santy wouldn't get dirty. Then Larry had to have his door left open so he could hear Santy when he came and also stay awake to keep reminding the rest of us to go to bed so Santy could come. When all was finally quiet Mom & the Britisher & myself trimmed the tree very badly with Dad sitting comfortably in your chair giving orders. There was no tinsel at all this year so all the wires showed and the bulbs were so old that all the lights were never on at once. Added to this you cannot buy any new ornaments and Larry so wanted a star on top this year and I couldn't get one. It was O.K. though and when everything was put around the tree we all went to bed. I slept in the third floor and thought about you.

Christmas morning I got down in time to put in a photoflood bulb and take movies for you plus the lousy enclosures. I'll get a good picture of Larry's skis as soon as we have some snow. The children were thrilled to death with everything which consisted entirely of guns & forts for Larry & dolls for Georgia excepting what I got for us to give them—skis, skates & Mom gave Georgia a coat, leggings, & bathrobe & Larry a sled that had been Jack's & mine. Dad gave each of the children a $100.00 war bond and us a $1000.00 one. Be sure to make a proper fuss over them when you write him.

About 11:00 o'clock we finally tore the children away from the tree and took them outdoors down to the play yard. Mr. Hvolbeck had gotten it all set up without them seeing it. They really were thrilled. It looks like this:

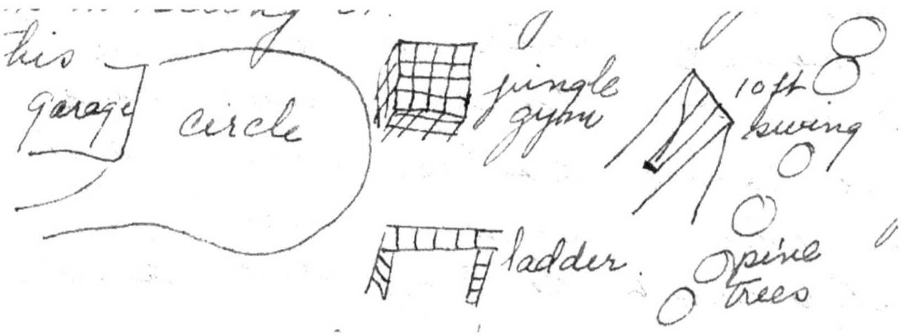

[hand-drawn diagram with labels: his garage, circle, jungle gym, 10 ft swing, ladder, pine trees]

We could almost have a nursery school here. So as far as the kids went they had a lovely Christmas.

In the afternoon we went down on Crowley's pond to skate. Dad was good but Larry was better than the Britisher. It was fun anyway. The next day, Sun. Dad got the Britisher working at brush burning. He was fairly good at that. Poor boy was overwhelmed at the kindness of taking him in, I guess. He said about ten words all the time he was here and was very dull besides—not much like the other two, but in his way I'm sure he thought he was enjoying himself. He went back to N.Y.C. on Sun. night. He didn't add much to our Christmas but if we added to his, that's what matters.

The rest of last week I wrote you V-mail so now I'll skip to New Year's Eve. I received two gorgeous green orchids from my very best beau along in the afternoon and wore them in my hair with my black taffeta evening dress with the gold & silver embroidered trees on it to the Greys. They had four houseguests from Long Island, Bowdens, Penn Bridge, Suley Ives and myself. We had a very nice time. Oh yes I [al]most forgot to tell you that it was exactly seven o'clock here as I pinned on my orchids to go to the party and I knew you were just ushering in the New Year so I thought and wished lots of things for us really knowing that at that second you were doing the same. Unless perhaps Stipp & Allen and that bottle of bourbon were still around. I got home at <u>3:30</u> and was up at 8:30 to get breakfast and take the children to N.Y.C. Yes, I decided to take them to the Savoy for New Year's dinner with Mamie & George. They behaved beautifully and ate in the dining room without a mishap. We pleased Mamie & George by going and the kids loved the train trip so it was well worthwhile. I got them home about 4:30 and then still wearing my orchids after going all the way to N.Y. with them I went to a cocktail party at the Somers. You haven't met them but Pat is an Ogontz girl that I found lives here and Ed is a very swell guy. They have a boy Larry's age and live over near the Gortons. I came home early last night after a couple of egg nogs there and went to bed. I put my orchids in water next to my bed and they are just like new still this morning.

Now we are up to today which is about half gone. I took Tina to church in Greenwich & went on to the Wards for a visit while church lasted. The kids had a great time together and they are all coming up here to skate this afternoon.

I'll close this by saying I'm so glad the holidays are behind us, but I am already looking forward to next year's as I hope you'll be here to make them worthwhile then. This is the 2nd day of 1944. How happy I'll be when we can sit by our fireside and look back on the events of this year. I love you so very much.

All yours, Peggy

[Peggy to George]
[V-Mail]

#111
Tues. P.M. Jan. 4

Darling,

I'm up late tonight as the eleven P.M. news is just coming on. I have spent the evening sewing up in our dressing room—letting down Georgia's dress, patching holes in Robin's shirts where he has cut his teeth on them, darning my own socks, and hemming a skating skirt for myself. During all of this I have been glancing up every few seconds to admire my New Years orchids. They are just as fresh tonight as the first day of 1944. This letter didn't get written this morning as we had four inches of snow during the night and it had started raining hard by breakfast so we couldn't get out to the mailbox in time. At precisely five last evening I was sitting in front of Robin's high chair in the kitchen feeding him and thinking of you. I could only wish you might peek in on us. He was teasing me between mouthfuls of egg and pablum with his toast. He'd push it at me and when I'd try for a bite, he'd pull the toast away and hold it behind his head and then squeal with laughter. Larry and Georgia were in the center of the floor showing off their new dances, Larry with wild gestures of arm swinging and much stomping of feet called his the "shadow" and "rhinoceros" dances. Georgia's was slower but not so wild and known by her as the "<u>u</u>salunt" dance. You've asked several times about the heat. We are warm as can be and everything about the house is perfect except that you are so lacking from every room, chair, and <u>my</u> bed. I'll describe the upstairs next time. I love you so very much. Peggy

[Peggy to George]
[V-Mail]

#112
Jan. 6, 1944

Dearest George,

    This is my first morning as cook, cleaner and all the rest and I love it. Anna left yesterday noon on the Doctor's recommendation and we parted happily. I wrote her a good reference for use when she is over these spells and paid all her Dr. and drug bills. The reference is a bit on my conscious after the poor work she has done the last six months but everything I said, she has been once so may be again after a rest and in a new position. Tina seems happier too since she left but of course I have my fingers crossed. I hope she stays but I can manage fine even if she doesn't. It's pouring today on top of four inches of snow so you can imagine the mess. Larry and Georgia are thrilled to play in the attic room today. They were equally thrilled to use their new sled on Crowley's driveway yesterday. Larry directed Georgia to lie on her tummy "way up front." Then he would push from behind and flop on reaching over her to steer. This way they proceeded at a snail's pace in the wet snow for a few yards. Here Larry would try to get Georgia off to pull the sled back up. She always hesitated moving as long as she dared. Finally, he would stomp his foot and say, "Georgia you're just plain ornery, go in the house." This would get her to her feet. I love you. Peggy

[Peggy to George]
[V-Mail]

#114
Jan. 8, Sat.

Darling,

What I wouldn't give for you to be a fly on our kitchen wall this weekend. Right now we have just finished breakfast. Robin is up on his toidey and Larry and Georgia are waiting to add a P.S. to this. Since Tina left yesterday morning they have been good as gold. Bernice brought her two at noon and we fed them all together and after napping they all played out of doors. Then I bathed Robin & Larry & Georgia bathed themselves and got pajamas, robes & slippers on and came down for supper. Larry set the table and correctly too. He helped making all the toast and fixing dessert in the dishes. Afterwards I washed dishes and they each had a towel and wiped for me. You can't imagine how cute they looked with their faces screwed in concentration and the towels hanging to their toes just working away. After the dishes I had hoarded four letters from you all day so we climbed up on the couch and I read them all to them. Larry particularly enjoyed your nice long one about your Christmas. We were so happy to know you had some fun. The Rebillets certainly were sweet to fix the flowers & note. Oh! Oh! Larry's turn [scribbles].

[Peggy to George]

#115
Tues. 1:30 P.M.
Jan. 11

Darling,

The hours for writing you have suddenly changed quite drastically with Anna's departure. Breakfast time is out because of dishes and evenings are usually busy until nine when I go to bed. It won't always be thus but every cupboard, closet and dish is in such awful shape I have to clean everything before I can use it. What she did the last six months I'll never know. You'd think this lovely clean new house would have inspired her if nothing else. Oh well, she's gone and I really am enjoying the work <u>if</u> I can just keep Tina.

Saturday afternoon the Wellingtons stopped for some tools. They have bought Frank Beane's house and had come out to find the outside awning broken and they had to take it down. I knew by then that Wayne M^{ac}Farlane was coming for the night so I asked them and the Bowdens for dinner. I dashed around and got the children fed & Larry & Georgia dried their dishes again and put themselves to bed. I really could manage fine alone with them but Robbie sort of spoils our schedules yet.

We had pot roast, cauliflower, potatoes, gravy and succotash plus coffee and a <u>swell</u> devils food cake that I made. The girls helped me do the dishes and we had a good time. After a little conversation they all went home.

Sunday Wayne didn't get up until noon so I had time to get the housework done etc. etc. <u>All</u> the children had dinner with us in the dining room. Robin in his high chair next to me by the bay window, Larry on my left and Georgia on my right and Wayne, the bachelor, in your chair cutting up the roast chicken in small pieces for the kids to eat. He was very handy I must say and certainly raved about the food, bed, leisure at least once an hour while he was here. I lent him an old pair of your pants & a blue flannel shirt and he wanted me to be sure and tell you that your shirts certainly are soft. He talked about it so much that he really must have gotten a thrill out of the change. Quite different from the British boy we had X-mas, but I think the fellow had an equally good time. I've made a bargain with Wayne that he can come any weekend starting next Sat. and work for his board & room & what fun I can throw in so he won't feel obligated. He was thrilled & so am I. I can't get any man to come during this cold weather and I just can't do it all. Next Sun. Wayne is cleaning the garage, the incinerator, moving a half cord of wood inside. I'll let you know how he gets on.

Yesterday was wash day as usual only I had the cleaning to do as well. I finished & did a better job than Anna used to just doing the cleaning & we all went skating in the afternoon. Larry's getting really good & he loves it. We also skated Sun. afternoon with Wayne. Robin gets spun around on his sled. I really am better myself.

I must draw a plan of our bedroom and sitting room where I spend evenings now—also where I am writing this—before I close & go to Greenwich for groceries. Now I must dash but please answer these questions[:]

1. Have you received Time's pony edition?
2. Did the Rebillets get the plum pudding?

3. Have you forwarded letters to frenchman Seymore?

I love you more and more and hope you have started receiving mail again. Yours is coming through fine.

Love, Peggy

[Peggy to George]
[V-Mail]

#116
Jan. 12/44 Wed.

Dearest George,

This time you find me in the hairdressers. It seems as if the days of leisurely writing you a daily letter are over. However, except for that one fact I love the work. Slowly, I am getting my cupboards and closets back into the order I like them and Tina helps very cheerfully. In fact I approached her on the subject of staying if I did the rest of the work, this morning, and she said it was all right with her. Consequently we moved Anna's bed to the store room and I fixed that room up as a really nice sitting room for her. She seems cheerful most of the time and likes the improved cooking enough even to say so. I get such a kick out of the children. They rave so over each meal that it almost is embarrassing. Tapioca the other day nearly brought the roof down. Anna never had time for anything but Jello lately. So you see we are settled very happily again except for needing you so very much. It is so much fun to keep house in our lovely home that it reminds me of playing house when we were children. Tonight I am going to Maggie Seymore's for our girls' discussion evening. On the events tonight I have to give a resumé of Far East history up to 1000 A.D. I've learned lots of things I can't remember ever having in school. My hair is curled up now ready for the dryer so we just came out even. Yours, Peggy

[Peggy to George]
[V-Mail]

#117

Thurs. Jan. 13.

My darling,

    Today you catch me after supper for our little daily chat. We all ate in the kitchen about five thirty, then I cleaned silver, mixed up a cake which is now in the oven and should be baked by 8:30.— Remind me to take it out. Will you? We might get too interested here together to think of that, though. Doxie is at my feet and a bunch of finished mending is next to me on the couch plus my needlepoint. I have taken that up again in hopes of finishing our dining room chair seats before you get home. Don't wait for me, though. I had a nice time last night at Maggie's. Incidentally, she had a Christmas cable from Michel from Cairo so she is very happy. In looking up my little topic I discovered that Japan has been governed by military men or groups since the middle of the eighth century with the emperor only a figurehead and often deposed by the army heads.[161] Did you know that? Also the Chinese civilization is several hundred years older than Japan's—the latter being started by Koreans[162] and the first government was modeled after that of China.[163] You are such a history student I know this is a waste of time. Today Larry & Anne Bowden & I went to the Peter's for lunch. We picked Hodgey up

---

161 Rather than military groups or an army leader, it was usually members of (or the head of) a rival clan who initiated the deposing.
162 These statements are misleading oversimplifications. Beginning around 400 BCE, migrants started arriving in Japan from continental Asia, including many from the Korean peninsula (including people from China who had migrated there earlier). During the 4th century the influx increased and many Koreans were present in the Japanese government. Depending on one's point of view, at this point numerous aspects of Korean culture were either integrated with the aboriginal culture or Korean culture replaced the original culture. Regardless, since people were living in Japan prior to the arrival of Korean migrants it would not be correct to say that Japanese civilization was created by the newly-arrived Koreans. Given how "civilization" was defined in the western world in the 1930s and 1940s, it should not be surprising that the resources Peggy used for her research made this erroneous claim. For the same reasons, the assertion that Chinese civilization is older than Japanese by several hundred years is problematic as well.
163 Prince Shotoku (b. 574, d. 622) ruled as regent of Japan for nearly three decades. During his reign he advocated for closer relations with China and adopted many Chinese characteristics of government, including restrictions on who can impose taxes, the abolishment of nepotism among government officials, and the elimination of corruption. Most famous is perhaps the ethical code he is credited with inspiring, entitled, "Seventeen Article Constitution" (Cartwright, "Prince Shotoku.").

at school for Margie & I showed Larry around. He was absolutely inarticulate. I know he is going to love it. I read your letter about the elephant to the kids for the sixth time. They love it, obviously. Peggy

[Peggy to George]

#118

Sun. P.M.

Darling,

I cannot tell you how I hate to send you this clipping, but you'll have to know.[164] It has had me so upset for three days I just couldn't write. Now I have managed a poor excuse of a letter to Kay. What horrible hours of waiting word of his safe landing she will have to look forward to. I do hope she hears soon and that it is convincing. Poor girl and what hell for him if he is O.K. and cannot send word. Several times a day the picture comes to my mind of you and Webb darting hysterically around the yard playing with that toy airplane of Larry's. Do you remember what fun he had and how hard he laughed. Then I think of him marveling over the minuteness of Georgia's toes when she first came. How wild he was over that baby! Oh nuts, what's the use of these reminiscences.

This morning I took the children over to see Robin Peake. He's gained plenty of weight which makes his face round like yours used to be when you sat on your fanny like he does. He only has another month at Fort Sill before he is reassigned. The Peakes had a real reunion this week. All the children are home. Allison's husband is in the Pacific, however. Cam has been rejected by the draft board finally due to his malaria so he is job hunting. Dave is in the marines. Allison is home having a baby in March. Robin is on leave until Wed. Mr. and Mrs. Peake certainly looked happy.

---

164 On January 6, 1944, a brief announcement appeared in the *Omaha World-Herald* titled, "Lt. Webster Bull Missing on Raid." Webb left the United States in September 1943 to serve as pilot of a B-17 (Flying Fortress) stationed with the 388th bomber group in England. On December 22, 1943 he was declared missing in action after failing to return to base from a raid over Germany.

Wayne was here last night but he left early this afternoon as he had a bad cold and was afraid of giving it to the children. Last night Anne Hannan included him in a farewell party for Moon and he came back out with me afterward. Moon has his own ship now and is heading for the Pacific. Friday night the Gortons gave a farewell party for a Navy friend. They had Ray to bartend, an accordion player and thirty guests. We all dressed and it seemed almost like a prewar party except for all the uniforms. I was the first to leave and it still was 2:30. I've had quite a gay weekend. Even during the course of this letter the Peters phoned and I let them persuade me to change my nightie for a dress and go down there to a party. That was exactly one hour ago. I'm still dressed but they were all so far ahead of me I slipped my coat back on as soon as I could and came back to finish talking to you.

I was thinking today how much the children have changed since you left and am going to try and give you a description of each of them right now. Larry has grown about 2 inches and looks very much a little boy now. He isn't much heavier but his appetite is excellent and he looks fine. He has acquired a great deal of self confidence and is oftener the aggressor than Georgia now in their little spats. He is very mechanically minded and I often blush to think how disgusted you'd be to the answers I give him. He even tried to discuss "steam" with me last week. I nearly phoned Colby in my dilemma. Where do you suppose he gets <u>that</u> trait? He has all of your <u>good</u> qualities too. He is most dependable. I never worry about him being reckless or leading Georgia in mischief. He has an excellent sense of responsibility and is a big help and comfort to me. He is very affectionate and sentimental. A few times when he has found me a bit tearful he always reminds me that he will take care of me "as Daddy told me too."

Georgia has lost all her baby-ness too. She is a <u>very</u> pretty, imaginative child. Except for Tina's extra discipline she could easily get out of control as she doesn't listen to instructions and seemingly goes about in a cloud which nothing breaks through but definite punishment. Then tears fall with absolutely no effort and stop as easily leaving the patient completely unaffected until next time. She has grown at least three inches since June and is now wearing size 5 dresses and the same size shoes as Larry. He is still a head taller but they weigh the same.

Now for Robin who you would hardly know. He is as solid as rock and very large. He still hasn't had his haircut so the baby curls at the nape of his neck keep him a cuddly age but he really is outgrowing it. He races madly in his taylor tot and takes whatever the other two can give in rough housing without a whimper. His legs are so fat the tops of his socks won't pull up. He wears Georgia's shoes which she wore at two. He says "light," "bye-bye" "Dox," "Do-da" (Georgia) [and] "mum-ummmm." He has a marvelous sense of humor and seems to already realize he can be funny. When he gets a laugh for some prank, he continues it by the hour. And that my darling is the picture I see each day of the three wonderful children you have given me and which it hurts so to watch knowing you are not able to share the joys they bring with me. I try to think of how I can ever make it up [to] you, but have no answer except that we might have a couple more in our old age.

Robin suggested today that you might get a chance to come home after a few more months. That isn't possible, is it?

I must go to bed now and get ready for wash day tomorrow. I love you so much, my darling, and sometimes really feel one more day of this separation will be more than I can stand. Usually, though, I manage to keep so busy that I drop into bed and sleep fairly quickly. Also, I have Georgia sleeping nights in your bed now so it doesn't seem so empty. I often listen to her breathing in the dark and tell myself it really is at least half your breathing. She can even snore, at times.

                    Loads of Love, Peggy

[George to Peggy]

[#]79
18 Jan. 44
Tues.
Capt. GR Steiner
AFHq G-4 Sec APO 512
c/o P.M. New York N.Y.

Peg dear,

You were neglected last night, at least so far as correspondence goes, because down at dinner Callahan, Hayes, and Sowman wanted to play bridge. That lasted until about one o'clock so I am a bit sleepy tonight. I did think of you though and thought along about ten o'clock you might be feeding Robbie. I sure would like to see that little guy. It was interesting to see how closely his weight compares to Larry's at one year.

Stipp is still here waiting for transportation. He just came back from dinner and is sitting over at his desk bothering me with talk about one thing and another. I am going to miss him, he is a good gent.

Yesterday I sent you $1,740 through the War Dept., so you will probably get a check from the W.D. in several days after receiving this letter. How about getting Larry and Georgia each a $1,000 bond and put the other $240 in your own bank account to get something you may want for yourself? Miss Finn knows what I get per month from the Army so you won't have to write her, except I guess it would be well to send her the bonds. I figure if we can put something aside now and then for the children, it will be a surer and easier way to take care of their education and perhaps have something for them to get started on when they get out of school. We won't forget Robbie either, we will give him something next time we get a bit ahead. Sure am glad we have such a nice home of our own all free and clear.

Ran into a class mate from Yale who was in our ROTC unit, Capt.

Echols.[165] He is a good gent, was down at Sill with Robbie for a while and is now working with the same outfit that Duncan Lee is with. You remember I told you about Duncan on the phone coming across. He went on out to India though.

Schutz has to stay pretty close to the C in C so we don't see much of him now. That is a nice gesture on the part of an English officer to take an American aide.[166] Our relations with the British here are very good. Calahan who I played bridge with last night is from London, had a stock brokerage business of his own, and Sowman comes from Edin[bur]gh, just one of those bloody heathen Scotchman according to Calahan. The latter has a boy and girl about 7 and 8 nice looking kids. Sowman plans to get married when the war is over and wants to come over to the U.S. on his wedding trip. I invited him out to dinner, will that be all right.

I don't remember if I told you what I did about Tripier. You can tell Margaret that I will keep trying to get in touch with him and probably will one of these days. I have written him telling him the situation and asking him to write me or get in touch with me if he is in town. I have kept Margaret's letters but told him briefly what she had written. I have tried getting in touch with him several different ways, so thought it better to hold the letters until I was sure I could get them to him. If I get any news of him I will surely let you know right away.

All my love dear, George

---

165 Emmett Deering Echols (b. 1913, d. 2002) served in the OSS during WWII. As George writes in a later letter, Echols was born in Milwaukee, graduated from Yale in 1935, and ranked as a Field Artillery captain in the U.S. Army during WWII. During the Cold War, Echols will serve in the CIA as the director of personnel.

166 British General Henry Maitland "Jumbo" Wilson was Commander-in-Chief, Middle East and then replaced Eisenhower as Supreme Allied Commander, Mediterranean.

[Peggy to George]
[V-Mail]

#119
Jan. 19, Tues.

Dearest George,

You catch me in the queerest places these days. I just arrived at the Park Lane Grill in Greenwich and am waiting for Jessie Bedford and Bernice to meet me for lunch. Previous to this I got lunch for Tina and the kids, washed the dishes and went to the bank. This morning I did the washing of sweaters which were not finished yesterday and all the ironing. This probably bores you but I really love it and am only surprised at the amount which can be done with little time and a bit of system.

The children are grand and thrive on my cooking. Georgia came down for lunch after supposedly washing. There still were smudges here and there but she doesn't notice that. As she climbed into her chair I said "Georgia what a clean face you have." She said, "Yes, isn't it wonderful?" Oh yes, I forgot to tell you that Larry wouldn't let her touch something the other day and announced "That's too <u>trescious</u> for you to handle, Georgia." Well, Jessie's here so enough for now. Loads of Love. Peggy

[Peggy to George]
[V-Mail]

#120
Jan. 20, Thurs.

My Dearest George,

Your family is at the breakfast table here in the kitchen. The same table you and I ate at so many times in the alcove in Forest Hills. Robin is in his high chair pulling off his slippers and putting his feet in his mouth. Larry is finishing his toast and honey (some you brought home from Congers last spring.) Georgia has finished and gone. My system is improved this morning by the alarm clock which got me up an hour earlier so I had breakfast ready for all when they got downstairs. That has allowed me to finish eating first and now have a moment to write this. Larry and I will go to the mailbox in a minute. Incidentally our name which mysteriously disappeared from the entrance to Oakley Lane months ago has just as mysteriously reappeared. Consequently I was trying to replace it in the ground a few days ago and Larry watching me remarked "Are you doing that Momie, so that Daddy can find us when he comes home from Africa?" He cannot believe that you won't go to the old house looking for us and not be able to find us anywhere. Last night I took a pot full of sauerkraut and spareribs up to Bill & Bernices. Penn came with a ginger bread for dessert so we had a community supper. Bill furnished drinks and Bernice mashed potatoes. Yours, Peggy

[Peggy to George]
[V-Mail]

#121
Jan. 21, Fri.

Darling,

We are all through breakfast and Tina is washing dishes while I write to you. Then she goes off for three days and I snuggle into our wonderful house with the children. I really mean snuggle in as we are so closed in by the fog this morning that we cannot see a thing. I just heard Larry say to Tina while he and Robin were giggling at one another "Isn't he wonderful, Tina?" He reminds me so much of the way you acted with him [your]self. Neither of you are very interested in tiny babies like Georgia and myself, but as soon as they can play you both can hardly tear yourselves away. Thanks for the advice on Marg M[ac]Cagney. I know you are right. Besides nobody but you could live with my system and efficiency without going whacky. She does have to take care of her Aunt too. Tina is working out fine alone if I can only keep her happy and maintain some degree of authority. I must say Anna's hundred bucks is pretty nice. This month I am having that circular couch from the 1941 Knox amusement room upholstered with it in your favorite color too—a lovely blue. I love your letters so dear. I really don't know what I'd do without them. Peggy

[George to Peggy]
[V-Mail]

No. 81
Friday 21/1/44

To a Girl I love,

    Time's passing, three weeks of this year gone already. That one year they called me to duty for has certainly stretched out a bit. I am duty officer again tonight. Hope I get a good night sleep, but have my doubts. Just finished a letter to your father with thanks for the very generous Christmas present. Take a look at the picture on the back page of Stars & Stripes for 15 of Jan. Our general and colonel are both getting some very well deserved recognition from the British government.[167] They are good men and very capable. Your letter telling about Christmas day was most very welcome today, particularly the pictures. Robbie sure has grown. I wrote Larry a letter for his birthday tonight. Now you just guess a few of the things I am wishing tonight for they have quite a bit to do with you. Goodnight my dear. Yours. George

[Peggy to George]

#122
Fri. night

P.S. The gal on the radio is singing "I wish I could hide inside this letter." The words are cute. What fun it would be to pop out at you!

---

167 Likely another reference to Brigadier General Adcock and Colonel Heyduck. On January 11, 1944, England's King George VI honored U.S. service members with decorations for their service. Among those acknowledged were Adcock and Heyduck. The former was awarded the honor of Commander of the Order of the British Empire and the latter, Officer of the Order of the British Empire ("18 U.S. Generals Honored by King.").

Darling,

I am sitting in our dressing room listening to the radio with my nightie on and red bathrobe with a new cashmere blanket (green) over my knees. I bought it with some money Mom gave me for Christmas. I think you will like it. It's so warm and soft and goes so prettily with the yellow upholstery and wall paper. The children have been tucked in for a couple of hours now. Tina left again this morning for her weekend so we are alone and getting on fine. After doing the supper dishes I let the two, Georgia & Larry, write you the enclosed letters while I put that fat little Robin to bed. They were still scribbling away at the kitchen table when I came down. Georgia said she had written you a song about Goldylocks. Also she asked you to put her "farmer" (wooden man belonging to farm blocks) in the closet. I've forgotten what his misdemeanor was. Larry wrote you about the flag Grandma sent him from Chicago. He says now he needs an electric fan to make it wave!!! Can you tie that? He's very proud of the flag and can now put a jig-saw map of the U.S.A. together with very little help and can find you on the globe. After Christmas morning when Dad showed him how the jig-saw went just once, Larry heard Dad telling about coming through Colorado on his way from the west. Larry picked him up and said, "Colorado is the big square one away out other side on my puzzle."

I had some shocking news tonight. I told you about going with Pinky one night to have dinner with an old Dutchman, Mr. Timerlaine[168] (Bea Hekma's father). It was before Christmas. I was his partner at bridge. He's a sweet old man about 75 with a terrific accent. He naturally has been very depressed about relations etc. in Holland and today he jumped from 40 Pine where his office is located.[169] Poor Bea. Her sister did the same thing, the first summer

---
168 Floris W. ter Meulen.
169 Mr. ter Meulen was a representative for a Dutch banking company and honored by Dutch Queen Wilhelmina for furthering the interests of the Netherlands in the United States. On January 21, 1944, Mr. ter Meulen jumped or fell 20 stories from his Wall Street office, landing, as Peggy writes, along Pine Street where he narrowly missed pedestrians. At the time of his death, he was in his sixties.

we lived up at Hekma's.[170] Do you remember?

I have just reread your letter telling me all those sweet thoughts and desires you have these days. Darling, just to read those words gives me a thrill. I wish I could say the similar wishes and memories I have each night but you know how badly I do it even when I have you in my arms. It's too bad wedding rings cannot talk. I put a special message with yours which should be repeated every single night to make you know how much I love you and need you. Perhaps the message is telepathic since you say rubbing brings you vivid memories of moments together.

      All my love, Peggy

[Peggy to George]
[V-Mail]

#123
Mon. P.M. Jan. 23

My Darling,

We've had a busy date so far tonight as I have Anne Hanan here with Kenneth since yesterday noon. Everything has gone fine but I am a bit weary tonight as the washing, scrubbing of laundry, kitchen, cooking, dish washing must go on Mondays despite house guests. Despite all these also I attended the funeral services at 11 a.m. for Mr. Ter [Meulen]. It was very sad as only a handful appeared at Christ's Church. They held it in the little chapel where Georgia was christened. No pall bearers either. How dreadful for his daughter, Bea. This afternoon Anne and I took all the children except Robin for a walk down the bridle path. I never go along there that I don't think of the day we discovered it and ended up looking like tramps at Mrs. Bigelow's doorstep. What a beautiful day that was with you and the sunshine and a summer's day. Will the[re] ever be another I often wonder. I had a letter from Cecil today and she arrives for a visit next

---

170   Bea's sister was Yvonne Borden. On May 16, 1940, Yvonne perished after plummeting six stories from her residence in Greenwich, CT.

weekend. There's no chance to say "no" as her letter was written on the train and mailed in Wash. D.C. I'll be glad to see her but I have just about all I can handle at present. Your letter of Jan. 10 arrived today. So glad to hear of Schutz's good fortune. What is it? Please number your letters again, and tell me how mine are coming through. Yours always, Peggy

[George to Peggy]
[V-Mail]

24 Jan. 44 Monday

Dear Peggy,

Good morning. I just walked down the hill, had breakfast with Boger, and came up here to find Allen and Stipp busy writing their families. Stipp is still with us, but Allen was telling him yesterday that he ought to back up to the window to collect this month's pay. He has let down on the work a bit naturally enough since he knows he will leave any day but we get a lot [of] fun out of kidding a bit. I still think he is doing a lot more than ninety per cent of the people around here. Received your parcel with the wool shirts and underwear. Thank you. And here a V-mail just came in from you. Will write you again tonight. Love, George

[Peggy to George]
[V-Mail]

#124
Jan. 26, Wed.

Dearest George,

I have just returned from New York with Mary Ward and am staying at her house for dinner. While she puts the children to bed I thought I could grab a few seconds to write you. We showed the Stony Wold movie to the annual meeting of all the auxiliaries in N.Y. today and it was very well received. Mr. Sandy the Pres. offered to pay my way and furnish the film if I'd go back and do a more extensive job. I told him my present job was too demanding I fear, but it was a nice compliment. After lunch with Mary and Peggy Gerli I set out to buy Larry a suit for his birthday and get "paper snappers" and candy baskets and a "pull pie" to decorate the table. I won't go into the difficulties, but after six stores looking for the suit I bought the only size 6 cotton blouse De Penna's had and the only size 6 wool pants any store had & they were at Lords & Taylors. Anne Hanan & Kenneth stayed until this morning and she drove me into the city. Last night I also had our discussion meeting group for dinner so I am pretty tired. I'm going straight home to bed after dinner. Hope to find a letter waiting for me. Guess from whom!? Love, Peggy

[Peggy to George]
[V-Mail]

#126
Conn. Jan. 29, Sat.

Dearest George,

Again we are finishing up breakfast and I can look forward to a quiet day doing odds and ends. Our house is cleaned from top to bottom and I finished my paint jobs yesterday. How I wish you could peek in and see it. There is still one piece of furniture to come for the living room and then I'm going to attempt so[me] indoor pictures for you. The check came from the war dept. and I am doing as you said. Thank you for the dividend. That will pay for the children's play yard which I had intended squeezing out half this month & half next from my allowance. I also am buying five more bonds the same size as the children's against taxes this month. Last night I had a lonely spell and climbed into bed after hearing the dreadful news of the Jap atrocities to our prisoners.[171] I got in all right without a light so as not to awaken

---

171   In spring 1943, ten U.S. service members escaped the Philippines after roughly a year as Japanese prisoners of war (POWs). Three of them reported to the U.S. Army and Navy on their experiences. In early 1944 their sworn statements were summarized and made public, along with the Army-Navy account of atrocities in the Philippines.
   In April 1942 after the surrender at Bataan, 78,000 American and Filipino troops were marched 65 miles over the course of 5-10 days in what became known as the Bataan Death March. An estimated 10,000 of the above service members died from starvation, dehydration, exacerbated and untreated health issues such as dysentery and malaria,

Georgia. Just as I settled under the covers a wee sleepy voice said, "I got lots a kisses for you from Daddy. Momie, You must 'a got.'" I could hardly believe my ears. Needless to say I took every one she had. I love you so much, darling. Peggy

[Peggy to George]

#127

Mon. Jan. 31. 6:40 PM

Darling:

Perhaps you would like to know how we have spent our date. We all had supper of waffles, salad and home baked beans, coffee in the kitchen at five except for Robin who ate pablum, boiled egg and banana. Larry and Georgia helped to dry the dishes and put them away and by six we were finished. Then we settled ourselves around the phonograph to hear "Peter & the Wolf." (Colby's gift has become a great favorite.) Larry sat in his rocker, I in my chair, Georgia on a cushion and we heard all about Peter catching the wolf. Larry's eyes are something. I'd love a painting of him as he waits for the wolf to swallow the duck. The last ten minutes have been spent at hide & seek only Larry cheated. We turn all the lights out and Tina & I hide from them. If we find too good a spot Larry switches on the lights to bolster his courage and always catches us peeking out from behind something

---

and cruelty inflicted by their Japanese captors (Groom, 1942, 177.). There is no lack of documentation detailing random beatings, bayonet stabbings, beheadings, and cases of service members buried alive. One survivor remembers seeing a Japanese soldier guide a sick prisoner toward the road only to toss the sick POW in front of a line of tanks (Ibid., 179, 180.).

Those who survived the march found conditions equally as bad at the POW camps. At Camp O'Donnell for example, there was one water spigot for tens of thousands of POWs. The Americans and Filipinos imprisoned at the camp were told they were not prisoners of war, but captives without rights (United Press, "Survivors' Statements on Japanese Abuse of Prisoners on Bataan."). As such, disease, starvation, and dehydration at their peak killed Americans at Camp O'Donnell at a rate of 550 POWs per single day (Groom, 1942, 183.).

It is worth a note that historians seeking to explain the Japanese brutality point to poor planning (only 25,000 POWS were anticipated on the march), cultural differences (surrender was regarded as a criminal act in Japan), and the simple fact that the Japanese had never ratified the Geneva Convention (Toland, *The Rising Sun*, 301.) (Groom, 1942, 182.). However, for a select few Japanese it was a racial war and, as an article in the *Japan Times & Advertiser* declared, "to show [the Allies] mercy is to prolong the war" (Toland, *The Rising Sun*, 295, 301.).

Perhaps the only thing that equaled the excesses of the Japanese soldiers were those of the U.S. forces as the tide of the war turned and American service members sought to avenge the gross mistreatments of their military and civilian brethren. American aviator Charles Lindbergh (who toured the Pacific) remarked in his diary, "We claim to be fighting for civilization, but the more I see of this war in the Pacific the less right I think we have to claim to be civilized." (Ibid., 678.)

or other. Now they are being tucked into bed and I can sit down and have a chat with you.

Being Monday, I don't need to tell you that I've done the washing and cleaned the kitchen pantry & laundry. Also I hand waxed the floors today so my hand is a bit stiff. I do manage to get the heavy work done by Friday so that Sat. & Sun I only have the cooking, dishes & beds except when Tina is off. Now for the weekend. Cece didn't show up but she will this week. Wayne did, however. I spent all day with Frank, gardener, cleaning up more of the woods and had to take Doxie to the "vet" again as I met Wayne on the 6:52. I had a roast lamb in the oven so we had a good daiquiri and dinner. He is very smart and interesting and very helpful in the house so I am glad to have him come since it seems to give him so much pleasure. I darned children's socks after dinner & we listened to the radio. Sun. Wayne cut brush up by the garden and watched the children while I took Tina to church & did dishes. About noon we went to Mary and Bill Ward's for a cocktail party. It was very nice and I always enjoy them so much. This was followed by lunch at the club with quite a group. Peters, Dodges, Terbells, Linens. I haven't been there in months and it was quite fun. I underlined Linen because Jim is back having been for three weeks in Rebillet's home town and only left there two weeks ago. He tried to contact George but had no luck and since he'll be back eventually he suggests that you tell Geo. to call Dick Hollander or Peggy Pollard at P.W.B.[172] They would be very worthwhile contacts and could call Geo. when Jim arrives. Incidentally—Jim's address was Maison Agricole. The Hoggson's came for supper after we returned from the club and we went to the kitchen and made lamb sandwiches and a salad. I love Sun. nights like that if you are home. It's chummy anyway with good friends but not nearly the fun. I always think I need you to light the fire and put up the bridge table. Strange isn't it? Now I'll read over your last letters

---

172 The Psychological Warfare Branch was a collaborative organization of American and British military and civilian personnel. It primarily used radio and leaflet propaganda to wage psychological warfare.

again and see if you asked any questions. ----- Yes. I'll send the tobacco tomorrow, but right now here's all my love & bushels of hugs & kisses.

Peggy

[Peggy to George]
[V-Mail]

#128
Feb. 2, Wed

My Darling.

 I had a blissful awakening this morning. As I started to wake up I had the wonderful dream that you were home and just then a tiny body crawled into my bed and with a lusty kiss announced "That's a kiss from Daddy again. You haven't had one in a long time, have you Momie." I told her that I was just thinking of you and nothing pleased me more than to have your kisses. With that followed this "You know Momie, that kiss Daddy really gave to God and God gave it to me for you. Then Daddy put the kisses in his letters to come by mail. That's how I know when he gives them to God." Do you think we have a small philosopher or spiritualist on our hands? Certainly a very sweet thought and I am sure your ears were burning about 7:30 this morning. I am struggling with my bank balance this morning. If I could disagree by a few dollars, it would seem worth the effort, but it is a miserable 60¢ that is driving me batty. Going to Bill & Bernice's for supper. Bill's about to be drafted and they are both a bit nuts on the subject. All yours, Peggy

[George to Peggy]
[V-Mail]

4/2/44

[An image of two hearts with an arrow connecting them.]

"VOUS ÊTES TOUJOURS DANS MON CŒUR!"
"YOU ARE ALWAYS IN MY HEART!'

[Peggy to George]
[V-Mail]

#129

Feb. 4. Fri.

My darling,

    There was no chance to write you yesterday as I spent 24 hours wearing a path between my bed and the bathroom with tummy flu. Fortunately the butterflies are dying this morning and I have kept [down] a dish of grapenuts, scrambled eggs, toast and now as I write—a cup of tea. I say it's fortunate because Tina leaves in about half an hour for her weekend. I surely hope the children don't come down with it or the birthday party Tues. will have to be postponed. That would be a major tragedy. They talk of nothing else and I have fourteen kids coming and 10 Mamas and all the decorations collected. Robin is full of the devil this morning. He's here in his high chair playing peek-a-boo with his bib and giggling away. If all goes well I hope to get some good snapshots on the birthday. Larry has a few words to say. [Scribbles.]

[Peggy to George]
[V-Mail]

#130

Fri. P.M. Feb. 4.

My Darling,

    Larry and I hardly finished our letter to you this morning when the postman brought him your sweet birthday letter and me the nice one I have before me now. If you could have seen Larry's face when I pulled his out of the mailbox. He jumped up and down squealing and tore it open looking for kisses. I love the questions you ask me about our kitchen. Your guess is good that it is the place where you could be sure to find me most any time you peek in. Everything about it is perfect. I knew that even before you mentioned Mme. Rebillet's hardships by contrast. In fact I enjoy cooking there so much that recuperating from yesterday's tummy flu was even easy. I feel fine tonight. It's about ten P.M. and I had a phone call from Cecil. She just reached N.Y. tonight. She arrives Greenwich 10:24 A.M. tomorrow. I have the Bowdens & Peters coming for dinner tomorrow night. She'll probably stay for Larry's party. Oh boy! Am I busy! I'm getting everything done this year, so when you come home we'll forget friends & relatives and at times even the children, I hope, and enjoy each other alone. The Italian business doesn't sound very good tonight.[173] I love you. Peggy

[George to Peggy]
[V-Mail]

No. 89-A

7 Feb. 44 Monday

My darling Peggy:

You see I have not forgotten about Monday night. It is only nine P.M. though. Went down to see a movie at the Red Cross with Allen after dinner. It [was based] on the book "Confessions of a Nazi Spy," trouble was it was all in french.[174] The author of the book, a former G-Man, was there to give a very interesting talk.[175] He had been brought up and educated in foreign countries[176] and had a very sincere

---

173 It is likely Peggy is referring to the Allied efforts to push farther into Italy. Allied forces in Anzio were met with strong Nazi counter-attacks while a separate Allied group was able to land behind Cassino and the Nazi lines. The Allied troops pushing toward Cassino found themselves engaging Axis forces at point blank range–their perilous advance sensationally described across the media (Sulzberger, "Tanks and Troops Battered Cassino.").

174 *Confessions of a Nazi Spy* was a 1939 spy movie starring Edward G. Robinson. It was based on the book *Nazi Spies in America* by Leon Turrou and was the first obviously anti-Nazi film produced by a Hollywood studio.

175 Leon Turrou was a special agent to the Federal Bureau of Investigation (FBI). At the FBI Turrou worked on a variety of cases (including the kidnapping of Charles Lindbergh's son) but is best known for his work in exposing the Rumrich spy ring in 1938. The Rumrich spies had stolen and sent technological military secrets from the U.S. Armed Forces to Germany. Breaking with his G-man oath, which stated FBI agents were not permitted to expose information about their cases, Turrou began writing articles on his experience exposing the spy ring. Turrou was dismissed with prejudice from the FBI and not entitled to any of the benefits he would have received had he resigned. His articles later became the book *Nazi Spies in America*.

176 Turrou's often contradictory revelations about his background were complicated by his propensity for exaggeration (Jeffreys-Jones, *The Nazi Spy Ring in America*, 34.). He was born in what is today a part of Belarus, but at the time of his birth was part of the Russian-controlled partition of Poland. Throughout his life Turrou adamantly claimed he was not Jewish, however, recent research indicates otherwise (Ibid., 34.). According to Turrou he travelled to and lived in numerous countries, including Australia, China, Japan, Egypt, Singapore, Germany, and England and he spoke five languages by the time he was 13. Adding another two to his total, his multilingualism became quite an asset for the FBI (Ibid., 35, 39.).

belief in the advantages of a democratic government. It seems a person has to experience the evils of oppressive government to fully appreciate what a privilege it is to live where the rights and freedom of individuals are respected and protected by the government. Necessary as I realize it to be, I resent the loss of freedom and personal liberty entailed in military service. From the abuses which we see many people make who are suddenly (another sheet)

No. 89-B

given great authority, it becomes painfully evident how prone man is to use position to advance his personal interests and comforts even though it is to the disadvantage of his fellows. Such acts are particularly ironical when they are performed by high officials in an organization which is dedicated to the advancement of democracy. Not that such conduct is the general rule among our leaders, but when you do see some individuals taking unwarranted advantage of newly gained positions, it makes you angry. The beauty of democracy is that the rights of individuals are protected against abusive acts on the part of high authorities, and that when the misuse of position becomes too great we can always vote them out of office, or at least have the opportunity to do so. All this chatter and I do have so[me] news too. (another sheet)

No. 89-C

Yesterday a naval officer was up on some business. He came from Chicago so we got talking about that part of the country with the information emerging that Fitz Gerald was out here with the navy. So I had dinner with Jerry (Lt. Cmdr.) out at their mess which sure has ours beaten a dozen ways. Covey (Ens.) ate with us. We had a big highball before dinner and [a] couple after, fried chicken, new peas, and all well served. Quite a contrast to the sloppily run Army mess. Jerry is married and has a little girl four years old. Covey is a nice fellow. It was a very pleasant evening. Jerry was back to the states about a month ago but only stayed a week. Tomorrow will be a big day for me at home with Larry's birthday. Hope my cable got through. Wish I could hold you in my arms right now and tell you how much I love you. Goodnight my dear. George

[Peggy to George]
[V-Mail]

#131
Feb. 7, Mon.

My Darling,

 A mad rush this morning. Cecil has been here since Sat. and is going to N.Y. on the early bus in a few minutes for the day. Two men are here already working on the humidifier. They hope ---- Tues. ---- Wed. night ---- (The humidifier is working). Too many people were hollering at me at this point and I've carried this letter for two days trying to find a minute somewhere to finish it. Now I'm cozy in our upstairs dressing room on the chaise with the radio and Doxie so I'll end this and write you an Air Mail too to make up for the delay. Cece left this morning and that makes life quite a bit simpler. I surely enjoyed seeing her though. We took up our friendship like an old comfy slipper after not even writing for two years. Good friends are really so few and far between we should value them much more than we do in this hustling life of ours. Doxie's another and I have hardly taken time to pat his old head all day. Yours, Peggy

[Peggy to George]

#132
Wed. 7:30 P.M.

Darling,

 I just finished a V-mail begun on Mon. and I was talking of Cecil's visit. I must continue to give you news of Steppy. It makes me so happy to know our first baby is so well cared for. Cece runs a riding school and uses Steppy for her own horse and holds him up to her best pupils as reward if they learn to ride well enough by the end of the year. She took him on a show circuit last year and showed him in "good hands" and "manners" classes and won $65.00. Isn't that marvelous! My sweet baby. I'm so thrilled as she really seems to love him as I do.

Monday Cece spent in town and I rushed around baking Larry's birthday cake and getting ready for the great day yesterday, and it surely was something.

Larry came into our room at day break and I opened an eye and said "Happy Birthday" which was all he needed. With a squeal he landed on my bed and we had a big hug and kiss. Then he wanted to know if he really was 5 years old. I said "yes." With that he looked very puzzled and said "But, Momie look at me—my 'jamas still fit and so does mickey mouse (watch)." He had expected to grow at least 6 inches over night. We finally convinced him he was a little bigger than when he went to bed. With presents from Cece & me at breakfast the day began. I gave him an Army bomber with torpedo tubes underneath it. When we wrapped it up Cece & I saw a tiny envelope in the box & nearly threw it away before opening it to find small wooden sticks (torpedoes). When Larry opened the plane in the morning he looked it over and then started scrambling through the wrappings. He came upon the envelope and without opening it said "Oh goody! The torpedoes!" Were you ever that smart? Now for the party. Thirteen children arrived about three—Hodgey, Anne Bowden, Luke & Judy Ward, Timmy Somers, Candy & Terry Ives, Kenneth Hannan, Carlise Bowden, Fitzy & Katie Boussevain, Larry & Georgia. They played out in the play yard first & then came in and went up to the third floor. About 4:30 I showed them two Mickey Mouse movies I'd rented from Eastman. They all sat perfectly still and the remarks were priceless and how they laughed when Mickey got into trouble. I had Ray from the club to help. He served the 12 Momies tea and sandwiches &

cookies I had prepared while I showed the movie. Then he served the supper. I had the table in red, white & blue. The table cloth was navy blue crepe paper. The plates blue & white (paper). Then I had candy dishes with blue sailor boys for the boys and red sunbonnet bab[ies] for the girls. In the center was a huge red, white, & blue drum full of favors with strings attached that they pulled out (birch bark boats for the boys and tiny green plastic doll forks, spoons & knives for the girls). Then the boys had blue snappers & napkins & the girls red. To eat they had creamed eggs on toast, spinach & cottage cheese.

Behind Larry's chair was a high chair with two big balloons tied to it and [a] blond headed little smiling boy in it all dressed up in a little white suit with blue embroidery that his Momie & Daddy had bought in Cuba for his great big brother <u>long</u> ago. He never missed a trick and ate everything the rest had and laughed at all the jokes including his own. Larry sat in your chair at the bay window and had the poise of a 16 yr. old. He stood on his chair and bl[ew] four candles out with the first breath and the last with his second. I tried to find out what he wished but "it's a secret." I used photo floods and took movies for you but my Christmas movie was no good so I'm not very hopeful. The film isn't worth a darn now. They replace it but that doesn't help any. As you can guess, Cece and I were glad when they all left but it was nice to know that they all had such a good time.

Today we dragged ourselves out of bed and took Cece to [the] 10:00 train and Larry, Georgia & I went to the dentist. They love to go so it was great fun. After the teeth cleaning I took them to the Woman's Exchange for lunch. They ate so perfectly I just puffed my chest out and let the women all around talk about them <u>pretending</u> not to hear.

So that's the latest on our cute babies. As for us it's the same old story. I love you so much and wish I could take you by the hand and take you with me right now to a place where it's so much fun to try and show you just how much I love you. P.

[Peggy to George]
[V-Mail]

#133

Feb. 11 Fri.

My Darling,

    Oh! how I wish for you this morning. It has been snowing hard all night and is still coming down fast. Larry and I are dressed for skiing and he is going to try the skis you gave him for Christmas. Doxie is closer than my shadow. I know he remembers these clothes and wants to be sure he doesn't get left behind. I'll let you know how we proceed to the mailbox with this letter tomorrow. I climbed into bed after finishing your Air mail Wed. night and was asleep when I thought I heard the phone. I dashed downstairs and the party had hung up. Then I worried for fear it was news of you or Mom or Dad. I just got settled when it rang again and this time I got there. It was your cable to Larry. I even woke him up to tell him and he was *so* thrilled. He told everyone about it yesterday. Incidentally, *I* was thrilled too that all is well and you are thinking of your family who love you so much. Peggy

[George to Peggy]
[V-Mail]

No. 91

13 Feb. 44 Sunday

Peg dear;

    Received a V-Mail today from you dated 2 Feb. so I am getting up to date. You tell Georgia that I surely would like to be awakened by having her climb up on my bed. She must be a sweet little girl. I sure would like to see her and Larry helping dry the dishes, that is quite a picture. You thank them both for the nice letters they wrote me. We have been pretty busy today, it is ten P.M. and we have just finished up. Last night there was a dance, it being Lincoln's birthday. Jerry came in to try our mess, which is quite a let down after the Navy mess. Then we went out to the navy mess, sat in their bar, had a couple of drinks, listened to the radio and talked with Covey and some other Navy officers. On the average the Navy draws a better type for their officers. Went down to take a look at the dance and got to bed late. My love, George

[Peggy to George]

#134
Feb. 13. Sun. P.M.

Darling

　　Will you be my Valentine? (in about 3½ hours) Do you remember what you gave me the first Valentine's Day after we were married?—a perfectly beautiful frying pan! For the sentimental feeling I hold for this favorite of all my pots and pans I have scrubbed it with each use since Anna left until now it shines again like it did six years ago tonight. Other times I've had lovely red roses which hardly need to say "I love you" because you were always there to do so much more convincing a job of it. Many thanks again, my dearest, for the sweet thoughts you've given me on St. Valentine's Day as well as every other day in every year we've been together. I'll carry them as usual in my heart this year and pray that next year I'll hear you whisper in my ear, "I love you more than ever."

　　It seems ages since I've had an evening in which no housework waited to be finished while I snatched a precious moment in which to write you—my favorite occupation incidentally. But tonight is the third since we've been snowbound and such fun we've had. Larry got on fine on Friday so we went out all afternoon and again yesterday through the snow storm. I've taken him for three hours today on the bridle path through the woods wishing so hard that since you can't share it with us that you might just be given the ability to look down through the fairy land over our heads and peek through at us poking along. Since the snow is at least six inches deep I lead the procession to make a trail for Larry. It won't be necessary to tell you how I look, but I will. First of all there is a faraway look in my eye which takes me skiing with you in other places, but I don't miss the dazzling beauty of this trail in our own back yard which we shared twice in summer but not in this new startling dress. The wind has not blown the snow as yet from the branches of each tiny pine and stone or from the taller trees which reach up to a bright blue sky. But to get back to how I looked today. I have on the same blue ski cap with the ear flaps tied on top for the weather is mild. My jacket a very thoughtful boy brought me from Vancouver once. My long light blue ski pants the same boy found for me at Sun Valley, I believe. The rest are boots & skis. Next comes a perfect little gnome with peaked cap in a one piece green snow suit. The hood is attached and lined with red. A red scarf surrounds his neck tied fast behind. If he catches you peeking at him he will break into a whimsical smile and show his rosy cheeks and his Daddy's love of praise, but if you look without him seeing you, the expression you find will be most intent and breathless as he plods along struggling to coordinate skis, feet and poles all into Momie's trail. Doing rear guard duty is a dark brown furry creature with tail erect and emanating intense interest in the whole excursion. In fact the reduced speed of this particular outing suits his ageing tastes. There are many stops which allow time for lying down and carefully chewing snow and ice from between the toes without fear of being run down in the process. We end up down a piece on North St. and come back by Oakley Lane so that Momie with a rope harness affair can pull Robin['s] sled back to the house from where she left it earlier to be filled by the milkman with six quarts of milk. In the meantime Larry robs the mailbox of a loaf of bread left by the Bowdens and we all ski home wishing at each drop of the pole that Daddy could see how wonderful his little five year old boy is as a skier. He learned to climb by side stepping today and practiced coming down a tiny slope in the yard with "knees bent & weight forward." He really acts as if he'd been on skis for months instead of 3 days. Before I end this subject and forget to tell you, I just got Mr.

Hvolbeck on the phone and he has promised to get us plowed out to No. St. tomorrow morning. I really have enjoyed every bit of it & (we have plenty of food yet) with the exception of Tina's foul disposition.

I just finished a marvelous book called "The Little Locksmith." It's written by a girl who was strapped to a board from the age of 5 to 15 with T.B. of the spine. Despite the treatment she got up a hunch back and the story is of her fight to make some kind of a happy life for herself with this terrific handicap. She lived in a family of means with two brothers & a sister all of whom loved her but never spoke of her trouble or offered help mentally. She had a nervous breakdown when she realized that boys were repelled by her physical unsightliness and that she could never have any hope of marriage. She turned to writing and disciplined herself to spend hours each day writing poetry or stories and finally tore herself away from her family. Until this book came out of her life she has had very little published but she stuck at it throughout her life. She bought a large house in Maine and finally realized happiness there alone. Here there was no one to pity her and she came to know the humility of faith in God. She had a very interesting idea which I'd like to give you. In speaking of what God has given us in the way of senses and the human mind and the heart she says; "And although everything appears to have been planned to make us feel at home on earth, aren't we really in the position of guests? We came from we do not know where, and we return we do not know where. And in that case what incredibly rude guests! Taking all this for granted, and then complaining and cursing God and asking for more. I tried to think of some way to make amends and it dawned on me then to pray. Then that is what prayer is for! It is the natural expression of those who are not so stupid & so rude as to have forgotten they are guests."

Well, darling, it's been wonderful to have an hour's chat with you again. I always have so much to say & so few words to say it in. I love you.

Peggy

[George to Peggy]

#92
Capt. G R Steiner
AFHQ G-4 Sec APO 512
c/o PM New York N.Y.
15 Feb. Tues. PM

My darling:

Your letters are so very welcome. You tell me things I like to know about. What you do, who you see and of course most important what the children are doing and saying. It is a shame to have Robbie growing up without me there to enjoy it all. Still I know you have a lot of troubles, work, and loneliness, but you seem to find a lot of bright spots in it all to appreciate, then tell me about. You always have been good at adding a lot of pleasant spots to living. One feeling I am constantly aware of is your absence. There are not many experiences we have shared together that I have not brought out of my memory to treasure for a while, even way back to the time Tommy McCann and I didn't get down to say good bye when you were going to South America. I had a box of candy for you from Ivey's, but since we missed seeing you we ate it ourselves. When you took Faustania over the bars you made some army officers look mighty foolish. You were very convincing one summer evening when I kissed you goodbye on the deck of the Bremen. I wish now that I had forgotten Harvard Graduate school and we had gotten married that summer. Then you were working so hard and so interested at N.W. hospital. I am sure you could have been a very good doctor, but when I see our children I am convinced that you chose a much more important occupation in which you have no equal. I sure am proud of those children. Yale will be pretty lucky to get a couple of boys like Larry and Robbie, now how about Georgia, where is she going?

You know I wish there were two martini glasses with the little shaker Monie gave us on the coffee table in front of our fire place, with some of our favorite Hungarian gypsy music playing, some bright embers glowing, you sitting near me with just a lot of things to talk about. That will be fun to do that again, and I can give you some more lessons at backgammon.

It has turned quite chilly again, maybe that is what made me think of the grate fire with you sitting very near me, or again it might have been something else.

Hope you got my V-Mail valentine. There is a gold ring here which has a lot of promises for the future. X Larry X Georgia x Robbie. You will have to wait for yours.

My love dear. George

[George to Peggy]

[#]93
Capt. G.R. Steiner
At Hq G-4; APO 512
c/o P.M. New York N.Y.
17/2/44

My darling Peggy:

Here I was duty officer last night and I didn't even write you a letter. Trouble was several back copies of Time and News Week arrived along with a new edition of Readers Digest which is now printed in four installments by Star and Stripes. Then a long distance call came in that took some time to settle up. Finally Allen stuck his homely freckled face in the door to say good night and we got talking about one thing and another until it was way past a reasonable bed time so you didn't get a letter which by all rights you should have had.

So in lieu of above mentioned letter, which inadvertently was not written, a package is being forwarded to you at an early date. So far as you are concerned the contents will remain a mystery until arrival in Greenwich. I hope you will like it as I took some time and pains in selecting the contents which consists of two items. One is tan in color and the other as you might guess is blue. I looked over a good many of them before choosing these, opened them to see how they were put together and felt of the texture to get a nice soft one. The work on them is not as well finished as I would like, but the material appears to be of good quality.

It was my day off and Allen being an ugly sort of guy chased me out after lunch. So I took a walk about town and looked into a number of shops, even got myself a couple of pairs of socks. At one point I found Capt. Downer down by the water front watching the goings on which is always an interesting occupation in any port. That reminds me of one trip you and I made on this same sea. Then a bit later I ran into Lt. Col. Starr just walking around with a day off. We took a look into a shop that must have been quite a place for tourists in prewar days with all sorts of native weapons, a bit of french statuary, and some rather handsome mantel clocks along with a lot of Arab brass work.

After dinner tonight Maj. Simons and Col. Bolan wanted to play bridge but we couldn't locate a fourth. So we ended up throwing darts of all places in a big bath room next to the room where we stay as duty officers, Maj. Simons being it tonight.

Now it is going on to ten o'clock so I will be on my way to bed to think about a girl I love as I fall to sleep. You guess what I will be wishing.

My love dear, George

[George to Peggy]

>Capt. G.R. Steiner
>AFHQ G-4; APO 512
>c/o Postmaster N.Y.C.
>19 Feb. 44

Peg dear:

Got a very nice letter from you today with a picture of Larry and Robbie by the Christmas tree. Robbie surely isn't the little baby I left with you anymore. I noticed a pair of ski poles off to one side, a coaster that Georgia and Larry must have fun with. Further study of the picture gets my curiosity aroused as to why my old flight bag with the ATC stickers on it appears off to one side in the door way. Just what could you have been using that for.

Remember that dandy little pocket knife I always carry? It is just like the one we bought for me when we were looking for a Christmas present for Colby a couple of years ago in that little cutlery shop on Madison across the street from the Biltmore. No I didn't lose this one but last night after dinner Hayes, Walker and Knifflen were very insistent on playing some bridge. Unfortunately we picked up a bottle of wine. Not having a corkscrew I tried extracting the cork with my knife. So I ended up by breaking off that neat little nail file on my knife.

Allen came back for a while tonight so we have been talking things over. We are both pretty discouraged about the personnel policy or rather lack of one in this section. The way the section is set up there is no chance for promotion with no inclination to change the situation. After the build up we got from Marshall in OPD this has been a sorry let down. With the very uncommon training, background, and experience in staff work which we both have had it is more than annoying to see far less qualified officers with nominal duties in sections whose very existence would be difficult to justify getting promotions. Allen was G-1 of a division when OPD selected us for training last year, and I sure would jump at the opportunity to get my job back. Well the luck has to turn back again sometime, and I am not missing any opportunities to help it along. In the meantime I can honestly say we are doing a pile of work here and doing it well.

It is getting late now so I will have to be getting to bed. My study of french has been sadly neglected of late, the few nights we have not been working here I have been playing bridge so I haven't talked french for a long time. So I guess in our travels you will still have to do the talking when it is in French.

Good night dear, George.

[Peggy to George]
[V-Mail]

#137
Feb. 19, Sat.

Dearest George,

I am sitting in the bay window of our living room with the sun coming through listening to Larry and Robin play on the terrace and waiting for Georgia to get dressed and go out after her nap. I can see Frank burning brush up by the vegetable garden. He watch[ed] Larry and Scott Pearson this morning while I drove to the village for errands with Robin and Georgia. As we came back the boys ran up to the car and Larry said, "Momie, can Scott stay for lunch with me?" I knew Scott put him up to it but I couldn't say no. So I fed all four and Doxie at once in the kitchen. Then Larry and Scott played outside while the other two napped. Now Scott has left and Larry is trying out all the new expressions he heard Scott use—on Robin. How fast he is growing up. There's a regular loud mouthed roughy to replace our quiet shy baby boy. He just screamed "Boy! Robbie was that a dirty one!" I don't even know what he refers to. Last night after the children were tucked in the girls met here and had roast pork from our own pig. It's very good but too expensive to try raising again. We discussed Russian history last night. Georgia is very excited about her doll which is to come from Africa. You're awfully sweet to do that. I think Covey is the boy's name under Hewitt that Mart told me about. Love, Peggy

[George to Peggy]

#94
Capt. G R Steiner
AFHQ G-4 Sec APO 512
c/o P.M. New York.
22 Feb. 44

Peg dear:

Your most very nice Valentines letter came today. Larry and you on your skis was a very well drawn picture. Of course I cannot figure what you mean by referring to his inherited liking for praise. My reaction on such occasions has been mistaken by you, for my expression is really one of surprise at such a seldom heard remark. [doodle] (fish hook)

Jerry Fitz Gerald called up late this afternoon to ask me out to dinner. He and Covey came by to pick me up about 6^{30}. We had a drink at the Navy bar which is more than welcome and enjoyed an excellent meal with good company. One thing I notice about the Naval officers is that they take much more pains to carry on a good conversation even though they do not know each other and take the trouble to straighten out names all around the table. Most of them are better mannered and educated than the average officer you eat with in our mess. I think on the whole they have been more careful in giving commissions than has the Army.

Played ping pong with Jerry for a while after dinner for the first time since I have been over here which for some reason made me think of playing with you at the Manor House in Morton Hempstead if you recall. And you did not care for a Tom Collins made from Holland gin. And do you remember the fine "Nordic" specimen who was there showing his great friendliness for the English people?

Well anyway I rode back here about nine o'clock with a Naval officer Lt. Sweet who was coming into town. Finding Allen, Barnhill,[177] Little, Ream, and Heartzca[178] playing poker I got in the game for a couple hours lost a lot, made it all back to end up with only 30 francs ahead.

So now I will remind you that I love you very much and say goodnight.

Yours, George

[George to Peggy]

#95
Capt. GR Steiner
AFHQ G-4 Sec APO 512
c/o P.M. New York.
23/2/44

Peg dear:

For the moment we have a lull in this great paper battle.

24/2/44

The above is one of the shortest letters I have ever written you. Allen insisted we leave the office before something else got tagged on to us, so we went down to dinner about 6^{15} yesterday.

Today being *mon jour libre* I got a haircut before coming up here. We have a pretty good barber shop with some very good barbers from among the Italian prisoners.

This place I went out to have lunch with Echols is quite an interesting old place. Echols says it is about 500 years old. It is one of these Villas that some Arab built. When the Army took it over however it had been modernized along French lines. The water for the

---

177 Likely Colonel Lester H. Barnhill.
178 Likely Lt. Colonel Wayne S. Hertzka.

plumbing fixtures was gotten to a tank on the roof by wheel driven pump, the wheel in turn being driven by the Arab who in turn was driven by a frenchman.

Echols I have mentioned before as a very good gent (i.e. Yale 35) who comes from Milwaukee, was at Sill with Rob for a while, and was in our R.O.T.C. field artillery unit. Also Betty Seymore, Bill Houses old mountain climbing companion is working in the same outfit as Echols.

Went down to see a movie at the Red Cross last night after dinner. Tonight I am going to pick Hayes up on the way to dinner, see if we can find someone to play bridge, if not go to a movie. It is cold and wet around here now.

My love, George

[Peggy to George]
[V-Mail]

#139
Feb. 24 1944 Thurs.

Darling,

I am on my way to N.Y.C. and shall attempt to tell you something with each stop. This is Rye. I am going in to have dinner with Frank & Helen and do the errands I couldn't do on Washington's Birthday. (Mamaronek.) Frank came into the hotel from the plant before I left for Greenwich Tues. and he is looking fine. He said to tell you they just got the [S]perry gyroscope order which runs about 5 thousand a month. (must be a year?) Uncle George had another spell but is better. Helen got a new mink coat for Christmas too. (Harrison) Tues. night I stopped at Pinky's for dinner and our weekly meeting before getting home. Yesterday I worked around home as usual and took all three children to Dr. Close for a check up in the afternoon. If you have a yard stick you can see how tall each one is: Larry—43½ in. & 39½ lbs. Georgia—40in. & 35 lbs. Robin, 30 in. & 25½ lbs.

(Larchmont) Last night I sewed on my lamp shade which I am making for an indirect lamp in our living room. Then I can put the radio on my sewing cabinet where the table lamp is now. (New Rochelle) This morning Larry and Georgia were out in the brook with an old piece of pipe making "chocolate pudding with nuts (stones) in it." Robin was upstairs crawling in my bucket while I washed windows. They all had lunch and are in bed for their naps while I change from charwoman to lady in her minks and go to town. Glad to know you are at Navy mess. Peggy

[Peggy to George]
[V-Mail]

#140
Feb. 25, Friday

My Darling George,

    We have just finished a very strenuous game of hide and seek. Larry scared me nearly to death by jumping at me from the dark coat closet here in the sitting room and I bumped my knee on the door much to his delight. Georgia hid once in the cupboard underneath the pantry sink and no one could find her until we heard her knock over a carton of coca-cola. Robin was screaming lustily in bed to miss it all because he went there when he refused lima beans for supper and returned the mouthful he tried with a great blow. Last night with Frank & Helen was very enjoyable. We had drinks in their room which was the one Mrs. Alworth usually has with Mr. & Mrs. Catlin, George Benninghoff—Frank Mihelich. Mr. B. got arguing with me about the hopelessness of a peace with Russia & the inevitability of another war in our lifetime until I could hardly control myself. Frank finally broke it up and we went downstairs for dinner. Only the Catlins joined us. They were very nice, I thought. I took the ten o'clock express home and found everything O.K. Today believe it or not I cleaned our red sofa and chair myself and they are fine.

They wanted $40.00 over [in] town to do it. I must admit it took all morning but surely my mornings aren't worth more than that. I love you so very much dear. Peggy

[Peggy to George]

#141
Mon. Feb. 28. 8:P.M.

Darling George,

We had our date in the kitchen as usual tonight. I wish each time that you could peek in at your great big family. I really am kept busy cooking for all those mouths and how grateful I am to still have so much good food available in this country. We really get everything we need in abundance and almost anything one could ever want except perhaps filet mignon. The children really are developing so fast and look fine. Tina rides pretty heavy handed on the discipline but working side by side each day I know whatever goes on and although sometimes she definitely takes out her lousy morning disposition on their fannies I grit my teeth and say nothing as long as none of them are cowed by her as Larry was by Kathe.

The weekend was quite gay. Wayne took me out Saturday night. We had cocktails at the Biltmore, dinner at Persian Room in the Plaza. Then went to see "Mexican Hayride" which was a good musical based on mexico and very elaborately scened and costumed. This wasn't even all. We went to the new Monte Carlo night club afterward for a couple of drinks and then took the 1:25 A.M. train home. Sat. nights in N.Y.C. are something awful. The crowds are so terrific, it's impossible to get in any place without reservations, a taxi is like a needle in a haystack. We took [a] trolley Sat. P.M. I must say most of the crowds have a predominance of men in uniform and the rest are Jews or people with more money than they have ever seen before and how they can spend it!

Sunday (yesterday) morning I had to get up at eight as usual to get the children & Tina their breakfast. However, I did get back in bed about a half hour later and slept a couple more hours. I gave Wayne coffee and we went to Bowdens for lunch. Bernice did it all herself and it was very nice. She had 12—Hites, Lewises, Wainwrights, Marj Peters, Peggy Gerli, Wellingtons & Wayne & myself. About three thirty we left because Helen & Frank borrowed your old car from Crawford and drove "Chiffon" (dog with red hair ribbon) up to see the house & children. It was a foggy, icy day and I tried to get them to come by train but that didn't suit the dog. Consequently, they barely arrived when Frank got [fidgety] about the weather and they left in about an hour. I felt badly as I had planned supper for them and Bill & Bernice were coming. They loved the house and the children showed off well so I guess it was O.K. Anyway Bill & Bernice came and I made waffles and a salad which we had on the card table in front of the fire. I also had a fresh devil's food cake & coffee. It was appreciated by all but me I fear. I wanted to do it for Frank & Helen so I could talk about the night you and Frank got supper for Helen & me. It would have made last night so much cozier. Do you remember what you fixed[?] I do. A can of tomatoes plus olives I believe because that was the closest you could come to finding mushrooms. Then we had scrambled eggs and toast—both of which were excellent. They all left early so I got into bed and tried not to hear a little voice which kept saying; "How much longer, how much longer will I have to go on like this?" I always tell myself that it is so much easier for me to live alone when I have the comforts of these wonderful babies of yours and our lovely new house. You only have the great satisfaction of being part of this great conflict and doing a superb job of it. That is a lot as not a day passes that I don't wish I could really get in and do something. I tell myself that by doing Anna's work I have released one more person to do defense work & can buy more war bonds, but it's not too convincing. If I could only do something to bring you home more quickly to say nothing of a few million other boys.

My love dear, is always with you but Mon. nights I really do feel a little closer and can hardly wait for the day when we can really make a weekly occasion of these little telepathic dates. I love you so much and miss you more each day.

      Yours, Peggy

[Peggy and Larry to George]
[V-Mail]

                Feb. 29, 1944

To whom it may concern: This is Larry's idea of Georgia in the house looking out the window at him fishing on the dock at Grandmas. He claims you can see the fish. The hugs & kisses follow & his newly acquired signature.

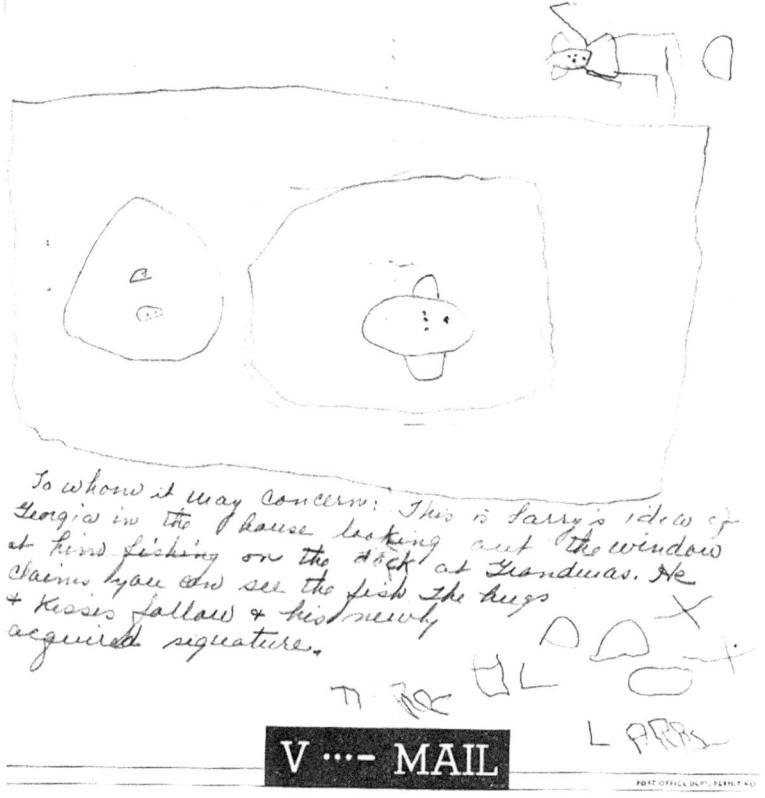

[Peggy to George]
[V-Mail]

#141
March 2, Thurs.

Dearest George

This letter I am writing so Chloe Bouscaren can take it into N.Y.C. to mail. I feel as if I have deserted you for days but boy! have I been busy. Tuesday, I had Pinky, Maggy & Pat Somers here for dinner and our discussions of Russian history this time. (After ironing all day!) In the midst of the evening Chloe called from N.Y.C. to say that Pete was on his way to New Haven for his Army physical & could they spend the night here. They arrived about ten and have been here ever since. Of course yesterday I wanted to entertain for Chloe so I had ten for cocktails & Bill & Bernice for dinner. This besides the children's meals. They leave today and Tina goes off tomorrow so I just planned to do the housework I've skipped over the weekend. About ten minutes ago word came that Bernice's father died last night so now I've offered to take Anne for the weekend. When it rains it pours! I feel fine though and surely have enjoyed Chloe. Pete says our house & grounds are the loveliest of any he knows in Greenwich & I believe he means it. He just raves about it. They both send their best to you. Yours, Peggy

[Peggy to George]
[V-Mail]

#144
Mar. 4 Sat.

Darling,

We are still at the breakfast table. Robin at my right gnawing on a piece of toast with Doxie catching all the stray crumbs. I have my back to the window and a cup of coffee left beside me. Georgia is opposite me trying to down her vitamin pills before Larry finishes his toast. He has eaten three "dogs" this morning, i.e. we had sausage and scrambled eggs. Now you have the picture. Here's hoping it stays comparatively stationary until I can finish this sheet. It is almost time for the postman and as I didn't even get to the mailbox yesterday, I am particularly anxious to go now. I got the house cleaned O.K. and the children cared for and Larry and I even had time to build a circus wagon out of his building logs that Ki gave him for Christmas. Today there isn't much to do besides meals. Mrs. Collins from the farm at Hekma's is coming to sit with the children while I go to Peters for dinner. It is a party to say farewell to Margie. She is leaving for a month in Florida. She "needs a change." Isn't this war awful on some people. I hope I can keep my thoughts to myself. All yours, Peggy

[Peggy to George]
[V-Mail]

#145
March 7, 1944

My Dearest George

Right now I have arrived early at Pat Somers for our weekly meeting as I have been to a Garden Club meeting in this part of town and don't have the gas to go home and come back. Anyhow I'd rather write you. Sat. nite I had a very nice time at the Peters' party which is unusual as I have become very critical of those of our friends who still spend money and drink in a wild war hysteria to forget they aren't doing their part. At best that seems the only possible reason. However Sat. was very pleasant, and several besides me left early so I felt O.K. about going for once. Sun. I was alone all day with the children and thoroughly enjoyed it. They all were good as gold. While they napped I did the family wash so that Mon. I could go to N.Y.C. which I did. The morning was busy scrubbing and waxing all the linoleum floors but I got away about two. I did a few errands and met Frank & Helen at the Hotel just about five. I almost let them on our date but preferred to keep it just for us so I said nothing. We had a very good martini and went to Brussels restaurant for dinner. The last time I went was with you and Frank & Helen for lunch. Do you remember? This really was a nice thought for last night's date. I love you so much dear. Peggy

[Peggy to George]
[V-Mail]

#146
March 8, Wed.

My Darling

    This is a lovely sunny morning and the children are outdoors helping Joe & Frank burn brush. We nearly have all the property cleared now so that when the ground is soft I have a plow & tractor ready to get out the roots so we can plant hay. I hope to have a pasture all ready for you when you get home. It makes the house so much fun to get each thing done thinking forward to the day I can show it all to you. Then as Georgia says "Daddy will be the farmer and build our barn." I have lots of plans which cannot materialize until after the war. One which I really anticipate is putting my favorite post and rail fence across the house end of the woods where the wall that comes through the center of the land stops at the garden path and east to the wall on that side of the property. It would look nice from the house and we could sit on the porch and watch the horses graze. That is a real dream isn't it. But we will do it—just wait & see. Love & Kisses. Peggy

[George to Peggy]
[Handwritten on American Red Cross Stationery]

[#]102
Capt. G.R. Steiner
Hq SOS Natousa[179] G-4 Sec.
APO 750 c/o P.M. N.Y.C.
9 Mar. 1944

Dearest Peggy:

Reported in to the above headquarters this morning. It will take a little while to see how I stand around here. There are a lot of people around here whom I know. It may turn out all right, if it does not look too good, I am sure of being able to get a transfer back to the Air Service Command in this theatre. There was no possible chance for a promotion for anyone in the section I left. Allen is trying to get in a position to move out to some outfit where he has a chance, but I would be mighty surprised if they will let him go.

Had dinner tonight with Maj. Boyd who shared the apartment with Howder and Allen. He was with the group that preceded us in that OPD training course. His group got the same kind of treatment on assignment as we did at least in this theatre. What was done with the officers that went to the other theatres I do not know. Boyd has been transferred down here also.

This is not a bad place to be assigned, much better than at (I just can't mention the name 'cause it would be censored you know). There is a very good officers' club, the Red Cross Club is excellent for a theatre of operations, in fact it would pass well in the states. The mess is excellent in both food and location. It is located in what had been a first class restaurant.

---

179 On February 29, 1944 George was relieved from his assignment at AFHQ in Algiers and transferred to Headquarters, Service of Supply (SOS) North African Theater of Operations, United States Army (NATOUSA) located in Oran, Algeria. (It should be noted that SOS, NATOUSA is not the same as NATOUSA, which had its headquarters in Algiers near AFHQ.) Activated in February 1943 SOS, NATOUSA absorbed much of the AFHQ G-4 section's work freeing up the AFHQ G-4 to manage matters of more importance (Wisbith, *Allied Force Headquarters during the North African Campaign*, 63.). Responsibilities of the new SOS, NATOUSA sections included centralizing stock control, making requisitions on the port of embarkation, and maintaining necessary supply levels in the many supply depots of NATO. By February 1944, SOS, NATOUSA had been transformed into a legitimate communications zone organization, about to experience its peak.

Right now I am living in a transient billet while I keep an eye open for a permanent location. However, there is hot water and a shower so you sure cannot complain on that. I was in that one spot in AFHQ for too long a time without ever getting away. This is a very welcome change indeed. I was sorry to leave Allen as we were getting along fine. He is O.K. There are not many people I have run across with as keen a mind as his. Along with it he has the sort of solid integrity that keeps him on the job even though he has gotten a mighty poor break promotion wise. With that amount of experience, background, training, and native ability it is not very heartening to have some of these screw balls in military government, P.W.B. etc. with direct commissions as major and lt. col. com[ing] in trying to tell you how things should be handled.

Well I will say good night dear. I sure do miss you, but as Allen reminded me upon saying goodbye, I am very lucky because I will be a couple of hundred miles nearer home than he is. A helpful friend isn't he?

All my love dear, George

[Peggy to George]
[V-Mail]

#147
March 9, Thurs.

My Dearest George

Your nice long typed v-mail letter came yesterday. Don't worry about my reading those you write as I haven't missed a word yet. Both have merits. I like the extra news you get in when it's typed and I like to see the handwriting which is so familiar to me. Your stories about using the ready-made cables are very funny. I'd like to know if Allen's wife did get the house and where she lives. I guess it's not around New England. Joe and Frank and the children got quite a bit done yesterday. When they left, Frank said he had a "lady friend" who he'd like to have cook for me. He's bringing her out to see me tonight. I'm getting along fine as it is—except for losing a few pounds and having a few of our friends comment on how tired I look I wouldn't bother with anyone until next summer. It seems silly to train someone in now even if I am lucky to find one and then go to Mpls. this summer and either pay wages while I am gone or let her go. However, I don't intend to go until August as I hate to miss my garden and the pretty place here. How I wonder when you'll be home to enjoy the spring at our new house. It seems a thousand years since last June when you left and I feel a thousand years older. I hope I don't look it. My independence galls me so I can hardly wait for you to come back so I can be a clinging vine. It's gotten so the boys who are drafted ask me to look after their wives!! Peggy

[George to Peggy]
[Handwritten on American Red Cross Stationery]

[#]101
10 March 44

Peg dear,

    Last night, I slipped up on the letter number, got one ahead so I will take care of that tonight. From the above you will see that I am down at the Red Cross again tonight.

    Thought that I would take up the study of French seriously. So I have just been in a french class for an hour and a half.

    I wanted to put some time in at this before but with the way Allen and I were working evenings and all in AFHQ, there was no time left for that. Perhaps we were taking things too seriously, but then you keep thinking about what the boys are up against in the front while we lead a physically soft and comfortable life back here. Then you put that together with the unusually excellent training we had for staff work, and you just have to see that the work is handled properly and cleared up every night. They sure left us in the cold on promotions in our section, but it was satisfying to find how the work came our way and more and more people came in to Allen and I for answers. Then when our work went up to the front office for signature they were very ready to trust our judgement and send it along.

It looks like a fairly decent set up here. I will let you know how things go.

Darling, I sure miss you, and that part of it never will get any better, until I get back.

My love dear, George

[Peggy to George]

#148

P.S. On rereading I find just telling you this has raised my spirits 100% so thanks, darling, for listening. I wish you'd send me a new snapshot of yourself. <u>No cigar</u>

Friday

Darling

I've had two rather hard days since I wrote you. Friday besides the cleaning I had Anne Bowden from nine a.m. until Sat. noon. She's not exactly an addition as she becomes more like Janet each day and is very critical of anything different from the way it is done at home. Besides she eats nothing to speak of. Just after she left I went up to change my clothes as Pete had asked me down for a drink. The children were in the kitchen having supper as I came down & I walked out to catch Tina in the act of threatening Georgia with my laundry stick if she didn't eat faster and stop crying. I screamed at her and she put it down but I've hardly been able to speak to her since and I couldn't sleep a wink last night. I try to stake her past actions against the implications of this act and make myself believe that she wouldn't have hit her, but so far nothing's convincing. I'll let it go another day or two, but I don't believe I'll ever feel comfortable about leaving her alone with the children again. If that's true I'm paying out $100.00 a month for nothing as she certainly is doing no work. The spurt she had just after Anna left has long ago worn itself out. I wrote you about the girl Frank was bringing for an interview. They came and she wasn't bad. She only was getting $130.00 plus room and board at the place she has & was willing to consider this place at the same figure. It reminded me of the $85.00 a month (minus room & board plus a college education and 6 months training without pay) which I fought for and had refused to me as laboratory technician.[180] Another woman (German) Frank has sent to see me tomorrow. She sounds too much like Kathe over the phone and is worth $125.00 says she. I'll go home to Mother before I pay it. I'd do all the work anyway, I'll bet.

I haven't been any lower since you left. It all seems so futile trying to cope with food rations, shoes, gas, oil, lousy help, if any, and you so far away and no end even in sight. Excuse the griping but you know when you read this, it will be all straightened out some way for a few more months.

I had a letter from Kay Bull and she really has something to worry about. There's been no word from Webby, but she heard from a fighter pilot who was escorting him. He said Webby went down over Holland & was still under control until he lost sight of Webby going into a cloud. He wasn't seen after that. They say she probably won't hear directly for months.

Darling there are so many things I want to talk to you about tonight. Most of them have to do with the different outlook I have on many things since you left. I'd like you to straighten out my critical feelings towards everyone not in this war, somehow either at home or abroad. I find I can't have a ten minute conversation with one without throwing a few sarcastic remarks around. Perhaps it all comes from living alone and thinking too much about where this life takes us and

---

180 After she graduated from college, Peggy lived with her parents and worked as a lab technician at Northwestern Hospital (now the Abbott Northwestern Hospital) in Minneapolis.

why we are here. I have to have some purpose besides just to love you now. That was so easy and required no thought. Now I resort to reading and trying to figure out what I can give and what I want to get out of this life. The children well mannered, well educated, thoughtful of others, and clear on their purpose in life is what I hope to give. Peace, organized by farsighted statesmen, backed by an international police force and <u>you</u> <u>home</u> is what I want from life. I'm working hard on my 3 donations each day and also reading and talking to bring forth my hopes of peace organization into the minds at least of the few people I contact. But what I really need and want the most—<u>you</u> I can do nothing more tangible about than writing letters and buying war bonds.

You'd have had a laugh out of the children tonight. I read them their nightly story and they were so full of the devil that they raced around and asked a million questions to put off prayers and goodnights when the reading was over. Finally, I got Larry down to say his prayers and tried to hog tie Georgia until he had finished. In spite of this she talked incessantly. When Larry finished he said, "Whew, I'll bet God had a hard time hearing me tonight." <u>What</u> I'd give to have you see how he's developed! He's just as sweet & obedient, but he's a regular fellow now. And <u>very</u> good looking, if I do say so.

I love you so very much, dear, Peggy

[Peggy to George]
[V-Mail]

#149
Wed. Mar. 15.

My Darling,

I haven't written since Sunday as I wanted to be able to tell you the domestic outcome. Mon. a.m. I took the floor with Tina and for once was mad enough to hold it and not let her argue. The results are good so far. That afternoon the applicant for cook arrived. She was french instead of german and I liked her very much except for her age. She was too old, also she wouldn't work for my $100.00. Smug act. All's well now though and I'll get a cook at my price eventually. How I wish I could be with you on your birthday Mon. I've been thinking of the fun we had driving to New London two years ago for the big event. We'll have a real date next Mon., though. I'll even mix us a drink, a fire and think over all we'll do next year to celebrate. I am mailing you a photograph I had taken as a birthday present. It could be better but you'll like it anyway, I hope. Many <u>Happy</u> returns dear and <u>please</u> let's have the next one together. Larry has been so worried because we cannot send you a cake. He had great fun, however, substituting the cards. Frank is here and the brush is all cleared today. It looks wonderful but there is so much more to do. Larry helped clean the garage and sift dirt to start our seeds this a.m. We need a greenhouse but use the guest room. Peggy

[George to Peggy]
[V-Mail]

No. 102
16 [March] 44

Peg dear:

    After not hearing from you for a couple weeks I got three V-mails and two air mail letters yesterday with a birthday card today. The birthday card got here in a hurry, it was mailed March 7 and had to be readdressed from AFHQ. You know when you move into a new headquarters like this there sure are a lot of new names to remember. And before you can be of much use around a headquarters you have to get acquainted with a lot of people, know what they do, and how to get ahold of them. There is a good bunch of officers here. Think I will stop in for a French lesson tonight. It is kind of nice for a change not to have the pile of work Allen and I were confronted with before. My love dear. George

[Peggy to George]

#150
Friday 7:30 P.M. Mar. 17

My Darling George

It seems quite a coincidence that I should reach this particular letter number when you change your location for the first time. I wonder if I'll write a hundred and fifty letters to this new A.P.O. It surely seems ages already.

You seem quite satisfied with the change so naturally I am happy about it too. I wish Allen could have gone with you as you seem to be so congenial. Your birthday present was held up a day in <u>mailing</u> which is fortunate as I could put the new address on it. Don't worry if it is late as it weighed a little too much to go Air Mail. I must say your new location improves the length of time it takes mail to get home. The letter you wrote March 10<u>th</u> arrived yesterday (6 days.) I feel lots closer to you if that's any help.

My throat is hoarse from nursery rhymes. Tina is off this weekend and I read and sang the whole of Mother Goose almost tonight after Larry and Georgia helped me with the dishes. I want you to know I never dried one dish or pot tonight. They did the whole business. I wish I could remember all of the funny things they have said today. It makes me furious to forget them so quickly. One thing I remember is that Larry was on his favorite subject of you and the barn you are going to build. Today, he figured out just how he wants the barn door. He even told me how many hinges to buy for you—<u>three</u>, if you please.

Not much has gone on this week except the domestic struggle which I have given you round by round. I believe it is ironed out again for the time being, at least. Last night I had Pete Peters and his partner from Chicago and Pinky for dinner. Margie being in Florida and their couple off Thurs. leaves Pete to get his and Hodgie's suppers so I took Hodgie after school & kept him & fed him & put him to bed.

Pete picked him up when he left. It was a pleasant evening although the men arrived with several drinks under their belts. I had dashed around after the children's supper to fix spareribs, sauerkraut, mashed potatoes, asparagus, hollandaise & a nifty barbecue sauce for the ribs. Also had a compote of fruit & cookies & coffee. They ate second helpings but I don't believe they knew what they ate. I had all the dishes to do after Tina left this a.m. and that made me think I was foolish to have fussed so much.

I just let Doxie in out of the rain. He's soaking and lying by my feet here in front of the fire. Whew! Stinko! There's no doubt about him being a dog. I built the fire so you and I could have a cozy date but you might be glad it's only telepathic if you could get a whiff. There's a pile of mending knee deep on the other side of me which I'll have to tackle when I've finished bothering you. I also have the morning's oatmeal on the stove which must be turned off now.

The flight bag you noticed in the Christmas picture I have laughed about more times. I gave it to the British Navy boy who was with us Christmas. It's easy to see I can't even get away with giving out your things when you are several thousand miles away. You are too observing altogether.

I suppose I better get to work on Larry's socks.
      Goodnight, darling & a great big X & O. Peggy

[George to Peggy]
[Handwritten on American Red Cross stationery]
Capt. G.R. Steiner
Hq SOS Natousa G-4 Sec
APO 750; C/O PM N.Y.C.
19 Mar. 44

Peg dear;
    Je viens d'une leçon français, mais je ne parle bien parce que pendant que je restais au Alger je n'avais pas le temp libre pour etudier.

Cenpendant, maintenant j'etudierai chaque jour.[181]

This is not too bad a town, although I have not gotten too good a place to live yet. Only trouble is it is too crowded, double decked beds with eight officers to a room. Then of course, there is no place to put your clothes. However, there is a shower and hot water, even if it is salty like Key West.

The work here is just about the same as we were doing at AFHQ, G-4.

On the whole they have a pretty good bunch of officers, on the average not so capable as at AF but good fellows. The chief of section and his assistant are of course regular army.[182] The former has some of the fine qualities of Eugene Alder, while the latter could easily be mistaken for Doug Hemming. A letter from Lt. Col. Peairs[183] informs me that Hemming has just received a well earned promotion.

There is a new colonel in charge of the subsection to which I am assigned, who just arrived who seems to be on the ball. Strange to say he is not a ring bearer, but a reserve officer. An HBS[184] man who had been interested in getting in that Task Force Officer's class of Marshall's, but was a year too old. I guess he won't feel so badly about missing it after he found the kind of jobs we were all dumped into upon arrival over here.

Remember your troubles with Nan Miller? Well I have the same situation on my hands with a major here.

Guess I am getting to be an old man, tomorrow I will be 31. Wish I was home 'cause I am sure I would get a nice party with one of your wonderful angel food cakes. Chances are I will remember two years ago when you gave me such a pleasant surprise by bringing the family up to visit me. I sure was surprised to have Larry come running over

---

181   Translated: "I come from a French lesson, but I do not speak well because while I was staying in Algiers I did not have free time to study. However, now I will study every day."
182   Regular Army refers to the full-time, active-service section of the Army. Regular Army members make a career of their service.
183   Likely Chalmers A. Peairs, Jr. who was stationed with George in Rome, New York. Peairs was a major at the time.
184   Harvard Business School.

to my chair in the hotel when I was just expecting you, then to see Tina with Georgia. Thanks again for that nice surprise. I won't be expecting anything like that tomorrow.

Gee, but I miss you darling. There is a dance here at the Red Cross tonight. I sure wish I could take you out on the floor, I would be mighty proud to let the other fellows see what a pretty, charming girl I have. I expect to keep your date book well filled up when I get home. Sure resent missing a year shared with you my dear.

George

[George to Peggy]
[V-Mail]

No. 104
20 March 1944

Peg dear:

Here I am 31 years old today. Wish we could be together to have a birthday party. If this goes on much longer I will have an awful time blowing out all the candles. I got three letters V-Mail from you today, one from a fellow by the name of Larry, a big box of candy from Aunt Gertrude, and a big jar of my favorite Walnut tobacco. Thank you very much also for the Leica film and the razor blades, both of which are very welcome. I received the letter with all the pictures of the kids and the house. Gee I better not forget you and Doxie, give him a pat on the head and remind Mrs. Steiner that she is the pretty, likeable, capable wife of a man who is very much in love with her. I am being rushed to go to supper—will write you more tonight. My love. George

[George to Peggy]
[V-Mail]

No. 105
20 March 1944

My darling:

    Wonder what you are doing right now, it is Monday evening so of course I am thinking of my best girl. I am writing on my bunk with another officer on the tier above me reading an old much worn copy of the "Robe." To write on, I am using that fine photo book you gave me after having looked at pictures of you which has gotten me to longing a bit more than ever to have you with me. I sure have an attractive pretty wife, but you are much too far away right now. Wish my fingers were touching your back right now and you had had one of those pretty nighties on. That is the birthday present I want next year so don't forget now. There is only one person I want at my birthday party, but I do want lots of care giv[en] to wrapping my presents, and I want to unwrap it myself, maybe taking all evening to find just what I am to get. My love dear. George

[Peggy to George]

#151
Sun. P.M. 7:00

My Darling George,

    Happy Birthday dear! If you are still up, this is already the great day. I do wish you could have spent the last fifteen minutes with us here. The problem was to get two hellyuns to bed. They listened quietly while I read to them until 6:30 and then the trouble started. Both went wild—crawling under chairs, tables, the piano etc. etc. I finally got them separated to get one brushing teeth while I heard the other's prayers in our dressing room. If I let them stay together the rough house reaches such proportions I cannot cope with it single handed. After all preparations were finished we had a tickling bout and then Larry refused to say goodnight to Georgia. This worked to prolong things a little more. Finally that was accomplished with a slight twist of Georgia's neck and a lusty smack. Georgia tried to rub the kiss off but Larry insisted he had put it on so hard she couldn't get it off. I fully expect to still see it in the morning as a black & blue spot. That got Georgia to bed. I still had to tackle Larry. When he finally lay on his back in bed I leaned over to kiss him and he hugged me so hard I fell on the bed. This was worth another three minutes of giggling on both sides. At last the door was closed on the last night of this weekend alone. I cannot pretend I don't enjoy their vitality and spunk but neither can I pretend I don't feel relaxed when they are finally in bed. Arriving down here to write you I came upon Doxie with eyes ablazing and the newspaper in shreds between his paws. He couldn't have said more plainly, "Now it's my turn!" He doesn't compete while the children are up, but he certainly comes to life immediately after they are in bed. The three of them surely have been feeling their oats all day. At noon when I called them in for lunch, Georgia came in covered with mud from the brook. I said, "You're a devil, Georgia." The answer was: "I'm not a Devil, Georgia. I'm just <u>plain old Georgia</u>." Enough about our remarkable progeny.

 I phoned Mpls. this morning and found Jack reported this noon to Fort Snelling for his physical. Mother was in an awful state. I suppose she'll have to take in Thelma and the boys. Little Georgie has been sick all winter too. He had measles last week as the last of a long chain of colds, flu, diarrhea, fevers etc. He weighs two pounds less than our Robin and is 8 months older than Georgia. It makes me sick as I know how it worries Mother. She often writes that she fears they'll never raise the little fellow. If I had a good nurse and cook and Thelma was willing, I'd like to take him for a few months. The responsibility would be too hazardous though in his present condition. I'm sure she is doing everything possible, but the change in climate might help.

 After writing you Friday night I actually did start my mending, but the phone rang and it was Pete Peters, his partner, Pinky and another business associate. They had been to the Club for dinner and wanted to come over to amuse me. Well, they did! and what's more they got me pretty high. Pete brought the first bottle of bourbon I've seen in months and it tasted fine! They already had had plenty except for Pinky. It was good to really laugh. I haven't done it in so long I'd almost forgotten how good it makes you feel. The third member of "Free & Peters" was a born comedian & with a few drinks and St. Patrick's Day to celebrate, he really was funny. I trust you'll forgive the dissipation. It was harmless but enjoyable only because it's such a novelty to me. With most that crowd, it is a steady diet and that would be unbearable.

Yesterday, Sat. we all walked to the mailbox for a letter from Daddy and found two. They were from the old A.P.O. One letter told of your present coming to me and believe it or not the box came in the same mail. How I love my bags. They are beautiful. Already the blue one is in everyday use as my knitting and darning bag. The tan one I am saving for my spring suit. Many thanks darling. Leather goods [are] impossible to find in any quality. These are beautiful.

I have gotten pretty upset about Russia's attitude in Poland[185] etc.

---

185   As the Nazis retreat west across Nazi-occupied Polish territory, the Red Army of the Soviet Union advances for a second time through areas that belonged to Poland before the war. A lack of publicized post-war plans for Poland's eastern border and the absence of normal diplomatic relations between the Polish government-in-exile and the Soviets seemingly indicate the USSR's ambition to remain and incorporate those areas. Soviet leader Joseph Stalin has gradually separated Poland diplomatically from its neighbors, courting alliances with the Czechoslovakian, Italian, and Romanian governments. The Polish government-in-exile is isolated from events in Poland but despite expressing its concerns about Soviet post-war intentions the U.S. and British governments offer no assurances of support.

During the Russo-Polish War (1919-1920) the Curzon Line was proposed as the demarcation line between Poland and Russia. However, the final treaty reflected Poland's victory and awarded nearly 52,000 square miles east of the Curzon Line to Poland. The Curzon Line was largely forgotten until the Nazi-Soviet Non-Aggression Pact in 1939. Secret sections of the pact, surfacing in 1946 and denied by the Soviets until 1989, allowed for the USSR to occupy land east of a demarcation line nearly identical to the former Curzon Line while allowing the Nazis to invade and occupy all of Poland to the west–which is what happened, effectively erasing autonomous Poland from the map (Zawadzki, *A Concise History of Poland*, 253, 255.). During the two years the Soviets occupied eastern Poland, around 315,000 Polish citizens were deported, nearly 110,00 arrested, 25,000 perished while in Soviet custody, and 30,000 were executed (Snyder, *Bloodlands*, 151.).

As the Red Army approached the Curzon Line in spring 1944, concern they would remain after the war and prohibit an independent Poland reached a peak. The government-in-exile was especially worried about a propaganda war promoting Soviet communism. Their worries were well-founded as the USSR established civil institutions in the newly-liberated (or newly-reoccupied) Polish lands to rival those of the government-in-exile (Zawadzki, *A Concise History of Poland*, 267-268.).

In response to the silence from the United States and Britain on the "absence of a precise Soviet commitment to respect the pre-war Polish-Soviet border," 36 educators, jurists, publicists, and religious leaders issued a statement

Also our seeming lack of any postwar foreign policy. Please write me your ideas on the subjects. I am forwarding several articles from Life & the Post soon.

My love and X X X, Peggy

[George to Peggy]
[V-Mail]

21 March 1944

Peg My darling:

One of these days I am going to get so damned disgusted with the dumb observance of form by people who would like to pass themselves off as genuine staff officers. This headquarters is the real dumping ground for worthless old regular army officers. With clouds in their heads, lead in their tails, and eagles on their shoulders, they swagger arrogantly about with riding crops in their hand desperately trying to convince people of their importance. Unable to grasp major problems or to comprehend fundamentals they busy themselves with petty details. Of course the key men are not this type, but they put up with having too many old fuddlebuts. Yours, George

[Peggy to George]
[V-Mail]

#152

Tues. Mar. 21 1944

Dearest George

Our birthday date last night was a bit confused. Five o'clock is a bad hour for me to fix myself a cocktail as I had planned and toast

---

reminding the world that Poland was the first nation to fight Hitler's advances–while the USSR originally aligned itself with Germany (Ibid., 267.). The group argued that if the demarcation line from the Nazi-Soviet pact was determined to be Poland's eastern border after the war, Poland would lose 46% of its pre-war territory ("Russia's Attitude on Poland Scored."). The Polish government-in-exile later expressed in a letter that Churchill and Roosevelt's reluctance to discuss Poland's post-war borders indicated "Poland, who was the first to oppose Hitler and who ever since has fought Germany at a most appalling cost, is to be more harshly treated than Germany" (Associated Press, "Poles Ask About Charter.").

Unbeknownst to the public and the Polish government-in-exile, at the Tehran Conference in 1943, Roosevelt and Churchill had agreed to Stalin's insistence that the Curzon Line should form Poland's eastern border after the war (Snyder, *Bloodlands*, 297-298.).

next year's celebration. Robin was screaming in his high chair for his scrambled eggs and spinach. Tina had the other two upstairs washing their hair and they would be down in a minute. So I just thought about you instead.....Wed. a.m. I didn't finish this yesterday and last night Pinky and Maggy came and we did celebrate your birthday. I got out a bottle of champagne and wished you all sorts of Happy Birthdays—all of them at home. This is a beautiful day but we have four inches of snow to welcome the spring. Frank & Joe came to fix my garden ready to plant and now I don't know what I'll do with them. We've had literally hundreds of birds outside the bay windows here in the dining room trying to fight their way to the feeder. There are chirpy sparrows, song sparrows, Nuthatches and a flock of birds that look like thrushes but aren't and no one has been able to tell me yet. We can hardly wait to get down in the morning to see which ones are here. They even sing in the snow storm. Yours, Peggy

[George to Peggy]
[V-Mail]

> Capt. G.R. Steiner
> Hq SOS Natousa G-3 Sec.
> APO 750 c/o PM N.Y.C.
>
> No. 106
> 23 Mar. 44

My darling:

The V-Mail processing station is downstairs in the building I am living in. A very pleasant young sgt. from New York showed me through the other night. It was very interesting. The letters go onto a 16mm film just like our home movie film but it only has holes on one side of the film. It is a real line production process, the place runs on a 24 hr. schedule. Four films, negatives run into a big machine which guides through a diesel-oper solution, an acid stop, hypo, wash, dry and rewind. The printers are ingenious, it looks something like our leica enlarger with the negative feeding thru continuously from reels at the top while the paper, feeds from a roll at the bottom. The paper and negative both run continuously without stop except to reload the rolls of course, the paper being exposed thru a crack about a half inch wide.[186] Note from the above address I am now in the G-3 section. No better, no worse. The col. who is G-3 came over from AF, so went to the C S to get me transferred, my previous chief objected but was too late. I wish, I wish you guess what. I am going to bed, good night — George

[Peggy to George]

#153
Friday 8:15 P.M.

My Darling,

    My letters to you have been few this week so I am indulging myself with a long one tonight so bear with me. I cannot tell you how I look forward to writing you each day and how disappointed I am when I can't find time. This is the first time I have sat down today except to eat. That is 12½ hours. The house is cleaned. All the meals cooked etc. etc. and then I helped Frank put up the screened porch this afternoon. Since supper I have finished painting the old green picket fence play yard white for Robin and swept the basement floor. Now I relinquished the blue jeans, took a shower and donned a blue & pink chiffon nightie you may remember and the blue crepe negligée with feather top that Jessie gave me years ago (the first Xmas after we were married) on the couch. The radio is playing "When Day Is Done." Tina is out and the children are all asleep. Now you have the setting. Would you like to be here nearly as much as I'd like you? I wonder, (but not much 'cause I know you too well).

---

186   George's detailed description of the V-Mail printing process is complemented with photographs of each stage in an online exhibit by the National WWII Museum in New Orleans, Louisiana (as of the date this book was published) at: https://www.nationalww2museum.org/war/articles/mail-call-v-mail.

Wednesday morning we had a heavy snow again. I got the car out early and was O.K. Frank & Joe were here as I wrote you and before the day was out I fired Joe. They cannot work together and I'm sick of listening to fights in Italian and having no work done. Frank's the best worker. I suppose he'll get along all right alone.

Thursday was a big day. Unfortunately, it poured all day but for two weeks I had promised to take Larry and Georgia to N.Y.C. for the day, so we had to go anyway. The car is in the garage with <u>hiccups</u> (called sticking of the hydraulic valves to you) so a taxi took us to the 9:17 a-m train. We sat with another mother & two big boys in double seats going in. At least we sat. Another taxi took us to Altman's and I bought the children spring clothes. They had never been in a dept. store before. All the sales girls were having a field day with Georgia standing on the counter in her undies trying on all the cute dresses they could find. She looked so adorable in each one that I'm afraid I bought more than she really needed. However, except for dresses given her by Mom I've bought her only two so far and everything else has been Larry's hand me downs. I got her a cute blue & white checked coat (small navy check) with [a] navy velvet collar. It's either for a boy or girl so I got the boy's cap now to match so Robin can use it later. For Georgia I got a navy straw bonnet with flowers to go with it. Larry got three striped pair of knee length shorts & white cotton knit shirts to play in this summer, a blazer & a green cotton suit. From Altman's we went to Dr. St. Lawrence's. He's a fancy priced pediatrician of N.Y.C. Park Ave. but has a good reputation. I'm not at all sure that his $25.00 visit is worth a nickel more than Dr. Close's $3.00 one and I don't like him as well personally. But to tell you why I went. I haven't been satisfied in the way Larry's feet have developed. You'll remember we discussed the way he walked before. Well he cannot run very fast and I hate to have him start school with any handicaps so I decided to try this even [though] Dr. Close didn't think anything about them (two feet). This St. Lawrence gave him a thorough physical exam and took plenty of time and attention, I will say. The result—Larry's feet are structurally perfect, but he is very awkward. This he thinks can be corrected by a very much exaggerated change in the height of the inner sole of his shoe heel. He's going to throw his foot over further than is normal to force him to toe in for balance. Also he put him on a diet to try and put three or four pounds on him very quickly. This is a bit hard on my cooking but it's worth it if it works. He says a few pounds may change his general condition enough to help the feet also. Then he's given him a tonic to bring up his hemoglobin. None of this will hurt him any and it may help in which case I shall feel the money well spent. As I've said, Larry looks marvelous, as is.

From the Dr's. we went to Anne Hanan's apt. for lunch. It was a blessing as the rain was coming in torrents. I had promised to take them to Central Park Zoo, but since it was raining they played with Kenneth and we took the 3:32 home. That time we, all three, stood up all the way to Greenwich. We couldn't even get into a car but stood on the platform. The poor kids were more exhausted than I when we reached Greenwich.

The stuffed dates arrived safely and are delicious. If you want proof of their popularity Tina told me a good story yesterday. While we were in town she was vacuuming upstairs and Robin disappeared for some time so she went to investigate. Down here in the hall was Robin sitting with his back against the wall muttering "Mum mum" as he crammed dates in his mouth. Doxie was lying on the floor casually chewing on several others with the rest of the dish scattered around them. Fortunately I had only put a couple of dozen in a silver dish on the coffee table. The doll and boat are expected daily.

Larry smashed his finger under a rock last week and the nail is a funny color. Yesterday as we got all dressed up to go to town he looked at his finger and said "Oh dear, I must 'member to keep my gloves on so my finger won't show in N.Y." Georgia pulled a funny one today too. She gave me a big kiss and said "That's a blue kiss from Daddy 'cause he likes blue bestest." What's your new cable address? I wanted to send you a Birthday message. I love you so much, dear and miss you too much.

Peggy

[Peggy to George]
[V-Mail]

#154
March 26 Sun. P. M.

My Darling.

It's after ten and my bedtime but I want to say a few words to you first. The oatmeal is cooked for breakfast and Doxie is in for the night so we're all set for bed. The Cleveland Orchestra is playing Strauss' Emperor Waltzes on the radio. The trip to N.Y.C. was hard on Larry. He's in bed with a cold but doesn't seem to mind very much. We modelled indians of plaster this afternoon which was a treat for both of us. Santy Claus brought the props and we haven't used it until today. Tomorrow we take the indians from their molds and paint them. Larry says he knows they must be all red but he wishes their eyes could be blue. Last night I went to the Hoggsons for dinner. Connie had twelve and it was very thrilling to go to a party again. Few people have the food or courage to entertain without help. Lt. Bartrans was there having just returned from commanding a LCT[187] in the Mediterranean. He suggested asking you if you have a fine view of MER.[188] Today has been very warm, and Robin, Georgia and I painted the old blue chair on the terrace while listening to Churchill through the dining room windows which were wide open and no need to worry about wasting oil. Churchill disappointed me in not mentioning the many problems of political difficulties which we are all talking

---

187 A landing craft, tank (LCT), also called tank landing craft (TLC). LCTs generally launch from a "mother ship" and ferry their cargo a short distance to the landing site.
188 The Mediterranean Sea was often abbreviated MER. Peggy could also be using the French word "mer" which means "sea."

about these past few weeks.[189] I hope you aren't too lonely in your new job. It's hard to have to keep making new friends, but you can do it. Yours, Peggy

[George to Peggy]
[V-Mail]

No. 107
Monday

My darling:

Glad to hear mail is coming thru more quickly. Maybe it is because I live right in the same bldg. with one of the V-Mail plants. I have picked up a sore throat, cold etc. which has been going around, so I took a couple of long drinks from some J.W. black label along with a couple of aspirins and will get to bed early which ought to fix it up. I have kept that bottle and protector which we picked up in Washington which is handy when I can keep something in it. The paper war goes on here just about as at other headquarters except for a few more halts and breakdowns. It is seldom around here that I run into an officer who has the 'know how' on getting staff work processed. If all the training given our group had gone to some colonels or generals, it could have been put to much better use. *C'est la guerre.*[190] All my love dear, George.

---

189   On March 26, 1944 British Prime Minister Winston Churchill delivered a speech titled, "The War and Conditions in England–Our Greatest Effort is Coming," in which he provided general updates on the war's progress and reassured Britons that domestic promises made in 1943 (such as education reform and a national health service) had already been outlined and presented to Parliament and the public. Domestic issues and updates make up the latter parts of his speech. In the beginning, however, Churchill reminds his audience that "unity of aims and actions and singleness of purpose among us all–Britons at home and our allies abroad–will make [victory] come sooner" (Churchill, "Address by Prime Minister Churchill on War and Conditions in Britain.").

Based on comments in Peggy's other letters expressing frustration with Russia's predatory attitude toward Poland, Peggy likely takes issue with Churchill's tribute to the USSR's contributions to the war. Churchill declares the advance of the Red Army from Stalingrad to the Dniester River "the greatest cause of Hitler's undoing." Churchill refers to his Soviet counterpart, Joseph Stalin as "a warrior leader" and proceeds to praise Stalin's ability to "impart a unity and concert to the war direction in the East." Churchill continues his speech by discussing the war against Japan and praising the United States forces for "shield[ing] Australia and New Zealand from Japanese aggression and mortal peril." No mention is made of the differing views of a post-war Europe held by Churchill, Stalin, and Roosevelt. Churchill chooses instead to emphasize unity and cooperation when he envisions, "the whole circle of avenging nations will hurl themselves upon the foe and batter out the life of the crudest tyranny which has ever sought to bar the progress of mankind" (Ibid.).

190   Translated: "That's war."

[George to Peggy]
[Postmarked Wednesday, March 29, 1944]

#108
Capt. GR Steiner
Hq SOS Natousa G-3 Sec
APO 750, c/o PM New York, N.Y.
Tuesday,

Peg dear;

Some good news. Remember Maj. Ream who was in our group at the War Dept. and went down to Trinidad with me? He walked in here today and is assigned to this section. A good fellow and capable officer so I am glad he is here. I am surprised AFHQ agreed to release him. Guess I told you Helms is down here too. You might remember him, a good looking Captain who was eating dinner at a table near ours at the Statler one of the last nights we were in Washington. Schutz is still busy as jumbo's aide.

They had a pile of back work when I came in here a week ago, but we have been working nights and gotten rid of most of it now. Someday I am going to get a day off to walk up the hill and investigate that castle[191] I told you about. Then I will really have something to write Larry about. I have wondered whether any of the packages I sent ever arrived, hand bags, stuffed dates, a doll for Georgia, some boats for Larry, a couple of picture books. I am looking forward to getting that picture of you.

Sure miss you my darling, all my love, George.

---

191 It is difficult to know exactly which castle George is referring to but the Chateau Neuf or Bey's Palace is a likely candidate. Originally a Sultan's fort and compound in the 1300s, Bey's Palace was used by the Spanish in the 1500s and the Ottomans in the 1700s. After the French occupation of Algeria in 1830 the palace complex served as headquarters of the French Army.

[Peggy to George]
[V-Mail]

#155
Mar. 29, 1944

My Darling

This is supposed to be a big day for me and Maggie as I have tickets to the theatre and am taking her to dinner. However, I feel Larry's cold coming on and I'd give anything just to go to bed. She hasn't been to N.Y.C. since last May, if you can believe it, so I wouldn't disappoint her for anything. We've planned this for months. All's well here otherwise. Georgia and Robin have not caught the cold so far. Tina and I had another set to over Georgia but not as serious as the first. I called Bob Crawford yesterday for advice on buying a secondhand mangle I found out here. He is drafted this Friday. Jack also. He passed his physical and chose the Navy last week. Poor Mom, I suppose he'll leave Thelma & children on her. I hear Hanger was called but got out of it due to Presidency of Ki's Airport or something equally ridiculous. It probably won't hold him back for long though. Pete P. is going to London with O.W.I. Too bad. It would do him good to be a private awhile. All my love and kisses XXXX Yours, Peggy

[Peggy to George]
[V-Mail]

#156
Thurs. March 30

Dearest George

Our day in the city was fun but I surely have a lousy cold today. It rained which was no help to my condition especially as it is hopeless to get a cab in N.Y.C. now. However we saw the army show "Winged Victory"[192] and it is great. All the management, music, costumes,

---

192 *Winged Victory* was an Army Air Force (AAF) show written and directed by Moss Hart. It debuted on Broadway on November 20, 1943 and told the story of new recruits and their experiences during pilot training. Hart was given full access to AAF bases in the United States to help him write the show and the original cast featured 300 members of the AAF. *Winged Victory* was initially a fundraiser benefitting the Army Emergency Relief Fund and it closed in May 1944 after 212 performances ("'Winged Victory,' Army Air Forces Show, Opens Tonight at the Forty-fourth Street Theatre.").

settings as well as actors have army personnel for the jobs.[193] It's a bit of a tear jerker but wonderfully done. We had a great many similar scenes of our own to remember such as cancelled leaves, goodbyes by the score etc. etc. The Yale Club gave us good cocktails and an excellent dinner. Maggie really had a good time and she deserves it: a letter from Mike last week said he went frequently to the St. George Hotel[194] for cocktails wherever he is. It's too bad you never could find him. It makes me feel so badly to hear how dissatisfied you are in the application of your training to your present job. It seems as if something could be done back here. What about a letter to G.M. A pet plan such as that school was would surely receive some interest. Don't you think? Betty Black F. is coming tomorrow for the weekend as Tina is off. She expects in August so has had to give up the Waves.[195] Her husband has gone overseas. Having lots of rain for May flowers. Loads of Love. Peggy

[George to Peggy]

[#]109
31 March 44
Capt. GR Steiner
HQ SOS Natousa G-3 Sec
APO 750, c/o PM N.Y.C.

My darling.

Here I am after breakfast down at our office. None of the other officers are about yet, some of the enlisted men are here looking at the Stars and Stripes, shining their shoes, and picking up a bit.

---

193 The show included 54 civilian actresses (Ibid.).
194 The Hotel St. George (now Hotel El-Djazair) was the location of the Allied Force Headquarters in Algiers, Algeria.
195 The Women Accepted for Volunteer Emergency Service (WAVES), established on July 30, 1942, was the U.S. Navy corps of female members (Black women were excluded until the final months of the war). Notably, the WAVES, unlike the WACs of the Army, were not an auxiliary corps and received status and benefits similar to the male members of the reserve. Many WAVES were assigned to administrative and clerical positions, however, there were opportunities for women to serve in naval aviation capacities including as instructors for pilots-in-training. Women with experience in mathematics and engineering were also recruited to work as "computers," calculating and solving equations that were compiled for use determining bomb and shell trajectories. In 1978 the WAVES will become a permanent part of the Navy, integrated with the male units.

Seems to be a habit now to get down for breakfast early, so I have time to look at the paper and write a letter when I get over here. The real reason I get [there early] is probably because being naturally lazy I find it much easier to take my time shaving, dressing and eating. When you get over late to breakfast everyone arrives at the same time, result is you have to wait for some time and don't get what you want.

Of course when I woke up this morning, my first thoughts were of you. I did wish very much that we were together then, and I thought of you sleeping away off on that other side of the world where it was still dark. My love dear. George

[George to Peggy]

[#]110
Capt. G.R. Steiner
Hq SOS Natousa G-3 Sec
APO 750 c/o PM N.Y.C.
Sunday eve 2 Apr.

My darling,

Just finished up a pile of work, surprising how much comes your way when they find out you know how to handle it. We have been working every evening and have not had a day off since I have been in this section. Ream ended up in another subsection of G-3. Wish they had left him in here with me as he really knows how to handle this stuff which most of these jokers do not.

Sorry I did not arrange to have some flowers for your Easter. Am I forgiven?

Received your air mail posted 13 Mar. today. Sorry you were a bit dejected, but this will all be over one of these days and I will be home. Then you will have me to bother you, leaving clothes all around, dirty pipes, ashes, tracking dirt in, papers left all over the desk, won't that be awful. Then when you want to go to sleep, I will surely keep you awake. You wouldn't have any trouble at all getting me up to bed. I still think we ought to get a double bed. Wish we were walking up the stairs together tonight, there is always such a pleasant anticipation, I like to watch you getting into your nightie knowing I will help you take it off when you get in beside me. There are so many ways I miss you, it just goes from one thing to another all day my darling, you are never far from my thoughts, and they are not all so naughty as this. Shouldn't write like this, but then you probably want to know what I think.

I have read and reread your remarks about a regular fellow with a sweet disposition who is handsome and well mannered. Tell him I am proud of him.

I really enjoyed reading your aims to have our children well mannered, well educated, thoughtful of others and clear on their purpose in life. I am sure that your continuing efforts at peace organization do have results on others. We all have to work on that. Hope your domestic troubles are smoothing out and you are not overworking. Wish I had my dear lovely wife in my arms.

Love, George

[Peggy to George]

#157
April 3 Sun. 7:00 P.M.

My Darling.

I am sitting before a lovely grate fire having just finished a hot rum drink and bath [which] are improving my cold rapidly. This is good as I was too miserable to go out for dinner last night and didn't feel much better in bed. Betty Black is still here and has been a great help with the children. However, I will be glad to see Tina. Georgia & Larry are up and except for a few sniffles are feeling too good for me to cope with. Robin, I fear, is just getting the cold tonight. I suppose Betty will get it too. She is staying until Thursday. Daddy phoned this morning and Dr. Rhodda has just discovered little Georgie has developed celiac disease. This is an intestinal allergy to fats and starch. It is quite rare.

Sparky Sparks was born with it. The diet is almost purely bananas and requires years (6) to cure. This is quite a blow and especially with Jack going into the Navy next week.

There's no news since Friday's letter as I really haven't been out of the house. My cold is much better as I said so maybe I'll have more to tell you next time. Our little group met here Fri. night and a friend of Maggie's knows a Russian historian. So I had the friend and russian both for dinner and we had a marvelous opportunity to learn Russian history. We started so far back that it was midnight before we got hot on the present troubles and feelings. This didn't get very far as she only answered to my question "Do you think Stalin's insistence on acquiring eastern Poland will block any possible plans to make peace as per the Atlantic Charter." "No," says she. "That land is Russian."[196] I should have told her that nearly every nation of Europe could claim part of a neighbor if they chose to claim all land that had ever been part of their state. I didn't, however. Somehow my disillusion is nearly complete now as far as the permanency of the peace is concerned. Man is still so selfish on the whole to be willing to make the sufficient sacrifices for world security. I have a very good book which I wish you would request I send to you. It is Herbert Agar's (former editor of Louisville Courier) "Time For Greatness." He is a very logical thinker and has a marvelous grasp of past & present troubles in this

---

196 By 1944 Poland is no stranger to conquest and occupation by its neighbors. Even before the Nazis and Soviets invaded in 1939, Poland's autonomy had been denied repeatedly for over a century. During the period between August 1772 and January 1795, Poland was partitioned three separate times and its lands annexed by Russia, Prussia, and Austria. While Prussia and Austria received the more economically valuable sections (in the first and third partitions respectively), Russia took the largest share of Polish territory. The third partition completely erased Poland from the map, reflecting the goal of the partitioning powers "to abolish everything which can recall the memory of the existence of the kingdom of Poland" (Zawadzki, *A Concise History of Poland*, 132.).

Much of the land Russia awarded itself was once part of the old Rus empire (also called Kievan Rus to denote the significance of Kiev as its central city), a geographic grouping of peoples in Eastern and Northern Europe consolidated into a state. Russian Empress Catherine the Great resurrected and popularized the notion of reuniting the Rus lands, deciding it was her "historic mission" to reunify the area that today encompasses Belarus, Russia, and Ukraine (Ibid., 128.). When the Rus coalition disintegrated in the 1300s, like Russia, Poland and Lithuania conquered and absorbed various areas (including Kiev) into their respective territories. In 1569 the Polish-Lithuanian Commonwealth was formed, combining the Grand Duchy of Lithuania with the Kingdom of Poland. Any future opportunities to develop into a single, unified country were quashed with the Russian invasion and subsequent partition in 1792. Peggy's observation that "every nation of Europe could claim part of a neighbor" is especially astute in this case as Russia and Poland have each claimed what could be deemed "part of the other" at some point over the centuries.

country and magnificently presents the state of mind, and heroic deeds necessary of Americans if this war should not have been fought in vain. Some of it may make you mad but it is good reading and excellent food for thought. I'm anxious to send it to you so do mention it in your next letter. If the fuddybuts your letter mentioned yesterday are able to read, it might be a good thing to pass around. The text is anything but conducive to egotism on the part of any man large or small. The job ahead is too big. If I receive many more letters griping about your present setup I not only become more disillusioned as to our place in this world but I may do some letter writing. Clare Luce[197] and I have

---

197 Clare Boothe Luce (b. 1903, d. 1987) was a writer, editor, playwright, war correspondent, and politician who was married to Henry Luce, the founder of *Time*, *LIFE*, and *Fortune* magazines. Renowned in her own right, Boothe Luce's accomplishments included work as Vanity Fair's managing editor and a critically-acclaimed book, *Stuffed Shirts*. Boothe Luce achieved a new level of recognition after the 1936 debut of her play, *The Women*. A satire about idle, rich women, the play broke Broadway attendance records for a nonmusical and earned $1 million in its first year (Morris, *Price of Fame*, 11.) (Wainwright, *The Great American Magazine*, 58.). Three years later it debuted on the silver screen to great success: Only *Gone with the Wind* grossed higher that year (Morris, *The Price of Fame*, 11.). As WWII began in Europe, Boothe Luce toured as a correspondent for LIFE, writing dispatches from North Africa and China.

Boothe Luce's foray into politics began in 1940 as she enthusiastically supported Wendell Willkie's 1940 presidential bid (see footnote 198, page 313). Like many of her fellow Republicans, Boothe Luce opposed most of Roosevelt's domestic policies, however her travels saw her align less with the isolationism of the Republican party when it came to foreign affairs. In 1942 Boothe Luce ran for a seat in the House of Representatives representing Fairfield County, Connecticut–which included Greenwich. Despite running as a Republican, Boothe Luce advocated for the inclusion of minorities (including Blacks) in the U.S. Armed Forces, declaring they were entitled to serve their country with equal dignity. She also argued for a guaranteed, adequate standard of living for all Americans after the war, including affordable housing, medical care, education, and minimum wage. Once elected, her internationalist perspective saw her break with her party; she supported strengthening the British-American alliance, the creation of what would become the United Nations, and the involvement of the United States in an international relief organization. Domestically, she backed the Equal Rights Amendment and endorsed the Women's Army Auxiliary Corps. Boothe Luce was also appointed a member of the Committee on Military Affairs. Serving on a committee that cartoonist Sergeant Bill Mauldin (see footnote 211, page 326) called so ridiculous "it defied caricature," Boothe Luce set a professional example, taking notes, talking with combat soldiers, and seeing more of the front lines than any other touring Committee member (DePastino, *Bill Mauldin*, 182.). Never content to be a wallflower, Boothe Luce sought out troops on the front lines and in field hospitals to experience a moment of their lives–including the mud and their rations, in order to better report back on their needs when she returned to Washington, D.C. (Morris, *The Price of Fame*, 104-107.).

Narrowly winning reelection in November 1944, the next year Boothe Luce again travelled to Europe, arriving in time for liberation. She toured newly-emancipated sites of significance (notably the camps at Buchenwald and Bergen-Belsen), bearing witness to the emaciated skeletons of the survivors and the piles of corpses that had been left where they fell. At one point she told a cameraman, "Everyone should see these films and never forget them" (Ibid., 129, 130-131.). Returning to the United States, Boothe Luce was a vocal opponent of Roosevelt's role in Poland's post-war fate. She also cautioned leaders about the Soviet Union's foreign policy moves and the spread of Communism in Europe.

In 1946 she will propose a bill to create a Labor Department bureau to ensure minority workers receive equal pay for equal work and she will co-author the Luce-Celler Act, which will permit Filipinos and Indians to immigrate to the United States. Despite opting not to run for reelection, Boothe Luce will remain active in politics, serving first as Ambassador to Italy under President Eisenhower's administration (becoming the first woman appointed to a major ambassadorial post abroad), then later on President Reagan's Foreign Intelligence Advisory Board.

Boothe Luce will be honored with the Presidential Medal of Freedom in 1983 and pass away four years later after a long battle with cancer.

already exchanged correspondence on the soldiers' vote (nothing's going to happen in time for the boys to vote). However I might have better luck next time. Colonel Smith might have a suggestion too. Maybe I'll write him. How about it? Trust me to try and help you fight your battles even at this distance. I used to really be amazed if you could drive a car and read a road map & still reach the proper destination without one along to either do the driving or the reading. This gave me a feeling of importance and I sort of miss it I guess even though the conceit was the most obvious characteristic. You do still need me though, don't you, my dear. Your children do anyway. And since each baby is at least ½ you—that means that more than one whole of you needs me. I'm a selfish soul, though, like most wives and I'm not satisfied with taking care only of your children. Hurry home. Or I'll be even more solicitous. I fear.

When I look at Betty waiting for her first baby with her husband overseas and their longest time together the 10 days of their honeymoon, I realize how lucky I am. We did have four wonderful years. How much more I'm trying to appreciate the next after you are home! I love you more even without enjoying the daily thoughtful ways you always remembered me in deeds and words. I don't think any girl ever had a husband as capable as mine in always making me feel so very essential and appreciated in every move.

Goodnight, darling, keep bucking those eagle sprouting dawdlers. The day you fail to gripe about them is when I'll really worry.

My love & XXXX, Peggy

[Peggy to George]
[V-Mail]

#158
April 4, 1944 Tues.

My dearest George.

    This is a lovely sunny April morning. I wish you could see the how the sun pours into this wonderful house of ours. It is always so cheerful and makes me think that everyone will always be happy under this roof. I even have some delphinium plants to put into the ground today. You'd be amazed at my efficiency in learning gardening. I sent to Max Schilling for these hybrids and I am testing the garden soil with my own little chemical testing set and adding the correct fertilizer and lime before putting them in. By the time you come home I hope to be producing my favorite flower just the color our bridesmaids carried. Silly, I suppose, with all the things I should be doing every minute, but I am fascinated by fixing up these grounds. I had a note from Ki the other day thanking me for a birthday card I sent him from the kids and myself. He said he had been to Miami a few days and saw Uncle George. He is O.K. again but of course is apt to have more attacks, I suppose. Ki said he and Teedie are doing the same as always, which sounded a bit interesting. He must get a bit bored with that job. Betty is still here and staying until Thurs. I'm giving her a few cooking lessons and she is doing a pile of mending for me. Tina slept until 8:30 this a.m. Nice life & profitable too. Love, Peggy

[George to Peggy]
[V-Mail]

No. 111
5 April 1944

My darling,

    Have a pretty fair place to write here. There is one of those folding wooden chairs in the room, so by starting to close you can turn the back up flat, then sitting on the edge of the bunk I can rest my head against the upper bunk. Nothing like comfort. The room is not what you would call neat with duffel bags, sleeping rolls, mess kits etc. scattered about. Of course if it weren't for the other five officers it would all be picked up. They are a pretty good bunch and we usually have quite a talk before getting to sleep because just about as the conversation dies down someone else walks in. Guess we are lucky to be as comfortably as we are here. Peg I love you very much. George.

[Peggy to George]
[V-Mail]

#159

April 6, 1944 Thurs.

Dearest George,

Believe it or not we've had another heavy snow storm. I had my delphiniums all ready to plant and we woke up yesterday with six inches of snow on everything. I hope the plants can wait. Betty leaves today. I have been teaching her to cook and she's been a big help. She says she cannot practice at home because her Dad is too fussy about what he eats. That's not hard to believe. I was quite upset about Willkie[198] dropping out of the primaries last night. What's the matter

---

198 Wendell L. Willkie (b. 1892, d. 1944) was a decorated WWI veteran, lawyer, utilities executive, and former Democrat who won the Republican nomination for presidential candidacy in 1940. While campaigning against Franklin Roosevelt in 1940, Willkie criticized Roosevelt's New Deal, arguing that more jobs needed to be created through policies that encouraged business expansion and investment. Willkie also decried the United States' lack of military preparedness and vehemently supported aid to the Allies as WWII spread through Europe. Willkie ultimately lost to Roosevelt and the latter became the first president to win a third term. However, Willkie's popular vote of just over 22 million was the largest ever won by a Republican candidate at that time (Neal, *Dark Horse*, 176.). After his defeat, Willkie publicly spoke to the importance of national unity when he declared, "[Roosevelt] is your President. He is my President...We will support him with the best efforts for our country...I want to see all of us dedicate ourselves to the principles for which we fought" (Ibid., 181, 182.).

Ironically, Willkie became a strong backer of Roosevelt's international wartime policies, alienating himself from Republican party leadership. By the summer of 1941, Willkie was advocating for greater national support of Lend-Lease and unlimited aid to the United Kingdom (recognizing its importance despite believing that the presidential authority it granted was too broad) (Ibid., 187.). He travelled to Britain, the Middle East, the Soviet Union, and China as Roosevelt's personal representative to better understand the war and how it could be won. In 1943 he published *One World*, a book on his observations while travelling that stresses the significance of international peacekeeping and cooperation after the war. *One World* also admonishes imperialism and recommends colonizing powers withdraw, enabling the subjugated peoples and states to achieve autonomy. Furthermore, Willkie suggests a colonizing power should assist its former colony, providing infrastructure for education, public health, and the development of resources. One million copies of the book sold within the first seven months of publication and Willkie donated the $350,000 he earned from the book to a trust fund benefiting civil rights groups, war charities, and various public service organizations (Ibid., 264, 266.).

with Americans. Because a man comes out and says we must pay for this war as we go along and must pledge ourselves to cooperate with the rest of the world to maintain peace afterwards, he fails to get a single delegate vote from a midwest state and the votes go to men who haven't opened their mouths.[199] It makes me sick. Mary Ward called this morning and we are taking the children to Rye Sat. to a marionette show. That will make up for the circus. I decided against that this year. It costs a fortune and I am not a war worker yet. Excuse the gripes. We both seem to have them these days. I wish you could have seen Robin last night. He saw Larry saying his prayers and ran over, knelt beside him and folded his hands. Then he put up his head and laughingly jabbered along with Larry until he finished. All love, Peggy

Willkie had long been a vocal supporter of civil rights. Before his foray into politics, Willkie was a lawyer in Ohio, fighting against the entrenched Ku Klux Klan. His commitment to equality continued during the war years. Willkie opposed the internment of Japanese-Americans in concentration camps and denounced antisemitic tendencies and articles in the press. In his article, "The Case for the Minorities" Willkie declares, "we are living once more in a period that is psychologically susceptible to...mob-baiting" and cautions the public, "each of us has within himself the inheritances of age-long hatreds...It is, therefore, essential that we...not be among those who cry out against prejudices applicable to themselves, while busy spawning intolerances for others" (Ibid., 271, 272.). Willkie supported Black leaders in their efforts to integrate the U.S. Armed Forces and identified racism as a national imperialism while declaring racial equality the most critical of national issues. In 1943, Willkie actively supported antilynching legislation and demanded a repeal of the poll tax. Recognizing the significance of stereotypes in the perpetuation of racial prejudice, Willkie travelled to Los Angeles with National Association for the Advancement of Colored People (NAACP) secretary Walter White and confronted Hollywood executives about the misrepresentation of Blacks in movies, resulting (for a brief period) in films featuring Black actors in serious roles (Ibid., 275, 276.).

Despite the success of *One World* and the recognition Willkie had received for his crusade for equality, he was unable to secure his party's nomination for the 1944 election as Republicans felt Willkie's internationalist view no longer aligned with a Republican party more and more driven to isolationism (Ibid., 277.). The Republican party in 1944 opposed further participation in foreign wars, any increase in federal spending, and Roosevelt's centralization of the executive branch's power. Neither party was willing to risk losing the support of Southern politicians by addressing racial inequality in any official form, although Roosevelt at least made vapid campaign promises to that effect. Willkie did not exemplify the Republican party platform as Republicans saw it, which resulted in a disastrous defeat in the Wisconsin primary. After Wisconsin, Willkie withdrew, clearing the way for more rightward-leaning, isolationist candidates to vie for the nomination. Thomas Dewey would go on to win the nomination–without Willkie's support.

On October 8, 1944, after surviving thirteen heart attacks in just over a month, the fourteenth will prove fatal and Willkie will pass away at only 52 years of age.

199   Willkie aggressively campaigned in Wisconsin, understanding the significance of its 24 delegates to any future success. Over the course of 13 days Willkie crisscrossed the state, attracting crowds of thousands and even travelling in a horse-drawn sleigh in areas where the snow made roads impassable (Ibid., 303.). Notably, Willkie was the only candidate who physically campaigned in Wisconsin. Willkie, like Peggy, was unimpressed with Thomas Dewey's failure to "discuss issues or take a stand" as the New York Governor relied on mail and billboard advertisements for his nomination and avoided public appearances. Harold Stassen (see footnote 205, page 317) and Douglas MacArthur also shunned Wisconsin–Stassen preferred local endorsements and mailing brochures over campaigning in person and MacArthur did even less than that (Ibid., 304.). Despite Willkie's great pains (and the lack of effort by his competitors), the delegate results from the Wisconsin primary were as follows: seventeen for Dewey, four for Stassen, three for MacArthur, and zero for Willkie.

[Peggy to George]
[V-Mail]

#160
April 8, 1944, Sat.

Dearest George:

Back to a breakfast letter at last. I've decided to let the dishes wait mornings and write you as I can never find a better time. Last night I had dinner down a[t] Marg. Peters. Pete is in Chicago settling his business before going into O.W.I. We had a delicious dinner and then the phone rang. It was King Ludington & Mario ? (only two men known in these parts and the first very intimate with Marg.) We played bridge up at King's house in deference to me, I guess. The rest showed little interest in the game. When I said I was a working girl and got up to leave, sober, at 11:30 and Marg. had to go too to take me home, they really were fed up. One doesn't have to be around ten minutes to see there is some understanding between Marg. & King. It made me sick so I couldn't sleep when I did get home. Then just as I started to write you at 8:30 a.m., Tinkle Brainard called to say, as one of her best friends, she wanted me to hear first from her that she [and] Bill are getting a divorce. I didn't know what to say so I said "I'm terribly sorry." Are they supposed to be congratulated? Wouldn't you think with this war and so many more important things to be done that personal feelings would be in the background. It makes me weak just to think how desolate I'd be if during these lonely, crucial months I didn't constantly have your love to give me hope in every move I make. Yours, Peggy

[Peggy to George]

#161
Sunday P.M. April 9.

My Darling George.

This has been a very pleasant Easter night. I have been lying here on the couch in my blue negligee listening to the radio and reading over a lot of articles I have been saving to mail you. Doxie is lying so close to me that I just put my hand down to pat his old shaggy head. Most of these articles are a group running in 'Life' the past two months by Charles Beard.[200] They are from his new book "Republic" and helped me a great deal in understanding the workings and difficulties of our particular form of government.[201] Besides these there is one on Lt. Henry McKnight & his L.S.T.[202] which I know will interest you.[203] Then there is a good searching description of the creation, circumstances & personalities of the Versailles Treaty.[204] Also a letter from a soldier to his wife which expresses so perfectly just how I feel about the all pervading power of our love over my mental and physical being. Some of the ideas he tries to convey aren't entirely clear to me but the general moving mood is wonderfully expressed. I wish I could express myself half as well to you. One political article I put in as it has proved to be a forecast of what happened to Willkie. He was a great man and refused to play along with the Republican bosses so they got rid of him. Also mention

---

200 Charles A. Beard (b. 1874, d. 1948) was an American historian and author of over thirty books, the majority on U.S. history and government. Beard's histories often stressed economic determinism—the theory that economic commitments and conflicts determine political and social change. Beard's application of this theory to the formation of the U.S. government, highlighted in *An Economic Interpretation of the Constitution of the United States*, was misunderstood and poorly received. Beard later clarified that economic conflict did not determine the form of government in the United States because no single thing determined another. He suggested merely considering its impact was an important new line of research. Beard's monumental, influential history *The Rise of American Civilization*, was co-written by Beard's wife, historian and activist Mary Ritter Beard.

An ardent supporter of academic freedom, Beard resigned his teaching position at Columbia University in 1917 to protest the dismissal of two colleagues who had opposed U.S. involvement in WWI. With the dismissed professors, Beard co-founded the New School for Social Research, a private graduate institution specializing in the social sciences and philosophy. Beard tended toward isolationism as WWII approached, although he would argue in vain that his focus was not isolationism but an avoidance of war and the strengthening of democracy and security within the United States. This theme in his later writings, along with his characterization of internationalists as infantile and his insistence that isolationists were mature, adult thinkers will make him a controversial figure ("Charles A. Beard, Historian, is Dead."). Despite the discord, in 1948 the National Institute of Arts and Letters will award Beard a gold medal (an honor bestowed only once a decade) and emphasize the award was not for his later but rather his entire life's work.

201 Ten of Beard's articles appeared in a series titled, "Conversations on Fundamentals" which ran in *LIFE* from January 17-March 20, 1944. The articles are listed in the bibliography.

202 A landing ship, tank (LST) was designed to deploy troops, supplies, and vehicles directly onto a foreign shore.

203 "U.S.S. LCI 226" by John Hersey appeared in *LIFE* on March 27, 1944.

204 "Tragedy of Versailles" by William C. Bullitt appeared in *LIFE* on March 27, 1944.

is made of the rise of Stassen[205] in Minn. I hope you find time to read them.

Last night (Sat.) I went to the Brosnahans for dinner. They are the Omaha friends of Kay & Webb's. I didn't know anyone there but the Ives. It was a lovely party but I was so tired the drinks only gave me a headache so I left about midnight. I did enjoy talking to one of the guests who works for "Time." I say I enjoyed it. I really didn't then as it confirmed my growing disillusionment of late as to the possibility of a lasting peace. However, Secretary Hull's speech tonight[206] has lifted my spirits again and I don't think "Time's" staff can predict any

---

205   Harold Stassen (b. 1907, d. 2001) was the 25th governor of Minnesota, a presidential assistant, an educator and lawyer, president of the University of Pennsylvania, and a WWII veteran. Despite these accomplishments, Stassen is perhaps better known for his nine unsuccessful attempts at winning the Republican party's presidential nomination. In 1938, at age 31, Stassen became Minnesota's youngest governor. As a Republican governor Stassen was fairly progressive, not only pushing through labor legislation but allowing the first Black officer into the Minnesota National Guard. He also overhauled a deeply-rooted patronage system in the state government, cutting the state payroll by 7,000 (Krebs, "Harold E. Stassen, Who Sought G.O.P. Nomination for President 9 Times, Dies at 93."). Although reelected in 1942, Stassen did not finish his term, opting instead to join the Navy. During the war he served in the Pacific theater as Chief of Staff to Admiral William Halsey. Stassen was also awarded the Legion of Merit for his service and promoted to captain. In 1945 President Roosevelt appointed Stassen to the American delegation to the first United Nations' (U.N.) conference where Stassen helped write what would later become the U.N. Charter. During the Eisenhower administration Stassen was in charge of American foreign aid programs and appointed Special Assistant for Disarmament–a cabinet position. Despite his disappointment about the rightward direction of the Republican party and politicians who relied on special staff members to enhance their public image during campaigns, Stassen remained involved in politics, especially in his home state, up until his death (Ibid.).

206   On April 9, 1944 Secretary of State Cordell Hull delivered a radio address titled, "If We Are Divided We Are Ineffective." In the speech Hull discusses the "simple and direct" foreign policy of the United States, "founded upon the interests and purposes of the American people" (Hull, "Text of Secretary Hull's Address on the Foreign Policy of the United States."). While Hull draws attention to the success of the U.S. people and government in "mobilizing our great natural resources, our vast productive potentialities, and our reserves of manpower to defend ourselves and to strengthen those who were resisting the aggressors," he cautions that Americans "cannot move in and out of international cooperation." As the Nazis withdraw, they will likely leave behind "a legacy of confusion." Without a unified American-Allied effort to establish control and provide aid to the formerly Nazi-occupied countries, "without an enduring understanding between [the United States, the British Commonwealth, the Soviet Union, and China]...the path is wide open again for the rise of a new aggressor" (Ibid.).

Regarding France, Hull recognizes the French Committee of National Liberation (headed by Charles de Gaulle) as a symbol of "the spirit of France and of French resistance" but states (as Peggy notes), "the Committee is, of course, not the Government of France and we cannot recognize it as such" (Ibid.).

Much of Hull's speech discusses the importance of an international organization to "maintain peace and prevent aggression." In establishing world security, "there can be no compromise with fascism and Nazism." While Hull calls upon the United States and its allies to rise to the challenge of agreement and compromise in order to create and sustain harmony in the post-war world, he reiterates that fascists and Nazis "can expect no negotiated peace, no compromise, no opportunity to return" (Ibid.).

It is not only necessary that the Allies are all of one mind but "the will of the American people in this field is not effective unless it is united as well." In the United States, 1944 was an election year and Hull reminds the American people and politicians of their responsibility in "avoiding needless controversy" and requests "sober and considered thought and expression." A hint of foreboding closes Hull's speech as he warns, "once before...we fell into disunity and became ineffective in world affairs by reason of it. Should this happen again it will be a tragedy to you and your children and to the world for generations" (Ibid.).

better than I. Hull was specific on several points of our foreign policy and expressed himself strongly for the immediate organization of an international council of nations & police force. The only thing I didn't like is that he said definitely that we would not recognize De Gaulle's[207] Committee as the existing gov't. of France. I cannot understand that. Surely De Gaulle is better able to give us aid & we have more to gain by recognizing him than any of the gov'ts. in exile which we already have recognized. If the morning paper carries a copy of his speech I'll enclose it.

Yesterday afternoon our trip to Rye to see the marionette show was a great success. We had seven children in the back seat and Marg, Pinky and I in the front. It was at the Apawamis Club in Rye. Do you remember when Peter Hite took us over there? I ran into Mrs. Peake, incidentally. Allison just had a daughter and her husband returned from [the] South Pacific. <u>Lucky</u>. Anyway the show was the story of Peter Rabbit & Mr. MacGregor's garden. You can't imagine how thrilled the kids were. Georgia & Judy Ward left their seats and walked right up to the stage to peek up and see how it all worked. She was chased out while trying to climb back stage. Larry laughed so hard when Peter hid in the watering pail that along with the other children they got that incident repeated five times. It really was a far bigger treat for them than the circus. This is because it is small and they can see everything and understand what's going on. They were given ice cream and cake afterwards. Now you know why I was too tired to enjoy my own party last night.

This morning we had an Easter Egg hunt. Tina & I dyed and hid the eggs yesterday. When Larry found the first nest behind the johnny

---

207   Charles de Gaulle (b. 1809, d. 1970) was a French political leader who served as Undersecretary of State for Defense and War in Paul Reynaud's government in June 1940. When Reynaud's government was replaced by that of Marshal Pétain, de Gaulle fled to England–opposed to Pétain's intent of an armistice with the Nazis. For three years de Gaulle broadcast his appeals to the French people to continue the war against Nazism under his leadership in London. In 1943 de Gaulle moved his group of Free French supporters to Algiers where it united with Henri Giraud's branch of Free French members and was renamed the French Committee of National Liberation. De Gaulle and Giraud served initially as co-presidents of this provisional government until de Gaulle out-wangled Giraud in November 1943. Both the U.S. and British governments were reluctant to recognize the French Committee of National Liberation as the legitimate government of France without it being elected as such by the French people.

in the back of the laundry he came running into the dining room to tell about it. He was so excited, his face was crimson and he had tears in his eyes. Imagine the little effort it requires to give such thrills at that age.

This afternoon we got all dressed up in our spring clothes and went to the children's Easter service at Christ Church. Marg. took Hodgey & Pinky, her two. The children each took a bunch of myrtle and snow drops from the garden. Then all the children in the congregation go up to the altar and put their flowers to form a huge cross. Georgia took hers and liked the altar so well she just stayed until nearly the last. All the rest of our troops had been back in their seats for minutes before I could even spy her. She was just sauntering around looking the choir boys over so I finally went all the way to the steps before I could get her attention.

Do you remember a year ago today at the Colby's? That was fun. I have a card from Colby I'll enclose.

Hope your cold is better, dear. I wish I could rub Vick's on you tonight and make you comfortable. It must come soon—the <u>comfort</u> not the cold. We all send our love—even Doxie. Let's hope the peace of Easter may come to us all soon. I love you so much, darling and again am hoping we can make a better world for these wonderful three babies. Excuse my slump of past letters.

– Peggy

X   X   X   X   X
M   L   G   R. Doxie

(over)

P.S. I wish you could see the children hug and kiss your letters when I tell them you sent one.

[Peggy to George]
[V-Mail]

#162
April 11, 1944

My Dearest George

    You have the funniest children today. They both had their heads in a hole they had dug near the big rock by their old swing. I had to find out what they had. Larry said, "We's digging for worms and already have three." I noticed his hands were not dirty except where the coveted worms lay & Georgia's were filthy. I commented on this and Georgia said, "Well Larry makes me do the diggin' while he has all the fun holding the worms." Then yesterday they came down from the third floor all excited telling how much fun they had. They gave a tea party. Larry said, "And only for grownups. No kids were asked at all. Just Hodgey and Anne Bowden were there. All grownups." It's a nice sunny day and I have my blue denims on ready to plant onion sets. Also a nursery man is coming to see about moving a couple of trees to let air into my drying yard and put them at the end of the drive. How I wish I had a full time gardener now. There is so much I want to do but it will have to wait. I am going to fertilize a lot though. My chemistry test showed we don't need lime at all but phosphorus instead. I'm glad I spent the $2.00 for my testing outfit rather than take Frank's word and get 6 tons of lime. Frank & Helen are back from Florida. I am going in tomorrow, if I can get away. They don't realize how hard it is. I love you. Peggy

[Peggy to George]
[V-Mail]

#163
April 12, Wed.

Dearest George

    It is about 4 o'clock and I am in Frank & Helen's hotel room awaiting their arrival. They left me a key so I am resting a bit and writing you. Two things I like most and do the least of nowadays. Yesterday was a pip. Mr. Hvolbeck came to look over the land I want plowed. He decided we need horses instead of a tractor with all the rocks. Before he left he started talking about the day old chicks he was about to pick up in Portchester and before the day was out Larry & I were proud parents of 100 day old chicks. By means of a hammer, saw and the blue canapé from the old blue chair plus an electric light cord and bow bulb we converted the top tray of our vegetable storage rack into a brooder. It was ready in an hour and the chicks came in two. I know you'll think I'm crazy and I don't blame you a bit. Perhaps you won't scold when I tell you Larry is going to take them completely off my hands when they are old enough to go outside. Besides I only have to keep them two months to have broilers and then if they are too awfully much trouble I can kill them all at once and put them in our locker. The children were all so thrilled that the $18.00 original investment won't be totally lost if I don't raise them all. The children's hugs may not help too much. Tinkle Brainard came for dinner last night and told me her sad tale. Bill has fallen for a married woman with 3 kids and the two of them are selfish enough to ruin 4 children's happiness and that of [their] own wife & husband respectively. Terrible that it's allowed. Tinkle is wonderful about it and is going to Reno shortly. My love, dear, Peggy XXOO

[George to Peggy]

12 Apr. 44

Peg Dear

Had a pleasant surprise the day before yesterday. George Doerr walked in with a big smile on his freckled face. I sure was glad to see him. He is with military govt. handling medical supply. He has gotten around the theatre quite a bit, and is now at AFHQ. We had dinner together last night and the night before. He is a good boy.

Fact is I am all caught up with the mess I inherited when I walked into this section so I won't be coming back here every night now. Even had time to get a haircut today.

Just read over a very nice letter received from you. It sounded like you were working yourself to death with the house and children. You mentioned Larry's feet, you tell him mine were just like his, so I had to have my shoes made special for quite a while when I was a little boy. I don't think it is anything to worry about.

It must be real spring there by now, if you are putting up the screens. That must make a dandy porch.

As for the blue and pink nightie I do believe that I remember something about that. Your belief is confirmed that I would have liked to have been with you on the couch, even might have helped you wash your back in the shower. Maybe I will do that one of these days.

All my love, George

[George to Peggy]
[Handwritten on American Red Cross stationery]

Friday
14 April

Peg my dear;

Another day just about gone. Made up my mind that I really would like to come home you know, but somehow I can't seem to get around to it. Hope they let us know when the war is ended here; as it would be horrible to go on fighting it here for a year or so after the peace treaty was signed. We got one more colonel in our section today so I am sure what work I can contribute will be much better now with another set of initials on it.[208]

---

208 This is neither the first nor last of George's ironic remarks as his disillusion with the Army and his role within it grow. Enclosed in George's portfolio of wartime documents, among George's orders and records, was a notice from the War Department Office of the Provost Marshal General issued on January 13, 1942 explaining the meaning of "completed staff work" which was the responsibility and purpose of a staff officer such as George. Staff officers were tasked with "the study of a problem, and presentation of a solution...in such form that all that remains to be done on the part of the head of the staff division, or the commander, is to indicate his approval or disapproval of the completed action" (Lerch, "Completed Staff Work."). Using precise language, Deputy Provost Marshal General Colonel Archer Lerch instructs staff officers not to consult their superiors nor to "worry [their] chief with long explanations and memoranda" explaining, "It is your job to advise your chief what he ought to do, not to ask him what you ought to do...Your job is

There is a radio playing down here at the Red Cross. Was a bit surprised to hear the Whiffenpoof song,[209] made me think a bit of Harkeness Tower New Haven,[210] 680 Yale Station, that chubby faced roommate and maybe a weekend in New York.

Took a walk at noon through a little city park in front of the Palais du Justice where someone had gone to the trouble of planting a lot of flowers which made me think of your garden. Sure miss you dear.

All my love, George

[Peggy to George]

#165
April 16, Sun.

My Darling

Doxie has just pranced in with a pair of Robin's red corduroy overalls which I had sorted out for washing on the laundry floor. Except for a few more gray hairs, he seems to have recaptured his old sauciness this spring. I'll never forget what that old dog's companionship has meant to me these lonely years while you've been gone. If only he can live until this war is over and I have you back. Larry came down to breakfast this morning and said "I have just been talking to God, Momie, and he said there is only one Jap left and as soon as Daddy finds him the war will be over and Daddy will be home." He also discussed the evils of war with me and ended up "When this bad old war is over, I certainly hope they never have another one." Perhaps I am imbuing him with too many of my ideas?

We've really had a lovely weekend alone. Friday we all spent out of doors. Larry & Georgia & I planted the onion sets and hollyhock

---

to study, write, restudy and rewrite until you have evolved a single proposed action…Your chief merely approves or disapproves" (Ibid.). The ideal proposal in its final form "results in a single document prepared for the signature of the chief, without accompanying comment" (Ibid.). In the sixth point of the seven-point notice, Colonel Lerch acknowledges, "the 'completed staff work' theory may result in more work for the staff officer, but it results in more freedom for the chief. This is as it should be" (Ibid.). All words underlined above are underlined in the original.

209   Founded in 1909, the Whiffenpoofs are a collegiate a cappella group made up of seniors at Yale University. The Whiffenpoof Song is considered the anthem of the group and is sung at the end of every concert.

210   Harkness Tower is an iconic element of the Memorial Quadrangle at Yale University. The tower is an example of Collegiate Gothic architecture.

seeds that I brought back from Minnetonka last fall. We also cut the seed potatoes ready to plant. It's rained ever since so they aren't in yet but I hope to plant them tomorrow. Yesterday, Sat., it rained so I cleaned the house, polished silver and baked a sponge cake. When the children saw the cake Larry said (mistaking it for an angel food) "Oh Momie, that's the kind of cake you always baked for Daddy, isn't it?" Of course I said "Yes." Then Georgia said "Let's pretend Daddy's having a birthday and this is his cake." They started to sing "Happy Birthday to Daddy" and I found the tears running down my face. They were so thrilled and just <u>really</u> believing they were giving you a party. They even each ate a piece of cake for you and insisted I do so also. Larry said "Now Momie you pretend you're Daddy and say "Larry where did you get this wonderful cake?" So it goes. ——— We miss you so terribly, Dear.

Yesterday afternoon Georgia's long awaited gift arrived from you. It's a lovely big teddy bear and she <u>adores</u> it. Naturally it's in bed with her now having had its teeth brushed and hair combed. Now if only Larry's boats come soon.

Our chickens are thriving—We haven't lost any yet. Mr. Hvolbeck couldn't believe it. Three of his have died already. Beginner's luck!

Last night Mrs. Collins brought her little girl and spent the night so I could go to the Peters' party. I think she also will come once a week and clean for me now. I have to spend so much time outside now. The party was fun. The Bowdens took me and I wore the dress you bought me in Paris. I always get so many compliments on it and a great many thrilling memories. They had 18 for a buffet supper. Bowdens, Joe Terbells, Tom Terbells, Redfields (house guests), Linens (Jim goes to London soon), Pinky & her brother (merchant marine), Peggy Gerlie, King Ludington, Mario Fernandez & myself. The Tom Terbells made their last appearance together. They're getting a divorce. Really it's almost funny if it weren't so tragic. Pete & Marg. I doubt will ever get together again after his sojourn in O.W.I. I guess

Mpls. is just as bad but it seems like an epidemic here. I surely have to laugh when these people remark on how sorry they feel for me "stuck out here in the country alone with the children & no gasoline & little help." My blessings are so great compared to their narrow unhappy existence. We are so much closer to one another even now than many of them who are still under the same roof—This is <u>true</u> and I know it so if it's any comfort to you just think about it sometimes. They admit that they never spend an evening alone together. They have nothing to say to one another. What a vacuum life would become!

I've been napping along with the children today as I stayed at the Peters until 3:00 A.M. Isn't that awful? It's rained today so I put the children in the playroom & it was easy. Tonight Larry completely fed Robin for me and quickly too. In the meantime I fixed our supper on a tray and built a gratefire. We put Robin to bed and had our supper on the floor in front of the fire—omelette, toast, buttered beets, milk and tapioca. We talked about all the Sunday nights we are going to do it with you and what we'll feed you. I'm afraid you might not enjoy some of Georgia's combinations.

Just as we finished Connie & Wally Hoggson stopped in. I had a drink with them, divided my Sun. paper as they hadn't gotten one and Connie helped me put the kids to bed. They are awfully good dependable friends.

I have to enclose two letters from the children. Georgia's is a thank you note for her teddy. She hadn't gotten him unwrapped properly before she sat him on her lap and insisted on writing it. Larry's is on his phobia (chicks). I love you, darling.

Yours, Peggy

[George to Peggy]

Monday
17 April

My darling:

Here it is Monday morning along about 8 o'clock. I have had breakfast and read the Stars & Stripes along with one of the *locale* French papers. The nice thing about the Stars & Stripes is that it is always cheerful, nothing is ever seriously wrong. They have a great knack for printing all the good news and omitting or belittling any bad news. Of course they never fail to build up our military leaders and of course never criticize. It may be considered necessary in war time as a policy, but it sure is insulting to the readers. In spite of all this it is good to have the paper and the boys that are putting it out in the face of all the physical and administrative obstacles deserve a lot of credit. Busy as you are I suppose you do take a glance at that Saturday edition when it comes. Those cartoons by Mauldin[211] really seem to hit the spot. It just brings out the world of difference between the way the fighting troops and us paper shufflers at headquarters live.

Just pulled out the new picture you sent me. I keep it in my desk drawer. Hope my thoughts did not disturb your sleep, maybe just a dream of a pleasant day together for you, and as for the other three I imagine the happy dream would be of a rough house with the poor old man at the bottom of the heap. I will try to get that picture you want. Still love you a little bit. George

---

211   Bill Mauldin (b. 1921, d. 2003) was a U.S. Army sergeant and cartoonist best known for creating Willie and Joe, cartoon characters who represented the unkempt, cynical dogfaces of the infantry. Mauldin's cartoon "Up Front" featured Willie and Joe wryly commenting on the ironies of war and the injustices suffered by infantrymen. A favorite subject was that of how far removed from daily life at the front pompous officers were, their useless advice often met with blank stares from the infantrymen's famously dulled eyes. "Up Front" appeared in the *Stars and Stripes* and the *45th Division News*. Willie and Joe's rough, filthy appearance (it is supremely difficult to maintain one's looks while slogging through mud then squatting in a foxhole for months on end) and Mauldin's propensity for highlighting the arrogance and ineptitude of those in higher command irked many traditional officers who felt soldiers like Willie and Joe should not be popularized–General Patton being one. Despite Patton's call for Mauldin's removal, other generals recognized that Mauldin expressed what infantrymen already griped about and they encouraged Mauldin's column as a harmless way to validate the infantry's frustrations (DePastino, *Bill Mauldin*, 107.). Mauldin won a Pulitzer Prize in 1944 for his WWII work.

After the war, Mauldin will continue his cartoon commentaries with the *St. Louis-Dispatch* and, in 1962, the *Chicago Sun-Times*. Mauldin also will serve two terms as President of the American Veterans Committee, author books and articles, unsuccessfully run for Congress, and star in a couple of movies. In 1959 he will win another Pulitzer Prize.

[George to Peggy]
[Handwritten on American Red Cross Stationery]

17 April 44

My darling:

Another day gone by. It has been cooler here for several days even rained one day. Think I will take my day or rather half day off to visit that old castle up on the hill this week.

I really miss some of the officers I was working with in AFHQ. Hope you meet Heyduck and Allen and some of the others when this is all over. Heyduck is a real gentleman endowed with a keen mind, common sense, a bit of humor and a lot of consideration for other people at least until they started trying to push him around. About all I can say for the officer I am working for now is that he is a nice old man.

The other night when George Doerr was here we ran into an interesting old arab. He was shabbily dressed and worked as porter in the building Doerr stayed in. H[is] face was bronzed behind a stubble of whiskers, with dark beady eyes touched with a bit of good humor. You would not have thought his short thick fingers could handle a pen to make the graceful arabic letters he was writing for us. He stated himself to be a "Professor of Languages" and he did speak English tolerably well. That was the result of several years spent in London. He knew a lot of old Arab folk tales. So now he has gotten the job of writing several of them in English for an American mother to read to a little boy and little girl I know. He is even putting a little Arabic writing at the beginning to let you see what it looks like.

I am going to stop back to pick it up one of these days [and] then you will have a couple of real good stories.

There is an Arab's house or rather hovel right down the hill a short distance from where I live. In fact I can look down into the courtyard from our balcony.

There is a little arab boy about ~~four~~ three years old who lives there. That is my guess as to his age. He is a cute little tyke, a bit dirty, but he is the favorite of the soldiers who run the V-Mail station. He wears one of those GI knit caps, a jacket that hangs below his knees and that is about all. He has learned a couple of English phrases like 'OK Butch' and 'Thanks for chewing gum.' They have trained him to take the paper off the gum they give him and carry it away across a parking lot to drop it in a trash container and also he has learned to salute. He is a very happy little fellow and answers to the name of O'Rielly.

It is a good spirit in men that treat strange little children kindly. It seems to be a wide spread attitude probably because they are confident that the child is not in a position to turn around and take advantage of them. Which leads to the thought of how we all might act if we were confident that the grownups we deal with would not take advantage of us. Guess the best we can do is to assume they won't at least until they do.

Oh I missed a most important detail about the old arab 'Professor.' When I asked if he had any children he said no but he hoped to in a couple years, but he has none now as his wife is only 14 years old!

It is a strange old world, kind of interesting though, but I do resent going thru part of it without you right with me. I sure do want to come home to you my darling.

George.

[Peggy to George]
[V-Mail]

#166
April 18, Tues.

Dearest George

Everything was ready for the children's breakfast this morning and I was going to sleep. But this is one of those heavenly spring mornings when all you want to do is get out of doors. So I'm about to take the children and drive around trying to find a team of horses and plow. My plans for plowing fell through. First Larry and I must care for the chicks. One died Mon. but we still have plenty. Yesterday I dug about half of last year's garden patch and planted potatoes. That's why I thought I'd sleep this morning. If I just had Frank enough to do all the heavy work, the rest is easy. Larry and I planted part of our new garden by the side of the drive too—peas, spinach, lettuce, carrots and beets. The tulips are coming up and the daffodils. Oh yes, I spread another 100 lbs. of fertilizer after supper last night and then mangled the clothes I washed in the morning. So you have a farmer's wife and I love it. Everyone says I'm thin (99 lbs.) but I never felt better in my life and I'm taking vitamin pills for you. Also now that I'll be outside most of the time Mrs. Collins is coming one day a week to work inside. I love you, dear. Peggy

[George to Peggy]
[Postmarked April 22, 1944]
[Handwritten on American Red Cross Stationery]

Friday

Peggy dear;

In the V-Mail I received from you today you were so presumptuous as to assume that after all the years (note the plural) that we have been living apart that I still belong to you and love you. Isn't that just a bit old fashioned. If we don't get at least one divorce our friends will think there is something wrong with us. When our children go to school the kids will whisper around about how their mother and father never got a divorce, that they still live together and of all things they all live in the same house, and their father hardly ever beats up on their mother. Well then they will probably just shrug it off as the old man being one of those psychopathic cases from the Ten Years' War and their old lady, well she got thrown off a hunter that refused a jump at a horseshow away back before they were married in the gay thirties, [in] which [said] fall touched her pretty bad in the head so much so that she has loved the old man ever since.

There are all kinds of things to tell you about tonight so I will take up our divorce up some other time. Robbie Peake will be able to handle all the difficult little technical details which may arise out of the fact that we will want to go right on living together anyway.

You know it is a shame that I should be sitting up here all by myself when I could be so entertaining this evening, but then you are the only person that I really want to be with so I may as well write you instead. Guess I would tease you.

After dinner this evening I took a long walk. Dinner itself was pleasant with Major Dean from Texas who went thru Annapolis, studied Chinese at Stamford, has been several times to China, and runs a big ranch in Texas. Quite a combination, and [a] very pleasant interesting fellow with some good ideas. Unfortunately he is shunted off on a bit of a dead end *pourquoi je ne sais pas*.[212] Then Lt. Col. Page came over to have a cup of coffee with us and we settled the war to our own likings. Page is one of those retiring fellows, smart as the devil, and you don't talk with him long before you know he is very considerate of people about him and understands them pretty well. One of the best officers in the headquarters.

Well before you got me off the subject I was saying I took a walk. I walked along the top of a Djebel (a hill to you) which has a big fort on it. You can tell the censor that the fort was built by the Spanish in 1563 so I don't believe it is any longer considered a military secret.[213] Wandering along the outside walls of this old fort I met up with a French captain who fortunately spoke no English so I had a fine chance to practice my very best French which somehow he seemed to understand—at least he was polite enough to let on that he did. He in turn told me the history of this town which I have for some time

---

212 Translated: "why I do not know."
213 George is possibly describing Fort St. Philippe, assuming some details were lost a bit in translation. Originally a Spanish castle called Castillo de los Santos (Castle of the Saints) and built in 1563, it was the French who rebuilt and repurposed the castle, transforming it into a fort. Alternately called Bordj-Beni-Zeroual by locals, Fort St. Philippe was razed in the 1970s by the Algerian People's National Army (ANP). The only fort built before 1563 and likely visible from Fort St. Philippe is the Chateau Vieux (likely the "old fort" George mentions). Also called the Kasba and the Citadel, Chateau Vieux was originally erected in 903 and rebuilt by the Spanish in 1509.

been trying to piece together. You may remember I have a failing for such things. The fort which we were walking by was called the new fort to distinguish it from the old fort which we could see silhouetted high on a hill in the distance against the setting sun. He told me of the Spaniards' fights with the Arabs, about the pirates who lived here (sorry pirates always infest a place) and how the French had finally taken the place from the Arabs after they had driven the Spanish out. Quite a story, maybe some evening I shall walk along that hill and tell you all about it. Then there are some nice benches in the gardens along the walk where we could sit and I could tell you another old story which you always like to hear.

On the way back I stopped in to my friend Benhamdoune the Arab "Professor." He had not finished the stories he promised me for Georgia and Larry, but said he would have them done next Tuesday.

Then yesterday there were a few things to tell you about too.

[The remainder of this page of the letter has been cut.]
[Continued on the back]

leather goods, all of which were sold after quite a process of bargaining and haggling.

Then I walked up a flight of stairs out of curiosity to find a Frenchman who sold furniture and was a decorator. His show room was

[The remainder of this page of the letter has been cut.]
[Continued on the next page]

big open troughs under little sheds with many colored garments hanging out in the sun to dry, quite a sight. Near there a stair way leads up into the old fortified native

[The remainder of this page of the letter has been cut.]
[Continued on the back]

very much I love you and miss your company. It would be so much more interesting to look around here with you. If I could just have you in my arms for a while tonight, or maybe all night would be better, I am sure I would convince you that I

[The remainder of this page of the letter has been cut.]

[Peggy to George]

#169
Sun. P.M.
April 23.

My Darling.

I'm so glad you like the picture. I read your letter to the children and they both said "When is Daddy going to send us a picture of him?" I agree perfectly. Let's have one soon.

This has been quite a weekend. I am in bed early tonight. My party for Pete last night went off very smoothly. Most of the cooking on Friday & then had Mrs. Collins to help Tina wash dishes last night. I had 14 girls and 8 men and that's pretty good for the present. Bowdens[4F], Brosnahans[?], Ives[USN(avy)], Peters[OWI], Hoggsons[4F], Linens[OWI], Wellingtons[4F] were the couples and Pinky, Maggie, Mary Ward, Betty Hite, Hattie Linen, Penn & myself were the extras. It's something now to give people a drink. I bought two bottles of rum, a half gallon of Cuban gin, one bottle domestic vermouth, one crème de menthe, one Calif. brandy, 12 beers, 12 Coca Colas and it cost me $35.00. It wasn't enough either. The food was easy as I had my good pig so we had ham, mustard sauce, scalloped potatoes, green beans, sponge cake & coffee. Some played bridge, others poker and we all had a good time including Doxie. It's so long since I had a big party that I was a little nervous doing it alone. However, except for the boredom of not having you to do things for, all was all right. I kept thinking how wonderful it will be when each of these girls except for poor Pinky, can come escorted to a party again instead of standing gazing hungrily as we all do at those in the room who still have husbands.

After I wrote you Friday a.m. Robin developed a swollen neck and fever which looked like more than cutting the teeth I wrote you about. In fact I was so sure he had mumps that I was all ready to call off the party. Dr. Close came that night and said it was tonsilitis and swollen glands. Now he takes sulfadiazine and today has a bad rash. Perhaps it is measles. Anyhow, it is not serious and he feels better today & his appetite hasn't failed him yet. He's so ---- cranky though that you can't get near him without being pushed away with shouts of "Don't! Don't!" Even Doxie got his tail pulled today for trying to be sympathetic.

I'm enclosing interesting clippings on Cochran.[214] He is doing a swell job.

I must stop & write Mom and Dad. First let me pass on the best wishes of all our guests of last night. Each one spoke to me and asked to be remembered next time I wrote.

Our room is so cozy here with the radio about to bring Charlie McCarthy[215] on the air. How happy I'll be when I can look up and see you beside me here. I often dream of our reunion and my imagination always fails me. It's really too great an emotion to imagine. What do you think we'll say first? Hello, Dear?

                    All my love, Peggy

---

214 The clippings likely detailed Cochran's success in the China-Burma-India (CBI) theater. Cochran developed the First Air Commando Force which provided aerial support during the invasion of Burma. Cochran's commandos were hand-picked for their skill and bravery. Most had already been decorated for outstanding achievements in other theaters or had extensive, years-long training (Associated Press, "Our Air Commandos Poised to Cut Burma Supply Lines."). In one estimate, from February 10-March 6, 1944 the commandos evacuated 700 wounded men from the Burmese jungles and "landed thousands of men, 500,000 pounds of supplies, mules, 75 ponies, oxen, and bulldozers for use in jungle warfare against the Japanese ("Philip G. Cochran, War Hero and Model for 2 Cartoon Figures.").

215 The Charlie McCarthy Show was one of radio's highest-rated programs during its run from 1937-1956. The comedy variety show was the brainchild of ventriloquist Edgar Bergen who was accompanied on the show by a wise-cracking dummy he called Charlie McCarthy. The show was inducted into the Radio Hall of Fame in 1990.

[George to Peggy]
[Handwritten on American Red Cross stationery]

#115
25 April 44
Tuesday

My darling:

    Suppose I have to write you a letter, what nuisances you women are. Don't you know what a chore it is to take the time to write? It takes you away for a while from all the exciting adventure of war back to those dull monotonous hours we used to be forced into spending together. Painful weren't they? Kinda would like to run my finger down that dip in your funny little nose and count your freckles just 'cause it annoyed you so. And I suppose you would come over to sit in my lap just so I couldn't read the new issue of Time, then I would probably get into your bed just to keep you awake. See how lucky you are, not to have to put up with such an ornery guy around the house.

    You took a walk with me tonight even though you may not have known it. You had to listen while I told you all about the history of the old fort we walked around. We ran into Capt. Price along the sea front with a couple of French girls. I stopped long enough for an introduction. They may have thought I was a bit rude to walk off by myself after they had invited me to go along with them, but then they didn't know, of course, that you were with me. We had a very nice walk, I held your hand and told you how pretty you looked which brought a becoming blush. Then we stopped back by Benhamdoune's to see if he had the stories written which he promised me. He had two finished and wrote out a couple of sentences in Arabic for us. I will mail them in separate envelopes, one to Larry and one to Georgia. The stories are a bit stilted so far as language goes, but that added interest for me. You can probably reword them a bit in reading them to the children and I think they will be interested. Benhamdoune says they were told to him by his grandmother. His penmanship is quite good.

I bought a story book with colored pictures and all in french by Pierre Jarry. It is all about *Pouichhove le petite pousin*.[216] I am afraid I will have to read it myself before I mail it to the children though.

I would like to have you mail me "Time for Greatness." Somehow the name reminds me of a verse from Longfellow — ~~Take lives of all great men~~

> Lives of great men all remind us
> We can make our lives sublime,
> And, departing, leave behind us
> Footprints on the sands of time;
>
> Footprints, that perhaps another,
> Sailing o'er life's solemn main,
> A forlorn and shipwrecked brother,
> Seeing, shall take heart again.[217]

It is one of those poems I like and repeat over to myself when I take a walk.

You mentioned that you were going to send me a piece you clipped from Saturday Evening Post; an open letter to my Wife. Strange that caught my eye too and I liked it. It is good but my dear you often do better in telling me how you feel and what our wonderful babies mean to you.

Now if I am not careful I will begin telling you a lot of silly things about how much I love you and miss you. And I never do stop thanking you for the loving care you give our babies with all the tiring work and patience I know it takes. Darling, one thing you can be sure of, I will love you more than ever when I do get home.

Sorry if I have groused around about some of the impediments placed in the way of victory by the worthless old baggage which the

---

216 *Pouichore le Petit Poussin.*
217 George is quoting two stanzas from *A Psalm of Life* by the American poet Henry Wadsworth Longfellow.

West Point Protective Society[218] foists upon us at times.

Guess I will get to bed now, I will be thinking of you when I fall asleep.

With all my love dear, George

[Peggy to George]
[V-Mail]

#170
April 26, Wed.

Dearest George

This is nap time for all but Momie and having just finished a month's mending I will write you before the crowd starts roaring again. What a troupe they are nowadays. I took Larry & Georgia marketing this morning and Larry insisted on taking along a snail he had just acquired from the garden mud. We hadn't hit North St. before I heard whispers & giggles from the back seat. Mr. Snail enjoying the warmth of Larry's hand was slowly emerging from his shell and sinister plans were being made for his disposal down my neck. By good luck I stayed on the road & changed their ideas but it just occurred to me now. I then promptly forgot the matter and haven't the vaguest notion what did happen to the snail. Perhaps I'll have a sequel to this story. The boats still haven't arrived and I fear I shall have to mail some out from N.Y.C. when I go in to assuage Larry's daily disappointment in his vain search of the postbox. He even insists on looking in Crowley's old box because it is larger than ours and the postman once used it when a parcel didn't fit into our own. The sun is out after days of rain. I haven't been out of the house since I wrote you Sun. until this morning. The chicks aren't so good. We've lost 14. I love you dearest. Peggy X X

---

218   The West Point Protection Society is an unflattering nickname given to Regular Army service members (usually by their civilian counterparts). The phrase reflects the belief that West Point graduates serving in the Army Officer Corps work together to promote and protect each other's positions and future careers at the expense of others. Critics assert that "West Point classmates learn to stick together, cover each other, and not to ask questions about the actions of senior graduates," leading to "clique leadership" and discouraging meaningful reform while "perpetuat[ing] a system of elitist control" (King, "Who Needs West Point?").

[George to Peggy]
[Handwritten on American Red Cross stationery]

[#]116

28 April 44

    Good Evening, nice night isn't it. Wouldn't mind taking a bicycle ride with you tonight. But I have a splendid idea to keep from getting wrapped around a tree on one of those dark roads you want to lead me around to get over to the Hoggson's. All we have to do is hang one of those 1\underline{^{00}}$ Ingersolls with a luminous dial on the end of Doxie's tail. Then we just tell Doxie to stay on the road. Simple isn't it.

    Spent a pleasant evening with Capt. Helms. I went out to his place for dinner which was a good change. He lives in a sort of sea side resort about 20 minutes ride from here. They also have a club out there and were having a dance tonight. You could not get into the bar without a blouse so one of the boys who lives with Helms was good enough to lend me his. So we went over and had a couple of drinks of eau de vie and talked over the general situation. Guess that will be about all for tonight my dear.

                   My love, George

[Peggy to George]
[V-Mail]

#172

April 29, Sat.

Dearest George

    This has been a glorious spring day. Betty arrived yesterday afternoon and while the kids napped today we took a sunbath on the terrace. The peas broke through the ground today, also lettuce an[d] the onion sets. We have one daffodil in bloom so we feel very much like spring has come again. This year it will be a cloudy one all over the world, though, I fear with the dreadful invasion seeming so imminent.[219] May we be successful and quickly. I am dressed now

---

219   Peggy is anticipating the Allied invasion of western Europe.

to go to N.Y.C. for dinner with the MacFarlanes. They are here a few days. Betty is feeding Georgia & Robin. Larry has gone to Fitsy Boussevain's birthday party with Hodgey. He looked pretty nifty in his new blue sailor suit and spring coat. I hope the girls don't mob him. I can't wait to hear his description of the party. I'll pass it on to you tomorrow. Guess I better run to catch the 5:45. I love you, Dear, and miss you so as the country gets ready for riding, golf, etc. Love, Peggy

[George to Peggy]
[V-Mail]

[No.]117
30 April 1944

Dear Peggy:

Thought I would go back to V-Mail for a change tonight. Being duty officer I suppose I should have taken the opportunity to write a more lengthy letter. But I got started reading some back issues of Time which I had not gotten around to reading before. Being well removed from the actual war back here in this paper mill, you get to trying to compensate in some way for the fighting, danger and physical hardships which others are facing. With the unusually excellent training and experience along administrative lines which I have had I can be of quite some use although my low rank is a positive handicap. Still I have been thinking I should get to some place where there is more war and less paper shuffling. Had a mighty nice letter from you today telling about Georgia getting her doll. All my love dear George

[George to Peggy]

[#]118
2 May 44

Dear Peggy:

Have had some mighty nice letters from you the last couple of days. Sounds like you were starting a regular farm. Hope you are not taking on too much. You don't want to go on losing weight, I don't like my girls too skinny. Bet you did look pretty in that Paris dress. Do you suppose that Agnes Drecoll is still in business on the Place de Vendome?

I saw a good movie in color last night with all the settings in Havana which reminded me of a pretty young lady sitting beside me in a plane over the Caribbean, those good daiquiris at Sloppy Joes, and an infant's shop on the Prado where we got a dress for Georgia when she was pretty young.

Took a walk with Helms the other night along the sea and thought of an awful bad sun burn we both got once along the shore of the same sea.

Our house must be pretty nifty by now. Sounds like you were fixing to surprise me a bit when I get home. I sure am looking forward to seeing all that you have done. But you will still have a little to keep me busy with.

A friend of mine was just in[—]an officer in french liaison section. I showed him that last large picture you sent me. He was very approving, but who wouldn't be. He mentioned that he would like to get such a picture. He has not heard from his family since the fall of France.

Guess we are mighty lucky in comparison to a lot of these people. Maybe more tonight.

                My love dear, George

[Peggy to George]
[V-Mail]

                                      #173
                              May 2, 1944

My Darling,

It was so good to get a letter from you today and know that you finally had a few hours off and found an interesting way to spend them. You must do that more often if it is possible. Betty is still here with me and will stay until Thurs. Today I took her to Jessie Bedford's for lunch & to the Garden Club meeting. I was asked to be President of the club which I consider quite an honor, but I couldn't accept the nomination with all I have to do at home. One job would be sure to suffer or I'd go bats doing both. The chickens seem to be recovering as no more have died. It's surprising how much there is to learn about being a farmer. It's quite a profession. The kids are fine. Robin still has a rash on his legs but he feels so well I haven't even bothered to call Dr. Close again. The place is beginning to look fine. I'll take some more pictures as soon as my new grass is up. Love, Peggy

[George to Peggy]

[#]119
3 May 44

Peg dear,

    Thought you might like a note this morning. I have this job pretty well in hand now, once caught up with what was dumped on me when I came down here, things will be pretty easy. Just wish I get a chance to do more. This is the same kind of work Allen and I were doing over at the other headquarters. They had a West Point Lt. Col. on this job who never made a mistake, so you can see why I have been busy. He is lucky enough to be on his way back to the states.

    I will drop Colby a line up in London, thanks for the address. That is the same pacificist that criticized me all thru Yale for taking military training. Wonder if he will get down this way.

    Today is my afternoon off so the way it looks this morning I will be taking it off all right. From where I sit I can see some eight officers, none of whom are occupied other than reading the Stars & Stripes, writing letters or just smoking. A busy place.

    There is one Maj. here who reminds me of GI Joe, who graces Sgt. Bill Mauldin's cartoon "Up Front." He has been through the mill with an infantry regiment until he made the mistake of driving a jeep over a mine. He is funny without intending to be. At first meeting he doesn't make much of an impression, but he has good common sense, a good heart, and is humorous in the way he accepts the futility of much that transpires here.

We just got a laugh out of the official document telling us what we have to do to vote. It contains 7 closely typed pages of legalistic phrasing which the Maj. says only a damn fool would read cause it's obvious that one way or another they will see to it that we can't vote. Yesterday he got a bushel basket full of mail dated back thru Sept. and Oct. last fall. He didn't even bat an eye.

I may be a bit critical now and then but on the overall picture I am proud of what our country and our army and navy have done. I am convinced that the goals we have set in the Atlantic Charter[220] are worthy of our best efforts. The difficulties in attaining them are great. Naturally we are going to make a lot of mistakes, and a lot of individual selfish actions are going to be taken. When you look back to the spring of 1942 though we have accomplished a lot. From an individual standpoint, I am not satisfied at sitting around here shuffling paper. Sure wish that I could have stayed along with Cochran. Thanks for the clippings. Boy what a job he has done.

My love dear: George

[Peggy to George]
[V-Mail]

#174
May 5, Fri.

My Darling.

I'm racing like crazy to get things in order so I can make the village for lunch and put Betty on the 1:42 train. It's a real hot day and I've done the cleaning and the silver polishing. Frank is here and I have

---

220 Released on August 14, 1941 by U.S. President Roosevelt and British Prime Minister Churchill, the Atlantic Charter was a nonbinding declaration that outlined U.S. and British goals for WWII. Specifically, the Charter publicly reaffirmed the solidarity between the United States and Great Britain against the Axis countries and outlined a vision for the world after the war–a vision of freer trade, self-determination, and disarmament.

one million things he must do which I simply can't but he says he will only have time to cut the grass today. Oh, for a full time man on the place! Tina & I finally put the awning on the porch this week and now we can't get the table up from the cellar. If I was helpless like most people, I wouldn't be left with all this impossible stuff to do. Oh well, you aren't coming home tomorrow so I suppose there is no need to get all this stuff done this year. Yesterday Pat Somers (Ogontz)[221] came over for the day with her boy, Larry's age. They played in the brook all day and were covered with mud, but had a marvelous time, of course. Must dash again. I love you. Peggy

[George to Peggy]
[Handwritten on American Red Cross stationery]

[#]119

6 May

My darling:

You know a fellow is pretty lucky to be over here. Just think of all the annoyances I escape by being over here. If I were to walk up to the house this evening Doxie would be all over me like a fur coat. Then I am sure I would have to play with the kids before dinner, Larry would want me to see his chicks, Georgia would want a story and Robbie I suppose would have dumped my tobacco on the floor. Of course I probably would not have enough gasoline to drive home from the station, but would have to have a bicycle.

Then those pleading brown eyes at dinner would make me feel so guilty that half my plate would be dog food.

With the man shortage what it is I suppose you would share me with your less fortunate girl friends. Of course I would have to give you a backgammon lesson. Another thing if I had just gotten home tonight chances are you would not even let me sit around and write letters.

---

221   The Ogontz School for Young Ladies in Pennsylvania was a boarding school Peggy attended when she was young. Ogontz also opened a summer extension program in 1912 in the White Mountains of New Hampshire. In 1923 the two programs separated and in 1950 the school was given to Pennsylvania State University. The extension program site became a summer camp which Georgia remembers attending one summer when she was eight years old.

So you can see I am smart enough to know when I am really well off. Maybe I won't even come home when the war is over. I don't know for sure, but I wish they would give me a chance to anyway.

Wish I was home to take some of that abuse.

My love dear, George

[George to Peggy]
[V-Mail]

7 May 44

My darling:

You know I didn't tell you about finally getting to visit that old castle I mentioned before. On my afternoon off I went along with a Red Cross tour 'cause you have to have a special permit to get by the French native guards and also, because it is a long way up if you walk. The Spanish built it away back in the first part of the 16th century. They didn't like the way the Arab pirates[222] were behaving so they came down here took over the city after quite an argument and then used it as a penal colony. A friendly Arab hauled water to the top of the hill on his burros every day while the Spaniards built the castle. When it was finished, the Spaniards took all the Arabs wives away from him and threw him in a deep dungeon where he died. Hope nobody does that to me especially 'cause I don't want to lose my wife. Love, George

[Peggy to George]

Sun. P.M.
#175

Dearest George,

You have been on my mind every minute today until I have reached the point of worrying that there may be some telepathic meaning to it. Last night I dreamt that a man phoned me to say you were in this country but could not see me or phone me as it was a

---

222 More specifically, Mers-el-Kébir was the bastion of the Barbary pirates.

secret mission. Then he hung up without even giving his name. I woke up miserable and as soon as I had finished the breakfast dishes and cared for the chicks I found myself baking an angel food cake. I couldn't seem to think of another thing which had to be done even though Tina had made ice cream for lunch. I roasted & stuffed a chicken, had mashed potatoes & gravy & wax beans & fully expected to have you walk in for dinner, I guess.

During dinner I remember that "Daddy should have some cake" where upon Georgia immediately left part of hers for you. I intend to enclose a lily-of-the-valley which we started picking today. Maybe I'll put in a cake crumb too.

Since this was my weekend "off" I decided to make the most of it. I went to the club yesterday afternoon & played tennis with Elsa Slocum. It was a good game. Then she asked me back to her family's where is where she lives now and I stayed for dinner. The place is one of the few show places of Greenwich which is still kept in A-1 shape. There are 85 acres of garden & lawn and not a weed among them. Elsa heard from Walt who is a seabee in New Guinea. He has just been made a Lt. Col. and is second in command of a whole battalion. She's thrilled to death, of course.

Today after our big dinner I went to the Club for more tennis with Clay & Martha Buckhaut, but it poured down rain just as we were starting. They had brought Bob Heiskell[223] along for a fourth. He's managing editor of "Life" and his wife just had a baby so she couldn't

---

223   It is likely Peggy means Andrew Heiskell (b. 1915, d. 2003), former chairman of Time Inc. and well-known New York City philanthropist. In 1937 Heiskell began producing and editing articles on science and medicine for LIFE before transitioning to the business side of publishing. In only six years Heiskell was named publisher of LIFE and shortly before Peggy's letter, Cornelia Scott, Heiskell's wife at the time, had given birth in to their son Peter.
   By 1960 Heiskell had advanced to chairman of Time Inc. As publisher of LIFE, he oversaw the magazine's transition to more text and many of his long-term projects as Time Inc. chairman remain successful (i.e., the expansion of Sports Illustrated and the creation of People magazine). Heiskell was as dedicated to his philanthropic endeavors as he was to his business ideas. Notably, Heiskell co-founded the Urban Coalition (community-based councils that address issues of urban blight) and the Enterprise Foundation (which advanced more than $600 million worth of housing in areas considered slums) (Kaufman, "Andrew Heiskell, 87, a Former Chairman of Time Inc. and a Civic Leader, Dies."). Heiskell is also known for his efforts to transform the previously ailing New York Public Library system and improve Bryant Park (abutting the main library). He is memorialized for his good works by a library branch bearing his name and a marker in Bryant Park.

play. We ended up at the Heiskell's playing bridge in our tennis clothes until 6:00 o'clock, & then Clay & Martha took me back to their house for dinner. I just got home now. Their two little girls 11 & 8 ate with us & they were perfectly mannered. Clay & Martha are so refreshing as they are among the few sublimely happy couples that we know here in Greenwich. They never take each other for granted and always speak so sweetly to one another. What a relief it is!

Doxie seems to be sick again. He's gone quite a while this time, but I guess he goes to the vet tomorrow. The chicks are growing fast and are not dying anymore. There's a weasel roaming up and down the brook which prohibits my putting them outside. How I wish I could shoot it! As it is, I guess the chicks will have to continue growing up in the garage.

The children are fine. Robin is bossier every day. This week Tina decided the bathtub would no longer hold all three at once so she made Larry wait. When he got in Robin was too far back so Larry tried to give him a shove forward with his feet. Whereupon Robin swung around hitting Larry across the face with his washcloth and yelling "Stop it" with the maddest look on his face. Must go but want to say again I love you more and more. Do come home soon.

Peggy

[George to Peggy]
[V-Mail]

No. 120
8 May 44 Monday

Peg dear,

Was going to do a little work tonight but I got into one of those talking sessions. First the duty officer came in to take a look around and we got to discussing one thing and another, then a couple of the enlisted men came along. They are nice boys along in their college years one of them wanting to go back to study medicine when the war is over, and one wanting to just go to college. When you see the general run of our soldiers over here compared to the local population it gives you a feeling of pride in our country. They are a pretty decent bunch of young fellows. Finally got a picture of your husband for you, it is all addressed here on my desk and I will take it up to get Helms to censor it for me in the morning. Hope you get it for your birthday[.] My love dear George

[George to Peggy]
[Handwritten on American Red Cross stationery]

[#]120
Capt. GR Steiner
Hq SOS Natousa G-3
APO 750
10 May 44

Peg dear,

    Had the afternoon off and wished more than ever that you were here. You see I pulled out a lot of my clothes which had reached that point where you either put buttons on them or throw them away. At least I am more appreciative now of those jobs you take care of for me. As button sewer on[-]er I am not so good. So now when I say that I miss you, it won't be so hard for you to tell just what I mean. Well maybe there are one or two other reasons.

    I suppose you miss me too. It would be handy to have a man around to help fixing up the house and yard. So you see I understand what you really mean when you say you miss me. Or do I?

    I wonder what that will be like when I see you for the first time again. I sent the picture along so you would be sure to know me when you see me. Also I guess it will have to serve in lieu of all I would like to do for you on your birthday. Maybe next year I will be home. I really think I will be so don't emphasize the maybe. Principle reason I would like to be home though would be so I could help you eat your birthday cake. Then too I would like to get you all dressed up to go to a show then someplace to dance where we could split a bottle of champagne. It's been a long time since we did that hasn't it. Sure will be fun to do it again though. I sent you some flowers which I would really like to pin on you myself. Then do you think we should stay in town or come back out home. I would like to be faced with problems like that. Maybe with the champagne it would be best to stay in at the Savoy. How about making that a date? We will have the cake in the afternoon so the kids can join the party then go in town for the evening.

    I have been reading those articles of Beard's and he really has an understanding of how our government works. They are very interesting, thanks for sending them.

My love dear, George

[Peggy to George]
[V-Mail]

#177
May 12, 1944

My Darling

    This is another beautiful morning and Tina is about to leave for the weekend. I'd give a lot to not have the children this weekend as the tennis would be perfect. But that's a mighty little complaint. Margie & Hodgey were here overnight. The boys slept in the guest room and what a time they had. Very little sleep but great fun. You should have seen the condition of their beds this morning. It was some sight. Margie and Pete signed a legal separation paper Tuesday so she was pretty upset. What a world this is. I like them both so much and I feel that they love one another but have grown so far apart with all their high living that neither has the desire to break down and give in so that an understanding can begin again. They aren't telling Hodgie as Pete leaves the country soon anyway. Joe Bridge is home on leave so

I had them over for cocktails last night and took them and Margie to the Club for dinner. He looks marvelous. Must have lost 15 lbs. and from the right spots too. Love, Peggy

[George to Peggy]
[V-Mail]

No. 122
14 May 44

Peg dear, Sorry I was not home to tell Larry about Mother's day.

Seeing that I committed myself this morning to writing again tonight guess I had better do it to keep peace in the family. About all I have done in the meantime is to write a lot of rather dull answers to a lot of rather dull papers. The flower from our garden with the cake crumbs arrived. Just to show you how much I would like to be home I would even help you weed your garden and I would leave half of that angel food cake for the rest of the family. If you would send me some more Walnut tobacco about now it would be appreciated. Also you might pick two pipes off of my rack if Larry will allow it. There is one with a curved stem and a silver band and another with gold band which I like. There should be two with gold bands, one I want has a little wider mouth piece. Put in a roll of dental floss. Thank you. My love, George

[George to Peggy]
[Handwritten on American Red Cross Stationery]

[#]121
Hq SOS Natousa G-3
APO 750 c/o PM N.Y.C.
Sunday
14 May 44

My darling Peggy:

Here it is Sunday morning. They have set it up now so we get half a day off on Sunday, today I drew the morning. Usually I have had too much to get done so have not taken advantage of it before. I guess [paper cut and removed by censor] days delay won't make much difference in this red tape mill. Wish I could [paper cut and removed by censor] where I could really see the results of what you do, both good and bad. Here you seldom know the difference. You can take [paper cut and removed by censor] finished job or just slide [paper cut and removed by censor] and you hardly ever learn what the final result is. Most of us try to turn out the right answers, but it is difficult to have much enthusiasm or interest in this kind of work.

Your letter written last Sunday arrived yesterday, there is a bit of evidence that things are well handled. That was a strange dream you had, but I don't think you had better put much stock in it. By the way what is our new phone number out there? Every now and again I run across someone returning to the states and several times had wanted to ask them to give you a call when they get to New York.

Maj. Williams and myself plan to drive down to see how the [paper cut and removed by censor] live next Sunday. There is one of their headquarters about [paper cut and removed by censor] from here where there is an interesting museum. A liaison officer who is in [paper cut and removed by censor] is going along.

I am on duty tonight so if you don't object I will probably write you again tonight.

Sure would like to have spent this Sunday morning in Greenwich with you. This dreaming must be contagious as I dreamed you were in bed with me last night without your nightie and that I-----well it is the end of the page any way.

My love dear, George

[Peggy to George]

#178
Mon. May 15
8:00 P.M.

My Darling.

It's not possible to put into words how much I would give to lead you by the hand out onto our terrace for our evening's date and show you our azaleas in bloom. There is a solid mass of red against each side of the door and then a huge mass of pale pink on either side of the bay windows. I have taken snaps so it will help a little.

Tonight I am enclosing the snaps I tried in the house. They came out fairly well so I'm going to do the rest of the rooms for you and other angles of these. The other enclosures I believe you can figure out for yourself. Don Fullerton's letter I'll let you answer yourself. You know I'll never get to it.

Larry was in a stew tonight because he had so much to write you and I made him put it off until morning. Your letter came today about the possibility of toy Jap subs having sunk his boats. They arrived four or five days ago and have been in constant use ever since. He feels you should be informed immediately so "Daddy won't worry anymore." Also the beautifully written stories arrived today. I am about to read them when I finish this. Larry wants to tell you about those too even though he hasn't heard them yet. Then he has to tell you that the potatoes are up but Bambi walks all over them every night and they don't get a chance to grow. The old garden fence we are using in the empty garage space to keep the chicks in. So if you get a letter from Larry and it's not perfectly clear, these are a few things he said.

As for me I got a nice letter from you today complaining of the trials that beset you at home and how much better off you are where you are now. You certainly keep up to us in your imagination. I often wonder if you can visualize the children as they are rather than as you left them. This letter is very convincing. You guessed exactly what would happen if you should drop in on us.

Tomorrow Isabel Haskins Hartmann & her two boys are stopping for the day on her way back to New London. I haven't seen her since we spent an evening with her two years ago your last birthday. Do you remember. Fred is a Navy Doctor in the Pacific now. She still lives up in New London. I'll tell you more after tomorrow. Unfortunately I already had Betty Bowden & her child coming up before Isabel called.

Mrs. Alworth is in town. I went in last Wednes. & had dinner with her and she is coming out Sat. for lunch and spend[ing] the afternoon. She is a wonder, really. I hope I always maintain a superior interest in life and people as I grow older the way she has done. She says Uncle George seems fine again. He goes out for dinner parties etc. and looks great. He'll go quickly, though, with one of those, I imagine.

I am anxious to get at Benhamdoune's stories so excuse me darling. You're already hidden behind a magazine so you haven't listened to my idle chatter anyway. Thank goodness, you don't spend nights doing field artillery problems anymore. 'I always told you' that was a waste of time.

I love you, darling, and miss you more and more each day. Hurry that —— war up in your part of the world and come home.

You may have a chance someday soon to tell someone what you think you ought to be doing. Don't let the opportunity slip.

Love, Peggy

[George to Peggy]
[V-Mail]

No. 122
17 May 44

Dearest Peggy:

Just finished lunch at the Red Cross, so now it being my afternoon off, I have the rest of the day to myself for whatever I can devise to do with it. The way it is starting to warm up now I think next week I will go out to the beach for a swim. We are back in cottons again. You must be doing a lot of work around the house dear, hope you can get some more help and ease up a little bit, it sounds pretty strenuous. The trouble will be when I return, you are going to be so used to shifting for yourself, you just won't know what to do with a husband around. It was about three years ago that you called me up down at the office to let me know that I was in the Army. Wish you were here this afternoon—it is a beautiful day, I would ask for a date tonight too. My love, George

[Peggy to George]
[V-Mail]

#179
May 17, 1944
Wed.

My Darling.

I have just ridden the bus to Greenwich and picked up the blue car which has been hospitalized for leaky radiator trouble. It's O.K. now and I am at Maggie's early so have a moment to write. The weather stays divine during the day and rains enough nights to keep the garden in good shape. I took some more pictures for you today. Isabel arrived yesterday morning and we had a marvelous day. Her boys got on swell with our three despite not knowing one another. It doesn't make any difference at that age. Isabel had taken hers to the zoo on Monday and had seen D[indecipherable]y I'd presumed she was a "wave" or "wac" by now. I haven't ever heard from her. Evidently she looks grand and is about to get married to an Amherst boy. Isabel couldn't remember his name and I'm dying to know if it's the one she pined for all through school and years afterwards. There's a dance at the Club Sat. and I have asked Wayne out for the weekend. Mrs. Alworth has wished another young man on me so I'll have to dye my hair and be a gal again with <u>two</u> dates. I forgot to tell you last Sun. Larry rode a pony at Anne's birthday party and I trotted it with him on and he <u>loved</u> <u>it</u>. Yours, Peggy

[Peggy to George]
[V-Mail]

#180
May 18, Thurs.

My Darling.

 This letter was left for tomorrow a.m. ten minutes ago and I had lights out & was almost asleep. Then the phone rang and now I'm wide awake again. You'll get a laugh out of the message. A man's voice said "Did I wake you up?" It was George Hite (he's still stationed on Staten Island). He asked me to come in and do the town some night next week. I jumped at the chance and said I'd love to. Betty's having a baby soon so I figured she'd suggested it to give him a little fun and had made sure he picked a safe woman. <u>But</u> after I accepted he said "Of course you'll have to keep quiet about our date or there'll be hurt feelings at home." With this promise I took an about face and said I couldn't do it if Betty hadn't been told and approved first. Do you think I'm prudish too, now? Most Greenwich does, but I don't believe you will. Had a swell tennis game today with Martha Buckhaut and two very nice British Navy officers. It was quite a fancy game. The men were really good. We had lunch at the Club and then I went to Greenwich to have my hair done for the first time in months. The children hardly knew me when I got home. Doxie howled. I love you darling, <u>very</u> <u>very</u> much. Love, Peggy

[George to Peggy]
[V-Mail]

No. 123
19 May 44

Peg my dear:

You know I would like to walk in and surprise you tonight. With the garrison you have in the house though it would be difficult to get in without being seen. Think I will do that when I do get home, just arrive without telling you. I would like to see the smile on your face. Good news. Allen was here yesterday and today, Maj. Doherty along with him. Of course we had dinner together, Ream also. As good a bunch of officers as I have run into in the Army. It was interesting conversation and good company. All seems to be going along about the same up at AFHQ. There is a possibility of getting a transfer up to where Stipp went. I would be glad to get up there. Did you ever hear any more news about Web Bull. Sure hope he is all right. My love dear, George

[George to Peggy]
[V-Mail]

No. 124
20 May 44

Peg dear;

It is getting a bit late, we had an extra job so worked tonight. Unlike AFHQ there has not been so much of that here. I have been wondering what kind of a Saturday night you would have this weekend. Wish I were with you whatever it is; out to dinner or staying home with the children either would suit me well if I had your company. I got a letter from Colby up in London said he was going to be there for a couple of weeks. He is fortunate to get over and back like that. Maj. Williams and I have tomorrow afternoon off provided something doesn't interfere so we got ahold of a jeep to drive down to one of the Foreign Legion[224] posts with a french officer to look things over. Had a laugh this morning at a native french soldier, a fine looking fellow loading a french poodle for its morning walk. He didn't appear to relish the job. I miss you right now. My love, George

[George to Peggy]
[V-Mail]

No. 125
22 May 44

Peg darling:

Had quite a trip yesterday. Maj. Williams, a french lt. and a french major from the Foreign Legion, and myself drove down to a little town about 50 miles away where the legion has a post.[225] Reminded you of Beau Geste.[226] They knew the officer of the day, a french captain, who showed us around. They had a very interesting collection of uniforms, trophies, weapons, pictures etc. all connected with the history of the legion. The old sergeant with 18 years' service did most of the explaining. The legion has fought everywhere, Mexico, (1860s) Crimea, Indo China, Dardendalles, Madagascar, Narvik (1940). Between 1920 and 1935 they had 2,000 killed in the years of peace.[227]

---

224   The French Foreign Legion is a branch of the French Army, commanded by French officers but consisting of volunteers from around the world. Originally founded in 1831 as a way to repurpose unwanted male immigrants in France and to defend French interests in Algeria, the Legion has since fought all over the world (Gilbert, *Voices of the Foreign Legion*.).
225   George likely visited Sidi Bel Abbès, site of the Legion headquarters until the 1960s when it was moved to Aubagne, France. Barracks onsite at the headquarters housed a French Foreign Legion museum until it was also relocated to Aubagne.
226   *Beau Geste* is a novel by P.C. Wren. Published in 1924, the book describes the fictional adventures of three British brothers who enlist in the French Foreign Legion. A silent film of the same name was released in 1926, starring Ronald Colman, and a 1939 remake with sound, directed by William Wellman, starred Gary Cooper. General Paul Rollet (responsible for supervising the entire Legion) felt *Beau Geste* misrepresented legionnaires, lazily relied on cliché characters, and advocated values in extreme conflict with those of the Legion (Porch, *The French Foreign Legion*, 429.). The mutiny at the end of Beau Geste resulted in a censure of the 1926 film in France and a complete ban on the 1939 version. The ban was not lifted until 1977. Despite unflattering portrayals of the Legion in films like *Beau Geste*, Legion recruitment increased as many Europeans were inspired by the antiquated idea of the Legion as a "small band of white men doing battle [against] people of color on the distant frontiers of the empire" and prevailing over "treacherous and ungrateful natives" thanks only to the legionnaire's "discipline and loyalty" (Ibid., 429, 439.).
227   During the interwar years, the French Foreign Legion was active during the Rif War (1921-1926) and the Druze Revolt (1925), however, George's claim that 2,000 members died in the interwar period remains to be verified.

Most of the non-coms are German.[228] The discipline is terrific. They showed us through their prison which had nice inner spring concrete bunks. Guess you know how bored I was with all this. All my love dear, for Larry X Georgia X Robbie X and you XX George

[Peggy to George]

#180
Monday May 22
8:10 P.M.

My Darling

I received a letter from you today, but it had several holes in [it]. That's only the second time that has happened and I enjoy getting even the holiest ones even though my curiosity fairly burns a hole in me too.

The weekend was very gay. You probably guessed that when I haven't written you since Friday. That day was spent cleaning the house from top to bottom and I do mean from the attic to the basement. Mrs. Collins has never showed up again. Guess I worked her too hard. I really don't mind the cleaning though and the house looked so pretty when I finished.

---

228 This claim is unlikely. It is doubtful the majority of non-commissioned officers (NCOs or non-coms) in 1944 were German for the simple reason that they were not French. Promotions and positions in command favored the French as emphasis was placed on their grasp of the French language instead of their merits or leadership capabilities (Ibid., 388.). Aside from language proficiency, French legionnaires were promoted because they were also the least ideologically-suspicious group in the Legion's ranks. German legionnaires had a reputation for desertion, often encouraging others to desert as well. As a result, ex-officers or NCOs from the German army were prohibited from enlisting in the Legion. While the interwar years saw an increase in new recruits, by 1936 the number of German recruits had sharply decreased. In 1935, for example, Germans in the Legion declined to around 19% from the previous year's 37% of legionnaires. After the annexation of Czechoslovakia and then the Anschluss, remaining German legionnaires (regardless of their political or ideological affiliations) were viewed with suspicion and their loyalties to the Legion questioned. Once the war began, the Legion kept German legionnaires from sensitive posts, such as radio operator (Ibid., 437.).

Loyalty to France and the Legion was of primary importance–another reason Frenchmen, tied to their country in many ways, and not Germans, were favored for command positions. In 1934, 35% of the Legion's corporals and NCOs were French even though the French represented only 16% of legionnaires. The Germans, during the same year, constituted nearly 45% of all legionnaires but only 21% of corporals and NCOs. Five years later, the percentage of Germans in the Legion dropped to match the 21% of corporals and NCOs that were still German, while the minority French comprised 41% of the corporals and NCOs (Ibid., 386.).

It is worth noting that for a brief period in the early 1830s, many NCOs were German. Thus, it would have been correct for George to write, perhaps, that in a certain regiment or at a specific time in the past, most of the NCOs were German.

Saturday I had Curt Swift for lunch. Mrs. Alworth asked me to introduce him around Greenwich. He's the son of some friends of hers who even have enough money to impress her. He's about 26 and has been discharged from the Navy for a "nervous stomach." This defect he immediately informs you of upon meeting him. Anyhow besides a suite at the Savoy he has one at the Pickwick Arms for the summer so that he can ride. That he's been doing at Round Hill. However after making him help get and serve his own lunch I took him up to Fillis's and rode with him. The river ride was gorgeous but every time I commented on it, he was so busy complaining about the mosquitoes that he had no time to enjoy it. Then when I rode faster to get away from the bugs, he was frightened. On the way back to the barn he came out suddenly with how much he liked the horse and wanted me to give a guess as to what Fillis would take for it. I'd never seen the beast before, but I guessed $300.00. We hadn't gotten our feet on the ground before he asked Fillis what he wanted for the horse. Fillis said $350.00. Curt offered $300 and the deal was closed. It disgusted me a bit that anyone could be so spoiled. With it all he's not bad. My main objection is that he's like an old man talking about his ailments all the time. Sat. night I had 16 for cocktails before the dinner dance at the club. Martha Buckhaut was going to have it but she had the Freeman's who built our house down from Mass[achusetts] for the weekend, and I wanted them to see the house. So there were Buckhauts, Linens, Freemans, Blacks & Hawleys (I didn't know them, but Martha & Clay had asked them before I took over) also two British boys I had played tennis with & Curt & Wayne MacFarlane. The Freemans were thrilled over the house and thought we had improved it a lot. They were so very enthusiastic and such charming people that I was so glad I had gotten them over. Mr. Freeman walked all over the place with me and gave me loads of ideas. The guests drank daiquiris & martinis & I made those cheese sticks, tiny wieners and spiced ham *hors d'oeuvres*. Every drop was drunk and every cracker eaten. There is no waste in America today. I had a good time at the party and danced every dance until 2:30. Curt brought Wayne and me back home complaining all the way about how acid the drinks had made his stomach.

Sunday, Wayne and I spent at the Club playing six sets of tennis against the British boys and winning all but one. We changed our clothes just long enough to have lunch. Wayne plays a superior game of tennis. Really almost professional and his form is beautiful. He gave me a lot of pointers. We came home and played with the children about 4:30. Hodgie & Pete were here as we arrived. I got a martini together and we enjoyed that and watched the kids until they left. Then Larry climbed to the top of the apple tree for Wayne. After a ham sandwich & glass of milk Wayne took the 8:21 to town. By 8:30 I was fast asleep and never woke again until 7:30 this a.m. I've got a good tan to show you.

Today my fancy partying gave way to a huge washing. This took all morning. Then we had lunch on the porch except for Robin. The high chair is too hard to move. After lunch I dashed to Greenwich to do the marketing and buy materials for Frank to build an outdoor fireplace. My chicks are going to be ready to cook before I have a grill. Then with 2 (12"x18") tile flue, 3 bags of cement, 3 bags sand, 1 bag lime, 65 fire bricks and 25 lbs. of chick feed I drove to Round Hill and played 3 more sets of tennis with the English boys and Martha.

Now again I am in bed early and will go to sleep shortly. What a marvelous time we could have here if this war would only end and I could get some good help. This spring has already done a world to lift my spirits, but I always have the feeling that you could really fix me up so I would actually never have another morbid, depressing moment. There were some pretty bad ones for us both during those lonely, dark winter months I know. I believe I have gained back some weight even though the garden adds work. We had spinach & lettuce from it already.

I'm sure you have had enough dri[vel] by now. So here's <u>all</u> my love darling. Goodnight.

    X X X x. **X** Peggy
    L. G. R. D. ?

[Peggy to George]
[V-Mail]

#182
May 24, Wed.

Darling.

  Such excitement at this breakfast table this morning. Larry & Georgia and Tina are all dressed up ready to "go on the bus" and it's all a secret. Breakfast is going down a mile a minute and Larry is clenching his 15¢ for the bus driver. As you can guess it's about Momie's birthday. I gave Tina $8.00 and told her to have a secret with the children & go to Greenwich to get me a present. I even told her what book to buy me. They are all a twitter. When Larry woke up this morning I heard him tell Tina in a woeful tone "It's raining." Then very disgustedly he added "That old God!" I've even made myself a birthday cake so at best the children are enjoying my birthday. I will too. Your cable came already and I am so thrilled. Thank you, dear. You are always so thoughtful. Yesterday was also a thriller as I have had the driveway resurfaced and we had dump trucks, oil truck and a steam roller here. All my love, Peggy

[Peggy to George]
[V-Mail]

#182
May 26, 1944
Fri.

Dearest George

  You surely gave me a wonderful day on my birthday. Your picture arrived in the morning mail and I simply love it. It's the very best you've ever had taken. The finishing is very artistic too. Many, many thanks. Then in the afternoon the flowers arrived—bushels of them. There are gladiolas—pink—and peonies and snap dragons of all shades of rose and pink besides two gorgeous gardenias. I felt (and still do) like a bride again. Marjorie & Hodgie came up for supper and we had ice cream and a birthday cake. Larry and Georgia brought it in singing "Happy Birthday" to me. I wish you could have seen them. They gave me the book with great flourish at the same time and proceed[ed] to blow out my candles & unwrap the gift for me. Tonight Marjorie is coming back and Elsa Slocum & her sister are coming for dinner & bridge so I can show off my picture & my flowers. I love you. Peggy

[George to Peggy]
[V-Mail]

No. 126
28 May 44 Sunday.

Peg dear,

 It has been a busy Sunday. It is along after ten now so I have shoved all my papers away and decided to call it a day. It rained quite a bit today. That will help to clean this place up a bit. It is just about as dirty a place as I have ever been in. Got talking to another officer yesterday who comes from South Hadley, Mass. Does that remind you of anything. I would like to be driving up to that little tavern in the Notch to have dinner with you tonight. Sounds like Colby was getting in quite a bit of traveling. Says he is going out to the Pacific next. Wish he might get down this way. Everybody is working around here tonight or at least they are spinning their wheels at a great rate. The news from Italy looks good of late. My love dear, George

[Peggy to George]
[V-Mail]

#183
May 28, 1944
Sun. 10 P.M.

My Darling,

    I have looked forward to writing you a long letter tonight, but Marjorie just left and now it's too late. She has been with me almost constantly since she and Pete legally separated and seems so lost I haven't the heart to send her home. She was here all night both Thurs. and Friday. The latter evening I had Elsa Slocum and her sister for dinner too and bridge. Marg. had never met them so I got her off the subject of Pete one night. But I've had it all day & night today. I cannot think either of them right or wrong so I'm sure I don't know why she seeks solace in my company. Even with our awful separation I thank God more and more for the great love and admiration we hold for one another as we are closer even through these troubled days than most married people have ever been. It's almost laughable the way I feel so smug and fortunate as one marriage after another crumbles around me. Thank you, Darling, for being so wonderful a husband and Daddy. The children are all asleep. I just changed Robin & took a stroll in the moonlight with Doxie. You can't guess what I wished on a star, of course. Yours, Peggy

[George to Peggy]
[V-Mail]

No. 127
30 May 44, Tues.

Peg darling,

    They have me up here as duty officer tonight. There was not so much doing today so everyone else has gone home. I have that nice picture you sent me, taken in the living [room], lying out on the desk. Boy that is a wonderful family. Larry is certainly a fine looking little fellow. Georgia is going to be Peggy all over again, enthusiastic, friendly, pretty and intelligent. And I envy you a bit holding that cute little guy in your arms. Wish I was sitting there with you in our living room tonight. I miss you and want you so much my dear. Well a good part of our separation is behind us by now at least. How did Jack make out with the draft, was he deferred at the last minute? I understand a lot of them were. Well I guess I will be walking back to my billet and thinking of you when I fall asleep. My love dear, George

[Peggy to George]
[V-Mail]

#184
May 30, 1944
Tues. 9 A.M.

Dearest George.

    I've been up since six to work at the weeds in our garden. There isn't a hungry mosquito between here and Greenwich but we still have the weeds. Yesterday after the washing and marketing were finished, I spent the afternoon playing bridge at Jessie's. I felt very guilty. No one does such things nowadays. It was fun though. Last night I had dinner at Marjorie's & today I'm about to leave with Larry & Georgia & Marjorie & Hodgie for the Field Day at Country Day School. Larry is possessed to win the potato race and has practiced for days. If he doesn't he will be very surprised. I'm taking the movie camera. Last Wed. I had a conference with Mr. Webster, the headmaster, and liked him very much. He asked me to bring Larry as he wanted to meet him. He was a regular fellow and was interested in Larry and seemed to have a good understanding of little boys. I entered him but am not sending Georgia as it is $200 a piece. All my love, Peggy

[Peggy to George]
[V-Mail]

#185
June 2, 1944
Fri. a.m.

My Dearest,

    Again I find time to write you during the process of getting a permanent wave. This time I had a new fangled one which takes longer but is painless. Hope it's O.K. The house I left at 8:15 taking poor Doxie to the "vet" before coming here. He had his usual complaint. Larry waved goodbye with specific instructions about nails, wood, plaster etc. that I am to bring home for him to construct a sailboat for Georgia. Oh yes, and paint. This I am to use as he still remembers a spanking he got for mixing his watercolors with spit last time. I must say the result was equally good but the idea a bit nauseating. My garden is lovely but the weeds have gotten too much for me. Today Frank is there and I hope he'll have time for a change to do more than just cut the grass. The fruit trees need spraying, potatoes should be hilled, a bushel of rhubarb roots are waiting since Tues. to be planted etc. etc. You mentioned something about having shifted so long for myself that I wouldn't know what to do with a man around. <u>Please</u> don't count on that. You'd be snowed under most any day I can think of, but as I remember you preferred not to have suggestions made. These perhaps would be so obvious I wouldn't have to say a word. We'd probably play tennis and leave Larry & Georgia & Robin working. Larry picks spinach now. I do wish you could have seen him & Robin in barber chairs side by side yesterday.
Peggy

[George to Peggy]
[V-Mail]

No. 128
3 June 44

Peg dear,

Good morning. Was glad to hear that you had not been neglected on your birthday. Wish I could have given you my personal attention. Maybe next year I can. You better start thinking of all the things you would like to have and to do. You made me a bit jealous of that angel food cake. Wish I could have pinned those flowers on myself. Sounds like you are really going to have the place fixed up for me when I come home. I'll bet Larry got a thrill out of the work on the driveway with steamroller and all. Tell him to draw me a picture of the steamroller. Everybody else is starting to get in now so I can get started at work. I sure do miss you my dear, but it will all be over some day and just a bad memory. I love you, George

[Peggy to George]

#186
Mon. June [5].
8:30 P.M.

P.S. Just at our date time tonight, we all ate supper on the lawn & talked of "Daddy."

My Darling.

Roosevelt has just started his speech on the capture of Rome.[229]

---

229 On June 5, 1944 President Roosevelt delivered his Fireside Chat 29, "On the Fall of Rome." In the speech Roosevelt discusses the significance of the Eternal City as "more than a military objective," remarking that "since before the days of the Caesars, Rome has stood as a symbol of authority" and "the great symbol of Christianity." He lauds the international armed forces that assisted the British and Americans including, "the gallant Canadians…the fighting New Zealanders…the courageous French, and the French Moroccans, the South Africans, the Poles, and the East Indians." Declaring Italians liberated from 25 years of enslavement by fascists, Roosevelt alludes to an impending strike in western Europe while cautioning, "Germany has not yet been driven to surrender." To his critics, Roosevelt reminds them that the financial cost of relief for the Italian people "will be an investment for the future–an investment that will pay dividends by eliminating Fascism." Roosevelt concludes his speech applauding the efficiency of the U.S. Armed Forces, "all the various agencies working with them, and American industry and labor as a whole." A recording and transcript of this speech can be found by visiting millercenter.org and searching for the chat title or number.

I suppose you are hearing his voice too, if you aren't too sound asleep.

I have had another busy day and only half an hour ago came in from the garden to bathe and settle down to this pleasant moment of writing to you. The washing is done and ready to iron, the laundry, kitchen & pantry are scrubbed and waxed and the garden weeded and sprayed. Tina took the car today while I cleaned and went to Greenwich to get the groceries and Doxie. He's been at the "Vet" getting cleaned out again and clipped. Dr. Schofield has a good sense of humor. He left a fringe on him like a poodle and Larry thinks he looks like "Chiffors," Helen Steiner's mutt. She'd love that. It certainly is going to be a big help having Tina able to drive a car. I raised her to $110.00 before she asked for it. She has been very cooperative lately and everyone pays more for nothing. She was quite pleased. I'm also going to offer her a month's vacation with pay in Aug. if I go to Mpls. provided she'll come back and stick out another winter with me.

Today I believe I have located a man and his wife to come Wednesdays. He will do the outdoor work that Frank never gets around to and she will clean inside. If they are any good, it will be swell. I have to pay him a dollar an hour and she gets $5.00 from 8-3:00. However that much help will let me get back to writing you nearly every day again. Perhaps 3 more letters a week will be worth $15.00 to you. Am I conceited!? Yours are priceless so that's what made me think of it, really.

Frank came all day yesterday, Sun. and started our outdoor fireplace. It's going to be nifty. Better looking than Dad's, I think. It's much lower and is going to have a curved stone wall off the back going on each side which can be used for seating people or putting dishes etc. on. My perspective is pretty bad, but you can get some idea. As soon as it is finished, I'll send you a picture.

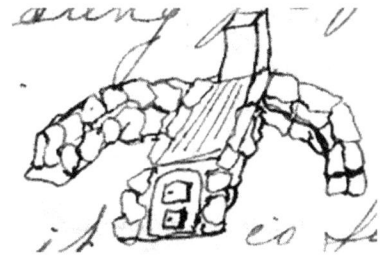

Wayne came out for the weekend and we had a good time. Sat. night I had the Wellington's for dinner and played bridge afterwards. I cooked one of my frozen salmon and served it cold with hollandaise. It made quite a hit. Also we had a salad and new boiled potatoes with parsley and butter over them. Then while I fed the children and Tina at 6:00, I whipped up an angel food cake and stuck it in the oven while I took a bath. My efficiency was in high gear on Saturday. I cleaned the house before this in the morning & met Mrs. Alworth on the 1:13 train. I gave her a nice lunch and daiquiri. She stayed until the 4:30 train so you see why I rushed getting dinner. I have your sweet picture here on the piano. It's such a pleasure to look up at that smiling face and know perfectly well that you were thinking, "I love you, dear," the very second it was taken. Everyone raves about how good it is but nobody else knows the reason like I do and I am very smug about keeping my secret.

Yesterday, Sun. I got Wayne to put up a new swing board for the children and spray the potatoes before I let him play tennis. He's a big help. He also looked over your guns with the idea of cleaning them. However he said the shot gun really needed a better job than he could do as the leather case had rusted it so he took them both into Abercrombie's. We played 6 sets of tennis (singles and doubles) and had lunch at the club. He's very good and has helped my game a lot.

I called the family tonight and all's well there. Georgie is out of bed again. Jack has received a 6 months deferment from the Navy. Dad's going to Chicago tonight for a few days. I wish he could get down here. I'm dying to show off our house in its summer finery and the chicks and garden. Larry was a scream today. While I was hanging up the clothes he and Georgia were playing in the play yard and talking back and forth. I offered a dime to which ever could swing themselves across the ladder without falling. Larry tried and tried but could only go two rungs. Finally he got up saying "I don't want a dime anyway. I have lots of money. My piggy bank is nearly full. Besides you said you'd give me a penny for picking spinach yesterday and you never did." Needless to say I paid up quickly after that. He'll earn the dime in another day or two and I'll have it ready if I have to rob the bank to get one.

If you want to buy anything other than bonds let me know. There is quite a bit of cash on hand. Also the second honeymoon account is quite sizeable. Should I get a $1000.00 war bond with that or invest it? All I really want to do is spend it quickly with you on a grand vacation. I have Mom all lined up to take the children so you'll have to see them a few weeks first 'cause <u>we're</u> <u>leaving</u> <u>them</u> <u>home</u>. I love you, darling … and can hardly wait to start having you annoy me again as you put it. X X X X.

Yours always, Peggy

[George to Peggy]
[V-Mail]

No. 129
5 June 44

Peg dear.

Here it is ten twenty, just cleaned up my work and I am a bit tired. Being Monday evening I know you are thinking of me particularly about this time. That ring on my finger brings back so many thoughts as well as holds many promises for the future. And I have not forgotten just where you put it on my finger. Think I will take it off some day just to let you give it to me just like that again. I wonder at how you can be so practical some times and again be so sentimental. Remember where we let Larry sleep the different times you came to see me at Manchester, Rome, and Key West. Sure was glad to see him a couple times and surprised too. Tell him and Georgia I miss them. Darling I love you and miss you so much. Yours with love, George

[George to Peggy]
[Handwritten on American Red Cross stationery]

> Hq SOS Natousa
> G-3 Sec APO 750
> c/o PM New York, N.Y.
> 6 June 44

Peg dear:

A nice letter arrived from you today. About what a swell fellow you married and what a happy married life you had. Point I couldn't make out was whether you were thinking of the first four years or the last three years.

The frenchm[e]n around here have of course let their hair down and really started celebrating today.[230] Can't blame them much. Adolph probably isn't so happy. Wish I could have had some small part in it. Guess it isn't all over. Williams who has been on two landings says he is very happy to be here today. He says it is all finished now except for the fighting.

We all got quite a kick out of Mauldin's "GI" Joe cartoon today. It showed a couple of weary soldiers talking over a meal of C rations. GI Joe is saying he figures on taking a good long rest after the war with no work to do, figures he will do a hitch in the regular army.

Well today is a big milestone. Guess I will go take a walk. I miss you much too much.

> My love, George

---

230 On June 26, 1944 the long-awaited Allied invasion of western Europe began with the Normandy beach landings. Codenamed Operation Overlord, the D-Day battles along the beaches of France marked the beginning of the Battle of Normandy which would last until late August of 1944 and liberate northern France from the Nazis.

[Peggy to George]
[V-Mail]

#187
June 6, 1944

My Darling.

It's a bit difficult to introduce the subject of this letter subtl[y] so here goes for the bare facts. Tina gave birth to a full term seven lb. boy about an hour ago. She never told me a thing even as I drove her to the hospital. Naturally I have been sure of it for some time although she carried it very well. Her boyfriend went overseas about a week ago and she hasn't seen him since this baby began and hasn't written or received as many letters since that time. She started labor last night evidently but never said anything until morning. Then she complained of nausea and diarrhea. This continued all morning. I couldn't get a Dr. as they were all tied up. Finally just as I was preparing to be midwife I got her a bed in the hospital. Marjorie came to stay with the kids and I drove her over. I waited a few minutes but had to feed the children so that's that. A Dr. Clapp finally delivered her and now I'm in a quandary. I feel sorry for her, but what can I do? She'll be over there 10 days and I'll have to decide. I found a 16 yr old girl to come in for about that long after school. She'll spend the night and help with breakfast. Gosh! What messes I get into without you. I try to figure what's right to do but I need your counsel so badly. The Dr. is going to call tomorrow after he talks to her & then he'll call me before I go over. More tomorrow[.] Yours, Peggy

[Peggy to George]
[V-Mail]

#188
June 8, 1944

My Dearest George.

Things are pretty well under control again this morning. A little high school girl, Vivian Wilson, from Banksville is doing the breakfast

dishes as I write and will mail this on her way to school in a few minutes. She is quiet and sweet with the children. Yesterday I had a cleaning woman who will come Tues. & Wed. of every week so I am O.K. for a while. I talked to Tina's Dr. and then went to see her yesterday afternoon. I took her some baby clothes and flowers from the garden. I also told her she could bring the baby back here for a few weeks until she had her strength and knew what to do. I am also writing a letter to the man in the case to try to arrange a marriage by proxy. Do you know the procedure for such an undertaking? For the baby's sake I'd like to make him as legitimate as possible before packing Tina out. Nobody here knows about it yet. I've told everyone she is in the hospital with peptic ulcers. What a situation for Greenwich gossips when I bring her home with a new baby! Larry crawled in bed with me this morning and I explained the difficulty to him as best I could. When I finished he said "Momie, we surely are lucky to have a good Daddy to feed us and keep us, aren't we?"
Yours, Peggy

[George to Peggy]
[V-Mail]

No. 130
10 June 44

Peg darling:

There were some mighty good pictures in your last letter. Robin sure is growing up. Not much like the cute little baby I left. Are you sure it is the same fellow? You mentioned that Larry was entered in school. Does that mean he starts next fall? The house looks wonderful. The dining room is really smooth. Sounds like you have a regular farm there now too. It must keep you mighty busy. One thing I really cannot understand is how you manage to get such good pictures without me there and no leica either. I suppose you just used a plain camera without any gadgets. You know I was looking over my calendar and noticed that the 26 June comes on a Monday. I kind of figure maybe you will be thinking about me that night. It has some pleasant memories. Next year we will probably be together for that anniversary[.] All my love dear, George

[Peggy to George]

#189
Mon. P.M. June 12

Dearest George

    I'm afraid you are going to be bored to death before I get you caught up on the last four days. It's quite a mess, thanks to Tina and her b———. Thurs. night I went into N.Y. having cocktails with Mr. & Mrs. Alworth. They were the first to know the story and seemed to think I was doing the right thing in trying to get a line on the Father and promote a proxy marriage. I worked through the Red Cross & Greenwich Center but so far he hasn't been located here or abroad. He gave Tina an A.P.O. number but mail so addressed has all been returned. Now she feels she only wants some support for the child & doesn't care about the baby's name. What sort of person can she be? I cannot go into all the problems that have come up & all the people I have had to talk to. It's too boring to write it after rehashing it day after day. The results seem to be that I am elected to care for baby & Tina here for two weeks until the Greenwich Center can find a foster home for the baby. Then according to Tina's deportment and attitude I'll send her along at the same time or keep her until I go to Mpls. in August. I am not at all dependent on her for help as this high school girl is through school next Friday (day Tina comes home) and will stay full time until Aug. if I want her. I'm taking her anyway. I also have the cleaning woman two days a week & her husband one day. So I'm better off every way if I never see Tina again, but my conscience won't let me turn her out cold and the baby. She's so unappreciative of anything I do or try to do that I know how little to expect in return.

However I'll get enough satisfaction myself out of knowing I'm helping, to make up for her cold receptive attitude.

To get back to Thurs. After cocktails I had dinner with Wayne at the Persian Room. We danced and had a lovely time. The only improvement would have been if I could have switched a sergeant for a certain Capt. I know. Then we went to Monte Carlo for a drink, more dancing. I got home very late obviously and was yawning at breakfast Fri. This brought forth a very severe scolding from Georgia. Something reminds me that I already wrote you that.

Friday I went to Helen Mayer's for dinner. She's just up here from Fort Benning a few weeks while John is in a school somewhere. The Grays were there and we had a very nice dinner & pleasant evening.

Saturday I had planned to go to New Jersey with all the kids and Vivian (high school girl) but Robin had kept me up all night & was running a temperature of 104° and had tonsilitis again. Dr. Close is out of town so I started the sulfa diazine on my own. He had ordered it last time and it worked. Robin is much better today but looks awfully pale. I'm afraid Dr. Close is going to want his tonsils out when he gets back. I hate to do it when he is so young, but they really must be bad.

Yesterday, Sunday, I left during the children's nap to get some exercise. I went to the club and played six sets of tennis before supper time. It wore me out but I got that good night's sleep which comes only after that sort of exercise. Somehow housework doesn't do the same thing. I brought one of the British boys home with me and made waffles & a salad for him. He's a nice sort, who tries very hard to hate America but is slowly giving up, I believe. The original feeling is based purely on jealousy, I believe.

My eyes are closing so I'll seal this up and ask you to excuse any incoherence—My mind doesn't work logically after this week of problems and at this moment the fatigue is pressing me too.

Loads of Love & Kisses, Peggy

[George to Peggy]
[V-Mail]

No. 131
13 June 44

My darling:

    This picture album comes in handy to write you on, then I can open it up to see you. Not that I ever really need a picture to remember how you look. You are along with me a good part of the time. There is a nice walk along below the walls of the old castle. There are a number of paths running through gardens along the steep hill that falls away to the water. You walk along there with me some mornings before I go to work, then in the evening after dinner we take a leisurely stroll, sometimes Larry and Georgia run along and make friends with the little french boys and girls. I kind of like the old castle, and people it with Spanish dons in steel breast plates, helmets and swords of damascus steel. Gay cavaliers and black eyed senoritas come out of the past. The old batteries on the walls throw their shot at Arab gall[eys] rowed by christian slaves. So you see you get in on some exciting scenes. Guess I better go to bed and dream you are beside me when I fall asleep. Can you guess how I miss you my dear. All my love, George

[George to Peggy]
[V-Mail]

No. 132
15 June 44

My darling:

    Just got your letter about Tina. I am sorry that you have that trouble to face. I agree that we should do everything possible to help her. I don't want you to take any more of the physical burden of it upon yourself, but there are two points I want to bring out. One is help her to get her morale up, she is fundamentally a good person and things like that will happen especially during a war. The other point is spend what money's necessary to see that she and the baby have proper medical care and get settled down where she can take care of it. It is most important that the man concerned acknowledge that he is the father of the child. If he does Tina can get a minimum of about $70 per month. I asked a catholic chaplin about it and he says that a proxy marriage depends on state laws where you live. I will check further. Hope you can get some more help.

    All my love dear. George.

[Peggy to George]
[V-Mail]

                #190
              June 16, 1944.
                Fri. a.m.

Dearest George.

 I've been struggling since Mon. to get a letter off to you again but this is the only way. I'm up before the children. Things should be better next week. Tina and her baby come home tomorrow and I have her rooms all ready for her—scales, sterilizer, bed, clothes, diapers, towels etc. etc. I never intended to get those out again even for our own. At least not for some years yet. The cleaning woman got a lot done and even watched & fed the children Tues. so I got in a tennis game. Vivian is here still nights and all our friends have been getting me away evenings for a few hours so it's not too bad. Larry is a big help and I fear I treat him in a way you may not approve. For a week he was the only one who knew about Tina. He was here with me and so practically in on its birth. I answered all his questions and even explained why Tina shouldn't have the baby. When we decided to take them back, he was the first to say we'd be nice to the baby and he got busy getting toys together for it. I suppose he'll be old & wise at six, but he seems to take it all in his stride, small as it is, and is a great comfort to me. Please forgive the dearth of letters. It won't be much longer. Yours, Peggy

[George to Peggy]
[V-Mail]
[No.] 133

Peg dear,

    Two letters came yesterday both with pictures of the children and the house which were very welcome indeed. It is sure surprising to see how Robin has grown. I agree he is a handsome looking little fellow. I like your idea about a trip when I get back. It should be a lot more pleasant than the kind of traveling that I have been doing for the last couple of years. Come to think of it, it is nearly three years since you and I used to live together remember? We saw each other every day, never wrote each other letters. Sorry to have let you down on letters lately, I will do better now. Love, George

[Peggy to George]
[V-Mail]

#191
June 22, 1944
Thurs. a.m.

Dearest George

    I wish you could listen to our breakfast conversation this morning. Tina and I have been in stitches. I asked Georgia what she had been doing when I caught her at the window talking last night at 9:30. She said "I was only talking to my sause." When I asked what she said to herself, the answer was— "I was telling my sause aren't those pretty little stars flying around on the grass." She had never seen fireflies I guess and had watched them by the hour chattering away. This was followed closely with a remark addressed to Tina inquiring why she hadn't brought home a baby named "Kenneth" 'cause "I likes Kenneths the bestest." To this she added she wished Tina had brought home three babies. I roared and Larry said "Boy, oh boy. Then Tina surely would have been fat she couldn't have hid three of them." She took it all very good naturedly with some remark about thinking one was bad enough. Nothing goes by those two. They are inflicted with my nasty trait of teasing, I fear. Robin is going to be the worst. You make the walks we take together sound so much more romantic than what I hope you do with me. We have been picking peas, beets, and weeding since 5:30 this a.m. How's that to come home to? Peggy

[Peggy to George]
[V-Mail]

#192
June 23, 1944
Friday.

Dearest George

Breakfast is over again but an hour earlier than usual thanks to Larry and his time telling. Now he came in from feeding the chicks having taken an old scab off his knee from a fall in the garage. You'd think he was killed. The original hurt came Sun. when he fell from the apple tree and he never said a word. It didn't bleed then but now of course it did so he still is sitting on the kitchen chair with a band-aid on his wound moaning and groaning. After the children were in bed last night I went to the club with Marjorie. We played tennis from 6:30-7:30 and had two really good sets. Then we showered and dressed, had a mint julep and dinner all by ourselves. We stayed and watched the kids and old folks dance and came home. It was loads of fun really. Thursday nights over there are quite different now. There are no men our age so the guests are either 16 or 46. I saw Mr. & Mrs. [indecipherable]. They expect their son home soon who has been in Guadalcanal district two years.

Larry has been razed into going out now. You should see him. One hand holds the shorts' leg up from that knee. The other furiously beats the ground with a stick and his lips are out a mile. I love you dear. Peggy

[Peggy to George]
[V-Mail]

#193
June 25th Sun. P.M.

Dearest George.

    Larry & Georgia and I left Greenwich & Robin & Tina & her baby yesterday morning and <u>drove</u> over here to Orange for the weekend.[231] We have been swimming twice and there is a marvelous instructor at the club who I have gotten to give Larry a little time. He is so timid about the water though. Georgia; I can't keep back but I didn't even let her put her suit on yesterday while Larry was having a lesson. Today she went with me and clung like a leech to the instructor until I let him take her in. Then she did everything perfectly in 10 mins. that he had worked on with Larry for 2 hrs. without even getting him to try. I do so want to keep her back athletically until he does everything fairly well. It's just like Jack and me, and I fear Larry will get the same inferiority complex, but when she has no fear and such perfect coordination it's not fair to discourage her either. What do you advise? I played tennis with Mac yesterday afternoon. This evening Ruth had several young couples in for cocktails for me. They were all very nice. I wore your lovely gardenias even though our anniversary isn't until tomorrow. Thank you my darling. I will put them under my pillow tonight and pray that seven is our lucky number and will bring us together before the next comes and goes. Yours always, Peggy

[George to Peggy]
[V-Mail]

26 June 44

Peg dear;

    Just walked back from the headquarters with Capt. Sheldon[232] and stopped up at his apartment where I am now listening to the news

---
231 Peggy and the children are visiting Ruth Atwood Black, Peggy's cousin.
232 John T. Sheldon of the Operations Branch.

from London.²³³ Price who lives with him just came in and decided to try to put some of the wallpaper back on the wall. For a month or so now it has been gradually rolling back from the wall. It was getting down to where it was endangering a couple of the Varga girls.²³⁴ The radio is playing the National Anthem so with Price on top of a French version of a step ladder we are trying to get him to salute. Of course one thing I have been thinking of all day is this date 7 years ago. Next year we will celebrate it together. Sheldon and Price say this is not a very appropriate letter to write on such an occasion. But they are bothering me anyway. My love dear. George

[George to Peggy]
[V-Mail]

26 June 44

Dear Peggy:

After walking back from Price's apartment I thought you might want a little more mail on a special occasion like this. Hope you have the flowers I sent. This was quite an evening for us seven years ago, so many friends gathered around from all over the country, with our families all there and so much good cheer. Your Father bringing you down the aisle, it was a pleasure to kiss such a pretty girl even with a church full of people watching. Only wish I could do it right now. Then there was a long reception line but I got you a couple of drinks of champagne to help out. Like every bridegroom I thought I was getting the best girl in the world, the strange thing about it was that I was right. My love dear, George

---

233 Operation Epsom was launched by the British on June 26, 1944. Part of the Battle of Normandy (and also called the First Battle of the Odon), Operation Epsom saw three British armies (notably the 15th Scottish infantry division) circumvent the city of Caen from the west while seizing bridges over the Odon River.

234 The iconic Varga girls (also called "Vargas girls") were pinup drawings known for their "elongated legs, narrow waists and sumptuous figures" (United Press International, "Alberto Vargas, Artist, Dead at 87."). Drawn for decades by Alberto Vargas (b. 1896, d. 1982) who was known simply as "Varga" during his time at *Esquire*, the Varga girls appeared in *Esquire* and *Playboy* as well as numerous calendars and advertisements. Popular during WWII, Varga girls inspired copycat artwork on bomber jackets and even bomber nose art. For example, the Flying Fortress of the 91st Bomb Group, nicknamed "Mount n' Ride," featured artwork based off a Varga girl who appeared in an *Esquire* calendar in 1944 (Roger Freeman Collection, Imperial War Museums, 2014).

[Peggy to George]
[Handwritten on stationery from 356 Forest Road South Orange, New Jersey]

#194

Mon. June 26th

Dearest George.

Here it is and goes—our 7th anniversary. It has been a lovely day with thoughts of you only a little more frequent in my heart and mind. How I prayed last night over your gardenias that this will be our last year of separation. There have been three awfully lonely, busy years and that is plenty for me.

Today the children went into the pool twice and Momie once. Larry did a little better today and Georgia attained the heights by putting her head under the water. Besides the swims I took a sunbath and Betty & I painted a chair, table and bureau to match our blue crib which I have given her. The room is going to be very cute. I sort of wish I could help finish the job but I must get home tomorrow afternoon. We talked to Tina and all is well with Robin & Doxie etc. there.

Tonight for dinner we ate fried chicken which I brought over to Ruth along with peas, beets and lettuce from my garden. These are the first chickens I have killed. Frank, gardener, showed me how and I did a very neat job although Larry nearly fainted when one, which I had said was dead, jumped out of a pail at him. He stalked into the house saying "I don't like what you are doing, Momie." Neither did I, but the death wasn't nearly as bad as the plucking and cleaning. However we both ate them tonight with great delight. They are delicious. Don't you think we are really farmers now?

My trip to Mpls. is getting more impossible every day. The railroads are so crowded it's impossible to get reservations more than 30 days ahead and then it's too late.[235] Besides that, they can put you off or cancel the entire car for any reason at all. It seems like a terrific effort with the added worry of not getting there when I'll have three children alone. On the other hand Mom & Dad haven't seen the children since Christmas and have opened the lake house solely for our prospective visit. With you away, it does seem as if I should do what I can to have them see the children for a summer visit.

This three day trip over here has done me loads of good. At least I realize how badly I need a rest. It's wonderful not to have to plan, cook & serve meals etc. etc. even though I couldn't get away from all the children. That will have to wait until you come home. Sometimes I am ashamed to get so impatient and tired of their fighting and chattering. It doesn't happen often with Larry, but Georgia is so exactly like me that I just cannot compromise with her at all. She even answers back in the same words I'd use. It's not a very pleasant feeling to see one's double and find them so intractable.

---

235   Railroads played a crucial role in the arsenal of democracy. Prior to the start of WWII, railroad freight ton-mileage (the volume and distance transported) had been in decline for decades, unable to compete with the logistical flexibility provided by trucks. When the war began, however, that trend quickly reversed and railroads experienced an increase in freight ton-mileage (Stover, *The Routledge Historical Atlas of the American Railroads*, 116.). The Battle of the Atlantic made shipping risky, thus railroads absorbed the responsibility of transporting supplies such as oil, coal, and lumber up and down the East Coast. In one example, two million tons of bituminous coal were moved overland by the Norfolk and Western Railway rather than via its normal route by sea (DeNevi, *America's Fighting Railroads*, 135.). As the United States officially entered the war, the railroads had two-thirds as many cars as in 1920 and nearly half as many locomotives. Despite this, in the first eight months of 1942 they carried over 600,000,000 ton-miles of freight. By the end of the war, railroads in the United States will be carrying 72% of all freight in the country (Ibid., 8, 73.).

   While freight traffic doubled, passenger traffic increased as well, quadrupling during the war years (Ibid., v.). By July 1942, railroads had moved the equivalent of 2 million service members per month since the beginning of the year. This pace was an enormous improvement over the previous war. During WWI, it took 20 months to move five million soldiers, compared to 11 million over only 13 months during WWII (Ibid., 125.). Average passengers per car and per train broke prior records and would continue to do so in the years ahead (Ibid., 50.).

   Advertisements updated civilians and offered tips and travel advice all while encouraging them to avoid unnecessary travel by rail (Ibid., 128-129.). Advice included avoiding weekend travel, limiting baggage, and remaining patient with overworked railway and swamped ticket-booth employees. Grand Central Terminal in New York City went as far as claiming in their *Wartime Guide to Grand Central Terminal* that their ticket office was 90% busier than before the war and their terminal information men answered 14,800 questions an hour (Ibid., 133.).

   As the war in Europe ends, passenger traffic congestion will worsen as troops return home or are reassigned. In late 1945 and early 1946 around six million service members will be returning to the United States. To expedite the movement of returning troops, the Office of Defense Transportation will issue orders mandating any passenger equipment to military use and restricting the use of sleeper cars on runs of 450 miles or less. That mileage restriction will free nearly 900 sleeper cars from civilian runs for exclusive use by military personnel (Ibid., 104.). However, that meant only one third of the entire sleeping car fleet would be available for civilian travel, resulting in more pleas for civilians to avoid unnecessary leisure travel well after the war has ended.

Tonight Ruth also had an anniversary cake for me. It had pastry flowers on the icing and (I S G 1937-1944) on it. You even had a place at the table but I must say the empty chair was worse than not having any. They are all sitting around and want me to send their love and congratulations. My love goes too as you know. How I wish I could really show you how much I miss and love you tonight! That will be waiting for you every day.

Peggy

[George to Peggy]

27 June 44

Peg dear,

This is a good opportunity to write a letter. I am back up at the headquarters after dinner, but can't get the papers I am working until the officer shows up who locked things up. Sorry not to have written more but I have not had a half day off for several weeks nor an evening for that matter.

Time goes pretty fast this way though before you know it another month is gone. I do resent having to waste away this part of my life in such a useless fashion. I should think we could figure out a better method of settling arguments.

You will note from my address that I am back in the G-4 section which is a much more satisfactory situation for me. Ream is still in G-3 and like everyone else is trying to pull a deal to get out.

Eating dinner with Ream we were laughing at how a year ago Gen. Marshall had us up in his office giving us a real build up, what a letdown this year has been.

Sorry to hear of all the trouble you have had with Tina. I hope she manages a marriage. It is kind of rough on a child to not have a father. Think it has been swell of you to take care of her as you have. It must be mighty hard on you, you hire a girl to take care of our children and end with you looking after hers.

Have you ever heard how Anna made out? Your servant problems went so well for a while, but the luck sure changed.

Well I have to go to work now, maybe I will get a chance to write a V-mail before I go to bed.

Sure miss you and the children. Sounds like Larry is getting to be quite a little man.

My love dear, George

Afterword

As the war continued, so did George's service overseas. In the next collection of letters, *Darling, Yours Always: The WWII Letters of Peggy and George Steiner, Volume III*, George writes from Caserta, Italy. Letters included in the upcoming volume share Peggy and George's efforts to remain faithful to their principles, their thoughts on the war and the world after the war is over, current politics as the United States prepares for another presidential election, and the adventures and many firsts of Larry, Georgia, and Robin, who are growing up quickly without their father.

Acknowledgments

This volume would have been difficult to produce without the support and assistance of a select group of fabulous people.

An enormous thank you to Georgia for tracking down family members, supplemental documents, and photos once again. Also, for her unlimited patience as world events forced a much slower pace on this volume than we had originally anticipated.

Without the copy of George's military records and discharge information that Andrew G. Steiner uncovered and shared, it would have been pure guesswork as to what George was doing and where. The documents Andrew shared included a list of those who served with George which was the reason so many of George's companions-in-arms could be identified this time. Thank you so much!

In memory of "the late and great Robin Steiner," Chichi Steiner generously corrected Peggy and George's French and provided English translations. I am incredibly grateful Chichi took on that responsibility.

Feedback is always necessary. Thank you to Cynthia and Carmen for useful comments on the first section, as well as Henry G. Fuette and Jess Pearson for recommendations on footnotes throughout. Kasia Majewski's patient explanations and thorough reworking of my citations and sources were also much appreciated.

Morale matters and my motivation would have waned without the support of Christina Williams, Caheri Aguilar, and Sarah Schwartz. Thank you for always asking how the book was coming along, offering advice regarding resources when asked, and expressing enthusiasm—especially when the milestones meriting said enthusiasm weren't visible to me.

A humble thank you to Talena Griffin who answered my ignorant questions about race and identity and who recommended relevant resources to help me better educate myself.

As always, thank you again to Agustin and Andre for the unique ways you provide support. You know what they are.

This project would not have been possible without the help of my mom who scanned original letters that Georgia unearthed, transcribed them during the COVID lockdowns, scanned and rescanned many of the images, and frequently went on scavenger hunts for papers I needed that were not with me. Your enthusiasm for this project and your belief in me kept the book alive through all of the challenges. Thank you for your patience with each silly question and your examination of every single comma.

With COVID-19 shutdowns, most of my research was only possible because of the efforts individual organizations have made to digitize their collections. When the libraries were closed around the country, a bit of creativity went a long way to find the articles and book excerpts I needed online. Thank you to each public library and historical organization that has taken the time to digitize their collections.

Primary Sources

Associated Press. "Coal Strikes Imperil War Pace, says WPB; Some Units Vote Work." *New York Times*, Oct. 25, 1943.

Associated Press. "Farm Tool Supply for '44 to Increase." *New York Times*, Aug. 1, 1943.

Associated Press. "Gen. Patch Dies of Pneumonia at 55; Led 7th Army in Victorious Drive." *New York Times*, Nov. 22, 1945.

Associated Press. "Hiland G. Batcheller Dies at 75; Steel Official Aided War Effort." *New York Times*, May 20, 1961.

Associated Press. "Our Air Commandos Poised to Cut Burma Supply Lines." *New York Times* Mar. 19, 1944.

Associated Press. "Poles Ask About Charter." *New York Times*, Mar. 21, 1944.

Beard, Charles A. "A Chapter from The Republic." *LIFE*, Jan. 17, 1944.

Beard, Charles A. "We the People Establish This Constitution." *LIFE*, Jan. 24, 1944.

Beard, Charles A. "Democracy and Rights." *LIFE*, Jan. 31, 1944.

Beard, Charles A. "A More Perfect Union and Justice." *LIFE*, Feb. 7, 1944.

Beard, Charles A. "Promote the General Welfare." *LIFE*, Feb. 14, 1944.

Beard, Charles A. "Congress as Power." *LIFE*, Feb. 21, 1944.

Beard, Charles A. "The Power of the President." *LIFE*, Feb. 28, 1944.

Beard, Charles A. "Critique of the Federal System." *LIFE*, Mar. 6, 1944.

Beard, Charles A. "Political Parties as Agencies and Motors." *LIFE*, Mar. 13, 1944.

Beard, Charles A. "The Fates and Fortunes of Our Republic." *LIFE*, Mar. 20, 1944.

"Charles A. Beard, Historian, is Dead." *New York Times*, Sept. 2, 1948.

Churchill, Winston. "Address by Prime Minister Churchill on War and Conditions in Britain." *New York Times*, Mar. 27, 1944.

PRIMARY SOURCES

December 24, 1943: "Fireside Chat 27: On the Tehran and Cairo Conferences." Miller Center. Accessed October 15, 2022. https://millercenter.org/the-presidency/presidential-speeches/december-24-1943-fireside-chat-27-tehran-and-cairo-conferences.

DeNevi, D. *America's Fighting Railroads: A World War II Pictorial History*. Missoula: Pictorial Histories Publishing Company, 1996.

"Dutch Banker Dies in 20-Story Plunge." *New York Times*, Jan. 22, 1944.

"Foe Slipped Away as Salamaua Fell." *New York Times*, Sept. 17, 1943.

Ford, H. S. *What the Citizen Should Know About the Army*. New York: W.W. Norton & Company, 1942.

Fowler, G. "James Linen 3d, 75, Ex-Publisher And President at Time Inc., Dies." *New York Times*, Feb. 2, 1988.

"H. Ford Wilkins, Ex-Reporter." *New York Times*, Oct. 25, 1983.

Hammond, W.M. *The Women's Army Corps*. Washington, D.C.: Center of Military History United States Army, 1991-1995.

Hull, C. "Text of Secretary Hull's Address on the Foreign Policy of the United States." *New York Times*, Apr. 10, 1944.

"Japan Bars U.S. Red Cross Ship With Supplies for War Prisoners." *New York Times*, Aug. 30, 1942.

"Kansas Department of Health and Environment Bureau of Environmental Remediation Identified Sites List Information." *Kansas Department of Health and Environment Bureau* Accessed April 22, 2022. https://keap.kdhe.ks.gov/BER_ISL/ISL_Pub_Detail.aspx?ProjectCode=C508571315.

King, E. L. "Who Needs West Point?" *New York Times*, Apr. 29, 1972.

Kress, James P. *A History of Military Training at the University of Minnesota 1869-1969*. 1971. Retrieved from the University of Minnesota Digital Conservancy, https://conservancy.umn.edu/handle/11299/121891.

Lerch, Archer L. "Completed Staff Work." War Department Office of the Provost Marshal General (PMG 312.2 Gen.), Washington, D.C., Jan. 13, 1942.

McAleer, J. *Farm Machinery and Equipment Policies of the War Production Board and Predecessor Agencies May 1940 to September 1944*. Civilian Production Administration, 1946.

Nelson, Otto Lauren, Jr. *National Security and The General Staff*. Washington, D.C.: Infantry Journal Press, 1946.

"Urges Senate Inquiry of Farm Equipment Output Hike Delay." *Chicago Daily Tribune*, Oct. 14, 1943.

"Victory: Official Weekly Bulletin of the Office of War Information." Vol. 3, no. 48 (1942): 9. http://www.idaillinois.org/digital/collection/isl3/id/20070.

Peterson, F. *Strikes in 1943*. Bureau of Labor Statistics. Accessed February 5, 2021. https://www.bls.gov/wsp/publications/annual-summaries/pdf/strikes-1943.pdf.

"Col. Philip G. Cochran, War Hero and Model for 2 Cartoon Figures." *New York Times*, Aug. 27, 1979.

September 7, 1942: "Fireside Chat 22: On Inflation and Food Prices." Miller Center. Accessed December 11, 2019. https://millercenter.org/the-presidency/presidential-speeches/September-7-1942-fireside-chat-22-inflation-and-food-prices.

Stark, L. "Labor Unrest Mounts Over Wage-Price Policy." *New York Times*, Oct. 24, 1943.

Steiner, George R. George R. Steiner to the Key West Art & Historical Society, Key West, FL, January 9, 1991.

Stout, R. "The Time And Its Opportunity." *New York Times*, Oct. 4, 1942.

Sulzberger, C. "Cassino Toe-Hold Won By Americans." *New York Times*, Feb. 5, 1944.

Sulzberger, C. "Tanks and Troops Battered Cassino." *New York Times*, Feb. 3, 1944.

"Race Bias Denied As Rioting Factor." *New York Times*, Aug. 3, 1943.

"Russia's Attitude on Poland Scored." *New York Times*, Mar. 16, 1944.

Trussell, C. "Soldier-Vote Bill Shifted By Senate To Let States Rule." *New York Times*, Dec. 4, 1943.

United Press. "Survivors' Statements on Japanese Abuse of Prisoners on Bataan." *New York Times*, Jan. 28, 1944.

United Press. "The Text of Prime Minister Churchill's Address as the Ceremony in London's Guildhall." *New York Times*, July 1, 1943.

Ulio, J.A. "Extract." *Special Orders No. 172*. War Department, Washington, D.C., Jun. 29, 1942.

Wilkins, H. F. "Close-Up Report on The Japanese." *New York Times*, Mar. 4, 1945.

"'Winged Victory,' Army Air Forces Show, Opens Tonight at the Forty-fourth Street Theatre." *New York Times*, Nov. 20, 1943.

"World Battlefronts: BATTLE OF ITALY: Ike's Way." *Time*, Nov. 13, 1943.

Secondary Sources

"AAIR." *Aviation Archaeological Investigation and Research*. 2009. Accessed September 16, 2019. https://www.aviationarchaeology.com/listPages/airforce/asp/AF_Monthly_1942Sep_O.asp.

"About Stars and Stripes." Stars and Stripes. Accessed April 2, 2021. https://ww2.stripes.com/about-us#history/.

Ageron, C.R. *Modern Algeria: A History From 1830 to the Present*. Translated by M. Brett. Trenton, NJ: Africa World Press, 1991.

"Allen." *Christian County Obituary Index*. Accessed March 1, 2021. http://www.westernkyhistory.org/christian/obit/a/allen.html#IRVIN%20L%20ALLEN.

Appiah, K.A. "The Case for Capitalizing the B in Black." The Atlantic. Accessed May 30, 2021. https://www.theatlantic.com/ideas/archive/2020/06/time-to-capitalize-blackand-white/613159/.

Beagan, C. "Frederick W. Boissevain (1904-1943)." *tclf.org*. Accessed March 4, 2022. https://www.tclf.org/frederick-w-boissevain-1904-1943.

Birnbaum, P. *Leon Blum: Prime Minister, Socialist, Zionist*. New Haven and London: Yale University Press, 2015.

Blatchford, F. "$1 Million Ransom Paid: Kidnappers Free Socialite." *Chicago Tribune*, July 30, 1972.

Blue, C. "Fats Waller (1904-1943)." *blackpast.org*. Accessed September 10, 2021. https://www.blackpast.org/african-american-history/waller-thomas-wright-fats-1904-1943.

Blum, A. A. *Drafted or Deferred: Practices Past and Present*. Ann Arbor: The University of Michigan, 1967.

Cartwright, M. "Prince Shotoku." *worldhistory.org*. June 8, 2017. Accessed September 15, 2021. http://worldhistory.org/Prince_Shotoku.

DePastino, T. *Bill Mauldin: A Life Up Front*. New York: W. W. Norton & Company, 2008.

"John Pillsbury Snyder." Encyclopedia Titanica. September 22, 2018. Accessed March 29, 2022. https://www.encyclopedia-titanica.org/titanic-survivor/john-pillsbury-snyder.html.

"Nelle Snyder." Encyclopedia Titanica. September 22, 2018. Accessed March 29, 2022. https://www.encyclopedia-titanica.org/titanic-survivor/nelle-snyder.html.

Ewing, Eve L. "I'm a Black Scholar Who Studies Race. Here's Why I Capitalize 'White.'" *Zora.medium.com.* July 2, 2020. Accessed July 7, 2022. https://zora.medium.com/im-a-black-scholar-who-studies-race-here-s-why-i-capitalize-white-f94883aa2dd3.

Gilbert, A. D. *Voices of the Foreign Legion: The History of the World's Most Famous Fighting Corps.* New York City: Skyhorse Publishing, 2010.

Groom, W. *1942: The Year That Tried Men's Souls.* New York: Grove Press, 2005.

Guénoun, D. A. *A Semite: A Memoir of Algeria.* New York: Columbia University Press, 2014.

Guise, K. "Mail Call: V-mail." *The National WWII Museum New Orleans.* Accessed Feb. 17, 2022. https://www.nationalww2museum.org/war/articles/mail-call-v-mail.

"V-mail." *Historian United States Postal Service.* Accessed Feb. 8, 2021. https://about.usps.com/who/profile/history/pdf/v-mail.pdf.

Huxen, K. "Operation Husky: The Allied Invasion of Sicily." *National WWII Museum.* Jul. 12, 2017. Accessed February 8, 2021. https://www.nationalww2museum.org/war/articles/operation-husky-allied-invasion-sicily.

Jeffreys-Jones, R. *The Nazi Spy Ring in America: Hitler's Agents, the FBI, & the Case That Stirred the Nation.* Washington, D.C.: Georgetown University Press, 2020.

Judt, T. *The Burden of Responsibility: Blum, Camus, Aron, and the French Twentieth Century.* Chicago and London: University of Chicago Press, 1998.

Kaufman, M. T. "Andrew Heiskell, 87, a Former Chairman of Time Inc. and a Civic Leader, Dies." *New York Times,* July 7, 2003.

Kinyon, J. "Air Mobility Command Museum: Air Transport Command—Airlift During WWII." *AMC Museum.* Accessed February 16, 2021. https://amcmuseum.org/history/air-transport-command-airlift-during-wwii/.

Krebs, A. "Harold E. Stassen, Who Sought G.O.P. Nomination for President 9 Times, Dies at 93." *New York Times,* Mar. 5, 2001.

Lichtenstein, N. *Labor's War at Home: The CIO in World War II.* New York: Cambridge University Press, 1982.

Littlejohn, D. "San Pedro's historic WWII 'Hey Rookie' pool ready for its $7 million makeover." Daily Breeze. Accessed August 18, 2021. https://www.dailybreeze.com/2015/02/12/san-pedros-historic-wwii-hey-rookie-pool-ready-for-its-7-million-makeover/.

SECONDARY SOURCES

Loomis, E. *A History of America in Ten Strikes*. New York: The New Press, 2018.

Lovelace, A. G. "Slap Heard around the World: George Patton and Shell Shock." *Parameters* 49, no. 3 (2019). Accessed September 14, 2021. https://press.armywarcollege.edu/parameters/vol49/iss3/9/.

Martin, D. "Stanley R. Resor, Vietnam War Army Chief, Dies at 94." *New York Times*, Apr. 19, 2012.

Miller, D. *Mercy Ships: The Untold Story of Prisoner-of-War Exchanges in World War II*. New York: Continuum, 2008.

"Minneapolis-St Paul Air Reserve Station." *United States Air Force*. Accessed February 23, 2021. https://www.minneapolis.afrc.af.mil/Home/Welcome/.

Morris, S. J. *Price of Fame: The Honorable Clare Boothe Luce*. New York: Random House, 2014.

Mueller, R. *Air Force Bases* (1). Washington, D.C.: United States Air Force Office of Air Force History, 1989.

"The Soldier Voting Act and Absentee Ballots in World War II. National WWII Museum. Accessed September 14, 2021. https://www.nationalww2museum.org/war/articles/soldier-voting-act-1942-absentee-ballots.

Neal, S. *Dark Horse: A Biography of Wendell Willkie*. Garden City: Doubleday & Company Inc., 1984.

"Lt. Charles Alfred Pillsbury." *Pacific Wrecks*. Accessed November 4, 2020. https://pacificwrecks.com/aircraft/f4u/17804/pillsbury/index.html.

Porch, D. *The French Foreign Legion: A Complete History of the Legendary Fighting Force*. New York: Skyhorse Publishing, 2010.

"Roger Freeman Collection, Imperial War Museums." *American Air Museum in Britain*. Accessed December 30, 2021. http://www.americanairmuseum.com/media/2840.

Scharch, S. "E.L. Scharch USNR." *scharch.org*. Accessed February 23, 2021. http://www.scharch.org/Ed_Scharch/06-nas-mpls-prim.htm.

Shafer, R. G. "'Your paper, first, last and for all time': How Stars and Stripes became a wartime force." *Washington Post*, Sept. 12, 2020.

Stora, B. *Algeria 1830-2000: A Short History*. Translated by J. M. Todd. Ithaca: Cornell University Press, 2001.

Snyder, T. *Bloodlands: Europe Between Hitler and Stalin*. New York: Basic Books, 2010.

Levy, Michael. "Buffalo Native Winston Burdett, 40-year CBS Veteran, Dies at 79." *Buffalo News*, May 21, 1993.

Stewart, G. "POST-WORLD WAR II DESTROYER ESCORTS." *Naval Historical Foundation*, July 19, 2016. Accessed February 23, 2021. https://www.navyhistory.org/2016/07/post-world-war-ii-destroyer-escorts/.

Stover, J. F. *The Routledge Historical Atlas of the American Railroads*. New York: Routledge, 1999.

Swanson, W. *Stolen from the Garden*. St. Paul: Borealis Books, 2014.

"The Battle of Manila." *The Battle of Manila Online*. Accessed April 21, 2022. http://battleofmanila.org/IG_Report/htm/IG_333_5_02.htm.

"Harlem Race Riot of 1943." *Encyclopaedia Britannica*, July 15, 2014. Accessed February 17, 2021. https://www.britannica.com/topic/Harlem-race-riot-of-1943.

"Walter H. Judd, 95, Missionary To China And U.S. Representative." *New York Times*, Feb. 15, 1994.

Toland, J. (2003). *The Rising Sun: The Decline and Fall of the Japanese Empire*, 1936-1945. New York: The Modern Library.

United Press International. "Alberto Vargas, Artist, Dead at 87." *New York Times*, Feb. 12, 1983.

van der Linden, B. "Air Transport Command and the Airlines During WWII." *Smithsonian Air and Space Museum*. Accessed February 17, 2021. https://airandspace.si.edu/stories/editorial/air-transport-command-and-airlines-during-world-war-ii-1.

Wainwright, L. *The Great American Magazine*. New York: Alfred Knopf, 1986.

White, Owen. "Introduction: The Empire of Wine in Algeria." *The Blood of the Colony*, 1–9. Harvard University Press, 2021. http://www.jstor.org/stable/j.ctv1b9f63c.6.

Whitman, A. "Paul Robeson Dead at 77; Singer, Actor, and Activist." *New York Times*, Jan. 24, 1976.

Wireless. "18 U.S. Generals--Honored by King." *New York Times*, Jan. 12, 1944.

Wisbith, T. *Allied Force Headquarters during the North African Campaign: A Study of Allied integrated multi-national command organization from August 1942-May 1943*. Columbus: The Ohio State University, 2018.

Wyant, William K. *Sandy Patch: A Biography of Lt. General Alexander M. Patch*. New York: Praeger, 1991.

Zawadzki, H. and J. Lukowski. *A Concise History of Poland*. New York: Cambridge University Press, 2006.

Index

A

Adcock, Clarence Lionel, 211, 250
Agar, Herbert, 183, 309
Air Service Command (ASC), 40, 59, 120, 190, 191, 283
Air Transport Command (ATC), 39, 40, 271, 390, 392
Albright, 24, 86, 99
    see also Key West, Florida
    see also Meacham Field
Algeria, 1, 7, 27, 55, 283, 304, 306, 330, 355, 389–92
    disenfranchisement of Algerian Muslims, 27
    French colonialism, 27
    Village Nègre, 109
    see also Blum, Léon
    see also Blum-Violette Bill
    see also France
Allen, Irvin L., 98, 102, 122, 138, 146, 155, 160, 161, 170, 172, 179, 194, 200, 201, 207, 208, 210, 211, 213, 216, 226, 228, 229, 235, 253, 259, 269–271, 274, 283–6, 289, 290, 327, 340, 354, 389
Allied Force Headquarters (AFHQ), 1, 2, 104, 125, 283–5, 289, 292, 304, 306, 321, 327, 354
    Hotel St. George, 306
    in Time, 104, 125
Alworth family, 48, 54, 57, 63, 77, 85, 159, 180, 187, 192, 193, 198, 201, 276, 351, 352, 357, 366, 371
    see also University of Minnesota
Antisemitism, 18, 55, 56
    see also Blum, Léon
Atlantic Charter, 309, 341
    see also Churchill, Winston
    see also Roosevelt, Franklin D.

B

Barnhill, Lester H., 274
Batcheller, Hiland G., 173, 177, 386
    see also War Production Board (WPB)
Battle of Normandy, 368, 378
    Operation Epsom, 378
    Operation Overlord, 368
Beard, Charles A., 316, 347, 386
Belden, Harry, 63, 72
Benhamdoune, 327, 331, 334, 351
Black, Betty, 15, 306, 308
Black, Ruth Atwood, 206, 377, 379, 381
Blum, Léon, 55, 56, 389, 390
    Algerian-Muslim rights, 55
    cabinet diversity, 56
    concentration camps and imprisonment, 56
    gains for workers, 55
    Popular Front, 55
    see also Algeria
    see also Antisemitism
    see also Blum-Violette bill
    see also France
Blum-Violette bill, 55
    see also Algeria
    see also Blum, Léon
Boissevain, Pinky, 119, 132, 134, 135, 142, 150, 153, 154, 172, 183, 186, 189, 251, 275, 280, 290, 296, 298, 318, 319, 324, 332
    Fitsy, 119, 156, 262, 338
    Frederick, 119
    Katie, 156, 262
Bouscaren, Chloe, 95, 99, 111, 123, 178, 280
Bowden family, 88, 89, 95, 99, 123, 135, 142, 150, 204, 235, 239, 242, 259, 262, 266, 278, 286, 320, 324, 332, 351
Brainard, Tinkle, 150, 153, 154, 315, 321

Bridge family, 113, 115, 124, 126, 134, 137, 142, 181, 185, 209, 231, 235, 249, 332, 347
Buckhaut family, 171, 344, 353, 357
Bull, Kay, 67, 81, 83, 128, 171, 243, 287, 317
Bull, Webster, 67, 83, 171, 243, 287, 317
Burdett, Winston, 168, 391

C

Camp Phillips, 110
Charlie McCarthy Show, 333
China, 187, 227, 233, 242, 259, 310, 313, 317, 330, 333, 355
    Ancient history, 242
    Cairo Conference, 227
    Chiang Kai-shek, 227
    China-Burma-India (CBI) theater, 333
        see also Cochran, Philip
    Clare Boothe Luce in, 310
    influence on Japanese government, 242
    Leon Turrou in, 259
    Wendell Willkie's visit, 313
    see also Judd, Walter Henry
Churchill, Winston, 13, 205, 227, 297, 302, 303, 341, 386, 388
    Cairo Conference, 227
    Guildhall speech "We Seek No Profit", 13
    post-war Poland's border, 205, 297
    "The War and Conditions in England—Our Greatest Effort is Coming", 303
    see also Atlantic Charter
    see also Poland
    see also Tehran Conference
Clow family, 37, 47, 48, 54, 61, 65, 70, 77, 78, 81, 85, 95
Cochran, Philip, 17, 333, 341, 388
    First Air Commando Force, 333
        see also China-Burma-India (CBI) Theater
    Milt Caniff's comic strip characters, 17
    Tuskegee Airmen, 17
Colby, Warren, 13, 102, 111, 167, 188, 210, 215, 244, 255, 271, 319, 340, 354, 360
Colman, Ronald, 133, 355
Command and General Staff College, 4, 93, 102, 162, 190
Covey, Preston, 82, 260, 265, 273
Crawford, Bob, 96, 98, 108, 118, 148, 152, 278, 305
Crosby, Beatrice and George, 62, 63
Crystal Bay, Minnesota
    see Hennepin County

D

Dayton family, 36, 42, 62, 63, 74
de Gaulle, Charles, 183, 317, 318
    French Committee of National Liberation, 317, 318
    see also France
    see also Free French Forces
Devevey family, 4, 18, 26, 29, 52, 57, 229
Doerr family, 53, 60, 62, 133, 153, 161, 211, 321, 327
Domestic help
    Anna, 31, 33, 34, 44, 79, 80, 81, 91, 94, 95, 104, 107, 112, 114, 115, 123, 126, 127, 133, 134, 142, 149, 154, 169, 171, 172, 175, 181, 196, 225, 237, 239–241, 250, 265, 278, 287, 382
    Hvolbeck, 47, 96, 107, 152, 167, 169, 186, 187, 208, 225, 234, 267, 321, 324
    Jesse Baxter, 47, 61, 68, 78
    Tina, 20, 21, 25, 34, 37, 40, 41, 53, 54, 60, 67, 72, 76, 88, 95, 98, 104, 112, 114, 123, 134, 135, 142, 149, 154, 169, 176, 181, 192, 223, 225, 233, 236–9, 241, 244, 248, 249, 251, 255, 256, 258, 267, 277, 278, 280, 286, 288, 290, 291, 293, 298, 299, 301, 305, 306, 308, 312, 318, 332, 342, 344, 345, 347, 359, 365, 366, 369–71, 373–5, 377, 379, 381
Donahue, Colonel Joseph J., 227
Doxie, 15, 20, 21, 23, 26, 27, 33, 44, 79, 88, 91, 96, 97, 103, 108, 110, 119, 135, 142, 148, 150, 155, 178, 179, 192, 214, 230, 242, 245, 256, 261, 264, 272, 280, 291, 293, 295, 301, 302, 316, 319, 323, 332, 333, 337, 342, 345, 353, 361, 363, 365, 379
Draft deferrals and classifications, 111, 112, 127, 204
Duluth, Minnesota, 48, 54, 56, 60, 75, 85

E

Echols, Emmett Deering, 247, 274, 275
    see also Office of Strategic Services (OSS)
Eisenhower, Dwight D., 104, 203, 204, 211, 214, 227, 230, 247, 310, 317
    and General Staff, 104
    appointment to Supreme Allied Commander of the Allied Expeditionary Force, 227, 230
    response to Patton's slap, 203

INDEX

F

Finn, Alice, 47, 65, 81, 96, 107, 128, 139, 246
Fitzgerald, Jerry, 260, 264, 273
Fleming Field, 63
Folsom, Myron, 100
　see also Salamaua, Papua New Guinea
Ford, Dexter, 205, 206
France, 18, 27, 55, 56, 66, 101, 117, 183, 317, 318, 339, 355, 356, 368
　antisemitism, 55, 56
　Free French forces, 183
　Popular Front, 55, 56
　Syria and Lebanon, 183
　see also Algeria
　see also Blum, Léon
　see also de Gaulle, Charles
French Foreign Legion, 355, 356, 390, 391
　and *Beau Geste,* 355
　German NCOs in, 356
　interwar years, 355
　Sidi Bel Abbès, 355

G

Gillette, George Lewis, 25, 31, 42, 44, 133, 143, 158, 187, 250, 264, 308, 333, 365, 366, 378, 380
　and the War Production Board (WPB), 172–4
　　see also War Production Board (WPB)
　impromptu speech in Chicago, 173
　　see also Minneapolis-Moline
　　see also priority classifications for farm machinery
　in Minnesota, 31, 32, 37, 39, 48, 49, 52–4, 60, 61, 65, 66, 71, 72, 78, 79, 82, 169
　visiting in Connecticut, 171, 172, 175–7, 195, 204, 213, 219, 223, 225, 230–5, 251
Gillette, Irene Isham Ford, 25, 87, 95, 128, 143, 145, 158, 176, 188, 251, 264, 287, 295, 300, 305, 333, 367, 380
　in Minnesota, 31, 32, 37, 42, 43, 48, 54, 61, 65–8, 71, 72, 74, 76, 77, 79, 82, 89
　visiting in Connecticut, 195–8, 204, 206, 208, 209, 213, 219, 223, 224, 230, 232–4
Gillette, John "Jack" Ford, 31, 36, 53, 72, 78, 176, 188, 234, 295, 305, 309, 362, 366, 377
　Thelma, 36, 45, 53, 72, 188, 295, 305
Gorton, Helen, 92, 95, 98, 151, 154, 174
Gray family, 115, 192, 209, 222, 372
Green-Lucas Service Men's Absentee Voting Bill, 202

Greenwich, Connecticut, 26, 34, 35, 42, 53, 65, 70, 71, 81, 90, 92, 93, 98, 101, 110–2, 115, 120, 124, 127, 131, 132, 137, 142, 146, 149, 154, 169, 171, 183, 184, 195, 209, 221, 223, 225, 227, 236, 240, 248, 252, 259, 269, 275, 280, 301, 310, 344, 345, 349, 352, 353, 357–9, 362, 365, 370, 371, 377
Gripsholm, 158, 205, 231

H

Hanan family, 76, 150, 154, 171, 232, 244, 252, 254, 262, 301
Harlem, New York City, 45
Harvard University, 133, 268, 292, 392
Hayes, Helen, 159, 209
Hayes, Lieutenant, 165, 211, 228, 246, 271, 275
Heiskell, Andrew, 344, 345, 390
Hekma family, 150, 251, 252, 281
Helms Jr., Lex C., 17, 18, 27, 34, 82, 98, 111, 144, 155, 208, 220, 304, 337, 339, 346
Hennepin County, Minnesota
　Crystal Bay, 2, 43, 48, 67, 81
　Minneapolis, 1, 11, 15, 23, 30, 34, 37, 39, 47, 50, 52, 54, 56, 63, 67, 72, 76, 77, 81, 90, 91, 93, 98, 138, 145, 159, 173, 184, 230, 285, 287, 295, 325, 365, 371, 379
　Minikahda Club, 37, 54, 58, 67, 72, 77
　Minnetonka, 31, 35, 38, 42, 65, 83, 177, 324
　Wayzata, 2, 31, 54, 58, 65, 77, 82
Hertzka, Wayne S., 274
Hestad, George H., 233
Heyduck, Lawrence E., 211, 250, 327
Hey Rookie, 170, 390
　see also Holloway, Sterling
Hickam Field, 24
　see also Pearl Harbor
Hite family, 88, 95, 99, 100, 103, 121, 278, 318, 332, 353
Hoggson, Connie and Wally, 23, 92, 96, 107, 115, 142, 196, 256, 302, 325, 332, 337
Holloway, Sterling, 170
　see also Hey Rookie
Howard, Bob and Martha, 36, 62, 63, 76, 81, 160
Howder, James D., 14, 80, 92, 198, 283
Hull, Cordell, 317, 318, 387
　If We Are Divided We Are Ineffective, 317

I

Italy, 2, 41, 89, 91, 204, 259, 310, 360, 383
　Allied push, 259
　surrender, 41, 89

395

J

Japan, 187, 227, 242, 254, 255, 259, 303, 387, 388, 392
    ancient history and culture, 242
    cruelty towards prisoners of war in the Philippines, 254, 255
    Prince Shotoku, 242
Judd, Walter Henry, 187
    see also China

K

Kee-Kaw, 33, 44
Key West, Florida, 1, 24, 86, 213, 292, 367
    see also Albright
    see also Meacham Field

L

Lee, Duncan, 13, 247
Lewis, John L., 19
    Federal Coal Mine Safety Act, 19
    United Mine Workers of America, 19
    see also Strikes
Libby, Donald Maxwell, 136
Linen III, James A., 31, 65, 86, 256, 324, 332, 387
    see also Office of War Information (OWI)
Luce, Clare Boothe, 310, 391
    see also United Nations
    see also Willkie, Wendell
    see also Wisconsin Primary, 1944
Lunn, Allan George Ramsay, 115, 126, 128, 133, 149, 186

M

MacFarlane, Wayne, 74, 231, 239, 240, 244, 256, 277, 278, 352, 357, 358, 366, 372
    see also Minneapolis-Moline
    see also Office of Strategic Services (OSS)
Marshall, George Catlett, 93, 102, 162, 190, 191, 214, 230, 271, 292, 381
    see also Task Force Officer's Course
Mauldin, Bill, 146, 310, 326, 340, 368, 389
Meacham Field, 86
    see also Albright
    see also Key West, Florida
Menjou, Adolphe, 117
Miller, Nan, 89, 95, 115, 124, 292
Minneapolis, Minnesota
    see Hennepin County
Minneapolis-Moline, 173, 174, 231
    see also priority classifications for farm machinery
    see also Gillette, George Lewis
    see also MacFarlane, Wayne

Minnetonka, Minnesota
    see Hennepin County

N

North African Theater of Operations (NATO), 14
North African Theater of Operations, United States Army (NATOUSA), 283
    see also Service of Supply (SOS)

O

Office of Strategic Services (OSS), 231, 247
    see also MacFarlane, Wayne
    see also Echols, Emmett
Office of War Information (OWI), 31, 102, 117
    see also Linen III, James A.
Officer Candidate School (OCS), 24, 88
Ogontz School for Young Ladies, 235, 342
Operation Husky, 21, 38, 390
    see also Sicily
Operations Division (OPD), 4, 93, 98, 102, 162, 271, 281
    see also War Department General Staff (WDGS)
Oran, Algeria, 283
    Chateau Neuf, 304
    Chateau Vieux, 330
    Fort St. Philippe, 330
Ordnance Corps, 125

P

Patch, Alexander "Sandy", 101, 386, 392
Patton, George, 203, 326, 391
    and Bill Mauldin, 326
    slap, 203, 391
Peairs Jr., Chalmers A., 220, 292
Peake, Frederick Robinson "Robbie", 154, 243, 318, 330
Pearl Harbor, 24
    see also Hickam Field
Pearson, Andrew, 202, 203, 205
Pierson, Charles "Carlie" Frederick, 44, 45, 62, 71, 72
Pillsbury, Charles "Chuck" Alfred, 62, 63, 391
    see also Pillsbury families
Pillsbury families, 36, 42, 62, 63, 71, 74, 390
    see also Pillsbury, Charles "Chuck" Alfred
    see also Pillsbury, Katherine "Kitty"
Pillsbury, Katherine "Kitty", 36, 62, 71, 74
    see also Pillsbury families
Piper, Catherine "Cocky" Gillette, 32, 36, 44, 62, 63, 71, 72, 74, 178
    see also Piper families

Piper families, 32, 36, 54
  see also Piper, Catherine "Cocky" Gillette
  see also Piper, Virginia "Ginny" Lewis
Piper, Virginia "Ginny" Lewis, 36
  see also Piper families
Poland, 205, 227, 259, 296, 297, 303, 309, 310, 388, 392
  Curzon Line, 296, 297
  earlier partitions, 309
  government-in-exile, 296, 297
  post-war borders, 297
  USSR designs on, 296, 297
  see also Churchill, Winston
  see also Roosevelt, Franklin D.
  see also Stalin, Joseph
  see also Tehran Conference
Priority classifications for farm machinery, 174
  see also Gillette, George Lewis
  see also Minneapolis-Moline
Promotion problems, 4, 5, 51, 92, 162, 183, 184, 191, 220, 271, 283–5
Psychological Warfare Branch (PWB), 256, 284

R

Railroads (in the United States), 157, 379, 380, 387, 392
  see also Strikes
Ream Jr., Edward F., 18, 52, 57, 92, 221, 226, 229, 274, 304, 307, 354, 381
Rebillet family, 22, 28, 29, 32, 34, 38, 51, 56, 80, 89, 139, 140, 151, 190, 194, 195, 228, 229, 238, 241, 256, 258
Regular Army, 292, 297, 336, 368
Resor, Stanley Rogers, 62, 391
Robeson, Paul, 209, 392
Rome Air Depot (RAD), 59, 120, 165, 211, 228, 292, 367
Roosevelt, Franklin D., 19, 112, 157, 205, 227, 297, 303, 310, 313, 314, 317, 341, 364
  and Poland's post-war border, 297, 310
  Cairo Conference, 227
  Clare Boothe Luce differences with, 310
  Eisenhower's appointment, 227
  Fireside Chat 27: On the Tehran and Cairo Conferences, 227
  Fireside Chat 29: On the Fall of Rome, 364
  on the drafting of fathers, 112
  Wendell Willkie and, 313, 314
  see also Atlantic Charter
  see also Poland
  see also Stassen, Harold
  see also Tehran Conference

S

Salamaua, Papua New Guinea, 100, 387
  see also Folsom, Myron
Schutz, J. Logan, 3, 17, 18, 26, 29, 30, 34, 52, 54, 57, 70, 82, 83, 92, 98, 101, 133, 137, 144, 145, 155, 189, 190, 191, 200, 204, 207, 208, 220, 221, 226, 228, 229, 247, 253, 304
Service of Supply (SOS), 283
  see also North African Theater of Operations United States Army (NATOUSA)
Sheldon, John T., 377, 378
Shewbridge, Benjamin B., 70
Sicily, 2, 20, 21, 22, 38, 92, 135, 168, 204, 390
  see also Operation Husky
Simons, Webster L., 136, 161, 179, 194, 270
Slocum, Elsa Domerick, 97, 138, 344, 360, 361
Smith, Milton J., 120, 155, 220, 311
Snyder families, 36, 42, 62, 63
Soldier Voting Act of 1942, 202, 391
Somers, Pat, 235, 262, 280, 281, 342
Sparks, Murray E., 52, 57, 92, 144, 155, 200, 211, 229
Spykman, Nicholas John, 47
  see also Yale University
Staff Officer responsibilities, 2, 322, 323
Stalin, Joseph, 205, 227, 296, 297, 303, 309, 391
  and Poland, 296, 297
  see also Poland
  see also Tehran Conference
Stars and Stripes, 66, 144, 150, 157, 166, 182, 204, 250, 306, 326, 340, 389, 391
Stassen, Harold, 314, 317, 390
  in Minnesota, 317
  in the 1944 Wisconsin primary, 314
  see also Roosevelt, Franklin D.
  see also United Nations
  see also Wisconsin primary, 1944
Steiner, Georgia, 1, 3, 9, 15, 20, 22, 23, 31, 33, 34, 35, 40, 41, 44, 47–9, 53, 54, 59, 61, 67, 68, 71–5, 77, 78, 81, 82, 84, 87, 89–91, 93, 94, 97, 99, 103, 106–8, 112, 113, 115, 118, 119, 121, 126, 128, 131, 133, 138, 143, 145–7, 153–6, 160, 163, 166, 168, 169, 176–8, 181, 184, 185, 196, 201, 206–8, 211, 215, 217, 222, 224, 226, 228, 230, 231, 233, 234, 236–9, 243–6, 248, 249, 251, 252, 255, 262–4, 268, 269, 271, 272, 275, 276, 279, 280, 282, 286, 288, 290, 293, 295, 300–2, 304, 305, 308, 318–20, 323–5, 331, 334, 336, 338, 339, 342, 344, 356, 359, 360, 362, 363, 366, 367, 372, 373, 375, 377, 379, 380, 383–5
Steiner, Harriet "Teedie" Talbot, 21, 48, 65, 69, 79, 81, 111, 128, 141, 157, 196, 201, 206, 312

Steiner, Jess McIvor, 47, 62, 94, 176, 195, 217, 228, 299
Steiner, Larry, 1, 9, 12, 15, 19, 20, 22, 23, 25, 26, 29, 31, 33-35, 39-41, 44, 45, 48, 49, 51, 53, 58, 59, 61, 66-8, 70-8, 81, 84, 87-91, 93-5, 97, 99, 101, 103, 106-8, 111-5, 118-21, 123, 124, 126-8, 131, 133, 138-40, 143, 145-8, 150, 153, 156, 159, 160, 163, 166, 168, 171, 175-81, 184-7, 189, 192, 193, 198, 199, 206-8, 211, 212, 214, 215, 222, 224, 226, 228-35, 237-40, 242-6, 248-51, 254, 255, 258, 259, 261-6, 268, 269, 271-3, 275-7, 279-81, 288-93, 295, 300-2, 304, 305, 308, 314, 318, 320-5, 328, 329, 331, 334, 336, 338, 342, 345, 348, 350, 353, 356, 358-67, 370, 373-7, 379, 380, 382, 383
Steiner, Lawrence "Ki", 11, 21, 41, 47, 48, 65, 68, 69, 77-9, 81, 83, 85, 128, 141, 145, 150, 153, 155, 157, 196, 201, 202, 206, 215, 281, 305, 312
Steiner, Robin, 1, 10, 20, 22, 30, 31, 40, 41, 44, 53, 59, 61, 67, 68, 70, 75, 81, 88, 91, 93, 95, 103, 106, 107, 110, 114, 115, 121, 123, 124, 126, 128, 150, 154, 163, 166, 169, 176, 178, 185, 187, 191, 192, 194, 196-8, 207, 208, 211, 214, 215, 219, 222-4, 228, 231, 236, 238-40, 245, 246, 248-52, 255, 258, 266, 268, 269, 271, 272, 275, 276, 280, 295, 298-302, 305, 308, 314, 323, 325, 333, 338, 340, 342, 345, 356, 358, 361, 363, 370, 372, 375-7, 379, 383, 384
Stepson "Steppy", 60, 88, 261, 262
Stipp, George, 28, 51, 82, 122, 138, 172, 179, 194, 197, 200, 207, 208, 213, 216, 220, 228, 229, 235, 246, 253, 354
Stony Wold, 97, 131, 133, 253
Strikes (in general), 19, 55, 157
    coal mines, 19, 157
    over wages, 157
    railroads, 157, 380
    see also Lewis, John L.
    see also Railroads
    see also United Mine Workers of America

T

Task Force Officer's Course, 4, 102, 190, 292
    see also Marshall, George Catlett
Tehran Conference, 205, 227, 297
    see also Churchill, Winston
    see also Poland
    see also Roosevelt, Franklin D.
    see also Stalin, Joseph

ter Meulen, Floris W., 251
Time Inc., 31, 38, 104, 121, 125, 130, 148, 157, 240, 269, 310, 317, 334, 338, 344
Turrou, Leon, 259

U

United Mine Workers of America, 19
    see also Lewis, John L.
    see also Strikes
United Nations, 189, 310, 317
    see also Luce, Clare Boothe
    see also Stassen, Harold
University of Minnesota, 48, 60
    Alworth Planetarium, 48
    ASTP classes, 60
    see also Alworth family

V

Vargas, Alberto, 378, 392
Victory Mail (V-Mail), 3, 12, 16, 24, 32, 35, 37, 39, 45, 57, 61, 64, 84, 90, 96, 97, 100, 105, 106, 116, 130, 139, 143-6, 149, 166, 177, 182, 219, 235, 253, 261, 264, 269, 284, 289, 293, 298, 299, 303, 328, 329, 338, 382
    censoring of, 130
    efficiency, 12
    process, 299

W

Waller, Thomas Wright "Fats", 180, 389
War Department General Staff (WDGS), 4, 93, 102, 162
    see also Operations Division (OPD)
War Labor Board (WLB), 157
War Production Board (WPB), 173, 174
    see also Batcheller, Hiland G.
    see also Gillette, George Lewis
Washington, D.C., 1, 4, 18, 23, 70, 80, 82, 93, 102, 106, 145, 172, 190, 230, 253, 303, 304, 310
Wayzata, Minnesota
    see Hennepin County
Wellington family, 95, 278, 332, 366
West Point, 336, 340, 387
Wilkins, H. Ford, 158, 205, 231, 387
Willkie, Wendell, 310, 313, 314, 316
    and civil rights, 313, 314
    and Franklin Roosevelt, 313
    in the 1944 Wisconsin primary, 314
    One World, 313, 314
    see also Luce, Clare Boothe
    see also Wisconsin primary, 1944
Wilson, Henry Maitland "Jumbo", 247

Winged Victory, 305, 388
Wisconsin primary, 1944, 313, 314
   see also Luce, Clare Boothe
   see also Stassen, Harold
   see also Willkie, Wendell
Wold-Chamberlain Field, 63
Women Accepted for Volunteer Emergency Service (WAVES), 306
Women's Army Corps (WAC), 75, 111, 120, 146, 170, 306, 352
   Women's Army Auxiliary Corps (WAAC), 75, 310

Y

Yale University, 13, 24, 47, 154, 206, 209, 246, 247, 268, 275, 306, 323, 340
   Harkness Tower, 323
   The Whiffenpoofs, 323
   Yale Club, 206, 209, 306
   see also Spykman, Nicholas John